INCARCERATED
WALKER

A Garrett Walker Novel

JOHN BEATON

Fulton Books, Inc.
Meadville, PA

Published by Fulton Books 2020

ISBN 978-1-64654-080-8 (paperback)
ISBN 978-1-64654-081-5 (digital)

Printed in the United States of America

CHAPTER 1

WHEN I STEPPED OUTSIDE THE terminal at the Boise airport, the late-August heat hit me like a blast furnace. Besides the 105-degree desert heat, I couldn't help but contemplate what lovely surprises the Idaho justice system had in store for me. When I missed my sentencing date with the Ada County District Court a few weeks before, I knew they would automatically issue a warrant for my arrest. It was now likely I would be considered a fugitive from justice. With a warrant looming over my head, I had flown over from Everett, Washington, where I had lived the past twenty years, and I was about to do something I had never imagined doing before: I was walking from the airport to turn myself in at the Ada County Jail and put my legal problems behind me. I wanted to show the judge I was taking responsibility for my actions by coming in voluntarily. It seemed better than getting tracked down and hauled into court by the police. By turning myself in, I was at least coming in prepared for incarceration, with all my personal affairs in order; I would be prepared as possible for what was ahead.

As usual, I was overanalyzing what I was about to do. I took a deep breath and tried to calm myself down. There was no turning back at this point. Since every journey begins with a single step, I decided to take the first one, and off I went.

Throwing my carry bag over my shoulder, I stepped out from under the shade of the airport overhang and out to the late-summer heat. I quickly made my way through the airport parking garage to the Chevron/McDonald's across the street, where I was grateful for the comfort of the air-conditioned building. With only $75 in my pocket, I bought a six-pack of Mike's Hard Cranberry Lemonade and stuffed it into my bag. Then I went next door to the McDonald's and ordered a cheeseburger, a large cup of ice, and grabbed a straw. I headed north down Vista Street as I poured a couple of Mike's into the cup. The last thing I needed was to be arrested for an open-container violation and adding to my existing charges.

The quality of my meals in confinement would not to be a five-star rating. I decided to make the best of my last taste of freedom by having a few cold ones, and at least I would enter jail with a full belly. After walking a mile or so, I reached Overland Street and headed west. By now my six-pack was almost gone, and I was dripping with sweat from the midafternoon heat. I stopped occasionally to cool off in the shade and rest my feet, the four-mile journey flying right by. Before I knew it, I was turning on Cole Road and I was less than a mile away from turning my life over to the man.

By now I was feeling a little buzzed, my heart was pounding, and I began to seriously contemplate if I was making the right move. I wasn't a career criminal or repeat offender constantly going through the revolving doors of the penal system. This was way out of my Brady Bunch upbringing and suburban lifestyle. I slowly tried to figure out a way to delay the inevitable. I thought about staying overnight in the woods, or in a park, and turning myself in come morning. But with warrants out for my arrest, looking like a homeless man in a city park might not be the smartest move to make. I wanted the judge to know I had turned myself in on my own accord. That had to look better than getting arrested and appearing in front of the judge. I quickly decided to pass on doing anything stupid and pressed on.

As I got closer to the jail, I felt myself get more nervous with each block I passed. How did an upper-middle-class, well-raised, semieducated man like me end up in this situation? I wasn't evil, dangerous, violent, or even close to being a threat to society. Jail was for criminals and brawlers, not middle-aged fathers or businessmen. Things like this didn't happen to guys like me; it happened to bank robbers, murderers, rapists, and junkies. I had never been in trouble my whole life, and the worst thing on my record until now was a traffic ticket. Now I was a fugitive from justice with a felony arrest warrant, and I couldn't believe I let my life get this fucked up.

I was born in Eugene, Oregon, in 1962 and raised in a middle-class neighborhood, the second of four kids in a loving family. We lived in the same house from the time I was five until I was eighteen. I was cocaptain of my high school soccer team and an honor roll student who graduated with the class of 1981. I guess life must have been just a bit too easy for me, and now I was finally paying the consequences for my three decades of continuous-partying lifestyle.

The jail was getting closer every minute, and fear of my impending unknown future was growing deeper with every step. I was desperate and intoxicated enough to want to try to figure a way out of this mess, and my mind was reeling with ideas and excuses to grant me yet one more night of freedom. I was now stalling at the intersection of Franklin and Cole, just two blocks from the jail. I looked up and noticed a sign that made me rethink my entire scope of possibilities.

In large letters, I read, "Ada County Work Release Center." Why hadn't I thought of preparing for that possibility sooner? I went into the little convenience store a block away from the jail and grabbed a newspaper so I could check out the help-wanted ads. I took it across the street to the Boise Towne Square Mall and found a quiet booth inside the Sizzler Steakhouse, where I could enjoy the air-conditioning and eat a nice steak dinner. I wrote down the phone numbers of a few roofing contractors who were hiring. I had been roofing for twenty-five years and getting paid by how much I installed, so getting paid by the hour was out of the question. The harder I worked, the more I made, and I always made decent money, so maybe things would work out. This way, I would have a few job possibilities if I was even eligible for work release and hopefully go home with some extra money.

Why wouldn't I be eligible? This was only my first offense. I wasn't a threat to society. I used to own my own roofing company. I flew over here to turn myself in, so I shouldn't be a flight risk. If I weren't eligible, who the hell was? Things were starting to look up, and I instantly began to feel optimistic after cooling off and getting a nice, juicy steak in me. I found four or five good roofing job opportunities as well as a couple of framing crews looking for help in the classifieds. I had been roofing since 1981, so roofing would probably be a better option for me.

If I qualified for work release, I could make a couple hundred bucks a day, which, even after paying for the right to be in the program, would still be profitable if not more exciting than the alternative. A few hundred bucks a week for six to eight weeks would make a little nest egg to go home with, since I would have nothing to spend it on here in Boise. Of course, by this late in the afternoon, anyone who did any hiring was already gone for the day. I knew the odds of me reaching management were slim, but what the hell else did I have to do? The jail wasn't going anywhere, so I got a few bucks in quarters and headed over to the phone booth to give it a shot. It only took a few attempts to confirm my suspicion, so I gave up after going straight to voice mail four out of four times.

Maybe I could convince my girlfriend, Beth, to put a hotel room on her Visa card for the night, and that would give me tomorrow morning to line up some work before I went in. This way, Friday morning I could get in touch with a couple of businesses and set it up so if I needed a job to get work release, I would be prepared. Beth and I had been together for the better part of eleven years now, with some split-ups during the roughest of my drug problems leading up to my recent downfall.

It only took a second on the phone for her to reject what I thought was a rather-rational and smart idea. She probably thought I was up to my old tricks and trying to avoid the inevitable, which wasn't the case for the first time in a long while. I was just trying to keep my possibilities open and be optimistic about the next couple of months. With $42 left in my pocket, I folded up my paper with numbers on it and headed out the door and back across the street to face the music.

I wanted to put some money on my account in jail, but I also wanted to make sure I had money once released. Since the jail does not give out cash but rather a county check, I wanted to plan and make sure I had some cash at my disposal immediately upon release. I found an isolated place along the railroad tracks and buried $20 under a railroad tie next to the signal switch to make sure I could differentiate mine from thousands of other ties along the track. I stopped in three other places and played with the rocks just in case somebody was watching me. I wanted to be extra cautious and make sure that money was there when I came back for it instead of somebody else finding it or an animal digging it up.

I still had $22 for the weekly purchases available from the commissary inside the jail. It wasn't much, but when you are locked up, the smallest things make a huge difference in your comfort level. I grabbed one more twenty-two-ounce cranberry lemonade at the store across from the jail, poured it in my cup, and drank it as fast as I could. I might as well show up with a smile on my face. Reluctantly, I crossed the street into the parking lot of the public safety building, which housed the jail along with some county offices and even a swimming pool. I threw away all my empties and checked and rechecked myself for anything that could be considered incriminating. Finding nothing that would get me into more trouble than I was already in, I apprehensively walked around the building to the jail entrance. Finally, it was time to do what I had been dreading to do for over three weeks now. I stepped through the door to voluntarily surrender myself to the whims of the justice system for the next six to eight weeks.

At least that was what my plan was.

CHAPTER

2

A T 6:45 P.M. ON THURSDAY, September 1, 2005, I walked up to the counter and said, "My name is Garrett Walker. There is a warrant for my arrest, and I am here to turn myself in." The officer behind the counter told me to step over to the side door and he would meet me there. As I stepped in the door, I was asked to turn around and place my hands behind my back. Once again, I found myself hating the unfamiliar, awkward chill of cold steel over tightened handcuffs around my wrist. The officer then grabbed my arm and my bag and led me over to the booking area to begin my intake processing.

There was no way I could possibly have drunk enough alcohol to make these moments tolerable. The finality of letting the system get ahold of me to do what they would was always a bit intimidating. The complete lack of control on my part and fear of the unknown was most difficult to accept. Although I had been mentally prepared for this moment for some time now, I couldn't ever imagine getting comfortable with it. I felt just as horrified now as I was when I was arrested for the first time back in January.

The intake process of any county jail is usually the longest, most tedious two to eighteen hours a person that is getting locked up is forced to endure, and I had no reason to think that today would be any different. I was led to a cement bench, told to sit down, and I waited in the cinder block intake area for roughly fifteen minutes. When a correction officer, CO, finally begin to process me, I was relieved to be moving forward, for better or worse.

"Stand up, turn around, and face the wall," I was instructed. As I did so, he began to undo my handcuffs, and I could instantly feel the blood rushing back to my hands.

"Place both hands over your head and lean up against the wall," I was told in a monotone, mechanical voice. Next was the two-handed pat-down along the arms, torso, legs, and the always-fun groin check.

"Okay, sir, turn around and sit back down on the bench and remove your shoes and socks." As I did this, the CO grabbed my bag and dumped it upside down on one of the nearby tables. Knowing what was going to be asked of me next from the last time I was here, I automatically took the laces out of my shoes before presenting them along with my socks for inspection. After he had made sure they contained no contraband, my shoes were placed in my possession bag along with its other contents, and my socks were returned to me to be put back on.

After the CO filled out two pages of personal information, such as names, address, phone, and employment information, it was time for a few more personal questions to complete the necessary paper-work before having me moved into the actual booking area. While the CO read the questions off the sheet as he was filling it out, I tried to speed things along by answering the next question as he filled in the last answer.

"Six feet tall, 190 pounds, brown hair, brown eyes, male, single, forty-three years old," I said, trying to stay ahead of the writing he was doing. This was followed by a long string of "Nos" regarding my medical history and other physical complications the medical staff may need to be alerted of before accepting me under their care. The same response came with the next questionnaire to determine my mental state, to make sure I wasn't suicidal or, worse, homicidal. After it was determined that I was normal and not a threat to the rest of the jail population, my bag was placed in my jail property bag until my release. Finally, I was escorted to the main booking area, where I was free to move about, sit down in a normal padded chair, make a collect call, or watch TV.

Sitting in the holding area, surrounded by strung-out, desperate people frantically calling anyone and everyone they knew to bail them out reminded me of how I felt eight months ago, when I was arrested for the first time in my life. Pleading and promising with anyone who would answer a collect call was the only lifeline from jail. Over the news on the TV, I could hear a variety of excuses and promises nobody on the other side of the phone should believe. I quietly sat and watched the drama unfold as a parade of people changed their stories with each call they made. I got to observe and privately analyze a wide variety of soon-to-be fellow inmates, both male and female, as well as hear part of their dilemma while they desperately pleaded for help getting bailed out. The spouses, parents, and lawyers on the other end of the phone call were promised the world from these people who would be locked up for a long time unless they could convince anyone with means to help them. All this really did was prolong the inevitable incarceration, as it did in my case. Back in January, I was one of these desperate people, so I completely understood exactly how these folks felt right now.

Most people getting booked into county jails are high and have been up for days, or maybe even weeks. These people have been awake for so long that getting arrested signifies the first time they have been deprived of their drug of choice for quite some time. Lack of illegal stimulants for the first time in weeks or months leads these folks to do some very humorous things. Some who obviously need it fall into a deep sleep right there in the chairs, with their heads bobbing and jerking them awake.

After thirty minutes of people watching, I heard my name called. I was led to the caged-off clothing-issue area. I was issued two tops and two pairs of pants in matching fire truck—red, scrub-like material. They allowed me to keep my underwear, T-shirt, and socks only because they were all solid white, like the jail-issued equivalents. Last on the pile was one red sweatshirt and a pair of worn-out blue canvas slip-on boat shoes.

The inmate-worker then pointed to a private changing area / shower, where I could change and wash up. When I finished up, he took my civilian clothes, put them in my property bag, and set my extra scrubs next to my bedroll with an ID card that had my name and picture on it. This way, when I finally was sent to my dorm, this assured my new wardrobe would go with me.

I went back to the sitting area and watched the continuing soap opera unfold in front of me, along with CNN, until my name was called once again. This time, I was fingerprinted, and my mugshot was taken, then I was told to return to the waiting area once again. All my public information, including my charges and photo, was then placed on the Ada County Jail website for anyone in the world to pull up and view. I wasn't too thrilled about finding this out, but public-information laws in a free country made it so there was nothing I could do about it. The CO mumbled, "If you don't like it, then don't come to jail."

"Garrett Walker!" I heard being called. I had to sign a piece of paper after a quick inventory of my property to be stored during my incarceration along with verification of how much cash I had so it could be placed on my jail account, commonly referred to as "money on my books." As soon as I verified I had $22 in my account, the CO riveted my new plastic wristband around my right wrist. This plastic-coated, perforated ID bracelet had a small copy of my mugshot, inmate number, birth date, and name thinly laminated for waterproofing. I was told to always keep this on, and if I destroyed it, I had to pay $8 for a replacement since that was how the COs kept track of inmates inside.

It was now 9:45 p.m., and the whole booking process had only taken three hours, much quicker than I had anticipated. Everybody going in had now been stripped off all jewelry, cigarettes, money, and any personal belongings so that the only items we entered the non-smoking facility with were the items they had given us.

I was now ready to leave the booking area and truly begin serving my time. Of course, just heading down the hall would be much too easy, so now I had to wait until there was a group of us ready to go all at the same time. This way, the COs wouldn't have to take us down the long hallway one at a time but rather in groups of ten. Soon enough, eight names were called by another CO as he gathered all the ID cards. We were given our bedrolls and spare clothing and told to put it inside a large twenty-four-by-twenty-inch plastic tub called a bin box.

When the door to the booking area was electronically unlocked and hydraulically opened for us, we all picked up our bin boxes and ushered into a small holding room called a sally. The door from the sally into the main corridor would not open until we were all inside and the door to the booking area was closed. This way, the COs could make certain of any unauthorized movement within the confines of one zone.

We walked quietly in a single-file line, hugging the right side of the corridor, as instructed by the CO, and looped around the guard's command center in the middle of the jail, referred to as hub control. From here the COs could monitor and unlock all the doors in sallies, hallways, dorms, and rec areas. Inmates called this the walk of shame, and every step I took, I understood why. The consequences of my actions had finally come back to bite me in the ass, and I was ashamed of what I had done with my life to get here. After thirty years of getting away with a variety of illegal activities and partying, it was finally time to pay the piper.

CHAPTER 3

THERE WERE BASICALLY THREE DIFFERENT housing possibilities in the Ada County Jail. Maximum custody was called max or seg (for segregation). High-risk offenders, escape possibilities, and violent inmates who needed to be separated from the rest of the jail population for safety reason or gang affiliation were housed here. Anyone else who got into a fight anywhere within the jail was immediately sent to seg for a cooling-off period and/or punishment for the violent infringement.

Housing was max, which meant twenty-three hours locked in the cell, minimum rec time, and limited commissary. The only good thing was, each cell was a single occupant, and some actually preferred the solitude.

The medium-custody unit was called MCU. Here there were four-man cells with rotating free time, or tier time, as they called it, divided among one-third of the pod's population. This way, the COs only had to contend with 40 inmates in the pod's 120-man population at any time, since the other 80 were secure in their respective cells. The minimum-risk inmates were housed in the dorms, which was where I was headed with all the other members of our group.

Dorm 5 was the intake dorm, where new inmates went until they met with the classification officer in a day or two. He evaluated the inmate risk factor, which determined where they would be permanently assigned. I was hoping to be assigned to the dorms permanently since I had no violent offenses, wasn't an escape risk, and really didn't like the confinement situations in MCU or max.

As we walked into dorm 5, it instantly became quiet as the forty other men who were still awake seemed to stop what they were doing at the same time and began to check out the fresh meat coming into the unit. Most were just checking us out to see if any of their friends had shown up to join them in jail. Slim chance of me knowing anyone, since I lived three hundred miles away, so I stepped up to the CO station when my name was called and received my bunk assignment.

"Walker, bunk 17, upper left," the CO called, pointing to one of the four-tier areas that divided the unit so I had some idea where to find it. I headed over to get my bunk made, stow my bin box, and organize my new living space. Normally, people go in front of the judge the next day for arraignment if they were here for three to five days, because many misdemeanor, alcohol, and drug charges carry this requirement. Most spend the next few days catching up on some much-needed shut-eye until they are released. These individuals stay in dorm 5 their entire visit, sleeping until released. This made me jealous. I might have wished to sleep away my entire sentence, but I was too high-strung to be lucky enough to do that.

I once heard that when you're locked up with this many other men, you don't necessarily have to stand out, but you do have to stand up. This was exactly what I was planning to do: keep to myself, not speak unless spoken to, and mind my own business. Follow these simple rules and life can be easy. Break them and your life will get complicated really fast. Unless you knew who the guy next to you was and what lit his fuse, the safest road to take was the high road or to turn the other cheek.

I found my bunk and began to unroll my bedding and inventory, my new personal possessions, compliments of the Ada County. Two sheets and one blanket, rolled around a small eight-ounce plastic cup that contained some liquid soap/shampoo, plastic spoon, small black comb, three-inch flexible pen, three-inch toothbrush, and toothpaste. Rule inside a jail or prison is for your bunk to be made if you are not on it or in it, so I checked the picture of the proper bunk in the photo on the bulletin board to make sure I didn't get in trouble my first few minutes here. As I had been in the military for six years, it took me no time to make my bunk look better than most of those around me, but still not quite what my old drill instructor would have accepted. I preferred a lower bunk because it was more convenient, but 17 was an upper, which made it easier to make but more difficult to get in and out of. After a few brief introductions from close neighbors who were not busy or sleeping, I ventured out of the tier to stretch my legs and check out my new home away from home.

My first order of business, as far as I was concerned, was to hit the book cart and find something decent to read. The intake dorm usually has the worst selection, because anyone who finds a decent book takes it to their unit with them once they are classified. Half the men in here were catching up on sleep after months of illegal-stimulant sleep deprivation and couldn't read *The Cat in the Hat* if their life depended on it. This allowed me to find a couple of good books to read, and I selflessly grabbed them both. What else was there to do in here?

Each inmate can keep two books and a Bible in their living quarters. I stowed my two selections in my bin box and headed for the CO station. As soon as I was booked, I was given a court date that the CO should now have on his computer. I stepped up to the counter and waited a few seconds, quietly and patiently, for the CO to finish what he was already doing. Finally, he spoke.

"May I help you?" he said as he looked up at me.

"Yes, sir! My name is Walker, and I was curious to find out if you could tell me my court date, please?" I was always polite and respectful to both COs and inmates alike when meeting new people until they treated me otherwise. After waiting for the computer to produce my information, he told me what I wanted to hear.

"It's September 6 at 9:00 a.m." That was it; my fate was sealed for the next week, and that was nice to know. Half the stress of incarceration is because you never know what the system has lined up for you. This may range from the amount of your bail, your next court date, or even what your final sentence may be. The uncertainty of the unknown is harder to deal with, no matter how devastating to your mental state the unavoidable outcome may be.

What a difference the last forty-eight hours had made in my life. Yesterday I was a professional contractor installing somebody's roof, making $500 a day's profit. I went home to my two-thousand-square-foot house, where I lived with my girlfriend and fourteen-year-old son. I had gotten up this morning and made bacon, eggs, and toast for breakfast before getting ready to head for the airport. I had been dropped off at the airport twelve hours and 365 miles ago. Now, here I was, getting ready for lights-out at 11:00 p.m. with ninety-five roommates and the rock-hard bunk 17. Still not too sure what to expect at court next week. I truly wasn't expecting to be locked up past my birthday in mid-October. I wasn't a career criminal and had only one felony to serve time for. I thought I'd be released in four to six weeks. I was more of a family man and businessman than those who surrounded me, but here I was once again and not too thrilled about being there.

From eleven to midnight wasn't technically "lights-out," but the lights were dimmed, and it was considered quiet time. We could still pace the dayroom quietly and watch the TV in the dorm with the volume reduced, but the card games and phone calls were done for the night, so those who chose to go to sleep early could do so. Most of the guys who were still up this late, including me, were gathered around the tube, watching the nonstop coverage of the storm headed for the Gulf Coast. CNN was predicting that over Labor Day weekend, things could be catastrophic for those who were too stubborn to evacuate as ordered to.

If you have ever been to the large cat display at the zoo, then what I'm about to say will make a little more sense. No matter what exhibit you look at, there is always two types of caged animals. One of the tigers, jaguars, cheetahs, or cougars is always just lying there, sunning himself on the rock or napping in the shade. These cats have accepted their captivity and just wait around all day to be fed and sleep as much of the day and night as possible. The other, however, is constantly pacing from one end of the exhibit to the other. These animals will never accept their situation, will long for their freedom, and are constantly contemplating the outside world. They accomplish this by training, and by strengthening, testing themselves for the day they will get their first taste of freedom or return to a life they once knew before getting captured. Out of the two animals, I am the latter. My plan was to keep as busy and productive as possible so that when I left, I, too, could be stronger and wiser for my time spent here.

No matter how upsetting my situation was here, all warm and cozy in Ada County's dorm 5, at least I didn't have to worry whether I'd be alive tomorrow; I decided at once to be productive and positive while I did my time. I grabbed a book from my bin and began pacing back and forth across the dayroom until it was time for lights-out, when we had to be in our bunk. I covered over seven miles that night as I caught glimpses from CNN on the TV of the floods and devastation that had begun in the Gulf of Mexico. Those poor folks in New Orleans and Biloxi were staring down the barrel of a killer category-5 hurricane that was headed straight for them. Whatever lay ahead for me couldn't possibly be worse than Hurricane Katrina. I decided to walk and read as much as I could while I was incarcerated and tried to make the most of my bad situation.

C H A P T E R

4

I READ FROM MIDNIGHT UNTIL I could keep my eyes open no longer. With the dim lights left on, a person could read all night if they couldn't sleep, and I am sure a few people probably did. I was up two or three times in the middle of the night, and this would probably continue until I got used to my surroundings. Deep down it bothered me that I even wanted this to happen. Getting used to jail can never be a good thing.

Nothing sucks more than waking up incarcerated at 5:55 a.m., except maybe having a CO yelling, "Breakfast five minutes!" I sat up and instantly realized where I was, and the first question that popped in my mind was, Why the hell did we have to wake up at 6:00 a.m. for breakfast in jail? I had no other plans today, so why couldn't we have done this at 8:00 or 9:00 a.m.? Knowing my opinion didn't mean squat, I quietly got up, threw on my shirt, and made my bunk. You can't leave the tier without proper uniform, so I got up and got dressed while others just rolled over and covered their faces. Half of the comatose junkies in the dorm didn't even bother to get up and get the one thing we look forward to three times a day, food. In some jails, it was mandatory to get out of bed to eat, but at Ada County Jail, all meals were optional.

When the CO called, "Upper left," I strolled out of the tier and stood in line with about fifteen of the tier's twenty-five men, with my plastic cup and spoon in my hand. My cup was not needed at breakfast since we were given an eight-ounce milk carton and a banana, two pieces of white bread, and an infamous bowl of Ada County Jail oatmeal. Overall, it was a pretty filling meal by jail standards, and the only part of the meal I had complaints about was the milk. It was fresh and even ice-cold, but eight ounces was like a shot glass to me, and I was used to chugging a quart or more at a time. What can I say? I love my milk!

I inhaled my breakfast and checked the bulletin board for my chore assignment. Each bunk had a specific cleaning duty that must be completed once a day. These were done three times a day, once after each meal was served, and inmates were required to stay in their bunks until chores were done. It didn't really matter at breakfast because everyone who did bother to get up and eat went straight back to their bunk after eating. Bunk 17 had to wipe the tables down after dinner, so I followed suit and got back in bed. Still tired after a long day yesterday, I fell right back into sleep until the CO woke me up again for a second time in an hour.

"Lower left, standing count!" was my wake-up call from the new CO, who had just arrived for the day shift. Twice daily at 7:00 a.m. and p.m. shift change, inmates were required to get out of their bunks and stand next to their bunks while the CO counted all the inmates in each tier. All inmates were again required to stay in or on our bunks until the count was cleared. Followed by razor call.

Having shaved yesterday morning but knowing Monday, Wednesday, and Friday were the only three days a week razors were available, I got in line to receive mine. I told the CO my bunk number and name so he could check me off when I returned it, because razors were kept very close track of in jail. We were only allowed to go to the sink area and wait in line until we shaved and then promptly returned the razor. Failure of all the razors being returned to the CO resulted in lockdown and shakedown until the missing razor surfaced. Safety first, right? It took about ten minutes of scraping the five-cent razor over my blood-soaked face to remove only 80 percent of my average-thickness facial hair. Having a mustache made it easier to complete, but between me and those before, the sink looked like MASH unit operating room when we were all finished.

By the time I returned my razor, I was wide awake, with no chance of going back to sleep, so I grabbed my book and headed out to the front room to enjoy some solitude while everyone else was asleep. When you have one hundred nineteen roommates, alone time is rare and valuable.

My first course of action was to determine the distance from the bottom of the outer staircases. This was the longest distance across the dayroom that a person could walk without breaking any rules. It was sixty-five paces in a large sweeping V. I figured down and back eighteen times would equal one mile, so I began to pace off one mile and watch the clock to verify my math. I could usually pace at three miles per hour, and when my eighteen trips took twenty minutes, it confirmed my math. Now, instead of counting each lap, all I would have to do was pace for so many hours to keep track of my distance.

Since the whole unit went back to sleep after razor call, I pretty much had the whole place to myself. I went back to my bunk, grabbed my book, and spent most the morning pacing back and forth on the empty dayroom carpet and reading. The morning was the only time to do both at the same time since I would be bumping into people the rest of the day. The TV wouldn't turn on until ten, and even then, the volume was kept lower than normal for the two or three guys who had enough energy to get up and join me.

I would walk and read for forty-five to sixty minutes on and off all morning until lunch at noon. It was much the same all afternoon except for a few card games. Before dinner at 5:00 p.m., I had read half of my four-hundred-page book and had walked over ten miles.

After dinner, I had to attend to my assigned chore, which was posted on the job chart. Wiping down the tables, sweeping or mopping the tier, scrubbing the toilets or the showers were among the jobs listed, and each was to be completed after the meal by the assigned inmate, before we were free to move about the dorm once again. The meal distribution usually took forty-five minutes. Once the CO had all the chores cleared, we had until 7:00 p.m. before we had to bunk up again for shift change and count time. Late in the evening, around 10:00 p.m., when the CO finally finished checking for contraband, escape plans, and porn, we would have mail call. Again, 11:00 p.m.

was quiet time and lights-out, and we were in our bunks and quiet by midnight.

This became my routine for the weekend, except for times that my feet hurt or I was worn-out, and then I would jump into my bunk to read. Ironically, this routine was relaxing and exhausting at the same time. The only departure of my new schedule came when I was invited to play card games. Spades was a jailhouse favorite. Tired from exercise, I found taking a break and chatting with my fellow inmates was a nice little break in my day.

Sunday was pretty much a repeat of Saturday, except after the beginning of the NFL football season. Also drawing our interest was news from the Gulf Coast in the wake of the damage caused by Katrina. I took several breaks from my pacing to view the utter devastation on CNN; the footage was just as difficult to turn away from as the 9/11 coverage had been four years earlier. What does it say about us that we are drawn to such horrible carnage with such curiosity? Does it make us feel better to know that our lives aren't as messed up as those of the people on the news?

Perhaps it's something different for each of us, yet it was absorbing enough that none of us were able to turn away. Here we were, locked up in jail, and yet we all felt sorry for everyone in the path of the hurricane. We were all safe, over two thousand miles away from what we were watching on television, and we didn't have to worry about our families this weekend. The folks in the Gulf were scrambling for their lives, and here we were, all locked up, wishing we could be with our families, having barbecues and ice-cold beer.

I was sent to classification on Labor Day, Monday morning, where my score was low enough for me to remain in the dorms. Apparently, COs did not get Labor Day off. I was an extremely low-risk inmate, with a record of good behavior and no fights. I would be moved over to dorm 6 for the remainder of my stay, according to the CO. They said they would be moving a bunch of guys tonight after dinner and asked if I wanted to fill out an application to be an inmate-worker since I had qualified. I told him I would let him know in a few days. This way, I could get the real story firsthand from those who had done it already before I ruined my chance of freedom.

By Monday afternoon, I had finished my first book and made sure I had another good one to take with me when I transferred to dorm 6 later that night. Since dorm 5 was the intake tank, most people rotated in and out rather quickly. Some got bailed out right away, and most were moved to their permanent housing locations within a few days. Others were here for the weekend or until they went in front of a judge and were released with time served or a later court date, depending on the severity of the charges.

My name was called around 8:00 p.m., and I was told to roll up my stuff along with five or six others who were all getting moved to dorm 6. Thank God I was finally getting away from all the drunks and strung-out guys who had not been to sleep for weeks until they showed up in dorm 5, where they could sleep for five days straight. Combine all the guys trying to detoxify with the added aggravation being allowed no cigarettes and you have a ticking time bomb.

By 9:00 p.m., I had a new bunk in dorm 6, located in the upper-right tier, where I started to make some friends. I was immediately greeted with bad news: This dorm had ordered commissary earlier this afternoon, and all the orders were turned in for the night, so as they say in jail, I was burnt. No commissary for me until next Tuesday, which really sucked. Since I wasn't in the intake dorm any longer, many inmates in this dorm would sell me what I needed. This was called storing out. Technically, it was against the rules, but it was still common, and those who did it were repaid double and it was profitable business for those who did it intelligently. There was even worse news for me than no commissary: dorm 6 was being closed for a week for maintenance and we were all moving to the medium-custody unit (MCU) tomorrow for at least a week. I had never been to MCU, but from what I heard from fellow inmates, there was not nearly as much freedom there as in the dorms.

I was a little nervous about court coming up tomorrow morning, and I tried to concentrate on reading a good book to help take my mind off my imminent sentencing. I was now on my second book, and I was beginning to enjoy literature as never before. I had never really been a reader until I was locked up in Everett back in February for thirty days and my friend had given me a book by Clive Cussler called *Inca Gold*. The adventures of Dirk Pitt and the NUMA gang, what Cussler wrote about, was not only interesting and educational, but reading about them also helped me mentally escape the confines of jail while I traveled the world in my mind.

CHAPTER

5

IMMEDIATELY AFTER BREAKFAST ON MONDAY morning, my name was called for morning court, and I was told to be ready by 7:00 a.m. Those of us called were also allowed the luxury of being the first to receive razors so we were on time for transport and presentable for the courtroom. A group of us walked the long hallways to the transport room under close supervision of the CO in hub control. This is a central control area that thoroughly monitors sallies, inmates, and hallways from a bank of video monitors. They can also open and close most doors from here, so every time inmates are moved from place to place, they do not require a guard to go with them. This ease of movement is a benefit to the low-risk inmates and the COs, while MCU and max are not allowed this luxury. Once we arrived at the transport room, it was a different story. All inmate transports were searched, handcuffed, and shackled around the waist and ankles to ensure against escape. We could take a book with us to court, since we would be gone from 8:00 a.m. to noon, with most likely only five minutes being spent by each of us in the courtroom. After sitting in the inmate holding area for an hour, I was taken upstairs for court at 9:00 a.m.

When my name was called, I informed the judge that my lawyer was not here yet, and that was when I heard some very interesting information from the prosecuting attorney. The prosecutor told the judge she had seen my lawyer, Kurt, in the building earlier and she was under the impression that he was no longer working on this case. All this was news to me since the last thing Kurt had told me was to call him when I got to town, as I did on Friday. I never talked to him, but I left a message saying I had court Monday morning, and now he didn't show up. The judge gave my case a continuance until Tuesday, September 12, which was eight days later. This guy was a real piece of work, and I instantly understood why lawyers have been negatively stereotyped by the public. First, when I missed my flight to Boise from Seattle for my sentencing hearing, instead of getting a continuance then or covering my ass like lawyers are paid to do, he told the judge he had no idea where I was. The truth was, I was at the airport, trying to reschedule my flight while calling him fifty times without success. I gave up after two hours and cursed myself for hiring the only person in 2005 who did not have a cell phone yet. I left him messages and tried to reach him repeatedly, but when I wasn't in court, he had thrown me under the bus, then he backed it up and parked it on top of me.

On the way back to jail, the guy next to me confirmed the bitterness many inmates have toward their lawyers when he asked me if I knew how to save a drowning lawyer. I shook my head no, and he smiled at me and said, "Take your foot off their head."

C H A P T E R

6

WHEN I ARRIVED BACK AT the jail, I was given a sack lunch consisting of two single-slice bologna sandwiches, an orange, and two cookies. I was told to take off my red scrubs and put on the god-awful orange-and-white-striped uniform of the inmates in MCU. As I walked into MCU, I was instantly disappointed with my new living arrangements. The dayroom was probably thirty-five feet across and one hundred feet long, with two floors of cells surrounding the perimeter.

Ringing the dayroom on the second level was a balcony catwalk with two staircases for access. Each cell was about ten by twenty and had two bunk beds in the back on both walls and one toilet/sink in the front by the door. Each cell would house 4 men, and there were 120 men. There were tables, TVs, chairs, and a bank of phone booths in the dayroom and a shower off to the side of the guard station. Everyone was locked down in their cells except for the 40 men who were out of their cells for what was called tier time. Tier time was once a day for four hours plus thirty minutes for each meal. "This is going to suck," I whispered.

The tier time rotated each day from morning, afternoon, and evening, and the rest of the time, you were locked in your cell with the three other guys. Since I was new to the dorm, this gave me a good opportunity to meet at least three guys. My name was quickly called, I went straight to my cell and could see all three of them had commissary. This meant they had been here a while. I hoped some-one would be nice enough to afford me some of their luxuries until I was able to order myself and pay them back.

"Good afternoon, gentlemen. My name is Garret, and can someone please tell me what the hell is going on around here?" A rather-strange way to introduce myself, I must confess, but it was effective. It drew a round of smiles from the trio, followed by a round of introductions and the customary knuckle bump. After some quick hellos, I was rather pleased with the new cellmates I was apparently stuck with for the next week or two. They were also glad that I showed, since they were under assumption that they would otherwise be missing the necessary fourth man needed for most card games.

My new cellmates were all younger than me, but not by too much. They were all from Boise, and all had legal problems surrounding their drug use as about 90 percent of inmates did. Scott North was a cocky, spoiled twenty-five-year-old whose parents were both dentists. He had grown up with a silver spoon in his mouth, but after becoming constantly frustrated by his erratic behavior, they had finally taken the tough-love approach. When he was busted for possession of oxycodone for the third time, his folks decided he was on his own. Like me, he was waiting to be sentenced. Because he was also a roofer, we had plenty in common and a lot to talk about. He said that if I was lucky enough to get into the work release program, he could easily get me a job.

Kurt Scriber was a good-looking thirty-four-year-old who had a twenty-two-year-old girlfriend and a new baby. He had violated his parole by disappearing for a year after doing two years in the pen a few years back on methamphetamine distribution charges. When they finally caught up with him, he failed a urine test, and he had been sentenced one-year inpatient rehab in Seattle. As a flight risk, he had ordered him to remain in jail until a bed opened up sometime in the next two months.

Then there was Sean Tyler. He was working on a plea bargain on counterfeiting charges. The $100 bills he had were so realistic they passed the brown-pen test and even had a dark stripe where the magnetic strip was supposed to be. At thirty-nine, he was closer to my age. He was short, bald, with a walrus mustache and looked like the guy from the board game Monopoly. Since he had used fake money and had the right look, his nickname was Monopoly.

After introductions, a brief recitation of our background and legal history, we spent the day playing card games and getting to know one another a little better. It was good to get a few of my questions answered by people who would give me straight answers and were familiar with the Ada County legal system. Work release turned out to be impossible for me to get, being an inmate-worker sucked, and the reason we were here instead of dorm 6 was a half-million-dollar repair to its air-conditioning unit. Evidently, it was hotter than hell in dorm 6, and since everyone was sick of breathing the stuffy air in 105-degree heat, MCU wasn't so bad for them.

On the upside, all these guys liked to read and had plenty of good books I could read in addition to their commissary stash. They also told me to put in an interjail mail request, called a kite, with the commissary officer, since I was moved on commissary day and I might get lucky. We got better acquainted over a few friendly games of spades, and finally, after dinner, we were allowed our tier time. We were allowed out of our cells from dinner at 6:00 p.m. until 10:00 p.m. After dinner, I called home and updated Beth about what had happened in court and told her I would call her again next week. Not knowing how long she would cope without my help financially, I wanted to keep the expensive long-distances collect calls to a minimum.

Bored with being in lockdown all day, I was anxious to hit the dayroom and pace, so I wouldn't be up all night. Soon enough, I would find out that it really didn't make much of a difference. The four of us stayed up all night playing cards and telling jokes until about 5:00 a.m., and just when we got to sleep, we were roused for breakfast. MCU sucked. I was already missing the freedom of the dorms. The next few days were filled with boring, never-ending games of spades. The other three guys seemed to have an uncanny ability to drift off with: sleep this was why I started reading in the first place. Not only did it pass the time without needing the others, but good authors also made good companies.

On Thursday, I received a postcard from my mom, who had just left her home in Washington's Long Beach Peninsula in her motorhome for a trip through the American Southwest during winter. The postcard had been sent from Montana a couple of days before, which ironically meant she had driven right by the Ada County Jail on Interstate 84 and passed within one hundred yards of me. She also sent me $50, so now I had $72 to buy commissary items with next Tuesday.

By the weekend, we had been in MCU for almost a week, and all of us were a little stir-crazy. We played spades all day Saturday and into the night, and by midnight, we were becoming loud and obnoxious, even by jail standards. We could pretty much do what we wanted if we didn't hurt anyone, but noise was the one thing the COs in MCU wouldn't tolerate, so we didn't disturb our neighbors. One night, we were laughing and making fun of one another that it wasn't surprising at all when the COs unlocked the door at 1:00 a.m. and told us all to step out of the cell.

We were lined up on the catwalk outside the cell while giggling and smirking like a bunch of schoolkids who had just gotten into trouble for farting in class. The silence of the rest of the unit quickly embraced us, and I knew we were in deep shit for how loud we had been. Once we gained our composure and quiet once again reigned supreme on the tier, a muscular, smooth-headed, and very soft-spoken CO named Sergeant Norton gave us all a very disapproving look.

"Since you four are obviously wide-awake and can't seem to keep the noise level down, I want you to come downstairs with me. I have something for you guys to do that might help us keep the noise level down," he told us. Once downstairs, we lined up in front of his desk as he stood next to us and yelled over his shoulder to his partner, "Hey, Johnson, someone got the grout in my cement floor all dirty!" He the pointed to a pile of toothbrushes on the counter and four spray bottles. "Let me know when I can come inspect the floors in the entire dayroom, gentlemen," he said in a voice so low it was intimidating.

We spent the next two hours on our hands and knees, spraying grout between the squares of cement and scrubbing them with toothbrushes. Occasionally, we would glance at one another and start to laugh to ourselves, or steal a quick smirk, but soon we were back in our cell, playing cards and laughing quietly through the night until breakfast. I had spent three months during basic training at Fort Benning, Georgia, and never once had to clean floors with a toothbrush until I had landed here.

We all spent most of the day Sunday sleeping, and I finally got ahold of my lawyer on Monday, one day before I would be in court. The chickenshit didn't even have the balls to talk to me man-to-man. He told his secretary to tell me to get ahold of a public defender's office since he wasn't interested in handling my case any longer. I was devastated at the lack of professionalism exhibited by this guy, not to mention the delay in informing me. For $200 an hour, a guy in my position expected just a little bit more bang for the buck, and once again, I would be up all night, worrying about court tomorrow.

The next morning, after the usual shackles, handcuffs, and a short bus ride, I waited again for three hours to go in front of the judge. Finally, at eleven o'clock, he called my name. When I told him I had no legal representation and why, he asked me a few financial questions and then let me know that I qualified for a public defender. The judge rescheduled my sentencing until October 14 and told me my new lawyer would contact me in jail. The stupidity of my old lawyer had cost me thirty-two days. Not taking my foot off his head was the first thing that went through my mind.

CHAPTER

7

I WASN'T DUE BACK IN court for five weeks. Five more weeks locked up with these guys in MCU, and I would go stir-crazy! It wasn't from the guys I was with but had more to do with the limited space I had to move around. These guys loved MCU because they could fall asleep at will. I was wired a little differently and had spent many hours being the only one in the cell wide awake, reading and pacing back and forth to occupy my time.

When I got back to the jail and into the cell, the guys were all awake and totally fired up for some reason.

"What's up, guys? Tell me some good news, 'cause court really sucked." I smiled and joined in their enthusiasm for whatever good news I was expectantly waiting for.

"We are going back to the dorms around dinner," Monopoly said with a big smile. A week ahead of schedule seemed too good to be true, and I immediately became skeptical. The three off them had ganged up while I was gone so they could mess with my head. Not a bad attempt, I had to admit, but I wasn't buying it until I heard it from a CO or somebody else. Three men alone all day will do anything to amuse themselves, and I had no intention of being the victim of their boredom. The air conditioner was fixed, and we were supposedly moving back to dorm 6 sometime before dinner according to the scuttlebutt or maybe even a cruel rumor started by the CO just to mess with us low-life convicts, whom most of them looked down upon. I was sure they were probably just as bored as we were, so why not have some fun? Locked up in our cell until dinner, we were only allowed to hit the intercom button for emergencies, and one could go to seg if one abused the privilege just to ask a stupid question. Getting reliable information up and down the chain of command here was a total crapshoot.

I told the guys what had happened in court and tried not to get my hopes up about moving until we were told to roll up. I always hope for the best but plan for the worst; I am usually prepared for whatever happens. Suddenly, the intercom blared out, "Roll up, gentlemen. We are moving back to dorm 6 in thirty minutes." The guys hadn't been bullshitting me, after all. Soon enough, the guards opened all the cell doors and told us not to come out until our names were called.

My name was called third out of ninety-six to be moved, and I smirked at the guys as I headed toward the freedom of the dorm before them. As I strolled down the long corridor, I felt a calming acceptance of my immediate future come over me and felt as if my luck were changing for the better. We could have been stuck in MCU for weeks, but after only six days, I felt almost like a free man. Compared to MCU, the dorms were practically freedom. I told myself to be happy from now on because things could be worse.

When I stepped inside, the CO told me my new bunk assignment, number 73 on the upper right. When I got up to my tier and found my bunk, I quickly switched my mattress for the thickest, fattest, fluffiest one I could find while making sure the CO didn't see me do it. As the others slowly poured in, I quickly made my bunk and situated my stuff while assessing my good fortune. Things were looking up. I had randomly scored the best bunk in the whole unit from just the luck of the draw.

It was not a bunk bed against the back wall but a single out in front against the second-story railing overlooking the whole unit. This gave me a view of the dayroom, so I could see what was going on, but also a front-row balcony seat above the only TV in the unit. Upstairs was always more secure, since everyone wasn't strolling through all the time as they were down below. I was in the middle of our tier, so I didn't have to be next to the toilet, and I could use the railing to tuck my feet under so I could do sit-ups. But one of the best things was the view of the bunk I had from the dayroom down below. I could see my bunk and my bin box, where my possessions would be kept once I ordered from commissary. From almost every table in the dayroom, I could keep a watchful eye on my bin box to make sure nobody ripped me off. After all, there was a bunch of criminals in here. Hungry men with no money were always ripping off goodies from those more fortunate than themselves, and one could not be too careful protecting what was theirs. This problem didn't exist in MCU since the only four men allowed in any cell was the ones housed there, so you would always get caught. The dorms were like having twenty-three roommates on each tier, and that meant inevitable conflict and inevitable crime.

For now, I was safe with my empty bin box, and turning around, I noticed all the guys from MCU bunked near me, giving me some friends on the tier until I got to know everyone else. Most gave me shit about my awesome bunk, and some even noticed my fat mattress. The last guy on the tier was doomed for some restless nights until somebody else left.

Once I settled in, I headed downstairs to find out from the CO what day commissary was for dorm 6, but my good luck held. I overheard someone talking about what they were going to order tonight, and I realized most of these guys had been in here before going to MCU, so they already knew we ordered tonight and would receive it tomorrow. We had until lights-out to fill it out, and it would be delivered tomorrow morning around ten. At last, there was light at the end of the tunnel. Nothing picks up a man's spirit in jail more than receiving commissary. Water from the fountain and three bland institutional meals a day, on a repeating and rotating basis, get old really fast. Yeah, we would get Kool-Aid with lunch and dinner and milk with breakfast, but an eight-ounce cup hardly quenched my desire quite like chugging a half-gallon of it ice-cold, like I would at home. God, I missed my milk! I tried not think about it, because it would just piss me off. It was my fault I was here, so there was no use dwelling on it. I will give the county credit for one thing: the water fountain was good and cold. Too bad it didn't dispense milk. I immediately headed over to the commissary list posted on the bulletin board to see what wonderful options I had to choose from. I had all night to figure out what to order, and we were limited to $50 to spend on food and $50 for hygiene items or stationery supplies. I also had to make sure I paid back those four candy bars I owed for the two I got last week. I didn't want to piss anyone off who had been nice enough to take care of me. I filled out my form and played cards the rest of the night in between miles and was looking forward to tomorrow. The small comforts from commissary became the highlight of each week.

We began to settle in, and our newfound freedom put everyone in a good mood. Friends separated in different cells and tier times in MCU quickly caught up with events that had transpired over the last week and exchanges of funny stories that always accompany isolated time with bored cellmates.

I got in bed that night contemplating my future and possibilities. I had already pleaded guilty and had a plea bargain with the prosecutor for 120 days in jail. By court on October 14, I figured I would have been locked up ninety days total for this offense, and Kurt had told me before he quit as my attorney that he was going to ask for time served at sentencing. I was only off by 30 days, so hopefully, I would be going home after court that day. With any luck, I would be home for my birthday on October 18, and this would all be behind me. I was glad to be out of MCU; I had a killer bunk, and my three buddies from MCU were on the same tier as me. These guys were quickly introducing me to all the guys they knew, so things were looking up.

Happy to wake up to the freedom of the dorms, I quickly got back into my pacing routine and walked and read for a couple of hours until the best part of the week would arrive in the form of commissary. It had been twelve days since I had any indulgences, accepting the two candy bars, and watching others who flaunted their full bin boxes was becoming extremely difficult. I didn't need much, but a few treats now and then made all the difference in here. We were told to bunk up and wait for our name to be called and come down and receive our purchases.

Once my name was called, I felt like it was my turn to open my Christmas stocking. I took my bin box downstairs and put it down next to my bag on one of the tables, where the inmate-workers had placed it for me. Before I left that table, I had to inventory my order and make sure what I paid for was there. Once I left the table, if I found discrepancy, there was no recourse, so I had to make sure it was right before I left. I inventoried everything I had received against everything they charged me for to make sure I didn't get ripped off. Once all was well, I went back upstairs. I had a big smile on my face, unaware of the vultures eyeballing my stash and making a mental inventory of who and what would be easy prey for them to steal from.

My first order of business was to pay back my debt. Nobody liked a man who didn't pay his debts, and I had no desire to be given that or any other label. Since sharing commissary and being in possession of other inmates' property were both against the rules, repayment of these debts must be done with a bit of discretion.

Technically, you were not supposed to have anything in your bin box or in your possession you did not have a receipt for. If you got caught, you could go to seg for a couple of days and lose your commissary for a week. This rarely happened, and the COs usually only did this when they wanted to mess with someone they had a more serious beef with and needed an excuse to dig deeper. I desperately wanted to stay out of seg and keep every bit of commissary, so I made sure to keep my receipts and be very careful when trading with others.

With the commissary passed out, we were back on free time, and I was glad to finally be able to eat when I felt like it. I didn't go overboard with goodies like some people did but saved a few high-demand items for future profit. I would stick with the same commissary each week, with coffee and cocoa to mix with it, Top Ramens, peanut butter bars, Tang, Skittles, saltine crackers, and a jar of peanut butter. I also got some hygiene products that were a must in here, including shower shoes, soap, and lotion, along with a couple of pens, legal pads, and envelopes.

The tier was abuzz with trading and debts being paid as well as arguments breaking out for those who did not honor their arrangements with their fellow inmates. Suddenly, as I looked downstairs, I saw a guy sitting on his butt, pulling himself across the carpet of the dayroom from one end to the other.

"What the hell is he doing?" I said to everyone around me as I pointed down to the man making a spectacle of himself.

"That's called the wormy dog," Monopoly told me. "That's what happens to guys that don't pay their debt. They are subjected to public humiliation, and nobody will ever store out to them again. They're burnt." We all stared and laughed as the hilarious scene was halted by the CO, who was less than amused. I was glad I paid my debts on time and wasn't forced to humiliate myself in this way. I also made a quick mental note as to who the welsher was, so I would be sure and not become his next victim.

As I observed what was going on all around me on the tier, I couldn't help but notice one fellow who appeared to be extremely popular all of a sudden. It was a guy downstairs named Reynaldo. The man had guys practically lined up at his bunk, and it was obvious he had more commissary than his box would hold. He must have been running store for a long time now and appeared to be making quite a huge profit doing it. The thing that scared me the most about running store was the COs having a clear view of the entire unit all the time. They even had cameras running 24-7 from the main office behind the CO station and could view three units. There was a one-way mirror with different cameras aimed at each tier recording everything that happened in case there was a fight. All the COs had to do was play back the tape, and they could file assault charges on the perpetrator after they found out what had really happened.

There truly is absolutely no privacy in jail. This is the first thing they take from you the minute you walk through the doors. While everyone else was eating goodies from their commissary and getting jacked up on the caffeine they had been denied the past few days, I didn't touch one thing in my bin box. As much as I wanted to, and as long as I had been deprived of most of these comforts, I knew that lunch was only moments away. The next commissary was still six days and twenty-three and a half hours away, and the man who had things to store out on Monday and Tuesday night would double his bin box by Wednesday. By next week, I wanted guys handing me stuff like Reynaldo received today. To be in business next week, it would require me to exercise extreme self-control for now.

CHAPTER

8

A FTER LUNCH, I ASKED REYNALDO, "Can I talk to you for a little bit?"

"Sure, but let's wait until we are in the rec yard in fifteen or twenty minutes."

Apparently, he and the rest of the unit were all on schedule for the next weekly Wednesday activity that was known as superexchange. I looked around, and the whole unit looked like it was rolling up and moving once again.

I asked Monopoly, "What the hell is going on now?"

"Gather all your clothes and linen in one pile and your hygiene issue into your plastic cup and take it downstairs to the bins they just brought in. Then, we go to rec for superexchange while the COs tear this place apart." Once a week, each dorm did this, usually immediately following the unit's commissary distribution. Everyone was to bring down everything, leaving only their two blankets and bin boxes, inspection-ready. They did it to make sure your receipts matched your property and that you weren't hoarding books or other people's property.

It was mandatory for everyone to go out for rec while the COs went through our stuff and searched the toilets, showers, and dayroom for unauthorized contraband and weapons. After about an hour, we would each be patted down and individually searched on the way back in, stripped down to our skivvies, and handed a new set of clothes, spare uniform, and bedroll. It was for a combination of security and hygiene reasons. Some people never changed their clothes, and this way, they were forced to do so at least once a week when we came back from rec.

We all headed out to the yard, which was a triangle about sixty-five feet long on all three sides, surrounded by a twenty-foot-high cinder block brick wall with concertina razor wire on top. Off to the side was a post cemented into the ground with a backboard on it but no rim, no net, and no balls to use. With around ninety-six guys, give or take a few, depending on how many empty bunks we had and who happened to be at court, the area was rather crowded. It was a nice, warm, sunny day, and everyone began walking in a nice, slow circle around the perimeter of the rec yard. After only five minutes, roughly 75 percent of the walkers all sat down against the wall and soaked in the warmth of the sun. I began to pace around the inside circle of feet made from everyone sitting with their back to the wall. After five minutes of my brisk walking, Reynaldo, who was sitting next to Monopoly, chatting, got up and began pacing with me.

"What can I do for you?" he asked as we strolled side by side, listening to the usual banter and whinny gossip among the crowded rec yard.

"I noticed you were quite popular once we got commissary. How does all that work?" I asked him. He explained how usually he made two-for-one item to guys who had established credit with him or could prove they had money on their books. Anyone could go up to the guard and ask how much money was on their books, or they could show the receipt they received during the mail call, when someone sent them money. I had received a receipt for the cash I had during intake and another with my mom's postcard, so I knew exactly what he was talking about.

Out of nowhere, some guy walked out to the middle of the rec yard and started doing push-ups, screaming at the top of his lungs, "I love cock! I love cock!" as he went up and down. He did this during twenty push-ups, and when he was done, he went back to his spot on the wall with a red face, a good round of applause, and his debt paid with public humiliation. This time, it wasn't from commissary transaction, though; it came from losing a spades game. Ronaldo also told me most people didn't pay their debt until after superexchange, so the COs didn't bust them right after commissary. Since we were limited to $50 worth of food, the key was to hold on to as much as possible until Monday or Tuesday, when everybody else was running out of stuff. They stored it out on Monday or Tuesday night and got back double on Wednesday. Not wanting to step on anybody's toes, I asked Reynaldo if he cared if I stored stuff out, and he said no problem. In fact, he was already so busy he couldn't keep all the profit in his bin box without drawing attention to himself and possibly getting caught, so he said to help whomever I could and he might even send some guys my way if I kicked him a little something back occasionally. "No problem," I told him as we bumped knuckles, and off he went. I walked the rest of the superexchange, and before we were told to line up in the hall and get searched, I was the only one left in the whole unit who was still pacing.

After we went back in and got our bunks put back together with fresh linen, the real paybacks took place. Now you had a week to either eat or use whatever didn't really belong to you before we got searched again. I told my three buddies from MCU and four other guys I had gotten to know from playing card that I was running store now and for them to let me know if they needed anything, and to spread the word to those who could be trusted. There were certain items I found out that would be high demand in this dorm. Top Ramen, stamped envelopes, and coffee were always good for trade, especially at the first of the week. For someone who was hungry all the time from the small amount of food the jail gave us, Top Ramen was a must and usually eaten around 9:00 p.m., so you didn't have to go to bed on an empty stomach. Stamped envelopes, or lopes, as we called them, were a form of money around here, and two of them would get you into the Texas Hold'em card table with playing cards with Xs on them, which were used for poker chips. One guy ran the game, and you had to buy your chips from him and get cashed out with lopes each day if you wanted to play, so he wouldn't get left holding the bag if he got searched.

Then there were the caffeine junkies, who were usually older guys that couldn't function without their coffee. These guys would do other people's chores for them, especially breakfast chores, in exchange for coffee. This way, the guy with money on his books could go back to bed in the morning between breakfast and count time. Some guys were so broke they ended up doing two or three chores for two or three meals just to get the goods they wanted or to pay of gambling debts from losing at spades games. The spades games were not just for entertainment; there was usually a wager of some kind. Chores, push-ups, commissary, lopes, and even sometimes more creative and humiliating ways to pay up, similar to the ones we saw during rec. Even though I could easily trade some of my coffee to get my chores done, it was after dinner and pretty easy. I saw no need for someone to do them for me, which would allow me more merchandise to be able to store out. Now, the key to making any profit was to just not eat it all, no matter how tempting or hungry I got. The more I had on Monday and Tuesday, the better off I would be for the rest of my stay. Some guys would get so much stored out to them the first week, before they could even buy any commissary, that they were always playing catch-up. With limits on how much you could buy each week, a person with a big appetite, no willpower, and lots of friends could end up paying off two-for-one for weeks or even months at a time. The only way to get ahead was to do chores, push-ups, or wormy dogs. Once an inmate lowered themselves to that level, they lost a lot of respect from the unit and were looked down upon the rest of their stay here.

My mind was made up. The more disciplined I was this week, the more stuff I could store out and double by next week. With only $20 on my books and no idea how or when I would get any more, it seemed like running store was the logical thing to do in order to be self-supportive. I knew Beth would send me money when she could, but the house payments, school clothes for Sean, and bills would rightfully come first. The only thing I could control from in here was the discipline to run store until it grew big enough to support itself. Along with my pacing and reading, having the willpower to run store would become my new obsession. One well-known fact that I already knew was that the busier a person is, the faster time seems to go pass. While incarcerated, that was the name of the game.

CHAPTER

9

IT WAS NICE TO HAVE a plan finally. As messed up as it was, it was still a plan to help keep me busy and my mind sharp. The next few days, I would always have breakfast and rest again until count time. I would then stay up and read or walk until 10:00–11:00 a.m., when the tier slowly came to life. After lunch, more pacing around fifteen miles a day before lunch. I was reading in between card games in the afternoon and at night more of the same until I was so exhausted I would get into bed and read myself to sleep usually before lights-out. I would occasionally store out a few candy bars to new guys who came in, or soup to some hungry friends who I knew would pay me back. Since everybody saw me walking on and off all day, guys would approach me and ask about my latest book or recommend a good one to me. I quickly had eight or nine books waiting to be read next or traded for other good ones with fellow readers as soon as they were done. Before long, I was reading so much I decided to keep a list of the books I had read, and I began to write them all down. I liked certain authors and their style, which led to more than a few discussions about literature with fellow inmates.

I was amazed at the extensive knowledge these seemingly idiotic people had when it came to our number one pastime, reading. Ironically, nobody did any reading once they were released. Instead of continuing to better and educate themselves through literature, they would immediately return to their illegal ways. In retrospect, when I discovered this, I also realized that I had never read since the last time I was in jail also, so who was I to judge? I wondered why that was the case not just for them but for me as well. I was quickly discovering that books had replaced cigarettes as the major trade commodity, even more so than commissary. A Top Ramen, and a cup of coffee, or a candy bar would be filling and comforting for five or ten minutes. A good book, however, would last a day or two for me, and most guys a week. Even though we weren't supposed to be in possession of another inmate's property, guys who had books sent to them were able to trade them for other good books or commissary, once they were done reading them. The better the author, the more it was worth, since the dorm cart was hardly ever worth looking into. Occasionally, the last few pages would be missing, or the book was broken up into three or four sections from excessive usage, and that sucked.

After looking at my short list of books with three hundred or four hundred pages each, it was motivational to see how quickly I was going through them. I also started keeping track of the miles I was walking. If I was here, I might as well get into shape and lose a little weight instead of sleeping all day and letting myself get soft. With evenings usually spent playing spades, it was a nice break, since I had usually walked all day, on and off, and sitting down to rest my feet felt pretty good. Everybody's ante into the Spades tournament was one lope, two men per team times eight, or usually sixteen teams added up to thirty-two lopes for the winners, and that translates into eight dollars for each team member. Some of the guys who were in jail a lot were pretty much card sharks, hustlers, and cheats. If you had no money on your books, the only way you could earn was to hustle others by whatever means necessary to get extra food or put your hands on a good book. The problem was, every now and then, in the finals, guys would catch someone else cheating or table-talking. Guys would have hand signals or tell one another what was in their hands by using code words, and both were considered forfeiture of the game. Controlling the behavior was extremely difficult in jail since most people couldn't follow the rules on the outside were even more difficult to control in here. This would usually end up in a fight, and then the whole tournament would fall apart since we weren't supposed to be gambling in the first place. The CO usually turned a blind eye unless something like that happened and then disciplinary action had to be taken.

I had my unique methods for occupying my time in here, but most guys did one of three things. Sleeping was an easy choice for those whose body would allow them to get eighteen hours each day. The younger crowd was usually in front of the TV in the dorm, which was not always on my choice of programming. Most guys played spades to keep busy. A simple-enough game, with two-man teams often challenging other two-man teams, which often included a small wager of some kind. The weird thing was, most arguments that led to fights involved two guys on the same team. One guy would get mad at the other for not playing properly and then blame his partner for costing him the wager.

I occasionally played in these tournaments not to win the prize, because odds were against it, but for the entertainment. Most people wouldn't play regular games for fun; they always wanted to bet something, so entertaining yourself in here did cost you something. One lope would get you two or three hours into most tournaments, which was cheaper and safer in the long run instead of wagering one for each of three or four games I would play if I wasn't in the tournament. I didn't like to gamble very much, because I knew some of these hustlers would fleece me, and I didn't want to lose what I should be storing out. A single ramen lost today is worth two next week, and four the week after that. Since I thought of it that way, a lost ramen would actually be eight or sixteen down the road, and then the cost of gambling now was just too high. I had no intention of ever going hungry like I did the first two weeks I was here. As long as I had something to fall back on in my bin box and I had access to some good books, the only really bad thing about being here was the fact that I missed Sean and Beth. I also missed my milk.

The repetition of the meals and the isolation from my family were really the only things that bothered me. I felt sorry for a few of my new friends here who had been inside here for ten months and still had two to go. One guy's judge gave him 364 days in the county jail instead of one year. Any sentence over one year would automatically get you sent to prison, but the judge didn't want that.

Supposedly, prison time was much easier than county jail. TVs in your cell, pool tables in the rec room, weight rooms, basketball court with actual hoops and nets, along with better and more plentiful food made prison life easier to handle than jail. The judge wanted him to be stuck in county so he would be forced to suffer more. Anyone I had talked to about it had said the same thing, but I wasn't planning on finding out firsthand.

By the time my third weekend here had rolled around, I was feeling comfortable with the guys in my tier. I was getting a good reputation as a quiet, keep-to-myself kind of guy, and that was what most people wanted in here. Nothing was worse or more annoying than some loudmouth, nonstop, obnoxious know-it-all who butted his nose into everybody's business. The other hated guys were the whiny crybabies, who wouldn't shut up about how the system or their wife or girlfriend was to blame for all their problems and they never did one thing wrong in their entire life. I was flying under the radar, keeping a low profile, and slowly getting to know most of the guys on the tier. Monopoly had introduced me to most of them, since he had been here a while, and he and I were quickly becoming good friends. He was also my spades partner most of the time.

If you played smart and didn't do anything stupid, it was mostly luck of the draw, although every now and then things that you just couldn't control would happen. Reynaldo began to send guys my direction over the weekend to store stuff out, and if he or one of the other guys in the tier would vouch for someone, it was good enough for me. We also got a new guy in on Friday night who was a perfect example of an overzealous legal system trying to keep the jail full. He was a baby-faced nineteen-year-old who came directly into our unit so he wouldn't get messed with in unit 5. This poor kid was so scared nobody was sure what he would do first, piss himself or start crying. Thank God they put him up on our tier, so we could take care of him, but that didn't mean we couldn't have a little fun with him first.

Jack Addison was the guy who was sentenced 364 days in county. He had a mean look to him, but he was a big teddy bear. He was a fellow reader and a big Dean Koontz fan, and his bunk was two bunks away from mine and almost as nice. The only problem I could see about his was that it was right next to the bathroom facilities on our tier. When you have twenty-three other tier-mates sharing a couple of urinals and two sinks and two commodes, the nights you have burritos or franks and beans can't be too pleasant, no matter how you slice it.

Jack went up to the new guy, Kurt, and said, "Have you made any friends here yet?" Kurt's eyes popped wide open, and the expression on his face showed just how scared this poor kid was. "What are you in for?" Jack asked slowly, deeply, and in a very intimidating way. Acting as if we didn't care, the rest of the tier had a watchful eye on the happenings but also giving Jack room to operate.

"My buddy said he would go pay for some ice, so I grabbed a couple and threw them in the cooler while he went and paid," Kurt explained. "The problem was, he only paid for one and I grabbed two. The clerk saw this and called the cops with my license plate number, and before we got back to the tailgate party, they pulled us over and arrested me for theft." Poor kid wouldn't get to go in front of a judge until Monday, so he was with us for the weekend at least. Jack looked into the kid's eyes softly and said, "Don't worry, I'll make sure we have a fun weekend, just you and me." Everyone held their smirks under their breaths if they could, but when we looked closely, the kid was in tears and turned to hide his face. Just then, Monopoly and I went over and put a stop to it. What Jack had done had scared the poor dude half to death. Kurt saw Monopoly and me headed his way, and a big smile crossed Jack's face and he knew it was just a joke.

"Sorry, dude," Jack said. "I was just messing with you. It's all cool in here. You're safe."

A small group of us gathered around Kurt, introduced ourselves, and told him not to worry about a thing. Kurt had even realized he had been pranked and cracked a small, cautious smile. We sort of took him under our wing and adopted him for the weekend to make sure he was okay. We were not a bad group of guys, just a little older and wiser, and probably bored.

Kurt was a student at Boise State who was from Bend, Oregon, and had never been in trouble his short pampered life. After what we did to him, I don't think he was so afraid of telling his dad what happened, and I think he grew up a little as well. Needless to say, we were a little more careful of how we handled new guys after that, and we saved the pranks for guys we knew a little better. So I guess us old-timers learned a lesson too.

Scott and Roger were bunkmates who were right across from me up against the back wall. They were also a couple of the older guys in their tier of mostly twenty- to thirty-year-olds. Roger was a huge, muscular, and tattooed ex-con that was probably headed back to the pen on his current meth charges and was sort of the tier boss. Nobody messed with him in the whole unit for that matter, and he was the guy who ran the Texas Hold'em card table. Deep down, Roger was a mellow guy who also kept to himself, but believe me, I wouldn't want to be on his bad side for any reason. In fact, he kind of got pissed off at Jack for what he did to Kurt over the weekend, but I kept thinking how much better Roger would have pulled it off. Kurt would probably have shit himself if Roger had done it. I only imagine what would have gone through my mind if Roger pulled something like that on me my first night here.

Scott was the tier matriarch, coming in at fifty-eight years old. He was in here for stealing horses and was looking at a trip to the pen for eighteen months. Both these guys pretty much read or slept all day; other than that, all they did was win all the time at Texas table. I was getting to know these two so well, because they would always be willing to buy stuff with lopes they won at the poker table. Two lopes were equivalent to a dollar's worth of commissary, and by selling to these two guys, I slowly began to gather a nice supply. Then I would trade the lopes to guys who would write all the time, who were willing to give up their food, so they could mail letters home all the time. As long as I came out ahead in the deal somehow, I would do it. Otherwise, I wouldn't. Business is business.

CHAPTER

10

SCOTT HAPPENED TO BE A veteran of the Vietnam War, and on Saturday, he was finishing up a book he was reading the last couple of days about the Special Operations Group in the war, known as SOG. These were covert Special Forces who would go deep into enemy territory and pull off missions that most troops couldn't handle. Highly sophisticated, well trained, and well equipped, these guys ended up with one of the highest ratio of enemies killed per US troop in the entire war.

"Hey, Walker, I see you reading all the time. You want this book when I'm done?" he asked me while showing me the cover title, *SOG: Special Operations Group in Vietnam.* "It is very well written and realistic. Believe me, I should know."

"Why's that?" I asked him.

"I flew choppers for the SOG for three tours in the midsixties."

I told him I would take it when he was done and thanked him for thinking of me. I had always been fascinated with the Vietnam War, seen most of the movies made on the subject, and I was always looking for something good to read in here.

I was in the Oregon Army National Guard for six years from 1983 to 1989, and during that time, I met, worked with, and talked to a lot of Vietnam vets. The secret I learned about getting the good stories out of them was to let them tell you at their pace. Never force it or ask about it but just listen, respond caringly, and be patient. Only after you had gained their trust and friendship did they truly began to tell the good stories. My system seemed to work with Scott as well, and after small chitchat about the war for a couple of days, he finally opened up.

"I was a helicopter pilot when I enlisted and volunteered with my childhood friend from Oklahoma," he began to tell me. "The two of us were crop dusters and decided to join the Army and go see the world together. I enjoyed my job and was really good at it, as most pilots who managed to survive over there were. During our second tour, while evacuating a group of SOG soldiers near the Cambodian border, I saw my buddy's chopper get hit. I watched helplessly horrified as my best friend since we were five ran out of his chopper and fell to the ground, slowly burning to death. Something inside of me snapped that day, and I lost it. I killed everything on the ground after that, and I mean everything." There was a long pause after I heard all that as he seemed to be reliving the experience all over again in his mind. He never signed up for a third tour, and once he got home, his life was different forever. Being in and out of trouble with the law and drinking and drugs took over his life as it did with many returning vets.

"If you are really interested in this shit, you could read about it in some of the short stories I wrote on the subject and submitted for publication. The VA psychiatrist told me that writing down my experiences and sharing them with others is cleansing for the soul and helps in the healing process." He was supposed to put some of the things that bothered him from war on a piece of paper so he could face it and deal with it. It also helped clear the conscience in case any deep-seated guilt was causing him stress. He told me I could read his stories only after I finished the SOG book, which he would give me later today to start reading. He finished on Saturday night, and with not much to do Sunday, I read the whole thing from start to finish that day. It was the first time I had completed a book in a day, but not the last.

When I told Scott the next day that I had finished the SOG book, he broke out a file about a half-inch thick with typewritten pages that his lawyer had brought him into the jail. He told me I could read them as long as I didn't tell anybody else about it and promised not to judge him too critically. Feeling his apprehension to let me into his private little world, I gave him my word to comply. He had seen me reading on and off the last few weeks, but who was to judge anyone at this point? It was one thing to have an opinion on published books by famous authors, who write for a living. By earning a living, that way, they practically invite it. It was a whole other subject to publicly criticize and possibly embarrass a fellow tier member who let me read his private memoirs, which had only been shared between him and his psychiatrist to this point.

I spent the rest of the day storing out commissary and reading the eighty or ninety pages of stories, atrocities, and events that continually cluttered Scott's conscience before, during, and mostly after the war. The events were disturbing to read about, but the thing I was truly impressed with was his ability to describe the way these events had stayed in front of his mind and haunted him over the years. His writing was interesting to read and very thought-provoking, to say the least. I was very impressed.

Finally, commissary day came once again, and it was truly the climax of the inmates' week. Now it was time to collect and see if running store was as good of a business as I had hoped it would be. If nobody repaid their debt and I lost all the merchandise I loaned out, what was the point? I carefully watched as all those men who owed me all came forward to receive their commissary. Fortunately, by the time we all came back in from superexchange, everyone who had owed me had paid up. So far, so good, and it appeared to me that running store definitely had its advantages. I was left with almost $90 worth of stuff repaid to me plus the last $20 I spent this week myself. I had turned $70 into $110 over the course of a week while being incarcerated, and that wasn't half-bad. I decided to keep doing it so I wouldn't have to buy as much each week and I would still be able to live comfortably. Why not? I didn't have much else to do, it was a great way to meet people, and I could control my comfort level rather that depend on anybody controlling it for me.

CHAPTER

11

THE BUNK NEIGHBOR NEXT TO me was Jay Burbury. He was a twenty-two-year-old habitual offender who occupied the only bunk in the unit that might even come close to being considered as good as mine. He was up against one of the three-foot-high cinder block dividing walls that separated the rows of bunks on the rail overlooking the dayroom. The guy on the other side of him was too far left of the TV to be able to watch from his bunk, so Jay and I had the two best bunks in the tier.

He was from the younger generation rapidly appearing in the system with credit card, identity theft, and fraud charges to answer for. They accounted for a large portion of the jail population than I had ever imagined before I arrived. How anyone ever thought they could get away with a crime that left a paper trail the way those crimes do is beyond me. His charges would continue to be added to his record as more of the checks he had fraudulently cashed or the sham credit card purchase he had sent to his house were discovered. Over a six-month period, his charges grew and grew until he was now going to court two to three times a week, with two different judges, to face fifteen separate felony charges against him. With all this over his head, I had to give him a little credit—the guy was usually in a great mood, easy to get along with, and never got mad as many of the fellow inmates did.

The thing I respected about Jay the most was that he had a routine that kept him sane in a place where total insanity surrounded him. Although it was a little strange, it seemed to work for him, so I had to admire it even if I didn't agree with it. The guy would eat his breakfast and get up for the mandatory 7:00 a.m. standing count, then go back to sleep until lunch and do the same thing again until dinner. The only time he was up during the day was when he had court. As soon as he returned, he headed straight for bed again. He had constructed a blindfold by wrapping a sock around his eyes and locking it in place with a comb. From dinner until lights-out, he became a bit more social and tried to earn a little something by engaging in a few games of spades. Then he would read all night long until breakfast. Only some people were able to do this, depending on how well-lit their bunk areas were. This, too, was another reason our bunks were so good: there was a light from the dayroom that enabled our reading 24-7, yet it was still dark enough for us to sleep if we were tired. On many of my sleepless nights, he and I would quietly share favorite parts of books we had both read or sometimes make recommendations to each other at 3:00 a.m., while the other inmates were snoring.

Most people had their own routine to pass time. Otherwise, it would get too boring and time would drag on. If you could manage to fill the day with things to do and schedule to keep, the days seemed to go by much more quickly. The busier I was, the faster time seemed to go by. This gave me a huge psychological advantage over the guys who sat around, pissing and moaning all the time, and believe me, most of them did, especially the younger ones. All they could ever seem to talk about was being screwed over by others, never taking responsibility for their actions. They tried to blame everything on others without looking at the true cause of their problems. It never accomplished anything but just seemed to bring people down. I tried to surround myself with more positive people to help keep my morale up.

Even though you live with one hundred nineteen guys, jail is quite a lonely place. The people you really care about and want to be with are back home, going on without you in their lives, and what hurts the most is to not be there with them.

The only contact we had with friends or family was through jail visits or collect phone calls. I would call every week or so, but I actually avoided calling home too much. It would make me sad to call and talk to them. I loved and missed them both terribly, but every time I would get done talking to them, I would get overwhelmed with sadness and grief, which made it that much harder to call them the next time. I was hoping to be home in a month, and this would all be over then. But it was still difficult to think of them out in the world while I was stuck in here, unable to help or support them in any way. I constantly worried that Beth would find someone else while I was locked up, but thoughts like that just make you a "hard timer" in prison, so I tried to stay focused on my routine and decided I would deal with the outside world when the time came. What could I do about it in here, anyways? It would be out of my hands. I was already having a hard-enough time just being locked up. Some repeat offenders were used to this life, and some seemed to enjoy being away from society for a while. I would never be like that.

As I paced and read throughout the day, I would catch bits and pieces of conversations between inmates or phones calls from wives, girlfriends, or children.

I would constantly hear the other guys constantly complaining about the same old stuff every day. It was a constant stream of bitching for the most part, so repetitive I could hardly stand it. Maybe that was how these guys coped with being incarcerated, so I tried to be understanding. That was why I enjoyed the morning so much. I had the whole room to myself, in total silence. Occasionally, I would get into an intelligent conversation with the CO and we would step out into the hall, where he could watch through the glass and the noise wouldn't bother anyone. It almost felt normal.

Some inmates were just plain stupid, uneducated, or young; they were so immersed in the criminal underworld that carrying a conversation about anything besides drugs or crime was beyond them. So I would put in my earplugs, lie down on my bunk, and read myself into another world. Authors like Lee Child, Michael Connelly, Louis L'Amour, Clive Cussler, and my new favorite since my arrival here, James Patterson, kept me from becoming totally bored. If you had a Patterson book that someone received in the mail, the waiting list determined who would get to read it next; it always had at least four or five names on it. The list would usually remain that long until everyone in the unit had read it.

When it was their turn, each person gave you something for the privilege of reading it—a lope, a dessert, a ramen, or any other good book. By the time some of the Patterson books worked their way around the unit, the owner usually had $5 worth of trade for the privilege of letting others enjoy a good read. If you've read Patterson, you'd understand why.

After I was done with the SOG book and Scott's Vietnam stories, I found a great little book on the cart. It was *Wise Guys*, the biography of Henry Hill, who was the main character in *Goodfellas*, the movie it was based on. I had only read a few good books back in junior high that had years later been turned into movies. It was usually disappointing to see my memory of the written version destroyed or interpreted on film in a way that I had not expected. When reading, a person is given the ability to use their own imagination and mentally insert certain images the author had described, or they were left out or replaced by the screenwriter. In a movie, you are forced to see it from a director's point of view or a producer's imagination, and this can never be as perfect as yours.

Goodfellas was the first time in my life I had seen a movie and then years later read the book that the movie was derived from. This was odd. I kept visualizing the scene from the movie while reading, yet some of the author's thoughts and feelings would occasionally be left out of the film, and now I was able to delve even deeper into the mind of Henry Hill and the circumstances of his torrid life. The other thing I learned from this book was that telling a story was a far cry from writing one. The main difference basically was the amount of time one dedicated to the task.

I remembered the time I had spent in both inpatient and outpatient drug treatments centers. You told your druggie life story to your group in one hour. I had made an outline and basically winged it from there on my own, but both times people in the group would give me praise for telling a good, funny, and exciting story and tell me that I should write a book or make a movie based on my experiences. I had always shrugged off the idea, yet it always stayed in my mind. I had never written anything other than for school assignments. Scott had done it with his Nam stories. Henry Hill told his with the help of a ghostwriter or a biographer, so why couldn't I? Of course, I needed to be released from jail first. One of the best ways I could keep myself from "hard-timing," besides reading, was to remind myself just how easy I had it compared to, say, the guys in POW camps or hard-core lockups like San Quentin, Folsom, or Rikers Island. In those places, you not only had to do your time, but you also had to watch your back so you didn't get hurt, raped, or even killed.

On Monday night, with everyone running out of commissary, Jay came up to me and asked, "Garret, can you spot me two lopes, so I can play Texas tonight? I will pay you back on Wednesday when we get commissary." This was a new concept to me, but a very intriguing one. I had sponsored people at the casinos before, but that worked a whole different way. "Jay," I told him, "have I got a deal for you! Tell you what I'm going to do for you tonight and see how it works for both of us. I will give you the two lopes, but here is how it's going to work. If you win, we split the profit. If you lose, then you only owe me one lope. Is that fair enough for you?"

"I can live with that," he responded, and then I went up to my bunk to get two lopes. Then I went to tell Roger what was going on just in case Jay tried to jerk me around, but I trusted him as much as anyone inside the walls, so I wasn't too worried. If he lost, I would be out fifty cents, no big deal. If he won, however, my share could be between $5 or $6, depending on how busy the table was, which wasn't a bad gamble in my book. With commissary only a day away now, I found myself storing out almost everything I had in anticipation of the payoff come Wednesday. The list of stuff owed to me was impressive, but I had to be careful that I never exceeded my receipts for fear of losing the store to the COs during superexchange. Between my purchase and my paybacks, I was easily looking at $200 total but with only $70 worth of stuff I had receipts for. I was now up almost $130, and I had to come up with a way to make sure the COs didn't take it from me.

Just before lights-out, I was lying in bed, reading, and Jay came up the stairs with a shit-eating grin on his face and a handful of lopes. I closed my book and sat up to see how well my investment in him was going to pay off.

"How did we do at the table tonight, partner?" I asked him.

"I came in second place by the end of the night. I am up twenty-two lopes, eleven for each of us." He handed me eleven lopes to add to my collection and then asked if I would give him a ramen so he could celebrate with some food tonight. I couldn't really make it a two-for-one after his making me eleven lopes already tonight, so why not give him a ramen for only one in return?

"Just don't tell anybody," I told him, hoping to not let it get out that I was soft. Besides, with the massive commissary I was going to be holding on to until Wednesday, I would need a few favors from people myself.

"You owe me one," I said as he nodded okay and headed down to get some hot water before it was too late. It is amazing what makes a person happy when they are in jail.

A half-hour later at mail call, I got a letter from Beth along with $50 on my books, just in time for commissary tomorrow. It was good to hear from her and get some news from back home, but it also made me miss her and Sean all the more, and that made me sad. Before turning in for the night, I asked Roger how Jay did tonight. Roger confirmed the number of lopes Jay had won, and I knew Jay was now one of the few people in here I could truly trust. Behind bars, or fences, this was a good asset to have.

CHAPTER
12

ON WEDNESDAY MORNING, I WAS pacing and reading after razor call and anxiously anticipating commissary delivery so I could check my payback results. Most people sleep in most of the morning, but around eight thirty, my buddy Monopoly came downstairs early and began pacing with me.

"Care if I walk with you?" he asked.

"Just as long as you keep up and don't slow my timing off," I told him.

I put my book down on the next pass of my table, and after a couple of laps adjusting the pace for two walkers, we got into a nice rhythm, and I slowly began to think this was not a social discussion but rather business related. He and I had talked plenty of times, and I could tell he wanted something from me this time. The other dead giveaway was that he was up this early.

"I need to talk to you, and I mean seriously talk to you," he told me with a hint of desperation in his voice. "A lot of times guys give each other shit and joke around, and it's difficult to have a serious discussion with anyone here." He got my attention right away, and I had a feeling that whatever problem he had was soon going to become mine as well.

"I am in deep shit with Reynaldo, and there are three or four other people I owe money to from spades, but by the time I pay everybody back, I will have nothing left the rest of the week."

"Is the stuff I gave you going to come back today?" I asked him.

"Well, that is what I wanted to talk to you about."

I let the silence of his pause linger as I absorbed this information and let him take a moment to gather his thoughts so he could drop the proverbial bomb I was anticipating.

"Since I know you better than all those guys, I thought you and I could work out a deal that was beneficial to you and would keep me out of trouble as well. I am going to be known as welsher if I don't pay everyone back, and then I'm burnt. Not to mention if I don't pay my gambling debts, I might get my ass kicked and then I would end up in seg for fighting. That might get me sent to MCU until I go to court, and I can't stand it in there." It didn't matter who initiated and who defended themselves; if you fought, you went to segregation in max—no commissary, no visits, only one book per week, a twenty-three-hour lockdown, and nobody to talk to. The only possible benefit for some people was that they liked the privacy.

After the COs reviewed the tapes of the fight, they would adjust the disciplinary action accordingly, even going as far as having assault charges filed against the aggressor. The victim would be allowed back into the dorm, but only if he just stood there and got beaten down without defending himself. With all the testosterone and attitude in here, that just wasn't an option.

Monopoly was in a tough spot, and I completely understood his reason for coming to me. We had spent time in MCU together, and by quietly discussing this with me while everyone was sleeping, he would be able to keep his pride and save face with the entire dorm later in the day. His fate was in my hands, and if I didn't help him, he was going to be in a world of hurt. I felt for the guy, but business was business. I didn't want to be known as the guy you screw over when it came time to paying your debts, but I didn't want one of my buddies to go to the hole. He had brought all this down on himself by gambling too much on his mediocre spades skills. By constantly getting stuff stored out whenever he was hungry, he had now dug a hole so deep that even if he got $50 worth of food each week, he wouldn't be able to eat a thing of his own for two weeks if he paid his debts off. I knew what he owed me and Reynaldo, but his spades debts incurred when he wasn't my partner were a different story. Those he kept to himself, and if he owed any hustlers or card sharks with no money on their books and survived on card games, he surely would be in a "world of hurt."

The dorm was slowly waking up by now with the anticipation of the CO walking into the dorm with two inmate-workers rolling in five-foot-high commissary racks filled with the simple pleasures that kept us sane in this otherwise-crazy place. I had mostly kept to myself in here so far and stuck to my reading-and-pacing routine, which bothered nobody and sustained my isolated existence. I tried to bother no one, and for the most part, nobody bothered me. Most of the store was to new guys and only when Reynaldo was out of stuff, so I didn't take over his turf, since I was the new guy, but also from always trying to cooperate with one hundred nineteen room-mates we all had in here. The easier it was for all of us, the easier it would be for me in the long run, and being comfortable in here was the only thing that made jail bearable.

"How did you get yourself in such a mess, Monopoly?" I had to ask.

"Listen, I can tell you all about it during superexchange, and we can work out the details, but for now I need to know what to tell these guys when commissary comes. Help me out, Walker, and I promise you it will be worth your while. I can even have my mom put money on your books, but that doesn't help me out with what I have to deal with today. You going to help me or not? Here comes commissary."

I let the silence hang there just long enough to let him think about the bind he had gotten himself into. I had to think about it myself and figure out the details to make sure he wouldn't put me out of business. I wasn't trying to be an ass, but I had a nice thing going, and he could see how well I was doing. Maybe he was just trying to work me and then get sent to MCU, where I would have no way to get repaid. I had seen a few guys do that to Reynaldo, but nothing on the scale Monopoly was talking about. I also understood where he was coming from, and I had been in his shoes a few times in the past. Occasionally, I needed only a small break to make the difference between getting by and living well. I didn't want the poor guy to suffer the wrath he had brought down on himself, but I did want compensation, and definitely a few answers.

"I'll help you, but only with a few conditions," I finally said. When I did this, I could almost see the weight lift off his shoulders and relief come across his face.

"What are the conditions, and how much is it going to cost me?" asked Monopoly.

"You tell me what's really going on, and I mean the truth about how this happened. I also want your salads at dinner and the *Liars and Thieves* book you are reading when you're done. We have the whole hour during superexchange to work out all the details. Tell everybody they don't get anything until we come back in from superexchange. Fair enough?"

"Deal. I owe you, buddy," Monopoly said. And with that, he walked away to let everyone know they would be taken care of when we came back in.

It was remarkable how commissary could make the entire dorm get up early. It was usually quiet until well past eleven, but for some strange reason, everybody's internal alarm clock managed to wake them all up at nine thirty on this day. The entire dorm was busy with activity; men were cleaning out the bin boxes in anticipation of impending arrival of commissary. By ten thirty, commissary had been distributed and we all started tearing apart our bunks so we would be prepared for superexchange. I found it ironic that we all looked forward to Wednesday for commissary and yet, at the same time, dreaded superexchange. The main reason I didn't enjoy it was that the whole dorm was outside all at once, making it very crowded. During the daily recreation hour, only ten or twenty guys would ever make it out, which was something I never completely understood. Being locked up for months at a time inside the dorm was even more constricting without breathing fresh air and seeing the blue sky. How some guys could only come out on Wednesday, when it was mandatory, was beyond me. Maybe shutting out the outside world in every way was their only way of dealing with jail, and if that was what worked, then by all means, they should stick with it. Myself, I had to have exercise, have fresh air, and most of all, see the sky. I couldn't stand to work in an office; I had been working outdoors for twenty-five years now. I needed to feel the sunshine and have a little room to breathe. As we prepared to go outside, I was quietly keeping an eye on Monopoly as he bounced around, making promises and reassuring everyone that he would pay his debts once we came back in. I was also making the rounds so I could make sure that everyone who owed me paid me when we came back in. This worked out well for all the concerns if the COs compared my receipts to my inventory during superexchange.

We were all shuffled outside as the crowd settled down against the wall. Monopoly approached me and began walking beside me in a brisk circular pattern around the perimeter, as I always did. I wasn't trying to be an ass by making him walk with me every time we talked, but when you are in motion, it makes it more difficult for anyone to hear everything that is being said.

"Okay, what the hell did you do to get yourself into this mess, Monopoly?"

"Here's my problem, Garret, but this is just between you and me, okay?"

"Okay, okay," I assured him, as I noticed him nervously watching a number of different people as we circled the small cement court.

"I have been getting my ass kicked at spades the last couple of weeks, and I also owe two-for-ones to Reynaldo just to pay off my gambling debts. On top of that, I already owe my desserts for the next week, and I am starving to death. The bottom line, Garret, is that I have a gambling problem. That's how I deal with being in here. You deal with it by walking and reading. I gamble on spades games because it is the only form of entertainment I enjoy."

The minute he said that, I instantly recalled the last couple of weeks and remembered the numerous times I had seen him give different stuff to a lot of different guys. This was him paying some of his debts off immediately, most likely to the people who didn't trust him, wouldn't wait until Wednesday, or knew he was quickly running out of his own stuff. Now these payoffs were starting to make sense, especially with his gambling problem, and because I knew just how shitty Monopoly was at spades. It was surprising he had lasted this long.

"All right, here's what we're going to do," I told him. "Do you have enough to pay everyone off and not have to worry for one week?"

"Yeah, but then I have nothing left, no desserts, and I am already doing three peoples' chores plus mine."

"Okay, from now on, you only play spades with me and you only store out from me. I'll keep a running tab for your debt, and if you were serious about your mom putting money on my books, the payoff won't be two-for-ones. I will give you a better deal. If she doesn't come through, we go back to regular juice on the balance. If you can survive without the gambling until we are square, I will find us games we can play for fun that will keep you busy with no wager to lose. You can live without the action for a week, or this is never going to end. I am not trying to be your mother here, but you are putting me in a bind by expecting me to carry your ass, so I have to have a few rules in place. Fair enough?"

"Yeah, I can live with that, but just one thing: I don't need the humiliation from everyone else about this. I get enough shit from everybody who hears me on the phone with my wife, so this stays between you and me," he pleaded.

"I understand, but you got yourself into this mess, and if you want to get out of it, we have to work together. That's all I am telling you. Show some sincerity and a little effort and you will go a long way with me. Don't do anything different. Blow me off and leave me holding the bag, and the whole unit will know the truth. Do you understand what I am telling you?"

"I understand," he said as we stopped and looked each other square in the eyes. "Thanks. You don't know how much I appreciate this. I owe you big-time."

With a deal struck and Monopoly able to save face, I felt good about helping him out. Although I wasn't trying to "parent" him or tell anybody how to run their life, the only way I could be secure in this little venture was to make sure he made a few small changes and stuck to the rules. I liked the guy, and we were getting to be as close as two people could under the circumstances, but if he wasn't willing to make an effort, why should I?

When we finally came back inside from superexchange was when the true meaning of commissary was finally absorbed. Everyone would pay off their debts, losers would feel the sting of humiliation from the victors' wisecracks, and everyone was wired from the large inventory of coffee available. Things were as good as they were going to get in county jail.

CHAPTER

13

ONCE THE INITIAL RUSH OF business was completed, I felt compelled to have a little chat with Reynaldo just to make sure what I was doing with Monopoly wasn't crossing any lines of jailhouse protocol that I was unaware of. Once Monopoly was busy on the phone with his wife, as he was two or three times a day, I took Reynaldo aside and asked him if we could talk privately for a moment.

"Did Monopoly pay everything he owed you today?"

"Yeah, he and I are even for the first time in three weeks," he told me. I had only asked to make sure Monopoly wasn't bullshitting me from the start and that he was paying everybody back, so I wouldn't get any excuse about owing someone else when it came time for me to collect from him.

"Well, let me tell you something about him that you have to promise to keep under your hat," I said to Reynaldo. "He's in way over his head, and I have sort of taken him under my wing and sponsored him, if you will, and if he is even with everyone today, I want to make sure he isn't storing out a bunch behind my back and getting in deeper. Do you understand what I am trying to do here?"

"Yeah, and that's cool with me. I am getting busy down here with guys from the lower tiers, and I was getting sick of carrying him, anyway."

"I'm not trying to step on anybody's toes or embarrass the guy by telling you about his dirty laundry. I am just trying to cover my own ass."

"I see what you are doing, and I also appreciate you talking to me about it. If you want to work with me the first of the week, I'll just trade with you one-for-one or just keep a running tally, and we can square up next week. Sometimes I run out of stuff that I know you have, but I am not going two-for-one, so I just let it slide."

"You scratch my back, I'll scratch yours—isn't that what it's all about in here?" I told him as we bumped knuckles on the deal and parted ways. I was pretty much the store for upstairs now, and Reynaldo covered the downstairs. It was also nice to know that he and I could trade straight across to balance inventories without profiting off each other. Monopoly was still on the phone with his wife but was curiously eyeing me as Reynaldo and I parted ways. He quickly ended his phone call and hurried to catch up with me on the way up the stairs.

"What was that all about?" he asked.

"I was just letting him know that I own you now until we are even. To not help you out with so much as a piece of candy, let alone a ramen or some lopes. I didn't tell him about your gambling problem or that you were about to get your ass kicked by two or three people for not paying your spades debts, so your secrets are safe. You got a problem with me checking up on you so I can cover my own ass? You tell me right now."

"No problem. Just trying to keep it between you and me, that's all," he replied. "You know how cruel the guys in here can be. I get enough shit from the unit already. They don't need any more ammunition from this."

"I just found out what I needed to know, and your secrets are still just between us, so relax, okay? I am the one who needs to worry now, because if you go to the hole or get sent to MCU, I am the one who is out a ton of commissary. When will your mom send the money?"

"I will talk to her tonight," he told me.

Monopoly had nothing to worry about, and if it weren't for me, he would most likely be in the hole right now, or he'd be in the medical unit with a busted jaw. He also said he would give me his green salads from his dinner trays until the money showed up since his desserts were already spoken for. In return, just to be nice, I would give him my vegetables unless it was corn. I liked my vegetables cold and crisp, and here that was not an option on the menu. He paid off his debts, called his mom, just as he said he would, and everybody left him alone. He quit playing spades with everyone but me, and we just played for the fun, with no ride or whatever, wherever we could find anyone else who didn't want to gamble, or we played in the tournaments. I would store him out a ramen in the evening, which was usually the hungriest time of the day not to have commissary with dinner at 5:00 p.m., and at 11:00 p.m., it was a long stretch to endure, followed by going to sleep on an empty stomach.

Around 10:00 p.m., groups of three or four guys made spreads that each person would bring whatever they had to contribute—ramens, tortillas, cheese sauce, refried beans, or rice—and it would all be thrown in the mix. Usually, the Hispanics would make burritos and everybody else would just dump the mix in a bowl and stir it up and spoon it out. During this time of night, it was very difficult if you were broke and hungry, because dinner was five hours ago and suddenly the whole place smelled like a restaurant. If you had nothing to eat and saw and smelled what was going on, it really made your mouth water. Most people don't like to go to bed hungry, so this was when I would help Monopoly out. I would also give him some honey buns or nutty bars during the day, or coffee and cocoa if he was up early enough to walk with me, which we had been doing more and more frequently.

I didn't really think he cared about the exercise like I did as much as I enjoyed the discussion of friendship we had been missing in here. A lot of guys picked on others' weaknesses in here, and he made himself a target of ridicule by playing bad cards, gambling too much, and letting his wife on the outside control his emotions while he was incarcerated. Many times, he had walked away from the phone call home with red or watery eyes, upset about her drug use and infidelity, angered that he could do nothing about it. If he showed weakness, the stronger animals would prey on the weaker one as if we were in the African savanna. Their version of this was to make them the brunt of their jokes, to publicly humiliate others for no other reason than just to feel better about themselves. According to the average inmate's way of thinking, your life really wasn't so bad if somebody else had it worse.

Later, Monopoly came up to me and said, "I just want to say thank you for helping me, Garrett. Most guys in here would have just let me deal with it myself, which would have really sucked."

"No problem, man. You have kept your end of the deal so far, and I'm going to come out ahead, so it worked out well for both of us," I told him. His mom was sending $50 to put on my books to cover his debt, and he was bringing me all the store business from the upper tiers now while Reynaldo took care of the lower. Monopoly had been in here for two months already and had two more to go until he was released. About a year and a half ago, he was here for six months. He was from Boise, so he knew quite a few of the people who were jailed here.

"You and everyone else in here know me and my wife aren't doing too well while I'm in here. I think she's cheating on me," he said. "She's always over at this guy Mark's house, and I know she is still using meth, and it drives me fucking crazy."

"What about you?" I inquired. "Are you still using? I mean, once you get out?"

"No way, man. I am done for good. If I violate again, I will get three years at the yard in Idaho State Pen. I'm done. She told me she was too, but I can tell when I talk to her she's high, and I can't do a thing about it."

"Do you still love her?" I asked hesitantly. Some guys can be friendly, but once you ask personal questions, they tend to get all tough and masculine. It's a defense mechanism. I know I wouldn't share such intimate feelings with anybody here.

"Yeah, that's the problem, but I don't know if she still loves me or not."

"Well, do you trust her?"

"I don't know what to trust when I'm in here and she's out there. How do you ever know what your girl does when you are locked up? It's a fucked-up situation, but I can't do anything about it until I get out, and it pisses me off." He sighed heavily.

"How does she make money and survive with you in here if you were supporting her before you got arrested?"

"My parents are rich, and they send her money sometimes when I ask them to, but she hustles and sells drugs on and off to help make ends meet. When she comes to visit, I can tell she's still using. I can see the signs. You know what I mean?"

"Unfortunately, yeah, I do. There's nothing you can do from in here, so don't make it any harder on yourself by hard-timing. Just let it be for now and hope for the best. It will all work itself out or it won't, but worrying about it from now until then is just going to make it worse. If she loves you, then it will be all good. If she doesn't, then come out to Seattle, work with me, and meet somebody new. The economy is booming. There's tons of work, and housing market is one of the best in the country. Get a fresh start and get the hell out of Idaho, where all your problems started."

I saw him nodding and contemplating what I had just told him. I hated to see people fail and go back to the drugged-up lifestyle purely for economic reasons. Although, all it took in any small market was for interest rates to rise, and the housing market would fold like a deck of cards, and with it the local economy would follow. Most criminal and addiction problems usually spike during tough economic times, and if he was serious about his comment, he should consider getting out of Boise.

Hopefully, he was serious about his future, but one thing I had learned in jail is, most people will pretty much tell you whatever it is they think you want to hear or what will make them look good before they will tell you the truth. And in here, it was all about appearance, not facts. Everybody had a hot girlfriend but no pictures of her. Everyone was innocent, but we were all in jail. Everybody in here was getting screwed over by their judge, prosecutor, and public defender, as if they had never done anything wrong in their entire lives. I was sick of hearing the same story over and over; it became old after a week, let alone now that I'd been locked up for almost a month.

As I paced, I would catch bits and pieces of many different conversations, and after a while, they all seemed to become like the same story. I did feel sorry for some people, but most had made their beds and now they were pissed they had to lie in it. The really sad thing was, most of the guys in here had been here before and hadn't learned anything from their previous incarceration. At what point in one's life is it necessary to take some responsibility for where you are instead of always pointing the finger at somebody else? I guess what it comes down to is that some people don't mind this lifestyle and jail doesn't bother them too much. They must not have families at home, because being away from mine was the hardest part about being in here. A person has to hate it enough to change their behavior, so they are not destined to return. This was my first offense, and rather than bitch about the situation, I chose to make the best of it and possibly benefit from it.

Monopoly was on the phone two or three times a day with his wife, which I found strange. It seemed to me that his conversations with her were the reasons for half of his problems here. He was constantly trying to deal with issues on the outside. From here, he could solve nothing, so why stress about things that you had no control over? All this did was make him miserable and be in a constant state of fear of what his wife was doing at home. If he didn't trust her, he should move on; if she was trustworthy, then she would be there when he got out—end of story. Since the whole unit was pretty much one big room, everyone saw Monopoly go through his routine on the phone with his wife. This made it easier for him to be abused verbally by others, and this would make him an easy target for hustlers and thieves. It also made it easier for me to avoid making phone calls home. Granted, his calls were two dollars and mine were sixteen, but when one is locked up, everybody misses their family. I missed Sean and Beth very much, but looking forward to a phone call once a week or so helped time go by more quickly, and it helped me not to worry so much about what was happening back in Seattle.

CHAPTER

14

B Y THE FIRST OF THE week, my investment in Monopoly was beginning to pay off. With commissary two days away, he was bringing me all kinds of business from guys he knew on the outside. Now he owed me a lot of "money," but I had personally seen the letter from his mom stating her intention to send the two of us money. Although it wouldn't be here by Wednesday, just seeing the letter gave me peace of mind. I was running out of money on my books, but I had everything I needed daily, so I was hoping to make it to the end of my stay from the profits I made running store. Also, he said he was going to have his lawyer get in touch with me to see if he could help me with my case. He could not be any worse than my last one, who never even contacted me once during any of his many visits to the jail.

This was extremely good news, since private lawyers had a much better chance of negotiating deals with the prosecutor than a public defender. Discussing your client's options over lunch or in the law library is much more efficient than trying to throw something together in the hallway five minutes before your courtroom appearance.

With the good news putting an extra bounce in my step, I was again feeling very optimistic about being home for my birthday in a few weeks and putting the whole ordeal behind me. By now I was quite comfortable in my routine. I was reading a book every two to three days, walking around twenty miles every day, and with my sit-ups, was exhausted by 10:00 p.m. and sleeping soundly through the night. I knew where I was when I woke up, and my dreams were not as disturbing as they had been when I first arrived.

When commissary showed up on Wednesday, I became the envy of the tier. I had so much stuff I bought in addition to everything that was owed to me that by the time superexchange was over and all the debts were paid, I had too much stuff to fit in my bin box. I was required to have a receipt for everything in my possession, and by now my inventory was almost three times what I had receipts for. I had to have a few people who were out of money keep things for me in their boxes so I didn't lose it if I got inspected. The problem was being able to trust these guys so they didn't eat or trade my stuff or get it ripped off, in which case I would lose it anyways. I made a couple of deals so the guys holding my merchandise also came out ahead. I also told them this could possibly be a weekly thing if they didn't screw me over; they would continue to profit as long as things went smoothly.

The scary thing about deals like this was the possibility of guys getting transferred to other units or, worse, going to the hole. The minute a guy got in a fight, the COs confiscated his property and searched through it. Then it went into storage until that person was out of seg, and that person usually ended up in MCU until they got out. No more dorms meant no more bin box full of commissary for me. The three guys that stowed my stuff for me were stable, so I felt comfortable, and all of them were on my tier. Everyone on the tier was always watching out for thieves, and most of us took care of one another. I would constantly give out coffee and cocoa to guys in need, but I was also careful not to let it get out of control and let them take advantage of my generosity.

After my inventory problem was solved, I was pacing when I overheard a guy on our tier had to stay in jail for sixty-eight days until his court date because he didn't have $100 to bail himself out. He had a wife and two kids, one a newborn, a good job, and they just put their $3,000 life savings down on a house, so they had no cash. If he was to stay here until his court date in nine weeks, he would probably lose his job. Being unemployed makes it very difficult to catch up on the house payments. I didn't have that on my books, but I had over $200 worth of inventory.

I thought of having Beth send it and put it on his books so he could bail himself out, but I knew she was hurting with me in jail and might not be able to do it. It was worth a try to help the poor guy out, and I knew it would come back to me from his buddies who were in here. They would do my chores, let me have the best books, and do other small favors that would make my life easier. The guy was apparently one hell of a nice guy to boot, so I really felt for him. I would hate to think anybody had to stay here for that long over something. Whatever happened to innocent until proven guilty? It wasn't about guilt, innocence, the level of danger to society, or even right or wrong anymore; it was just about the money when it should be about justice.

Later that night at mail call, I received a postcard from my mom from her continuing journey across the Southwest. The postcard said that she had also sent me $50 more for my books and that her friend Sharon had sold her bed-and-breakfast. Mom and Sharon lived a few miles apart down on the Long Beach Peninsula in Washington. This was great news for me, for two years earlier, I had done the roof on Sharon's place in exchange for overnight stays whenever I was down there. She was supposed to pay me in full the balance of $2,000 when the place sold, and now I would be able to collect it. I called Beth right away. She told me she didn't have any money right now but she would call my mom's cell phone and see if she could collect from Sharon as soon as possible since my mom wasn't at home but had to coordinate this transaction because the only way I had to contact people from jail was *via* mail or collect calls.

Luckily, she was able to reach my mom late that night and even managed to reach Sharon on the first try. Sharon told Beth she would send the money at the first of the week, and then Beth would be able to send some to me. After I told her about the $100, she said she would send it to him as well to help the poor dude out. It was a good play for us all. I was going to get $900 on my books, $1,000 for Beth and Sean, and I could easily bail a dude out. With my court appearance coming up shortly, I would only need some of the money, anyways, and then I could buy my own ticket to get home when I got out. Things were looking up.

With all the stuff I already had, I wouldn't have to buy anything else before I left, so it was all downhill from here. A thousand dollars would be enough for Beth and Sean to get by for a couple of weeks, and hopefully she would have some work lined up for me as soon as I got home.

The next morning, Monopoly had a visit at 8:00 a.m. from his lawyer. I don't think I had ever seen him up quite that early before, except for meals, court, and razors. I paced and read for an hour. Three miles and forty-five pages later, he came back in with some good news for me.

"Garrett, I talked to my lawyer and told him about your case. He said he would come and have a professional visit with you next time he was here." He told me all this with a big smile because I think he was happy to finally be able to do something nice for me in return for all I had done for him. It was awesome to see that returning the favors I did for him was on his mind. No sooner had he told me all this than the CO stopped me on my next pass and said, "Walker, you have a professional visit."

"He must have just decided to stay around and see you now," said Monopoly.

I quickly gathered what paperwork I had and headed for the conference room to talk to the lawyer. After introductions and an exchange of polite pleasantries, we settled down to see if it was worth his time for what little money I had to offer.

"This was my first and only offense," I told him. "My lawyer had arranged a plea bargain with the prosecutor for 120 days, but by the time I was to appear before the judge, I would have already served close to 90, and maybe we could get that down to time served. In the presentence investigation, PSI recommended probation, and all I really need you to do is to make a few calls to verify this and show up in court."

Silence filled the small room while he looked over my paperwork and analyzed the situation.

"Let me make a few calls to check this all out. Call my office collect on Wednesday morning, and I will let you know. This will be $500 if it isn't any more complicated than you say it is. How can you pay me off if you are in here? Do you have somebody on the outside I can be in touch with?" I gave him Beth's cell phone number and explained the money situation with Sharon. I told him to call her tomorrow so I could talk to her first and give her an update on the situation and discuss the options available to best resolve the situation. I wasn't even sure if I needed a private attorney, but some of the horror stories I had heard in here had made me extremely nervous about public defenders. Think about it: if the judge, prosecutor, and public defender all got their paycheck from the Ada County, who was working for me? I didn't care about the money at this point; I just wanted this all to end.

When I went back to the unit after my meeting, I was totally stoked for my meeting with Mark and was extremely confident that I would be out of this jailhouse shortly. Monopoly was the only one up and began doing a great imitation of me.

"He stole your spot on the carpet, Walker," the CO said when he finished searching me.

"Mark is a good lawyer," Monopoly told me after I put down my paperwork and joined him in pacing before the rest of the unit woke up. "He got me off my counterfeiting charge with a slap on the wrist." He looked around to make sure nobody was close enough to hear him, and he continued, "Just between you and me, I should have gotten ten years. They caught me red-handed with $30,000 or $40,000. He can work a deal with the prosecutor better than anybody. You will be out of here with time served, I think."

"I don't know about that," I replied "I still have thirty days left on my plea bargain, but if he is as good as you say he is, you may be right."

Later that night, I called home again to update Beth and tell her to expect a call from Mark tomorrow. I told her to either put it on her Visa card or tell him the checks in the mail. She let me know Sharon was going to overnight the money to her since she had been informed by Mom of my situation and was extremely sympathetic concerning the urgency. That was nice of her, especially considering

I was told I would be paid half the money the day I finished the job. Unfortunately, she didn't have the courtesy to tell me she didn't have any of the money until after the job was done. I was left holding the bag on $2,000 worth in roofing material. So I went out of my way to help her, and I didn't get paid for $2,000 in labor for me and my crew. I also had to pay $2,000 out of my pocket for the materials. Maybe things were starting to go right for me, after all. When I got out, I would have some money left after paying Mark, and I could get back to work as soon as possible.

Things were fine for a couple of days, until two days later, when I called him back like he had told me to. I was slightly disappointed to learn what my public defender had done with my case.

"He was so far behind with his caseload that he already petitioned the court and received a one-week continuance so he could prepare for your case," Mark told me. "There's nothing I can do about it now," he added, "so instead of going to court on the fourteenth, you go on the twenty-first." The public defender that had five weeks to talk to me was so busy he couldn't find the fifteen minutes that Mark did to save me a week in jail. No wonder they called them public pretenders in jail. He didn't do shit for me in five weeks, and I am sure he came to the jail at least fifty times during that period. Now there was no chance for me to be home for my birthday. I was happy that Monopoly got Mark involved with my case, or I would have been screwed. Mark heard the disappointment in my voice.

"On the bright side, I spoke with both the prosecutor and the PSI lady, and they have both said they will recommend probation. This means everything is on track for your plea bargain, and the only thing we have to worry about is whether the judge wants you to stay in for the rest of the 30 days to complete the 120 days or let you go with time served."

Hearing that took the pressure off, although I was destined to stay an extra week thanks to the public defender. It would be my last. Secure in the knowledge that things were taken care of, I was more relaxed now than I had been in a long time. I also had the added comfort of not having to worry about court for the next week and a half, for the most part, anyways. Even with all my assurances from other inmates and my lawyer, for some reason, I was, deep down, still a little nervous about court. I had heard too many stories of a guy who did nothing yet ended up getting the book thrown at him. It seemed to me that the judge was a little too free with the sentencing guidelines, and that was a scary thought. There was no such thing as a sure thing, and until court was over and I walked out the door, part of me would always have a sliver of doubt as to what my future would hold.

It was sad to think that my public defender was such a lazy, disorganized slacker that I had to spend another week in jail. With ten days left until court, I was pretty much on autopilot, continuing my routine, keeping up my store and my exercise each day. On Monday night, after talking with Beth, I found the money from Sharon had not only arrived but she had also sent it on to Idaho and had even sent the $100 to Raphael, the dude who needed it to bail out. She told me she had sent it on Saturday, so I should be getting it tonight or tomorrow at the latest. I would be a hero to the Latinos once their friend was released, and until then, I decided to keep it to myself, so nobody got their hopes up too soon.

Sure, enough, on Tuesday night during dinner, I received a notice that $900 had been added to my account, and as soon as it happened, I knew the money would be on Raphael's books as well. I walked over to Raphael and asked him, "Did any money show up on your books today?"

"No, not yet," he replied. That was odd, since it should have arrived at the same time as mine. Just as had happened with the visit from Mark, the minute I was wondering what was going on, I got my answer.

"Martinez, Raphael," the CO called out from the station, holding a receipt in his hand.

Raphael attracted a huge smile, looked at me, and asked, "Did you do this for me?"

"Si, senor," I replied with a big old grin on my face. "I told you my girl would come through for you, didn't I?"

Everyone knew what was going on when they heard his name called. There is no privacy in jail. They all gave him the names of their favorite bail bondsman to call so he could get the hell out of here.

Even though it was 9:00 p.m., he would be out of here in a few hours and would be able to work and support his family until his court date. But then he would probably get time served and have his case dismissed. It felt good to help somebody escape the legal nightmare we so ironically call justice. Asking for nothing in return, I only hoped this would create good karma for me when my time came in the courtroom. After a few phone calls and the professional-visit call from the CO station, Raphael's departure was imminent. It usually took four to six hours to get out of here after a professional visit, but tonight was slow, and he was gone in no time.

"Thanks for everything, Walker," he told me as he got ready to leave. Looking down at my tattered shoes, which had by now covered close to one thousand miles inside these walls, he commenced to repay me in a way that made my week. "Trade shoes with me before I go. It isn't much, but I want to thank you for what you have done for me."

My shoes that I had walk down to nothing where the same size as his brand-new pair, and we switched before he went out the door and on to freedom. I was being thanked by all his friends, and I knew I had made many friends with such a small, generous act that hopefully would be returned by someone at a later date. Most guys on here were all talk. But tonight, it felt really good to achieve results. Raphael was free, and one person's legal nightmare was over for now. I hoped mine would be over very soon.

CHAPTER

15

I WOKE UP THE NEXT morning feeling pretty good about what I had accomplished from the inside. It was worth every penny. When I started pacing after razor call, I felt as if I could go from twenty-five to thirty miles today. I was conflicted about the comfort level I had created for myself in here. I didn't have to worry about work and all the other hassles of the real world. The conflict came when I thought about how difficult it must be for Beth to carry the weight of the business without me. And for Sean not having a father to be there for him. It quickly brought me down off my high horse, and before I knew it, my eyes were watering. Moments like this made me glad I had all this alone time and the whole place to myself when walking. I kept walking most of the morning, and before lunch, I had covered about twenty miles. Usually, that was what I had completed by the end of the day, so now I was shooting for a twenty-five-mile day in a room slightly larger than a high school gym. My feet felt great. All afternoon, Raphael's friends were patting me on the back and offering up a list of items to show their appreciation for yesterday. By the end of the day, I had been given a better pillow, custom jailhouse contraband pens, too much coffee, a long list of good books to read next, and envelopes with drawings on them.

Everybody had their own hustle here, and some of the more talented artists were Latinos. They would offer to draw almost anything you wanted on your outgoing mail, or custom drawing with hearts, arrows, and ribbons with you and your girl's name on them. There was also some tattoo-style stuff with skulls, crossbones, flames, and lightning. You got to keep busy in here, or else time dragged on and you went crazy. I passed the time walking and reading. These guys drew. It was also their way to earn "money." Other guys wanted to send pictures home to their girlfriends. These guys were talented and broke, so this was how they got coffee and extra food.

Monopoly and I were now walking together all the time, and along with being spades partners and sharing an attorney, we had a lot in common. We both had girls on the outside who were carrying the load while we were away. The only difference was, he didn't trust his, and I did mine. The way I figured it, if they were going to be unfaithful, then we would find out when we got out, and move on. His court date was one week after mine, and he seemed more concerned about his outside social life than with his rendezvous with "justice." During the afternoon rec time on Tuesday, the CO said it was sunny and seventy degrees out, so Monopoly and I decided to walk the rec yard and get some fresh air. I would go out as often as possible, but Monopoly was one of the indoor guys who never went outside. Today he went with me. As we started to walk in circles, he finally opened up about court and his crimes for the first time.

"You should have seen the money I was making," he told me with a pride in his voice I had never really heard. "I was so good that it passed the pen test at the grocery store. Ask some of the guys in here, and they will all tell you how good I was. I would go to the mall sometimes and just drive around the parking lot, throwing $100 bills out the window until I had literally thrown away $5,000."

"What a waste. Why the hell did you do that?" I asked him.

"That way, when I went into the mall and spent $400 or $500, I would just be one of the 50 people flooding the mall with fake bills. I had to in order to be one of the 50 in the crowd instead of the only person doing it. I had to give away that much to make sure I didn't get caught."

I shook my head in amazement at the idiotic things criminals did to keep themselves from going to jail. Too bad he couldn't have directed his talent and intelligence toward something more lucrative and legitimate.

"It must not have worked too well. Look where we are having this discussion," I commented.

"Point taken, but I am not here for making money. I am here on probation violation for absconding and for drug use."

"How did that happen?" I asked.

"*Absconding* is when you aren't living where you told the cops you were living, not answering when they call, and not checking in when you are supposed to. When they found out where I was staying, they surrounded the house and had a warrant for my arrest, so I walked out to keep the cops from coming in and busting all my buddies who were inside, getting high."

"You took one for the team," I told him. "That was exactly what I did when I was arrested. I was in a hotel room with three other people and a big stash of various drugs. We were selling anything and everything to support our habits. Oxycodone, coke, meth, pot, Vicodin, scales, baggies, and probably some things I didn't even know about. Nobody trusted anybody not to steal their stuff, so we were all hiding shit under the carpet, in the attic, or in box springs. God only knows what was in that room." I paused. "We had all been up for days when I looked out the window because the news had said it was snowing. What did I see? Three Snohomish County sheriff's cars in the parking lot. I just about shit my pants."

"Was the room in your name?" he asked.

"Hell no. I'm smarter than that. It didn't matter, though, because five seconds later, there were four loud knocks on the door. 'Snohomish County Sheriff, we have a felony arrest warrant for Garret Walker. Open the door!' It was me or the whole room and all the extra charges that came with it."

"Why was it a felony arrest warrant?" he asked.

"Because I had felony charges in Idaho and I had missed my court date. Even though I had called the court and told them I missed my flight. I asked them if I could reschedule, and they said yes, but they had to issue a warrant that would be washed when I appeared in court. Beth bailed me out in January, so when I missed court, she had me arrested to make sure I showed up. All she had to do was tell me to turn myself in, but instead I was arrested. I spent twenty-five days in jail in Everett before they sent me on a six-day chain gang road trip in shackles and leg irons to get me to Boise. The funniest, or saddest, thing, depending on how you look at it, is once I got here, she bailed me out again."

"Any girl who calls the cops on me would never see my ass again," he said.

"That was how I felt until we talked it all out and she even bailed me out the second time, but by then the financial damage was done. I lost an easy $54,000 job I had already paid out $18,000 for the material of. When the contractor couldn't reach me, he had the supplier deliver for free and had somebody else install it. By the time I got home, I had lost all my customers because they had found out where I was. She didn't believe I called when I missed my court appearance until I showed her my cell phone bill."

"Some people would say you are crazy for putting up with that, and some say I am for letting my wife get under my skin the way she does. Women make men do some pretty strange things over time, but love is different for everybody. The time is an important factor too. You put up with a whole lot more in a long-term relationship than you would for a new one, that's for sure."

His comment made me think of all that Beth had put up with over the years of my drug using, as well as how destructive it was to our relationship. I had nobody to blame for being in here but myself. But couples who push each other's buttons need to be careful about how far they let things go. Once any issue comes between them, it tends to fester and test their trust from then on. I guess the more I thought about it, the more I saw that Monopoly and I were more alike than I realized.

His mom's money had shown up, and his debt was slowly becoming paid off. He was still consuming more than he was buying each week and losing most of his dinner trays each night. He just couldn't stop playing cards even if it meant giving up food. The gambling bug had a hold on him that was just as bad as having a drug habit.

Sometimes, I would pace in the afternoon or evening, and with nothing else to do, he would partner up with some lame spades player and try his luck. Usually, he would try to make friends with new guys by being their partner. The two of them would get hustled by experienced players who didn't have Mom's golden parachute to land with. The professional hustlers would signal, talk code, or deal off the bottom of the deck and rip him off every time. The irony of it was, when he did it, they would call him on it and he would have to forfeit. Either way, he would lose. Everyone knew they could take advantage of him and he was a pushover, because they had seen how upset he would get on the phone. He was an easy mark. It made me sick to watch.

A couple of buddies and I decided to finally help him out.

We would play as many games as possible throughout the day. We would put one envelope on each game, but all of us except for Monopoly had a private agreement to make sure nobody ever won or lost too much. Whoever won the first game would always give the losers a chance to win it back. This was where the deception would eventually help him out. If they won the first game, then they would throw the second game, and if we won the first game, then I would try to throw the second one. This way, he would just go back and forth over and over and never win or lose anything and still be able to play all day. The three of us agreed not to tell anyone so Monopoly wouldn't find out and be pissed. We were trying to protect his pride, and in here it was important to have some, especially for him. After all that he had been through, the last thing we wanted to do was hurt him. The plan worked well for three or four days, and during this time, we played on and off all day and all night with the win continuing to rotate among us, so everyone broke even.

Monopoly seemed to be happy not losing even though he wasn't winning either. He was able to eat his entire dinner and was quietly working his way out of debt. Since he wasn't losing his dinner trays, he didn't need to store out as much stuff, because he wasn't as hungry at night. By the next week, I would be paid off. The three of us were content with our little scheme since it was better for us to challenge ourselves to help Monopoly and not let him catch on instead of playing against others. As long as we all kept busy and nobody got hurt, everyone was a winner, because the time would move much faster.

C H A P T E R

16

B Y TUESDAY, I WAS BEGINNING to count down the days until court, and it seemed like time was beginning to slow down the closer I got to Friday. The days were dragging on and on even though I was busier than ever. I used to just do my thing all day and all of a sudden it was lights-out. Now I was constantly watching the clock, and instead of hours going by, it was seconds. I was supposed to call home tonight and talk to Sean and Beth, and just the thought of doing so seemed to bring me to an overwhelming sadness. I used to be my son's hero, and the thought of him telling me, "Happy birthday, Dad," on a collect phone call from jail wasn't sitting well with me. Even though I would be out on Friday, I thought that spending my forty-third birthday in jail was not something to write in most high school yearbook predictions.

I was nervous about calling home, because I knew it would upset me, and I didn't want to look weak in front of the guys. I kept the call home brief and found myself taking big deep breaths all throughout to keep from getting upset. They were both doing well at home and looking forward to seeing me this weekend so we could get back to living. What was upsetting to me was that my actions had not just messed up my life but theirs as well. They were victims of my so-called victimless crime and we're being punished just as much as I was daily. Having no father to talk to or be there for him during adolescence was hard on Sean, not to mention embarrassing. Beth had to take care of him, all his needs, physical and emotional. She also had to manage the roofing business, something I normally did. I am sure it was tough on both, and for that I was truly sorry. In a way, I had it easier in here than they did out there. They had to earn, pay bills, and continue with the daily struggle of life, while I just sat in here with money on my books, running store, pacing, and reading all day. I felt badly for them but not at all sorry for myself. I had caused this situation, and I couldn't wait to get home and begin making things better for all of us.

By the time commissary came around on Wednesday, Monopoly had hardly owed me, and since I was planning on getting out Friday when I went to court, I barely ordered anything. I could easily live off what was owed to me and what others were holding on to me for until the end of the week.

Right now, I was one of the most popular guys on the tier, and even the unit, for that matter. I had been generous, nonconfrontational, and probably inspirational due to my diligence and dedication to my daily routine. I was privately dubbed the unit librarian and was constantly shuffling books around to those whose literary taste demanded more than the casual reader. I got all the good books, could borrow whatever I needed, and could get just about anything I wanted. I also felt incredibly close to most of the guys on the tier. We had pretty much all stayed together since we got back from MCU, and since these were the main guys I was talking and bunking up with, over the past six weeks, we all had grown close. It was nice to know that the tier I would shortly be leaving was the most sought-after location, and I had hope that I had help to make it that way. In a small way, I had hope that my being here had made everyone's time here easier.

Beth had sent me twelve books that I had shared with anyone who like to read, and even though I was running store, there was not one guy in the tier to whom I hadn't given a cup of coffee or a soup to when they were hurting. I shared my good fortune with all those who helped me acquire new customers and kept the store and tier safe from the lowest of the low, the jailhouse thieves.

I had never had anything taken from my bin box the whole time I had been here, and part of the reason was my bunk location; the other was the diligence of the entire tier. Thursday afternoon, the tier suffered a huge loss when the transport list for the penitentiary was called out. Our two elder statesmen, Roger and Scott, were both told to pack up and be ready to go to the yard in thirty minutes. Both were assets to the tier. They were quiet, polite, and respectful to others, which was always important, because we were living so closely packed together. Sentenced a couple of weeks earlier, they knew what fate awaited them, but nobody ever knew when they would leave. For security reasons, they never let anyone know who was on each transport, or somebody might try to commander the bus to free their buddy. All the phones in the unit were also turned off from the time their names were called until the bus arrived at the pen, so nobody could make a phone call with the travel information. Seems a little paranoid to me, but I guess when somebody is looking at twenty years to life, a bus hijacking is not out of the question.

Scott and Roger both had to serve eighteen months at the state pen. Talking to them over the past few weeks, I had learned that both had already been there and this would be nothing new for either of them. With that in mind, I wondered how many trips to prison it took to make a man change his habits or his behavior.

Both these guys had been through this before, and yet it disturbed them so little; they changed nothing in their lives after they got out, and now they were heading back for another visit. That kind of thinking was common with way too many guys in here. They looked at jail almost as a social club where they could visit with all their friends and make new connections. Boise wasn't a very big town, and after two people started telling drug stories, it was inevitable that they would eventually discover that they both knew the same dealer or scored dope from the same house at some point. Then with a common denominator to build on, they discovered they were neighbors or worked at the same place or had gone to the same school. I honestly hoped both had finally learned their lesson and this would be the last time they were sent to prison. Other than when I talked to Scott about Vietnam and his writing, I never got to know him or Roger very well on a personal level.

They packed and were gone in thirty minutes, and the biggest question now was what two idiots our happy little tier would now get stuck with. Some guys would request to move up to where we were just so they would have access to the tier and be able to rip us all off. Nobody was technically allowed in any tier except the one that you lived in, but people always trespassed to get their buddies into a card game or just stroll through; rarely did they get into trouble. This was what made our tier so special in respect to security. We all knew who was supposed to be up there and who wasn't. We also knew everyone's friends and made sure those who weren't supposed to be there were watched or quickly ushered out. If some new guy who was a good guy came into the tier but his buddies were thieves, then it would disrupt the whole tier and the sense of security we all had in a place with no locks or privacy to ensure it. One day you could trust a guy since he had money and was winning at spades, but a week later, he was on a losing streak and his check from home didn't show up before Wednesday and he had turned into a thief just to survive. They would never be the stand-up guys Scott and Roger were. They would be sorely missed.

But now I was quite anxious and nervous about my impending court date, and even though I was confident that Mark knew what he was doing, the closer it got, the more nervous I found myself becoming. The days seemed to drag on forever, partially because I was watching the clock and overthinking the whole legal process, as well as going over in my mind all the horror stories I had heard from the others who were now permanently part of the system. Guys with first offenses get years, while habitual offenders get thirty days because the judge knows it won't do any good to send them to the yard yet again. The system doesn't make sense sometimes, and personally, from everything I had heard, the judges here had too much personal discretion. They had guidelines to follow, but they made the decision for each and made it based on their own criteria. You were at their mercy. So much seemed to depend on the mood they were in.

I've always believed there should have been a graph of some kind with criminal history on one side and the degree of the offense on the other. The judge or prosecutor sees this is your third offense and you were caught with X number of drugs, and that will get you this sentence. The way it was set up here, there was too much gray area in between, and that was why I was a nervous wreck. Until I heard my sentence, the gavel fell, and I knew my fate, I wouldn't be able to relax.

Later that evening, after shift change, the new CO was bunk-move-friendly, so we welcomed the arrival of Reynaldo to our tier, along with another guy named Hal. They both had previously been bunking downstairs.

Reynaldo was cool to begin with, and nobody had any problems with him at all. The same went for Hal. I think Reynaldo was a habitual offender with drug problems and Hal was a recently divorced father-of-two who was having a hard time being away from his kids. After doing six months in jail on his first DUI, he was being sentenced on Monday for his probation-violation charges—drinking while on probation and yet another DUI. He was a nervous wreck just like me. I had talked with him on and off over the past few weeks, but now he was in the bunk across the aisle from me, and since I was the only one he really knew, apparently, I guess I was now his buddy. At least until tomorrow, anyways, and maybe another month, if I had to stay until my 120 days were up. The last 30 days would be easy because at least I would know my release date, and that was half the battle in here. Uncertainty is a motherfucker.

Finally, Friday was here. October 21, 2005, I was to be sentenced in Ada County District Court before the Honorable Judge Young at 9:00 a.m. I had waited for this day since my arrest back in January and had spent the first four days of my life in jail. Then I spent another twenty-six after the sheriffs got me at the motel, and another six days were spent on the chain gang that carried me from Everett to Boise. There were other days in June when I didn't have my PSI filled out completely, and with the last fifty-one, I had served ninety-three days. Every one of those days behind bars had just been stepping stones on the journey that would hopefully end in a few hours.

I hardly slept last night in anticipation of court, talking with Jay into the wee hours of the morning. After only two or three hours of sleep, I woke up before breakfast for the first time since coming to Idaho and couldn't get back to sleep. The day ahead was weighing heavily on my mind, and my imagination was going a hundred miles an hour. I didn't even take a book with me to court because I couldn't stay focused on what I was reading with my head in a spin. Last night, I had found myself going over the same pages repeatedly because my mind was somewhere else.

CHAPTER

17

H OPEFULLY FOR THE LAST TIME, I was shackled and taken on the bus to the courthouse. Sitting in the courtroom still and quiet, I was thinking how fucked up my life had become and why. Drugs had so overwhelmingly taken over my existence that I was now sitting here, waiting to hear my fate from a judge who had total control over my future. When Mark came in, he came up to me and gave me an update and helped me calm down a little bit.

"How are you doing, Garrett?" he asked me.

"I think I could safely say this isn't my finest hour, but I'm okay."

"Here's the situation," he continued. "I talked to the prosecutor, and they are going to recommend probation with time served. Same goes for your PSI. We have a plea bargain for your guilty plea with 120 days, but we are hoping to get you out today with time served. The judge usually goes along with the recommendations, but the final decision is his. Let me do all the talking, or did you want to make a statement when he asks you?"

"No, thanks. I will leave that to you. You are the professional," I said, gesturing toward him. With two missed court appearances and not having my PSI ready when I was supposed to, not to mention the public-defender, new-lawyer fiasco, I decided that the less I dealt with the judge, the better off I would be.

Finally, the judge called, "*State vs. Garrett Walker.*"

It was showtime.

The prosecutor read my charges, stated his case, and ended with a recommendation of probation and time served. Mark stood up and told the court everything he had told me and asked the judge for probation, as my plea bargain had called for. When I was asked if I wished to say anything on my behalf, I replied, "No, Your Honor." Mark had done a great job, and the last thing I wanted to do was screw anything up by opening my mouth. The judge was shuffling through some papers, going over everything while my life hung in limbo. The dead silence was defeating. He put down the paperwork, folding his hands on his desk, and we locked stares.

"Will the defendant please rise?" he said, ending the silence. He blinked first and then looked down at his papers again. Mark and I stood up. "Mr. Walker, you have been found guilty of possession of a controlled substance by this court. Are you prepared to accept your sentence at this time?"

"Yes, Your Honor."

"Have you been promised anything by the state as far as your sentencing goes?"

"No, Your Honor, I have not."

"The prosecution and the presentencing investigator have agreed to probation in accordance with your guilty plea. Do you understand that I am not required to comply with these recommendations and final sentencing will be up to the court?"

"Yes, Your Honor."

"Are you aware this court can impose a sentence up to and including seven years in Idaho State Penitentiary or any sentence it deems appropriate up to and including the maximum term allowed?"

"Yes, Your Honor."

"Then we are all in agreement with your plea bargain, giving you probation, Mr. Walker."

I started to relax after he said this and he paused and shuffled some more papers while Mark looked over at me with a nod and a smile. All the stress and all the worry from stories inmates had told me had freaked me out for the better part of two months now. All the nightmares, all the what-ifs, and all the jailhouse scuttlebutt had all been for nothing. I could practically taste the Sizzler dinner I would be eating soon.

"However," he continued finally, "I am a little more concerned than they are about releasing you back into the community to continue your drug addiction. This court hereby sentences you to the custody of the Idaho State Penitentiary for a period of three years fixed and seven years indeterminate for your felony possession charge."

My heart stopped beating for four or five seconds while my eyes bulged out of my head. I couldn't believe what he just said. I was going to prison for three years. Holy shit. My world had just exploded and collapsed all around me. Mark looked at me, bewildered. When my heart started again, I could actually feel the blood coursing through my whole body with each explosive pulse. My life was over. No Sean, no Beth, nothing would be there for me when I got out. I realized that my worst nightmare had become my new reality when the judge began to speak again.

"I will suspend the three-year sentence provided you successfully complete the rider program at NICI, and I will retain jurisdiction over your case for six months. The case will be reviewed at that time. That will be all."

The gavel fell, and the bailiff guided me by the arm out of the courtroom without being allowed to ask Mark what the hell just happened to me.

"I will come see you at the jail," Mark told me as a door to the courtroom closed and I was locked in a holding cell behind the courtroom. I sat in eight-foot-by-eight-foot cement room on a cold, hard cement bench and tried to decipher what had happened. I had a thousand questions. There were no guards, no lawyers, no fellow inmates to help answer them. After everything I had heard or overheard from others and had been told by my lawyer, I was completely in shock. I remembered the judge saying seven years, three years, and something else about six months. Why couldn't I talk to Mark and have these explained to me now? Where was I headed? For how long? When would I be free again? Was I going to prison? I didn't have a clue as to what the judge had told me, but the bottom line was, I wasn't going home today, and possibly not for a long time. My Sizzler dinner was now a far-off dream. The ice-cold gallon of milk I was going to chug had just evaporated.

When I got back to the dorm just before lunch, my head was still spinning. I talked to some of the guys on the way back from court, and it seemed to them that I had just been sentenced to a rider, but I wasn't quite sure. The judge said he was going to retain jurisdiction, whatever that meant. It all had happened so fast and unexpectedly that I couldn't understand what was really going on. Not being too familiar with legalese, I had no way to decipher what the judge had actually told me. I needed to talk to Mark to find out exactly what happened and hoped he would come by and talk to me as soon as possible.

I went straight to the phone when I got back and called Beth and told her what little I knew. I wasn't sure if she had a cell phone number for Mark, but hopefully she could reach him and get some answers before I could. I told her to try to reach him and I would call his office from jail, but if he was in court with somebody else, my questions would continue to go unanswered. Ironically, I had been waiting for today so at least I would know what fate was in store for me, and yet even after court I found myself totally immersed in the unknown. When I got off the phone with Beth and couldn't get ahold of Mark at his office, I went up to my bunk to sort things out and maybe get some questions answered from my buddies. Half the tier sort of mingled around to see what happened to me in court. I kept my head down so they wouldn't see my watery red eyes. I could hardly talk without breaking down, and I just sat there shaking my head and giving as short of an answer as I could.

"How about we talk after lunch, guys? I need a little time to process a few things, okay?"

They all just dispersed, and I was given a little space to breathe. Monopoly, Jay, and Hal were close enough to sit with me at lunch and give me the skinny on what a disastrous turn my life had just taken.

The rider program was a boot camp in Northern Idaho for first-time felons to show the court that they would rather change their behavior and receive probation instead of going to prison. The program lasted anywhere from ninety days to six months, depending on your sentence. First, you had to go to the state pen for in-processing before being bussed to Cottonwood, Idaho, where the rider took place. After being in the dark that I was in two hours ago, I had learned more about my situation from guys on my tier: that meant I was going to prison.

During lunch, everyone who knew me thought I was trying to pull a prank on everybody with my sadness, and they kept asking me when I was really getting out. After I told them I was sentenced to a rider, they laughed at me and thought I was joking. I wish it were true. The confusion of the situation was extremely upsetting. Why can't they sentence you in plain English so you can understand what the hell is going on? Why wasn't I allowed to talk to my lawyer at least so he could translate for me and immediately? Was this method all part of the process to keep you in fear of the system, to prevent future crime? But the biggest question on my mind was when I was going home. After lunch, I called Beth back, but she had been unable to reach Mark and I had fallen to the grim reality that what had happened in court today was slowly sinking in. I was going to prison. Forget the plea bargain or the fact that this was my first and only offense. Forget the PSI and prosecution recommendations. Forget I was a parent, a homeowner, a business owner and that I had an honorable discharge after serving my country in the Oregon Army National Guard for six years. Forget the fact that I shaved the court's time and expense, pleaded guilty, and took responsibility for my actions when I turned myself in instead of running from the law. I guess nothing you do in life up to the day you get arrested really matters to the judge. You can live a pretty normal life for the most part, but if you screw up once in forty-three years, the state of Idaho thinks the best thing to do with you is send you to prison. If this had happened back home in Washington, I would have been sentenced to treatment after only spending the first weekend in jail. As it was, I had been locked up for ninety-three days total so far, and I was looking at possibly six more months before I would be home. Today did not turn out as I hoped. Not even close.

Mark finally came. He had to be in court with another client all afternoon and apologized for not getting to see me sooner. He seemed to know from experience that when this happened, his clients were usually left in the dark and had a million questions for him.

"Well, Garret," he said, "do you want the good news or the bad news?"

"Just give it to me straight. What am I looking at?"

"I know it sounded bad this afternoon, but you're not going to prison for seven years or even three. You have been sentenced to a rider up at Northern Idaho Correctional Institution, in Cottonwood. The court changed your sentence for six months, so they can give you a review hearing after you get back from Cottonwood. rider programs are anywhere from 90 to 180 days, and that information you will be given once they process you up there."

"Where exactly is up there?" I asked.

"Cottonwood is an old Army Radar Station built during World War II. It is just east of the Idaho border where Oregon, Washington, and Idaho all meet. I am sorry, Garrett. I really believed you would be going home today."

"Thanks for everything, Mark. I don't blame you for my sentence at all. I heard in court how you did your job, and it seemed like the judge had more to do with my sentence than my representation."

"The judges around here just have too much discretion on any given case. Look at the bright side, Garrett. I have seen similar defendants get seven years in the pen for this. Maybe if you look at it that way, you'll see today wasn't so bad."

"I'll take the rider, I guess. Thanks again for everything, Mark. Will I see you when I get back?"

"I will be in the court for your review hearing. They will automatically notify me from Cottonwood, but I won't come back to the jail to see you. Have a good rider, and once again, sorry things didn't go as planned."

"Take it easy, Mark, and thanks again."

After that, I slowly walked back to dorm 6. It would be my home away from home for a little while longer.

I called Beth later that night and gave her the bad news and filled her in on everything I had learned from talking to Mark and to the guys in my unit. Some of them had been on riders, and I made a mental note about who they were so I could play spades with or against them later and pick up some more information. Nothing is as scary as the unknown, and when I would finally get to go home was still unknown. I could accept and deal with whatever they dished out if I knew what the hell was going on and what to expect. What troubled me so much this afternoon was the incomplete information and how it was communicated. I still didn't have all the answers, but I told her I would get as many as I could and call her back Sunday night. She seemed a little sad at the verdict and the new predicament that I had now dropped into her lap, and understandably so. She wasn't the one who was headed for the Idaho State Penitentiary. I was.

I fell asleep early that night, after one of the most exhausting days of my life. Physically, I had handled much worse in basic training and sixteen-hour days tearing off roof during August in Pendleton, Oregon. Hell, I had pulled twenty-two-hour days gillnetting on my uncle's fishing boat the summer after high school. Compared to today, my first day of basic was nothing.

CHAPTER
18

OVER THE WEEKEND, I WAS probably the biggest pain in the ass in the whole dorm. First, I was planning on getting out, so of course I didn't buy anything on commissary, and my supplies by now had dwindled down to record low levels. Everyone was asking me to store stuff out to them, but with a depleted inventory, I had to send them over to Reynaldo, and it cost me a fortune. Second, I was busy asking everybody who had ever been on a rider everything they knew about Cottonwood. Third, I was gathering all the information about the pen from anyone who had ever been there, about the in-processing procedure, so I knew what to expect next.

My next big day would be like what Scott and Roger went through just yesterday, transported to the pen. My name was now on or soon would be on the transport list. The buses went out every Thursday in the afternoon, and just like Scott and Roger, I never knew who would go or stay until my name was called. Either I would be called next Thursday or stay here for another week and hope that my name would be called then. The sooner I got this over with, the better, and until my name was called, I was just wasting my time. Riders were going for 90, 120, or 180 days, and you never found out how long yours would be until you got to Cottonwood.

No matter how long your rider was, it didn't start until you got there, so from now until I arrived in Cottonwood, I was wasting my time. I had heard different stories about how long RDU took, stretching anywhere from ten days to two months, depending on how many people they sent. The flip side to that is, in order to move from the pen to Cottonwood, somebody has to complete their rider and vacate a bunk for the new arrival. The process I was now a part of had already been predetermined for me, but I had no way of knowing when the guys ahead of me would be sent home.

Roger and Scott had waited for two weeks after they were sentenced before going to the pen, but they were not going on riders; they were just going to the pen to do their time. Cottonwood's capacity had nothing to do with them or when they left the county jail, as it would with me. If it took me two months to get out of the county jail and begin a six-month rider, I wouldn't be home until June of 2006. If I was out next week and in process in ten days for a ninety-day rider, I could be home as soon as the middle of January 2006. This would be quite a big difference. This was what was bothering me the most now. How did anybody know what to expect? I was now part of a system that would not be adjusted for anyone. I was now a case number and a prisoner number waiting to be shuffled into a system that I absolutely had no control over. At least I understood what was ahead of me, at least for the most part, and the fear of not knowing had been diminished substantially. No point in stressing out over things I couldn't control, so I decided to relax and go with the flow.

I spent the weekend walking as much as I could each day. All day long on both days, different guys would come up and tell me how sorry they were about how I got screwed. Many of them were generous with coffee and cocoa, which I was out of and I had generously passed out when I was stocked up. This was the weekend I found out who my true friends really were. The shoes I had received from Raphael before I helped to get him out were holding up well, and since I was the only one up most mornings, I was now doing ten or fifteen miles after breakfast, before the bulk of the population woke up. With no court or razor calls on the weekends, this sometimes meant it was pretty quiet until almost noon. There were always exceptions to the rule, but I never understood how these guys could go to bed at midnight when the lights were out; with the exception of breakfast and two minutes for count, they could sleep until noon. I might pull that off for the first week or two, but after that, there was no way I could sleep that much. Maybe after being locked up as much as some of them had, I would develop the ability to sleep at will. I hoped not, since I was getting into very good shape and getting a lot of reading done in the morning.

Monopoly came down to pace with me on Sunday morning, and whenever he did, I always put down my book so we could talk with a bit of privacy.

"You need a hug, Garrett," he said, opening his arms and smiling as he came toward me.

"Maybe if we weren't in here," I said jokingly while smiling and nodding in appreciation of his attempted humor.

"Feeling better about going on your rider?" he asked me.

"Nothing I can do about it, so I might as well make the best of it," I replied.

I called Beth and Sean on Sunday night and let them know what I had learned over the weekend. I also told them how things that I couldn't control would affect the length of my absence. Although we were all disappointed, getting upset would do neither of us any good. Watching Monopoly at the phone booths daily was a testament to what getting upset would do to a man and his relationship on the outside. Setting your eyes on the next goal was the best way to handle setbacks. RDU was the next carrot dangling in front of my face, and now I had to reach out and grab it.

"Someday I will be walking off here and this will all be over," I told her before I said goodbye. The only question that gnawed at me 24-7 was, What day will that be?

CHAPTER

19

I STARTED THE NEXT WEEK with a positive outlook and an unyielding hope that my name would be called for transportation to the pen on Thursday, but in reality, I didn't expect this to happen for another week. Plan for the worst and hope for the best. I was definitely getting commissary this week; I had learned my lesson about planning for the best. It bit me in the ass last week, and that wasn't going to happen again.

I stepped up my walking to twenty-five miles a day, every day. It was my number one goal each day. I read when I could and did my stretching and sit-ups as well, but getting my miles was priority. Some days I would even go further to keep my mind occupied and help me sleep better. Walking was the only way to wear out my body; otherwise, I would be up all night, reading or bullshitting with Jay.

"What's the matter, Garrett?" he asked me one night.

"Can't sleep. Thinking about going on my rider," I told him.

"Man, you need to look at the bright side, Garrett. I have fifteen different charges and three priors. I only hope I'm lucky enough for the judge to show me mercy and give me a rider."

"Yeah, well, you are supposed to get three years, and you are hoping for a rider and you would be happy. I was supposed to get probation, and I got a rider and I'm still a little pissed, so cut me some slack."

"It's okay, Garrett. I still love you," he said in a sexy, sarcastic, humorous way that made me laugh. "Maybe we could ask to get bunks next to each other when we get there. Do you think they will let us do that?"

Jay had a way of making me smile, and he always had a good sense of humor. Even though I was in jail, facing a visit to the pen, at 1:00 a.m., he could still put a smile on my face. I appreciated that more than he would ever probably know. When you are locked up, it is always about making it easier on yourself, and that makes time fly. In my case, good friends, good humor, good books, and some sort of routine all helped make it go by quicker. What other choices did I have?

Jay and I would often have short little discussions in the middle of the night, conducted very quietly so we didn't get in trouble with the COs. It was probably more out of respect for the other inmates who were asleep. By 1:00 a.m., the COs were usually all gathered in the outer hallway, comparing testosterone levels or hunting and fishing stories. For as picky as they were about us making noise in the unit, they sure had no respect for the hundreds of men asleep in their tiers, where they could be heard. As disrespectful and loud as they were some nights, they wouldn't be able to hear a dump truck drive through the back wall over their constant need to one-up the last story. Occasionally, inmates would yell "Shut up!" anonymously from the tiers when the noise levels from the COs in the hallways were too loud. This usually brought a round of snickers from the all-night readers who were scattered about the unit and a little wake-up call to police the police. The other middle-of-the-night ritual was a high-pitched, passionate moaning of a female screaming, "Oh, fuck yeah!" This would pierce through the night silence, often bringing a round of laughter and the attention of the COs, who could do absolutely nothing about it since they were usually in the hall and had no clue which of the 120 had done it. What were they going to do if they did catch us, put us in jail? Nighttime was always hard in jail. Being alone with your thoughts, and in the silence, tended to make time go by slowly. If it weren't for my stack of books and Jay up all night, this place would have been twice as bad. Little things like that made all the difference in the world to me. I considered this part of my routine since we were there for each other from midnight until breakfast if necessary. Most people had to put up with whatever farting, snoring, and stinky busybody the COs assigned to be close to them.

The next day, both my friends Hal and Jay went to court in the morning for sentencing, and while pacing and reading, I repeatedly found it hard to focus because I was thinking of the two of them. Hopefully, their day in court would go better than mine had. Jay had been up all night, but with all his invested hours in the sleep bank over the last four months, I was sure he would manage to survive half the day. Sentencing for guys you were friends with in here was almost like a special event. Their life would change on that day and forever be altered, for better or worse, as mine had. I was hoping they both had positive outcomes, but I had already learned from previous experience that you never knew what was going to happen. Right before lunch, they both walked into the unit, and I could immediately tell by the joy and sorrow they conveyed what the results were. The telegraphed emotions were just as easy to spot today as mine most likely was last Friday. As I approached Hal to offer my condolences; he offered up the answer to the question before I could even ask.

"They gave me a year at the pen," he said. "The judge said I have a drinking problem, and since they caught me drinking while on probation, I reoffended and had a blatant disregard for the rules." He looked about as upset as I was on Friday, and I could tell he didn't want to be bothered right now; just like me, he would rather be left alone to sort things out and think it through. I walked over to Jay and, making sure Hal wasn't watching, congratulated him on the positive sentence he had received.

"I'm going to Cottonwood with you, Garrett. I got a rider just like you," he said with a huge smile on his face. Ironically, the same sentence that had devastated me oddly enough made him the happiest guy in the dorm. To quote Forrest Gump, "Life is like a box of chocolates—you never know what you are going to get." Oh, how true that statement was today! Jay had two or three girls he was dating but was serious with none, and he had no kids yet in his twenty-three short years, and if this would have happened to me at that stage in my life, it wouldn't have bothered me so much. Leaving Sean and Beth for such a long period was the most devastating thing about my sentence. I had endured, and would endure, almost anything and not complain once. Three months' basic training at Harmony Church in Fort Benning, Georgia, living in the same barracks used to train WWII soldiers, living alone as a single father to Sean from the time he was eighteen months old until he was four, and twenty-three years as a roofer, installing and tearing off some of the dirtiest, nastiest building material on some of the steepest roofs Seattle had to offer. I even spent three weeks on my uncle's thirty-two-foot gillnetting boat in Bristol Bay, Alaska. Twenty-two days with no shower, twenty-two-hour days covered in fish slime as the greenhorn with two of my cousins. I could handle anything life would throw at me, and I was hoping Sean and Beth would be able to as well. Although I did feel somewhat a sigh of relief knowing I would have a friend with me when Jay said he was going. You are always better off surrounded by people you know, more so than strangers. Expecting him to fall asleep the minute lunch was over would prove to be a false prediction on my part. Just as sadness had overwhelmed my sentencing day, happiness had taken his over, because instead of looking at three years as he assumed, he was now looking at six months or less.

I went to find Hal to make sure he was holding up, and much to my surprise, he had already turned the corner from disappointment to acceptance. It took me all weekend to get the answers I needed to reach that point, and I was proud of him for doing it so quickly. Albeit part of the problem he had with the acceptance of his sentence was most likely already dealt with subconsciously since this was his third offense. By previously being through the system, he should have already known the consequences of his actions and thus would have been previously somewhat prepared to deal with them. Had I revived my sentence after a second charge, I would have expected what I received and therefore been better prepared to accept it. I had been told by so many I was going home that I jumped on the bandwagon totally in denial of the worst-case scenario. Not my best move.

"How are you holding up, Hal?" I asked him as I cautiously approached.

"I was pissed and mad at myself when I first got back, but deep down, I was almost expecting something like this," he told me.

"What do you mean?" I asked.

"The judge warned me not to, but I went out and fucked up anyway. How could I not expect this? I was hoping for ninety days discretionary time, or maybe even a rider like you got." After a brief silence to contemplate his actions, he continued. "I need this wake-up call to sober my ass up. If I don't change something, I'm going to end up dead, and my kids won't have a father anymore. Maybe I need to go to the yard. This might just be the best thing for me."

"Would rehab have been a better option, or can you stop on your own? Do you want to stop?"

"I tried that last time, and it didn't work. Maybe being away from my kids for a year will help. Maybe having them come visit me in prison is the slap upside the head that will keep me sober. I need to make some changes in my life, and I am sort of looking forward to getting it started."

"That's a good attitude, Hal. I'm glad you aren't sitting here, whining like a baby, like so many of these punks tend to do. Take responsibility for your actions and change yourself instead of crying about the repercussions you yourself have caused. Like they told me in rehab, you can't do it for anyone else. You have to want the change."

"Well, I am ready for change. What I have been doing so far isn't working. When do you head out on your rider?" he asked.

"Nobody knows. They call your name on Thursday afternoon for transport or they don't. They never tell you in advance, for security reasons," I told him. "I am hoping to be on this week's bus, but it wouldn't surprise me if I wasn't until next week, or maybe the week after. No telling with this clusterfuck."

"Well, hopefully we can at least go to RDU together. We were only sentenced one week apart, so I am sure transport orders will be just as close. I'll talk to you later, Garrett. I got to make some phone calls. I haven't been able to reach my ex yet, and this will not be a fun phone call."

"Good luck, Hal. I'll see you around. I know where you live."

And with that, he strolled over to the phone booths with my respect for his positive attitude and sympathy for the call he was about to make. Even if he and his wife did not reconcile their differences, her life was about to change, as were those of his two sons. Through conversations with Beth and Sean, I had learned that all too well.

CHAPTER

20

BY MORNING, THE STRESS LEVEL on the tier was starting to rise. Things had started to change the day Roger and Scott had left. Slowly at first, hardly even noticeable at all, except those who really paid attention to the general atmosphere and didn't just focus on themselves. The average inmate didn't give a rat's ass about anything but himself in here. Helping other people out was not at the top of most people's priority lists, but as I observed the feelings of the tier in general, I couldn't help but try to help make things go smoothly for everyone who lived here. Time was so much easier to do in friendly surroundings, so why not try to make it easy for all of us?

Craig was diagonally across from me on the back wall, and ever since Scott's and Roger's departure, he was slowly trying to maneuver himself into the top-dog position on the tier. The problem with his idea was that he had no chance of replacing those two. Craig was one of the oldest men up here, but this was only his first time in jail and he was still relatively new to the penal system. As new guys would rotate in or bunk changes were made, Craig would try to buddy up with them to make new friends. The only reason he needed new friends was that all his old friends, including me, were really getting sick and tired of his crybaby attitude and his nonstop whining. I began to realize that with Scott and Roger gone, nobody else was keeping him in check. Craig saw this as an opportunity to share his whiny outlook with all the new guys and the rest of the tier. The two biggest problems were that everyone was sick to death of hearing the same old complaints over and over about our lives here, especially since the COs were not about to make any changes, and all this tended to do was bring everybody down psychologically, because with constant negativity, eventually people would begin to get depressed. It was affecting everybody. Many guys were acquiring Craig's attitude, and it was making life hard for the tier; this wasn't accomplishing a thing. He would sit up on the edge of the railing after we were bunked up at chow time and bitch during every single meal about how bad the food was. It wasn't like the jail was going to change their menu because of one obnoxious asshole. Three times a day, seven days a week, since the day we moved back from MCU, the other twenty-three of us on the tier had to hear the same sniveling crap for weeks now, and the entire tier was ready to snap because of the snowball one idiot had started rolling down the hill.

Hal joined me on Tuesday morning when I was pacing, and just as I did with Monopoly, I put down my book so we could talk as we looped around the dayroom.

"What did your wife say last night about your wonderful news?" I asked him.

"She wasn't thrilled, but I think she expected it more than I did. She thinks it will be good for me, and after talking to her, I am beginning to think the same. I will miss my family, but I got the feeling from her we might be able to work it all out when I return. I hope we can, anyway, if I stay sober."

"I'm not trying to rain on your parade, buddy, but are you sure she's not just yanking your chain to make you feel better while you're gone? I hope she isn't, but you need to look at it realistically so you aren't devastated when you get out. I see what Monopoly's wife is doing to him, and it makes me sick. I hope your wife is nicer than that."

"She's not like that, but I know what you mean. She has never played head games, but thanks for giving it to me straight. I may not like what you have to say, but at least you speak your mind. Not too many people are that honest."

"Anything to help a friend," I told him as he strolled off. As I watched him go, I could almost see his mind swirling around the possibilities; I had just made him realize what the situation was. Hal was a pretty naive guy, and although I hoped everything worked out for the guy, it was always better to hope for the best and expect the worst. I wasn't sure if I had convinced Hal, but I promised myself I would never again feel the way I did on Friday.

I paced that night until lights-out and then ended up reading most of the night. A few late-night comments from Jay kept a small smile on my face, but inside I was reeling. I had tried to be there for my friends in here, but that night I realized nobody in here really knew my whole story. Different people knew different pieces of it, but part of protecting myself in here was to not let anyone know it all. It was a wall I had put up partly to keep the freaks out but also to isolate myself from them so I could do what I needed to do to get by. I contemplated letting that wall down so I could talk to someone about the events unfolding, but the fear of opening the floodgates kept me from doing it. I knew once I opened up, the grapevine would take it from there. Even in a place where everybody had a courtroom story gone awry, I would be judged unfairly. I enjoyed my solitude in the morning while pacing before the dorm woke up and being able to escape to whatever location the characters in my book were traveling to.

I wondered if it was easier for others in the prison surrounded by friends they knew on the outside. How much different it would be if this had happened in Seattle? Odds there were better for my running into some people I already knew, and I would get visits from Sean and Beth. Maybe that would make it even harder on me, but I never really thought about it since I was so far away. Distance might have been a good thing, because I had a really hard time keeping it together on the phone when I talked to them. It made me sad. This was one of the hardest nights to get through since I had been locked up. I hated where I was and why, but mostly that night I hated the fact that I couldn't shut off my overly analytical mind. The night before sentencing, I found myself rereading pages over and over due to lack of concentration. I wished I had been able to get out of bed and pace all night, but I didn't make the rules.

The next day was Wednesday, and with it came commissary and superexchange. After being up all night and getting up for razor call, I was dead tired. I knew if I took a nap I would just be up all night again, and I would rather be awake during my free time. Even though I was half-dead, nothing was worse than a sleepless night behind bars. I had been sleeping well for weeks, so one night wouldn't affect me too much, but the mental aspect of my exhaustion was taking its toll. I was tired from overanalyzing and processing what happened the day before, and if I didn't stop, I would be miserable and start to hard-time. I forced myself to put it out of my mind and focus on positive things rather than negative.

Hoping to be on the transport tomorrow for the pen, I wasn't really stocking up as I normally did to build up my store. I was slowly lowering my inventory levels and exchanging everything I could for envelopes. I had heard from all those who left before me that when you left the county jail, all your books and commissary went on your property and you had to have somebody pick it up for you at the jail. You were not allowed to keep anything and transfer it to the prison. This was for security reasons. Nothing could be brought into the next facility and be blamed on the last one. The few expectations were legal paperwork, some personal pictures, an address and phone number book, and envelopes. That was about it. This meant I might as well trade for or be paid off in envelopes so I would have something to barter with when I arrived at RDU.

I had also learned there were two phases of the RDU process. During the first phase, there was no commissary and you couldn't have any books sent to you. Since it was just a receiving-and-transport hub, it almost made sense to not bother with personal property until you reached your final destination. Whatever the reasoning, I had to be prepared to lose the few comforts I had managed to gain at county or at least minimize the potential for RDU being the longest two to six weeks of my life. The only two things that made being locked up bearable were commissary and all the books I had been reading. Without either of them in RDU, it was looking like it would be a really shitty few weeks ahead of me.

Nobody had any idea how long it was really going to be, so now there were actually three things that I was concerned about. It wouldn't be too bad if I was in and out in a couple of weeks, but so far Lady Luck had not been shining too brightly on this particular episode of my life, and I had no reason to believe that anything was about to change soon. For all I knew, I could be in RDU for two months with nothing to read and no commissary, so in an act of final desperation, I began trading everything I didn't need for envelopes with guys who used them to play at the Texas Hold'em table.

I asked everyone who owed me to pay in lopes; that way, I could trade them for commissary with whoever was ahead of me and already had store of their own the minute I got there. This would give me a small amount of comfort and extra food if the meals were not enough to fill me up. I wasn't trying to repeat the first twelve days when I had arrived at county and was starving the whole time before my first commissary showed up.

Jay and Hal both saw what I was doing, and after a brief explanation of the reasoning behind my actions, they both not only agreed with me but also followed suit. Neither of them had too much to trade, but they both agreed that it was better to be prepared for transport tomorrow and have some bargaining chips with them rather than go in empty-handed like most people. Part of the problem with this was, if I traded everything for lopes and didn't go tomorrow, then I would have nothing for next week. I told everybody to trade back with me tomorrow if I wasn't on transport and we could do this all again until I left. This way, I was prepared no matter what happened, and over the last seven weeks, I had learned that life is much more comfortable if you prepare. I had adjusted to the jail environment and had become very comfortable. Oddly enough, going to prison wasn't bothering me as much as the unknown transition that was ahead of me. Without a working time frame to go by regarding books or extra food, I would be a nervous wreck for the next few weeks.

That night, as dinner was being served, one of the things I had been so worried about happening on the tier finally did occur. Craig the Whiner was hanging on the rail, pissing and moaning about the quality of the cuisine being served, and he finally reached for the straw that broke the camel's back. In the back-corner bunk of the tier was a guy named Kellogg, who was a huge convict with bulging arms and a few trips to the pen behind him and was now getting ready to go back in for at least a year, if not more. He pretty much kept to himself and his own world of push-ups and other forms of weight lifting that you learned to do only after years of previous incarceration. He never really bothered anyone, and nobody in their right mind ever bothered him, for obvious reasons. Tonight, he had finally had his fill of listening to Craig bitch about something that would never change and made his feelings about Craig's crybaby attitude be known to everyone.

After hanging over the rail and making sure the whole world knew that he thought the jail meals were dog food, too small, and deprived of questionable meat sources for the two hundredth time, Roger dropped his book on the floor quite loudly and walked over to Craig, never taking his eyes off the man who was about to be silenced.

"I have sat here for three weeks listening to you whine, piss, and moan about every fucking meal seven days a week, and I am sick of fucking hearing about it!" he shouted. Stepping up close to Craig's red face, he continued, "Nobody on the tier wants to hear your sorry ass complaining about something that is never going to change just because you sit up here yelling about how bad it is. All it does is make everybody hate the meals we have no choice but to eat. There aren't a lot of options in here, so either don't eat it or shut the fuck up, because nobody wants to hear you mouth off any more!" With that, Kellogg turned and walked back to his bunk and dead silence reigned in the tier. The confrontation and ensuing silence caught the attention of the CO serving dinner and the rest of the unit as well. Halting the chow line and looking up at the commotion on our tier, the CO yelled up to us, "Is there a problem up there?" You could have cut the silence in the whole unit with a knife until three or four guys simultaneously yelled back, "No problem!" After a short pause and a careful look around to verify this, the CO yelled for the upper-right tier to get their chow. As quickly as it had started, it was over, and Craig's red face, somber look, and silence told the whole tier that Roger's message had finally gotten through. I felt what Craig had received was long overdue, but I wasn't one to rock the boat, and most people in here felt the same. The more problems you caused, the more problems you got in, and most people just kept to themselves and did their own time. In fact, when anybody in here told anybody what to do, it was pretty much standard to reply by saying, "Do your own time."

Craig wasn't a force to be reckoned with, but fighting with anyone in the dorms got you sent to the hole for a week and then, most likely, back to MCU.

Anyone who was used to dorm life dreaded going back to MCU because of the loss of freedom it meant. If someone did want to fight you, the usual reaction was to do nothing but stand there and get hit. This way, once the COs reviewed the tape that was always rolling upstairs, they would see you hadn't participated in the fight. The person who did start it would be charged with assault, and you would be out of the hole in an hour and return to the dorm. Craig wasn't stupid enough to fight Kellogg, and Kellogg knew the system so well that he never got himself into any trouble.

Craig was the first man down to the chow line, leaving the scene of his humiliation as quickly as possible. He grabbed his tray of "dog food" and hurried back upstairs to eat in solitude. The buzz from the rest of us was relief that it had finally been said and praise for Kellogg, who had the balls to do what the rest of us would only dream about doing. Some actually praised and thanked him for shutting Craig up once and for all. We had all thought about it and wanted it to be done, but you never knew how people in here would react, and Craig was no exception. Maybe Kellogg was a psychotic, violent man when provoked, and nobody in here knew him well enough to know that side of him. Kellogg had reached his limit, wasn't too worried about Craig, and most likely did it for the good of the tier. On behalf of the tier, I personally thanked the man, as many of us did.

CHAPTER

21

THE NEXT DAY AT BREAKFAST, Craig was silent. The same went for lunch. The message he had been given was received loud and clear. After lunch was a tense time for Hal, Jay, and me, as we anxiously anticipated the two o'clock transport list we hoped to be on. Over the past week, I had also learned that when the judge had "retained jurisdiction for six months," it meant that I had six months from that date to complete my rider and go back in front of the judge for my review. That meant I would hopefully be out by April 21, 2006, if my rider and review went well. It wasn't ninety days, but it wasn't June either, so at least I had a date to finally look forward to. The quicker I left here, the sooner my rider would begin and end. If I wasn't on transport this week, the time I spent until I was called would accomplish nothing toward my release date. In here, this was called downtime. The guys who were just going to prison and not a rider began their time when they arrived in jail, so downtime for them didn't exist.

As it turned out, today was not my day. It wasn't to be for Jay or Hal either, and while I was disappointed for all of us, I was slightly hopeful that we would all go together. I traded back some store for the lopes I was now hoarding so I could restock enough amenities to be comfortable all week. I blew out a heavy sigh finally knowing my fate for today at least, then I settled in for another week. I noticed the guys who did leave all were sentenced one week ahead of us, so chronologically, the three of us should all go next week. This was all speculative and very optimistic, but if things next week went the same as they did this week, the next seven days here would be my last. The other good thing that came of this was that Monopoly was going in front of his judge, and now I would still be here to find out what fate awaited him. I wanted things to go fast, but with no commissary in RDU, I would actually rather be here with my store and minilibrary for another week than locked up in a cell for twenty hours a day with no freedom.

I had also found out the two phases of RDU were extremely different from each other, by talking with guys who had already been through it. Though it might have been years ago, and possible changes might have occurred, but knowing what to expect was always better than not knowing. First, we would be sent to unit 15, which was the first stage of intake. Usually there for one week, we would face tons of forms to fill out, educational testing, and medical screening. Once done, depending on how full it was, we would be moved to unit 7, where we were allowed limited commissary and waited transport to Cottonwood.

Unit 15 pretty much automatically took one week. Unit 7 was a holding area for bunks to become available in Cottonwood, and this could last anywhere from one to eight weeks, depending on the number of inmates that graduated on time. With all my new information, I found a bit of comfort knowing what was ahead. Now, if everything would just happen in a timely fashion, we would be moving along smoothly. I shared all I knew with Hal and Jay while walking, and the two of them added all they had heard as well. Slowly, I was beginning to accept what lay ahead and was not as angry about my situation as I previously had been. Whenever I felt upset, I just remembered that I could have received three years, and suddenly being home by April didn't sound so bad.

The new thing that began to eat away at me was that I would be in prison for Thanksgiving and Christmas. Sean's birthday just happened to be on Christmas as well, so that made it even more difficult, but I wasn't sure if it was more upsetting for me or for him. I had talked a lot to him while locked up since I had been expecting to be home a week before. It was one thing to not communicate with him for a few weeks, but now it was going to be months, and I needed to suck it up and talk to him no matter how it affected me. Since I hated having things looming over my head and eating away at my subconscious, I figured the sooner I dealt with it, the better.

I spent the weekend reading and pacing as much as possible. I even found myself jumping into conversations with other people that I had thought had either been on a rider or had gone to prison already, so I could get more information from them. Not surprising, the majority had information that proved useful, and I learned quite a bit by keeping my ears open and listening to what was volunteered. By the first of the week, I had heard every story and digested every piece of info that I could possibly gather from the entire unit. Fearing that I was becoming a pain in the ass, on Monday, I gave it a rest and focused on finishing all the books in my bin box. The books Beth had sent me had to go on my property list when I went to the pen and couldn't be left in the dorm or go with me. There were still two or three books I was looking forward to reading, and if I was leaving Thursday, I had to get to them or they would have to wait until I got out.

While doing my usual pacing and reading in the morning, I also realized that ever since Kellogg got in his face, Craig had stopped whining completely; he now pretty much kept to himself. Public humiliation and being put in his place in front of everyone had driven him into a shell he might not ever come out of, at least for the duration of his stay here. I was breaking my rule of planning for the worst and hoping for the best by counting on being transported to the pen when Thursday came. If my name wasn't called, I knew that I would be devastated. As much as I tried not to, I couldn't change the way I felt, and it really bothered me. I knew that if I expected to leave and I didn't, the letdown would be painful. At the same time, I knew deep down my time here was over, and chronologically I was next in line to go. The wheels of justice turn slowly, but they do turn, and it was my turn to take a step toward freedom.

On Wednesday, Monopoly went to court in the morning and I found myself nervous for him. He was expecting to get the balance of his sentence on the last of his charges and finally have a release date to look forward to. I found myself watching the door for the arrival of the morning court guys and his return with possible good news. There was so little of it around here it was just a matter of time before somebody got a break in this place. It might as well be him.

When I saw him coming down the hall to the dorm entrance, I could tell in one second that whatever happened to him wasn't good. His head was hanging low, and his dejected look and body language said it all. As the CO checked the guys into the dorm, something happened to Monopoly I had not seen in my seven weeks here. He was halted in the hallway, and they made him face the wall while the CO made a call on his radio. After a few moments, other COs showed up in the hall, and they all surrounded him and began asking questions. We weren't allowed to communicate through the glass or gather around the doorway for security reasons, so I just kept pacing while paying attention to what was going on as best as I could. After a few laps, I noticed they were putting handcuffs on him and then they escorted him back down the hallway. I was never able to find out what happened to him. That was the procedure for guys who had been fighting or who were hauled off to the hole.

When the CO came back to the dorm, he gave no reply when asked by others what had happened. He made his way up to Monopoly's bunk, rolled up his belongings, and put them all down by the guard station, ready to be picked up. Something was definitely wrong. Asking around to find out what could possibly have taken place drew a blank from almost everyone, and even Jack, who had been here longer than anybody, was at a loss as to any reason for the actions we had seen taken. The CO wasn't giving out any information, and those who had returned with him either were not in court with him or had seen nothing out of the ordinary occur during the bus ride back.

None of this made sense, but it wasn't the exception here—it was the norm. Poof! Just like that, Monopoly was gone. If I left tomorrow as I hoped to, I might not ever see him again. He had given me his phone number a few weeks back, but if he was in trouble, who knew if it would still be in service when either of us were released? I felt bad for the guy, because something had not gone right somewhere, and he was already hard-timing as it was. I hoped the best for him, and knew I would miss the guy. When two men live together, whether in school, in the military, during camping, or in jail, they share a bond that brings them closer than regular friends are. He was the first real friend I had on the inside. We were parting ways, and it was sad I didn't even get to say goodbye.

Once again on Wednesday, after superexchange, I traded my entire store for envelopes in preparation for transport on Thursday afternoon. I had said my goodbyes to everyone who mattered, because if I was called to go, they would only give us ten minutes to roll up and go. While waiting for the final minutes to tick away, I was given some news that I would have appreciated a few days ago. You were only allowed to take twenty envelopes when you left here. After all my trades, I had well over one hundred, so I had to think fast and solve the problem so I didn't end up walking away from eighty. The only viable option I could come up with was to share the wealth with Hal and Jay. I would be losing lopes to Hal, but helping him out since he was penniless felt okay. Jay could owe me and square with me later at Cottonwood. The rest I could take down to booking when I was leaving, and I might know somebody else who could use them before they were taken away. In two minutes, that was the best I could come up with, and Hal and Jay both thanked me with a smile. I was trying to create good karma that I knew someday would come back to me.

Within minutes of my giving away my lopes, my name was the first one called for transport. Next came Hal, but Jay's name was oddly absent. It wouldn't do me any good to get them back from him, and I knew he would catch up with me eventually. With some good-natured laughing in his face for not making it, I told him goodbye and asked him to try to find out what had happened to Monopoly if he could before he left. With that, I rolled up my stuff and vacated the best bunk in the unit. It would be highly sought the minute I left.

I strolled down the stairs, saying quick goodbyes to Reynaldo and Jack and a quick "Keep them in line" to Kellogg. Then Hal and I and a few other headed out the door of dorm 6 and down to hub control one last time. Ironically, I found myself upset to be leaving, even though I wanted to keep the process moving forward. I was probably more upset about a change of scenery and the unknown living arrangements awaiting me. I had become fairly comfortable here, and the step I was taking today was about as big a step as a person takes in his life. It was a scary situation I was facing, and I knew that by the end of the day, I would feel better. I took a huge breath to keep calm and help keep my eyes dry so my emotions wouldn't be obvious. Hal put his arm on my shoulder and comfortingly said, "Come on, Garrett, let's get the fuck out of here." The long walk down the hallway on the way to hub control, I was amazed to see the guys from MCU in their stripes out in the rec yard, pacing around in circles. Much to my surprise, the man in the MCU stripes staring back at me through the window was Monopoly. Holy shit! With no time to talk, he yelled one thing to me through the window.

"Call my mom's number I gave you when you get out!" he yelled to me as he turned to keep moving in his circles under the careful watch of the CO. He couldn't communicate with other inmates without getting in trouble any more than he already was, so he had to keep it short. I could only assume as we proceeded down the hall to booking that he said whom to contact in case his phone number was not in service by the time either of us got out. I could reach his mom, who was listed in Tucson, and she would know how to reach him. That was a smart move and quick thinking for Monopoly to give me a way to reach him when he saw me going by. It wasn't uncommon to give out parents' phone numbers to guys in jail since their numbers were usually more stable, with a better chance of being the same for years to come. Most guys in here were on the run before being arrested, and since the bill isn't usually paid when you are locked up, cell phones would often expire during incarceration.

Arriving at the booking area, I was still heavy with extra lopes, and when we all took a seat in the waiting area, I was pleasantly surprised for the second time today. Scott, the roofer, who was in MCU my first week here, was getting out-processed as well.

"Walker, what the fuck are you doing here? I thought you had a plea bargain and were going home a couple of weeks ago?" he asked me.

"I ended up getting a rider, so I'm going to Cottonwood. Are you going home, or are they shipping you off somewhere?"

"Same as you. I am headed to Cottonwood with you," he said.

"At least I will know one person on the way and when we get the fuck out of here."

I gave Scott twenty lopes to take with him, and we spent the next hour waiting to pack up and go. When they called my name, I was amazed that two months of running store had been whittled down to one large manila envelope full of notes, lopes, and other paperwork and the balance of the money on my account, about $700, which would be forwarded to the pen. At least I wouldn't have to wait for it to show up in the mail, since it was moving with me. I had to put everything else on my property and had authorized somebody to come pick it up for me. That was going to be more difficult than it sounded with everyone I knew in Everett not wanting to drive 381 miles to get my stuff. This was a huge problem, but the jail would keep it for two weeks; after that, they donated it to charity. I left two authorized names to pick up my stuff: Tiffany, my high school girlfriend, whom I had visited the day I got busted, and my lawyer, Mark. I added the books in my bin box to the ones I had already sent from the unit down to the property room because you weren't allowed to possess more than three at a time.

Looking at the box I had filled up with books was actually impressive. I was proud of myself for the miles I had logged, the books I had read, and the fact that I was trying to be productive while incarcerated, as opposed to what the others were doing. I filled the box with books and filled in the top of it with my personal clothing and what little I had with me when I had flown here two months ago. I was dressed in a white transport jumpsuit and shackled and handcuffed for the trip to the pen. Finally, after an hour and a half of out-processing, I was loaded onto the bus with everybody else. I was hoping to never be shackled and chained like this again after my last trip to court, but that was not to be. After a decade of getting away with a questionable lifestyle, I was finally going to pay the price for it. Next stop: the Idaho State Penitentiary.

CHAPTER

22

I REMEMBERED THE WALK OF shame down the hallway of the jail when I first arrived in Ada County. Today, it was the ultimate bus ride of shame that was even worse. If Idaho is known for its warm, dry desert air and the bright-blue sky, then why did the wet, drizzly gray day remind me so much of Seattle in November? We headed south out of Boise and into the never-ending desert and saw nothing but miles of absolutely nothing completely surrounding this place, as if it was just dropped out here already built.

We rose up to get a better view out of the windows, to catch a glimpse of our new home. Ironically, it was the inside view that really mattered to me, because that was all I figured I would be seeing of it, anyway. It was probably nice to get another perspective on the local geography and the lay of the land for those on the bus who might end up here for the next few years. I had accepted the fact of what was happening to me, but I still couldn't believe I was going to prison. Somehow, it seemed so unreal, like I was watching from a really good seat in a movie theater.

As we pulled into the main gate, it opened and then closed before the second gate would open. The area between the first fence and the outer perimeter fence was known as no-man's-land. Both were twenty feet high, chain linked with razor wire uncoiled and covering the top. These two fences completely enclosed the entire prison. The only things in no-man's-land were guard dogs that had about one hundred yards to patrol along with a doghouse. Just outside the fences was a paved road that was constantly being circled by a prison vehicle. My life was pretty messed up right now, but seeing this guy made me smile just for a moment. No matter what was ahead for me, at least I didn't have to drive around in circles forty hours a week.

We pulled all the way around to the back side of the prison and pulled up next to a long older-looking building that somebody said was used for death row inmates twenty years ago. Once our shackles were removed, we were all herded into a small fifty-by-thirty holding cell and waited for our name to be called. Two at a time, we came out of the holding area and we were led down the hall to a window with two inmate-workers behind it passing out clothes.

"What size jumpsuit you wear?" he asked me as I stepped up.

"Extralarge," I answered.

"What size shoes you need?"

"Size 10."

He handed a pile of clothes and a pair of deck shoes to me, and I followed the guy in front of me to the next line in the hallway. Something told me that getting a perfect fit wasn't top priority for these guys and we were just cattle heading for the corral as far as these guys were concerned. In county at least, you tried your stuff on right there; in case something didn't fit, you could exchange it right away. I had no idea how long I would be carrying this shit around and how far away from the window I would be when I realized I got the wrong size. Ahead of me, I saw guys going into the room two at a time, but they weren't coming out, so I could only assume this was the next stop on our journey. It was close to dark, so this had to go quick if we were to make dinner in the chow hall. The alternative was the standard sack lunch, which I knew from experience usually sucked.

As I slowly crept to the head of the line, I began to realize what was next. It was time for the infamous prison strip search before we dressed down into our jumpsuits, two men at a time. If I had ever feared a body cavity search before entering prison, it was time to face the music. Oh, what a lovely day this was turning out to be! As I stood naked with my back to the wall, the CO said to both of us, "Put up your arms," as he demonstrated with his own. "Show me the back of your hands," he continued in a monotone voice that slightly resembled that of a baritone computer.

"Bend forward and run your fingers through your hair." We leaned forward and pretended to shampoo our hair.

"Pull your ears forward so I can see behind them."

"Open your mouth." He looked inside. "Lift your tongue." He looked again.

"Spread your cheeks so I can see your gums."

After he was satisfied I wasn't smuggling any contraband, we finally got to the fun part.

"Lift your penis."

"Lift your scrotum," he said.

Here it comes, I thought.

"Turn around, squat, and cough hard two times."

"Get dressed," he said, and it was over.

After all the movies and the stories and the bullshit I had heard about what just happened in my forty-three years, I felt pretty good about it being over. Thirty minutes ago, I had not wanted to be the guy driving in circles around the prison, but now that was a much better place to be compared to being assigned to literally checking out assholes all day long. How long does the low man on the totem pole get this job before being bumped up the ladder? Seniority definitely has its privileges as far as the COs are concerned.

Surprisingly, everything fit pretty well. We were all dressed in a one-piece jumpsuit, with denim jackets and a black stocking cap. We had also been given a fishnet laundry bag that was like the bedroll we received in county, which I was sure contained all our bedding, hygiene items, and anything else they felt we would need for the duration of our short stay here. As we lined up in the hallway, we divided into two groups, yellow suits for the riders and white suits for the timers. The guys who were going to prison to do their time were now called *timers* by the COs. From here on out, the timers and the riders were not allowed to communicate with each other. This helped prevent the timers from enticing us into a fight and doing other things that might prevent us from completing our rider successfully. The timers had nothing to lose by getting us in trouble and often resented us for being much closer to being free.

Once the rider was complete, we would receive probation and all the check-ins and urinalysis that would be required of us for years. Although timers would not get out for a couple of years from now, once free, they would have no requirements placed upon them in most cases. The tradeoff was six months for me as a rider instead of three years as a timer. Although after my six months I had to follow the rules of probation for six years, this was something most timers didn't want to be forced into doing. The choice was easy for me because of Sean and Beth. Some timers chose to go to the yard for two or three years instead of accepting a rider so they could just get it over with, because if you failed at probation, they would file new charges against you on top of your existing sentence.

After ascending to the higher echelon of the county jail in dorm 6, I was a new guy, down at the bottom of the pecking order again. I watched the timers pick on some rider to "flop" or fail before he even left unit 15. I had heard of many guys flopping riders for stupid rule violations within weeks or even just days away from completion. Even after you leave Cottonwood, the judge evaluates your behavior until you step up to the bench and your sentence is reviewed. You could pull off the perfect rider and still go back to county jail, get into a fight, and end up spending years in the yard. From now until I went back to court, I had to do what I was told, follow the rules to a tee, and avoid fighting for any reason at all. Failure to do so could cost me the next three years of my life. Hal and I shook hands and said farewell. Knowing that they separated the two groups, we might not be able to talk again. We lined up in two groups and went out through the back of the building. We were now headed through the yard of the pen and over toward two large buildings, units 15 and 16, known as RDU.

"The Reception and Diagnostic Unit of the Idaho State Penitentiary is the first stop of your visit with us," the CO in charge of the in-processing paperwork told us. The twenty-five of us were now in a classroom, complete with six rows with five school desks in each row. When we sat down, we found a manila envelope sitting on each desk filled with paperwork. I had no doubt we would be filling it out before we got to eat dinner. Along with the in-processing paperwork, these folders included some instructional pamphlets that told us what to expect, how to behave, and the inmate rulebook we were to read and obey. The rules were similar to those at county, but the riders had additional rules we had to follow while at the pen in order to keep us isolated from the timers. It was our responsibility to read and learn these rules, and the CO even told us, "The timers will try to get you to break these rules. If you do, you may be joining them."

Glancing over them quickly, I noticed that they were significant. Things like no talking in chow, no communicating with the timers, no passing anything from one cell to another. They were easy enough to follow, but I could see the timers asking someone to pass a note to a buddy just to get a rider in trouble, and I knew some idiot would do it. We sat through the one-hour class and were told explicitly not to engage in sexual activity, even if it was consensual, which received some chuckles. If you weren't crazy, you would avoid any temptation to physical violence at all cost. This was especially true for the riders, since this meant you would flop. How to conduct ourselves during movements, what movements meant, and what lines painted in the yard we had to be sure not to cross for security reasons. Finally, you needed to know how to fill out each piece of paper in the envelope properly.

This would have taken me five minutes without step-by-step instructions that dragged into a forty-five-minute question-and-answer session for some of the stupidest people I had ever had the displeasure of being associated with. The dumb shits in basic training were Rhodes scholar compared to this lot. If they had known that each question was making us wait longer for dinner, they might have stopped asking them. We were told to expect to be in unit 15 for up to four weeks, depending on test results, medical needs, paperwork arrival from various locations, things from lawyers, and PSI. The prison had to have all their ducks in a row before we could move on to the next order of business, or we would remain here.

"Don't blame us for the delays during in-processing," we were told. "We are a well-oiled machine. Any delays are because of the courts, legal counsel, medical needs, prescriptions, and whether you are psychologically stable enough or intelligent enough to move on. Unbelievably, some of you are too stupid to be here. After your educational screening, we will let you know." This guy should do open mic nights. He was pretty good. Maybe it was a way to calm our nerves during our first hours here, but it was comforting and helped put us at ease.

He continued with his speech. "We need all this information so that we may give you an LSI number like your classifications in county. This will help to evaluate the level of security risk you are to us and evaluate your eventual placement level within the state's Department of Correction, or DOC, community. Before you leave this unit, you will be fingerprinted, photographed, given an ID card and will have medical and dental screening and a mental health evaluation. We will also take a sample of your DNA, give you an educational evaluation and your computed LSI score. If and only if you have all eight of these items completed will you be ready to move on to unit 16 if you are a timer and unit 7 if you are a rider."

While hearing this lecture, one by one the riders would step up and have their heads shaved to a half-inch-long trimmer like the ones used in basic training. This was a mandatory haircut required every two weeks from now until we left Cottonwood. In addition, there was a no-facial-hair rule. I had kept my hair short ever since basic training, so that was no big deal. My hair was only a half-inch long, anyway, so that didn't really bother me. What really sucked was that I had to shave off the mustache that had been with me for twenty-two years. This felt extremely weird. Once orientation was over, we were given our cell assignments and led over to the main part of the unit, where we would be housed until in-processing procedures were complete.

CHAPTER 23

UNIT 15 WAS ABOUT THE size of a basketball court with all the bleachers rolled back. There was a huge dayroom downstairs with steel tables that had seats welded to them. In the middle were rows of seats like pews in a church that faced a TV set and two banks of phone booths. In the middle, there was a guard station with two COs manning it who looked like they were ready to fall asleep or drop dead from boredom any second. The things I liked best was a six-foot-wide painted walkway that circled the dayroom for pacing. Now I wouldn't have to turn around five hundred times a day as I did in county. I could just keep walking in circles. On three sides of the first and second floors were thirty-three separate two-man cells with steel doors that were like MCU's but smaller. There was also a catwalk on the second floor. The CO told us, "riders upstairs, timers down, get your bunk ready and be ready for chow in ten minutes."

We said some quick and quiet goodbyes to the timers we knew and headed for our designated cells. I quickly made my bunk and put away my hygiene items. I had the lower bunk in a ten-by-ten cement cell; there was one set of bunk beds on the back wall. At the foot of the bunk, there was a six-foot-high, twenty-inch-wide locker that had no door on it. Next to the door, there was a sink, toilet, and water fountain. Next to my bunkbed, on one side was a steel table complete with a welded stool. On the wall side was a clear window looking out to the recreation area for unit 15. The window was not fogged over and had a small ledge on the outside that a few rocks had been tossed up onto. I had a room with a view. Though it wasn't much, it still put the cement triangle in county to shame. The rec yard was also a triangle, but it was four times as big and filled with things we could actually use. There were horseshoe pits, a volleyball net, basketball hoops, and even some workout apparatus for push-ups, dips, and pull-ups. Along with my pacing, I could start working out as well. The bunk above mine was made up, and one side of the locker contained some hygiene items and a laundry bag, but oddly enough, I had no cellmate.

"Riders, get ready for chow!" boomed a voice coming from the guard station. I grabbed my coat and hat, checked my bunk, and waited by the door for the CO to open it for me when the time came. A couple of minutes later, the door buzzed open, and all the riders assembled downstairs for dinner. After the CO had the proper count, he told us to head down to the chow hall. Not given any instructions or information about dinner, I was wondering to myself which one of these guys would be the first to do something stupid and get into trouble. I just went with the group and played follow-the-leader down to the dining hall. We came out of our little corner of the prison and walked past some cyclone-fenced cages that somebody said were the recreation areas for the guys in solitary. These cages were about the size of a small dog kennel, and if they got any recreation in there, it would be a miracle. High above the cages was a brick guard tower that had fences all around it and a guard on watch up in the windows. I imagine this was a combination between hub control and an air traffic controller at the airport. Whoever sat up there could probably see the whole prison. We continued down a long sidewalk past the prison's recreation center complete with basketball courts, pool tables, and plenty of weights. Some of the prison population saw us in our rider yellow and decided to make sure we heard what they thought about us. They could say whatever they felt like saying, and all I kept thinking was that I would be out in six months and they would be here for years.

Finally, we were in line at the main chow hall. It was about the same size as the dayroom but looked like a high school cafeteria complete with long tables that had fold-down bench seats. After waiting in line, we were handed a tray through a small slot and forced to sit down in the order we were served. We were separated from the timers by at least two tables and told that there would be no food sharing or taking food from the chow hall. It sucked, because some guys would go hungry while the guys with extra food they didn't want would just throw it away. The other drawback was not having anything to snack on until commissary was available, and that could be weeks from now. It was an average tray of institutional food: it had no color, taste, or for that matter, size. We were only allowed ten minutes to eat, and then the COs would tell us to line up to head back to the unit.

Apparently, we were being groomed for Cottonwood, where we would only be allowed eight minutes for each meal. I felt as if I were back in the Army; only my "camouflage" was now bright yellow, and they wouldn't let me carry a gun. I never understood this control thing they had about meals. We had nothing but time, yet we were only allowed ten minutes to eat. What was the rush to get us back to our cells for the night? I understood they had to feed one thousand guys a meal in a timely fashion, but if it took two hours and fifteen minutes, what was the big deal? Did the extra fifteen minutes for each meal really throw off the other twenty-one hours and forty-five minutes of our boring lives inside?

Once returned to the unit, I grabbed a book from the bookshelf before we were stuffed in our cells for God knows how long. I went upstairs to the cell, and when I stepped in, I was introduced to my new cellie, Jesus Villanueva. We exchanged brief hellos, along with a little quick background info, and settled into a nice chat about what really went on in RDU.

"I have been here for one week so far, and I have no idea how long it will be before I go to unit 7," said Jesus.

"How many of the eight things do you have completed?" I asked him. He named everything he had done, and he was missing two of the eight. I had to tell him what was left. He was nice, friendly, but his being from Mexico and with English as his second language early in life had resulted in his falling behind academically, and he never quite caught up. He was smart, but there were things he did not understand about what institutions operated in this country. I could only imagine that this must have been a very difficult situation for him to deal with.

I was born in this country, and it was difficult for me to deal with. Having the knowledge of the two things he was missing fresh in my mind from the lecture only an hour ago, I told him what was left for him to do. He had already done the prints and pictures, so all he needed was to wait for his ID card to be made and handed to him. The other, he was doing when I came into the room before chow. The way I figured, he would be gone tomorrow, since technically now he was done with all eight of the things required to move on.

Jesus was a devoted Catholic Latino with a wife and three kids who had the same judge as I did and was going to Cottonwood on a drug possession charge, the same as me. We were both here on our first offense, possession of a controlled substance, and had just spent the last couple of months in jail before coming here. The cool thing was, he was a week ahead of me, so I could estimate my departure date accordingly. When I finally settled into my bunk and began to read, Jesus sat at the desk for a while and began jotting down notes from his Bible.

I lay in bed that night with a million thoughts running through my head. It had been a long day, and bunk 74, on the upper-right tier, seemed a thousand miles away. When I got up this morning, I had been surrounded by guys I knew, a bin box full of commissary, and the freedom of doing what I felt like doing nineteen hours a day. Tonight, I would go to sleep with a guy I had just met two hours before, with no food and locked in a two-man cell twenty-two hours a day for the foreseeable future. What a difference a day makes!

Bright and early the next morning, my in-processing started at 4:30 a.m. with a blood draw, a TB test, a medical exam, and a dental x-ray—all before breakfast. Actually, part of it was during breakfast, because they had to bring it into the classroom and we weren't allowed to eat it until we were done with the blood draw and dental x-ray. Oatmeal, two pancakes, juice, milk, and a hard-boiled egg made the best breakfast I had eaten in two months. In county, the menu stopped after oatmeal. To top that, the inmate-workers brought too many trays down from the kitchen, so if we finished early, we were able to have an entire second tray for breakfast. I was now stuffed for the first time in months, but I really wished I had a gallon of milk to wash it all down. God, I missed my milk. When I went back to the cell, Jesus told me, "That was all I did my first day here. You won't do any more in-processing until Monday."

Eager to hear all the info I could gather, especially from a guy who had lived it days ago, I was glad to hear from Jesus that my RDU timetable was on track. I spend the rest of the day Friday and the whole weekend locked in cell 65 with Jesus. I usually began a new book each day. There were only a few exceptions to the constant lockdowns we were forced to endure: meals and tier time. Tier time in here was like what it was in MCU, but without the commissary. Nobody in the unit had commissary, so there were no cards, coffee, Texas poker, or even any good books to read. The few choices I did have were limited, and quite a few of the books had the first or last pages missing. To get a good book in here, I had to be diligent and consistent. Knowing that everybody here was just as bored as I was, I checked the bookshelf five or six times a day. Each inmate could have three books and a Bible, so not only did I make sure that I always had a book to read but also two or three on deck just as I had done in county. The difference was, when I finished one, I couldn't just go get another one until a meal or rec time. With the riders' usually short stay, we couldn't have books sent to us, where all the good books in county came from. If they weren't the ones Beth sent me, then I read the books that I traded others for, books they had sent to them. I would read a good book and then a jail book and keep trading them back and forth so I wouldn't go crazy reading bad literature and always have a good book to read. The bookshelf here included old Westerns and romance novels. None of them really interested me except for a book by Louis L'Amour and Zane Grey. My problem now was, I was reading faster than ever. I could knock out a 400-page James Patterson book or Michael Connelly mystery in a day. The Westerns were only 150 to 200 pages or so, and while being locked down all day, I could sometimes read a couple of them.

We were only allowed tier time three times a day. One hour in the morning, and two in the afternoon and evening. This could be delayed, shortened, or even revoked completely at the whim of the COs. With the need to conduct a med call, laundry distribution, or another administrative procedure, they would just bunk us up at any time, cutting short our few precious minutes outside the cell. As in county, they didn't care if we were bunked up or not, but it meant everything to us. The COs were assholes about inside or outside rec privileges. They said that we either had to stay in the dayroom or stay outside in the period allowed for tier time. This was a power trip for them and meant that if you went out, you were stuck there for up to two hours. Apparently, pushing the button of the electronic door so we could come in from the seventeen-degree cold after half an hour was asking them to go out of their way just a little too much. The COs didn't have a clock out there, so we never knew how long we would be forced to endure the cold or heat. It really sucked to be locked out for however long in whatever the weather was for absolutely no reason. If the COs were so bitter about having to push a button, maybe they should go back to perimeter driving or strip-search duty for a couple of weeks to get a little perspective on how easy it really was to push that button.

When we were lucky enough to get rec time and the weather was decent enough to go outside, I continued my habit of walking as much as possible. The restriction of my freedom could do nothing but lower the number of miles I would walk each day. Having no standardized time schedule so I could properly manage my available time forced me to walk every free moment I had. The COs would tell us to cell up at any time. We were not allowed outside during the evening tier time because it was dark. I just made my big loops around the dayroom while reading my book at the same time. While walking, I would watch the others come and go to and from the bookshelf, and anytime anyone approached it with a book in hand,

I stopped to check out what new possibility they had dropped off. If the book looked good but I was undecided, I would ask the inmate if he had liked it and either keep it or put it back, depending on his answer. Books were not allowed outside either, so when the weather was good, I just paced in circles and looked out into the prison yard from the cyclone fence enclosure. Compared to the last two months I'd spent cooped up inside the Ada County Jail, now that I was in prison, the view was as good as looking from a penthouse window.

Between breakfast and dinner, the timers in the yard were free to move about the prison as they wished—within reason. They had to follow the rules, which basically meant you had zero to five minutes after the hour allowed for movement to go where you wanted to go. The track and softball field, the recreation center, the computer lab, or even the library were among the choices, but once you were there, you were required to stay there until the next movement. This way, the COs only had to supervise the entire prison area for five minutes out of each hour instead of sixty minutes. With two or three COs in each area, the manpower to supervise the population at each destination was drastically reduced, and the security risk was minimized. Looking out from my restricted area into the prison yard, I couldn't help but wonder what it was like to live here for years or even decades at a time. To those who were sentenced to life, this was all they would ever know. It was sad in a way to think this might be all someone would ever see, and at the same time, I could not help but wonder if I would end up back here for my three years. The rules of probation would be hanging over me for the next six years, and all it would take was one screwup and I would easily become a member of this exclusive country club. Staring at the possibility of my life would strengthen my resolve to make sure that when I left this place, it would be forever.

The surrounding desert, which stretched out as far as the eye could see, reminded me of my past vacations with Sean and Beth visiting Palm Springs, Southern California, and Lake Chelan in Eastern Washington. The desert had always meant good times and a pocketful of money to me. I hoped this experience would not sour the memories that came with the golden-brown rolling hills, blue skies, and sage-brush-dotted landscaped. After I was arrested in January at the Boise airport, those wonderful dreams had instantly become nightmares. Exotic locations and lazy days in the sun with Beth and Sean, swimming, and going to amusement parks were replaced with court dates, legal hassles, incarceration, and separation from my family for long periods.

CHAPTER

24

A S IF TO ADD INSULT to injury, I had learned the hard way over the weekend that the Idaho DOC had a different policy for weekend meals than during the rest of the week. Instead of the usual three meals a day, we were only given two. We ate two large meals at 8:00 a.m. and 4:00 p.m. According to the jail staff, the calorie intake was the same. Overall, the meals here were much better than what we were given at county, but I enjoyed eating all day long. With no commissary yet, the two-meals-a-day idea was not to my liking. Sneaking food out of the chow hall was an option my hunger level had not demanded yet, but I was sure at some point it would. I enjoyed having my commissary available for hunger emergencies, and it was easy to save food from your meals to eat whenever you got hungry in county. Technically, it was against the rules, but the COs in Ada turned a blind eye to it, and most people saved certain food items to snack on later. I found it psychologically satisfying to eat when I wanted to, not when the COs told me it was mealtime. Also, for some reason, just knowing I could have food whenever I wanted it was better than waiting for the authorities to feed me. On Saturday, by two in the afternoon, I found myself counting down the seconds until chow was called, and this really sucked.

When we finally got to go to chow, I had to admit it was pretty good, and for the first time ever, a single meal from a correctional facility had filled me up. Don't get me wrong; I didn't like the system at all, but I wasn't about to become another Craig and piss and moan about it all day. I would endure and keep in mind that when it was finally dinnertime on the weekends, I would always be filled, sated and content for the rest of the night. This wasn't a common occurrence when you were incarcerated.

By the time Monday finally came, after talking with Jesus on and off all weekend, I was convinced that the worst was behind me. I just completed the longest and most boring weekend of my life. I had been locked down twenty-two hours a day with no progress in completing my eight items so I could move on. I read four books just to keep from going stir-crazy. We began our educational testing right after breakfast with a timed multiple-choice test and filled in the standardized test to determine our educational background and make sure, as the CO said Thursday, that "we were not too stupid to be here." We were back in the unit by 9:30 a.m., and according to Jesus, who had a perfect record so far, we were done with in-processing for the day.

On the way upstairs, I grabbed two books that had magically appeared on the shelf in the morning while I was testing. The Alex Cross novel *Roses are Red* by James Patterson, and *The Old Man and the Sea* by Ernest Hemingway. Patterson was always a good read with his uncanny ability to keep the story moving. I finished the book before dinner. Hemingway became the first classic author I had ever read. I began the Hemingway book as soon as we got back to our cells. I soon realized just how shitty the books I had been reading lately actually were. I was beginning to question how much of the garbage I had read out of boredom had managed to get published. Increasingly, I began to appreciate Hemingway and how he managed to totally draw me into the old man's struggle.

We went out for evening tier time, and I kept reading while walking around in circles. I had no desire to sit on a hard bench and watch a rerun of *Fast and the Furious*, which had completely interested the rest of the group. The rest of these guys would rather sit than move around after spending twenty-two hours in the cell. This was something I never understood. The only thing I could compare it to was a caged tiger at the zoo resigning himself to his captivity. While most of the novels I had read were written by current authors,

usually best sellers, they failed in comparison to Hemingway's storytelling ability. I kept reading all through tier time and only put
the book down long enough to get into the shower before quickly
picking it back up as soon as I got out, with drops from my hair
falling onto the pages I was reading. I thought to myself how I once
was unable to keep myself from getting high. Now, I couldn't stop
reading this book!

My life was changing, and the cool thing about it was that I was
realizing this as it happened. Change takes place for most people at a
gradual, steady pace, which is almost an unrecognizable process, until
they begin to look back at their lives. I was seeing it as it was happening in the present, and that made me appreciate it all the more.

We went back up to the cell when tier time was over, and I kept
reading until almost 11:00 p.m., and I had finished my second book
of the day. I was restless and stayed up late, overanalyzing the similarities of the struggles the old man faced and my own. Or maybe
Hemingway knew the story was supposed to reflect anyone's, and
I was just taking it personally when I shouldn't have. There will be
struggles throughout our lives; some we meet head-on, with a sword
in one hand and a shield in the other, while others are coincidental,
secretive, and last a long time, only to be dealt with on a private stage
and in one's mind. These struggles are harder to win, but if we are
lucky enough to finally overcome them, then the rest of our lives will
be much easier to get through.

Lying there awake in my bunk, I hoped my life was turning the
corner finally instead of going in circles. Sleepless nights were always
the hardest to deal with. Alone with my thoughts and cooped up in
my cell, thinking about things way too much, made for long nights.
I wasn't sure if I was feeling sorry for myself or having a life-changing
moment that would affect me for the rest of my days. Either way, I
stayed up until I finally drifted off into the warm void of exhaustion.

After only five hours of sleep, I was tossing and turning rest-
lessly in the early-morning, predawn coldness, when I rolled over,
trying unsuccessfully to get comfortable in my tiny rock-hard prison

bunk. I noticed that there was a huge potato that had been tossed up onto the window ledge. In a sleepy haze, I got out of bed and used the toilet before quickly getting back under the covers to keep warm. I stared out the window and noticed the first frost of the year had come to the high desert overnight and painted a dappled landscape on the prison yard. The floor was cold, and I began to rub my feet together, trying desperately to warm them, when I glanced again at the potato on my windowsill. How did it get up there when outside rec had been closed for eight hours before I had fallen asleep and I knew it hadn't been there when I fell asleep? Maintenance workers, the COs, or inmate-workers? Somebody playing a prank on the new guys? I shrugged it off and went back to sleep. I awoke a short time later to the white landscape that now had been taken over by a heavier frost. The cell was much colder than it had been before. Opening my eyes and seeing the potato in the window confirmed I wasn't dreaming. The sky outside was lighter now, and the ground had a white glow to it. I noticed a large rodent scurrying across the frosty ground, so I leaned on one arm to take a good look at it. As I did, the potato in the window suddenly turned its head, and I found myself looking into the eyes of an owl. I jumped back, scared shitless. As I did, the owl flew off and floated down. He circled over the rodent with his talons open. Quietly, he soared downward and pounced on the poor little guy, piercing his flesh with his sharp claws. With swoops of his powerful wings, he cleared the concertina wire and flew off to freedom on the other side of the fence.

Jesus was startled awake when I jumped back from the window, and he at least managed to see the owl flying off from the ground. In his freshly awakened state, he was lucky to have even noticed the owl at all. I began to tell him what he had missed when the COs announced, "riders, prepare for chow!" We now had ten minutes to get up, get dressed, make our bunks before we would be ready to march down to chow.

Today I would be getting my mental health evaluation and a follow-up on the blood work and medical work of Friday morning. "Breathe deep," the doc told me as he moved the freezing-cold stethoscope over my chest.

"Now, drop your jumpsuit and your underwear to your ankles," he told me while he put on and pulled his surgical rubber gloves on tight. Seeing my appendix and hernia scars on the front of my stomach prompted me to give him a quick rundown of my medical history. While I did, he gave me the old turn-your-head-and-cough routine.

"Get dressed," he said, followed by a long silence while he read my chart, flipping page after page on his clipboard. "Your cholesterol level is 238, which is pretty high," he told me. Not knowing much about cholesterol readings, I asked him, "How high?"

"Anything over 200 is considered unsafe physically, but there are basically three parts to your overall cholesterol count. The part of your count that concerns me most is your triglycerides. A normal triglyceride count should be in the 160 range, and you have a dangerously high 340 that should be addressed immediately. You're a heart attack waiting to happen."

"Can you tell me what causes it to be so high, Doc?"

"Diet is the major contributor. Butter, ice cream, cheese, and other fatty foods are the worst thing for it. Have you been eating a high-fat diet?"

"I will be honest, Doc, I used to have a terrible diet, but I have been in county for two months now and walking over twenty miles a day. I haven't had any ice cream, cheese, or real butter for at least that long, just an occasional candy bar or some hot chocolate for nine weeks now."

"High alcohol usage or long-term drug use can also have a negative effect on these numbers. What was your drug of choice before you got in trouble?"

"Crack cocaine was, but I have been sober for two months now, and my usage was much less before I turned myself in. I was using heavily a year ago."

"Sometimes it takes years to repair the damage the body endures during years of drug abuse. Cocaine thins out the lining of the heart, and that could be part of it. It could be from the sedentary lifestyle in county jail with no cardio exercise. It could be family history, or even possibly a genetic defect you have had throughout your whole life, only to be discovered now. There are many options to look at. Let's check it again in a few months and see if it has come down. Other than that, you are in pretty good shape. Get out of here."

On the way back to my cell, I started figuring out how many of the magic eight items I had completed. As far as I could tell, I was missing only a couple of things, but who knew what administrative holdups or bad luck from Ada County paperwork would delay my departure? According to Jesus, I was repeating his routine from last week to the day, yet he had done nothing since Friday and was just sitting here, killing time. Later that afternoon, Jesus and four guys who had arrived on the same bus as I had were told to pack up and head over to unit 7. My buddy Scott was among them, and he made sure I knew he was moving along at a quicker pace than I was with some good-natured teasing on his way out the door.

"See you in a couple of months, once they figure out your mental evaluation, Walker!" he yelled with a big grin on his face as he left. We had spent time together in MCU and traded books with each other frequently. He had introduced James Patterson to half the guys in Dorm 6, which I could never thank him enough for. I wasn't concerned too much by his joke but rather was happy to see some of our group moving forward more quickly than originally anticipated. This was good news, and I was optimistic that I would be right behind them in no time.

With Jesus gone, I now had the cell to myself. I could read without being bothered, but there was no longer anyone to talk to in my cell. Some guys just kept going on and on and wouldn't give their cellie any peace and quiet. Your first choice was to tell him you were reading and to leave you alone, but some guys just didn't get it. Your second choice was to sit there and nod and say "Yeah," "Uh-huh," "Yeah," "Uh-huh" again and again until he got the hint and left you alone. The third was only used in extreme situations, telling him bluntly to cut the bullshit and tell it like it was, no matter how much it hurt him. This was highly effective, but once it was said, it would be awkward to live with a guy who resented you. A good cellie in prison could make all the difference in how easy it was for you to do your time. I hoped to see Jesus when we were both at Cottonwood. He was a good guy, someone I could easily talk to, yet he also knew when to leave me alone.

Wednesday morning, I was finally photographed, was finger-printed, had my DNA sampled, and finally, had the tattoo screening. The DOC needed its own fingerprints for each man, and the picture was for a DOC ID card that everyone was always required to have visible. I had seen these cards hanging on the breast pocket of the inmate-workers who were working in the in-processing department. They looked like orange driver's license cards with a most-wanted picture on them. Wearing a yellow jumpsuit and holding a name-plate in your hands made for a great picture, but it was required, so what was I going to do?

Every tattoo on every prisoner was also photographed and cat-aloged for ID purposes. They said it was a way to positively ID peo-ple and have them recorded in case they reoffended, and the tattoo became a distinguishing feature. Some said it was so the guards would be able to add new charges to those who violated prison rules by get-ting more tattoos while in prison. Whatever the reason, we were all sat in a holding cell for two hours while the photographer took the pictures of each tattoo of all the gang members' skin markings. Some of the guys had twenty-five or more tattoos, and the process took forever. Once we were done here, we could go back to our cells. My name was called last.

When I stepped up and told the guy I had no tattoos, I think I made his day. He told me this was my last stop before going to unit 7. He was being friendly with me, so knowing the sooner I got my ID card, the sooner I would go to unit 7, I thought I would ask him to help me out.

"As long as I made your day better, what do you say you just take care of my ID before you deal with all the tattoo boys, so I can get over to unit 7 and be on the top of the list?"

"I think I can do that, since you were last on the picture list. All I will do is go back through the pile that you are on top of, anyways," he said with a grin. "Relax, you will be in unit 7 by tomorrow. We are moving guys through here in one week right now because it isn't too crowded."

"How full is unit 7 right now?"

"It's empty. You should be on your way to Cottonwood in two to three weeks."

"Two or three weeks?" I asked.

"Hey, you should feel lucky. Sometimes it's backed up for six to eight weeks. It's a slow time of year right now. You're done. Head back to your cell, and good luck to you."

"Thanks. Take it easy," I told him and left his room with a smile on my face, knowing my shuffle through RDU was not only on track but also moving rather quickly. All I needed now was the card he was going to make for me, and off to unit 7 I would go.

I had a new bounce in my step as I paced around the dayroom that afternoon, and finding three good books to squirrel away only added to my optimistic attitude. I figured I would most likely get another cellie tomorrow when the new bus came in from the county jail. However, I did not consider that I was the only one bussed from one county and forgot to consider every person from every county in the state had to be brought here and processed before moving onto any state prison in Idaho. There was a lot of guys here from Kootenai County, which was right across the border of Spokane, Washington, up in North Idaho, in the Coeur d' Alene area. It would later break down to 30 percent from up north, 50 percent from the Boise metro area, and the other 20 percent randomly scattered about the state's various little communities out in the desert and mountains. The group from up North had to be transported on the chain gang down past Cottonwood, 380 miles to Boise, and processed through RDU, before they would be sent back to Cottonwood 250 miles for their rider. Suddenly, my trip to the courthouse while all shackled up seemed like nothing to whine about.

Wednesday was the day that the bus from up North showed up, and just as I had joined Jesus, who was only waiting for this ID card,

I was now in his shoes when, just before dinner, I was given a new cellie. His name was Dustin, and we barely had time to introduce ourselves when we were called down for chow. Now I was the veteran answering the new guy's questions and waiting to move on to unit 7. When we got back from dinner, Dustin began telling me his life story like we were best friends, and I asked him for information—he wouldn't stop spilling it out. I was trying to be polite, so we talked for a while, but deep down I already knew that this guy was one of the obnoxious cellies. I had a bad feeling I was doomed to spend the weekend with Dustin and then leave at the first part of next week like Jesus did. Even though the tattoo CO had told me differently, I would trust what had happened to Jesus, right in front of my eyes, before I would believe any information coming from a CO.

When Jesus and I would talk, it was a mutual conversation and quite pleasant. It was the complete opposite with Dustin, who just happened to be the biggest, most obnoxious, farting, backwoods, country hick I had met in my life. He wouldn't take my hint and leave me alone even though I gave him signs that conveyed that I wanted nothing more than to be left alone. He coincidentally was from Cottonwood, Idaho, and had to travel the five-hundred-mile round trip from the local county jail and back in order to go to the state facility only fourteen miles from his house. He would talk non-stop about hunting, fishing, trucks, and the mechanical work he did on them as if I were a coworker in the same garage that he worked in. He might as well have been speaking Japanese when he started rambling on about all the mechanical mumbo jumbo I had no interest in and was unable to comprehend anyway. The thing I couldn't understand was how on earth he even thought I gave a flying fuck about anything he was saying in the first place. When he wasn't talking my ear off, he was sleeping and snoring so loudly I couldn't stand it. He also farted in his sleep, and for a 280-pound man in a two-man cell, it quickly became too much to deal with. I found myself with my sheet wrapped around my mouth and nose just so I wouldn't get sick. My luck was apparently starting to go downhill yet again.

Thank God Dustin had to get up early Thursday morning for the medical screening and I didn't have to deal with him for the rest of the morning. When he came back to the cell, he started all over again with his blah, blah, blah. After about an hour, I took it as a sign from the gods when the COs called a bunch of us down to the dayroom and gave us our ID cards. That was it; I had completed all eight items, and I couldn't wait to get the hell out of unit 15. The next thing out of the CO's mouth was the best thing I had heard in weeks: "You nine men roll up your bunks. You will be moving to unit 7 before lunch."

Finally, it was time to go, and now all there was to do was be put on the transport list to go to Cottonwood. According to the rumors and those that had been here, the longest, hardest, and most locked-down phase of the journey home was over. When my name was called to head over to unit 7, I had already packed five good books in with my sheets and was ready to move on. After a week in lockdown and being with Dustin, no matter what was next, there was no way it could have been worse than this.

CHAPTER

25

T HE SHORT WALK BACK TO the first building we processed
through when we first got off the bus brought me back into
unit 7, my final housing destination in the Idaho State Pen.
The in-processing was now complete, and all that was left for us
to do was to sit around until we boarded the bus for our ride up
to Cottonwood. Unit 7 was shaped like a big capital H, with all
the control, intake, and transport areas in the middle, and the four
prongs coming out of it were the tiers. Each tier was a cement rectan-
gle about seventy feet long and twenty-five feet wide. It was divided
in half, lengthwise, down the center, with all the cells on the right
and a long dayroom to the left. This was the old part of the prison,
and the nine cells were divided by brick walls on three sides and ran
the length of the building.

There were two-man rectangular cells about six by ten and
included the same bunk bed, locker, and toilet as unit 15 had, but
much smaller. Instead of being celled up behind closed and locked
steel doors, each cell had three cement block walls and an open front
side that was partitioned off by steel bars. I had never been in a jail
that had bars before; up until now, there were always steel doors with
a tiny window, and the bars helped ease the claustrophobic feeling of
the cells. We only had eight people in room 18, so once again, I was
given my own cell. The long skinny dayroom had two tables, a TV,
a shitload of books, and even playing cards. With all the amenities,
how could I not be more comfortable than I had been where I had
just come from? Also, in here the cell doors were open all the time
during the day. We did have to bunk up for count twice a day, followed by meals, which were delivered to the tier. No more marching

down to the chow hall three times a day, and we were able to trade and keep extra food in the cells, as long as we were discreet about it.

The dayroom was smaller, but the fact was that the sliding hydraulic steel-bar doors were left open and we could come and go from our cells at will, made things much better. The book supply was ample, and I even managed to bring along my current books from unit 15, wrapped inside my bunk roll.

I spent the rest of the day reading and pacing the dayroom with a small loop that I calculated took sixty laps for each mile. Compared to this, my sixteen laps in Ada was a piece of cake. This could have been extremely difficult considering how small the area was and all the other guys who could possibly be using it. Right now, everyone else was either playing cards or watching TV, and I wanted to make sure I wasn't cutting off their view or having anyone getting mad when I walked around behind them. Some people didn't like anyone walking behind them if they were gambling, and I didn't want to piss anyone off the first day here. By now, all these guys in here had seen me walking all last week, and the guys from county knew me well enough to know that walking was my thing.

With all the freedom I had, I was walking twenty miles a day in county. In unit 15, I was lucky to log five to six miles each day. Not only was it good exercise, but without some physical activity, I would also be up all night. Now I was going to be able to get my miles back up, maintain my sanity, and be exhausted enough to sleep. Since I only needed about six hours of sleep each night, I would never go back to sleep after breakfast and instead pace as much as possible all day, hoping to wear myself out by the time we were forced to bunk up.

Even though I enjoyed the openness of the bars on the front of the cells during the day, at night, it was a slightly different story. My first night alone in my cell in Idaho's former death row tier, I almost wished for a cell with a steel door, because the guys were up all night, talking to one another from one cell to the next. With cement floors and an empty dayroom, nonstop conversations echoed throughout the tier. For those who had trouble sleeping, it was rude of these guys to not lower their voices for the sake of everyone else. I would read until sleep took over my conscious mind and it was difficult to concentrate on the words. I couldn't sleep, so I needed to come up with another plan. I could order earplugs on commissary, but not until next week, and until then I would be miserable. In dorm 6, the room was so large and there was so much noise it all blended in with the background chatter with no one conversation standing out. It was easy to read even with all the noise in the dorm, but one conversation pierced the silence in a painful way. It made for a long night.

After breakfast on Friday morning, I was exhausted from a long, sleepless night. Having been through this scenario before, I knew that in order to get back on schedule, I would have to endure one long, hard day. Of the eight people on the quiet tier after breakfast, the only one awake was me. I wouldn't turn on the TV out of respect for those who slept, so I swept and mopped the tier with the cleaning supplies left by the shower area for us to use at our discretion. This was the first sign of independent responsibility I had been given in nine weeks. Until now, all the cleaners, brooms, and mops had to be checked out and checked back in so no one would use them as a weapon or use the cleaning agents to poison someone else. It wasn't only the first chance we had to show we could handle responsibility without a problem, but it was also a problem to screw up our rider if we didn't. And with responsibly came privileges.

Open cell doors, meal and food liberties, self-maintenance responsibilities, the quality and quantity of books, access to the TV remote, and even playing cards were the COs' way of giving us some rope to hang ourselves with. I swept and mopped the dayroom and then sat in my bunk while the floor dried. This was a good plan since nobody was going to mess up the floor before it was dry. Once it was dry, I would pace and read in a wonderful solitude while the whole tier slept until lunchtime. In a world that lacked privacy, the mornings were my salvation. No personal attitudes to deal with, card-slapping to listen to, background noises to ignore, or *South Park* reruns to be forced to listen to made it almost like being at a silent retreat. I could read my books, escape the confines of the concertina wire, and imagine visiting the locations the characters in my books would visit. It was better to be a cowboy riding through the West with Louis L'Amour, solving a DC murder with James Patterson, or scuba diving in the Caribbean with Clive Cussler rather than being an Idaho's DOC number, locked up in unit 7.

We were forced to cell up right before lunch for them to count the whole unit or perhaps the entire prison. We were required to be locked in our cells with the doors shut until count was cleared. After I had walked all morning and afternoon, it felt good to get into my bunk and let my feet rest. Lunch was brought to the main door of the tier, and each of us received one tray. Now we could trade with others instead of throwing out what we did not like, and everyone had more food in the long run. I always thought of it as wasteful when one guy would throw away corn but liked salad and another guy would throw away salad but liked corn. Now two people could end their hunger pangs and nothing was wasted. It was also much easier to keep a roll or piece of fruit to snack on later, even though it was against the rules, technically. It had to be done intelligently, and you couldn't leave a mess, or you would attract insects. The only time the COs ever came into the tier was for count time, and then our cells were shut away, so everybody got away with it.

The tier came to life after lunch, but now we all shared a common bond, had the same rules to follow, and with that came the same punishment should we fail. With a common goal in everyone's mind, discussions tended to be about information that could be shared, along with stories of what each of us had previously endured. We all had a bad experience, CO problem, or humorous anecdote that needed to be shared with the guys we knew but hadn't seen in a week, except at chow, when there was no talking. Introductions were made between the guys from up North, from Ada and Canyon Counties, as well as individuals from around the state. Everyone found it necessary to share their background stories and bullshit about the way they had ended up in jail. During this testosterone-fueled conversation, I continued to pace and kept to myself as much as possible. I had no immediate urge to receive or divulge any information with anyone I didn't know. There were four units I might live in once I arrived at Cottonwood, so the odds were 75-25 that I would never see any of these guys again after we got off the bus, so what was the point?

At first, I would receive awkward looks from people who thought I was crazy, but over time, I would gain their respect for my unyielding dedication. I had been walking twenty miles a day and would get back up to that level as quickly as possible, and by now my reading had reached an unprecedented level. Being celled up in unit 15 for twenty hours each day, I had nothing else to do, and that had not only fueled my need to fight boredom, but after I had read *The Old Man and the Sea*, it had fueled my literary curiosity as well. I had thought to myself, while reading some of the shitty books in unit 15, that I could write a better book than those I was reading, and I probably could. From then on, I was not just reading to entertain myself but also to educate myself regarding the style, plotlines, grammar, and character development used by successful authors to build the suspense and curiosity of their readers. I found myself reading most of the day since I wasn't interested in watching shows that the younger inmates enjoyed. While my schedule was repetitive, as are as most of ours while incarcerated, at least it was productive. These other guys were truly "wasting their lives" in prison. My theory was, as long as I was here, I might as well make the best of it and better myself both physically and mentally.

When Dan stepped into the cell and introduced himself, I was ecstatic to learn that he was headed back to Cottonwood for his third rider. This was a perfect opportunity for me to get all my questions answered and learn exactly what I had to look forward to and how long I would be there. All the information he could give me about what to expect would be beneficial not only to me but also to all those men in the tier whose fear of the unknown was as upsetting to them as mine was to me. If I could pick his brain and get an idea of what to expect and then share it with everybody here, we would all be better situated to succeed once we arrived at Cottonwood. I knew I would have to wait until we were bunked up tonight to talk, since that seemed to be when all the other conversations took place in the tier, and I wanted to let Dan get settled in so he would be more will-ing to volunteer the info and wouldn't think of me as a pest.

After we bunked up that night, I quickly found out that my strategy had worked perfectly. Dan started spewing out information about his experience without any prompting whatsoever.

"They are sending me on my third rider, and I just want to go to the yard," he began to tell me. "I have been on two riders already, and I don't want to go back." I compared what he was telling me to all the dreams I had endured after my military duty was over about returning to basic training. Even though it wasn't that bad, I often awoke in the middle of the night years later to the recollection of a disrupted dream about returning to day 2 or 3 of the biggest mind-fuck I had ever encountered at Fort Benning, Georgia, back in 1983. Not having had the rider experience yet, I couldn't really compare the two, but just hearing him tell his story made me a little nervous about what lay ahead.

"The rider program is always changing," he said. "It used to be like a boot camp with push-ups and marching when I was on my first one, but now it has changed into what they call a community model. The COs do not punish you the way a drill instructor would, but by your fellow inmates. Everybody tattles, and the punishment you get is passed out by the inmate coordinators, senior members of your unit, who govern the operations of each unit." Soaking up all the info like a sponge, I sat quietly and absorbed his story as he continued.

"I am sick of all the rules you have to follow and getting up at 5:00 a.m. every fucking day and having to attend evening meetings. The bullshit rules they make you follow, it's ridiculous.

"I want to go to the yard, but the judge goes by what the coun-selors at Cottonwood recommend. Mine wants me to change my behavior, and since I won't, he keeps saying that I should go back. I think he takes it personally that he can't save me or change me, and that is what they say it's all about, change. I have seen guys pick fights just so they flop and can go to the yard. I think that might be my next move, but then you get assault charges and even more time. The system is fucked up, but once you're a part of it, your life is fucked forever."

I didn't like what I was hearing, and the fear of not succeeding and going to the yard for three years or having to repeat my rider suddenly washed over me. That was all I needed. The thought of six more months after my rider was overwhelmingly depressing. I was seriously hoping that Dan was just a fuckup and most people were just shuffled through the process and sent home, but if he wasn't the exception, I had to make sure I did what I was supposed to so I didn't follow in his footsteps.

"How long should I expect to be here before I head out?" I inquired.

"That all depends on how fast they are getting people through RDU. Last time I was in units 15 and 7 for weeks before I left for Cottonwood, but the place was full then. How full is unit 15 right now?"

"The upper tier with riders in it was only half-full, but the lower tier with the timers was packed."

"That is a good sign, if the upper tier is only half-full. When I was here last time, it was full, which was why it took so long to get out. I have heard stories of up to two months, but it isn't all that full right now. You should be out of here in two or three weeks."

"How will I know when I am getting close, or is it just a matter of waiting for my name to be called to get on the bus?"

"Usually, if you just came from unit 15, you are not next to go. They will move you from here into another tier in unit 7 that you will ship out from, but I doubt if it will be from this one. The other three tiers have people in them, too, and they have been here longer and will go before you. Don't worry, you won't be here too long. It's definitely not full enough to be backed up two months. I can tell. Look around. This tier is only half-full. RDU can't be that busy."

"Thanks for the info, dude. I am going to read till I fall asleep, and we'll chat more tomorrow, okay?"

"No problem. Glad to help. I remember how I felt my first time heading up there."

With that, silence fell over the cell, but unfortunately, the tier was abuzz, most likely with the others having the same discussion we were. It suddenly dawned on me that tonight I was the guy I was bitching about. I made a mental note to keep the volume down at night since my voice was loud and I had no desire to piss anyone off the way I had been last night. I began to read, secure in the knowledge of what to expect for the next few weeks and glad to hear things were moving faster than as recounted in some of the horror stories I had heard. Hearing from Dan firsthand helped calm my nerves for the first time since county. I found myself relaxed as well as feeling secure knowing the sequence of events that would lead me to the transport tier was underway.

S ATURDAY MORNING, I WOKE UP rejuvenated and motivated from my chat with Dan, and the fear that had become part of my existence for so long had vanished. After breakfast, again with everybody else asleep, I swept and mopped the tier after wiping down all the tables from breakfast. After everything dried, I went back down to the end cell that was unoccupied and took the mattress off the top bunk and quietly set it on the floor so I could do my sit-ups and push-ups in between the miles I would log. With everybody asleep, it was easier to do my laps, because now I could pass in front of the TV without disturbing others. I made the most of the morning, logging almost ten miles, two hundred push-ups, and three hundred sit-ups before I was forced to bunk up for count at 11:00 a.m. and rest before lunch. After count, I was ready for lunch, but I had forgotten about the two-meal weekend schedule and therefore forgot to save some of my breakfast to eat during the long wait until dinner. Dan joined in pacing with me after I realized my stupid mistake, and once he started talking to me, I got even more information out of him.

"How many miles should you get each day?" he asked me as he came up alongside.

"Between fifteen and twenty," I told him, "depending on how my feet feel. So tell me, what happens on transport day?"

"Well, it all begins on Sunday night, when the guard tells those who are leaving to pack. That's when you know you are on transport on Monday. Just like in county, you can't make any calls after that for security reasons, but you can call your family Monday night when you get to Cottonwood."

"We don't get there until nighttime?"

"It takes about six hours, including a piss break at Adams County. You get to Cottonwood at two in the afternoon, but you don't have any free time until after 8:00 p.m. once you are done with all your programming. Anyway, you are out-processed and leave here by 8:00 a.m., and the bus is half riders and half timers. You drive about three hours north up to council in Adams County, where you stop for about thirty minutes so everybody can take a leak. Then you're back on the bus for Cottonwood. The whole trip takes about six or seven hours, depending on the traffic and the weather. It's too early for the weather to slow you down now, but it becomes an eight- or ten-hour trip sometimes. That's a long time to be shackled on a bus."

"Why do the timers come with us to Cottonwood? It's just for the riders, isn't it?" I wondered out loud.

"They don't stay there. The riders get dropped off on Monday afternoon, and the bus goes on to Orofino, about another hour north, to a medium-security state pen facility up there. They drop off the timers, and the bus stays the night there. On Tuesday morning, it takes all the transports from Orofino back to the yard and the going-home riders back to Ada and Canyon Counties before you get back in front of your judge."

"We don't come back here?"

"No. You go straight to county for your rider review hearing, where the judge says probation or the yard. They might even say you didn't get it right the first time, so you have to go do another rider, like they did with me."

It was nice to know what to expect, and not only did I learn what was happening when we left, but I also knew what to expect on the way back, no matter how long that might be.

"How come you didn't go back to county to go in front of your judge?" I asked him.

"Because if you flop your rider, you come back here for God only knows how long, until they take you to court. That way, if I get a third rider, I am ready to go back up North, and if I go to the yard, all they have to do is transfer me back to unit 15 and put me in with the timers."

"What is so bad about a rider that you would rather go to the yard?"

"My fixed time was eighteen months. Between the two riders I have already done, the county times, and RDU twice, I have already been in for ten months. One more rider will take at least four to five months for a total of fourteen or fifteen months' time served. If I go to Cottonwood one more time, when I'm done there, I will be on probation for three years afterward instead of being out of the system and 100 percent done with DOC in eight months. No hoops to jump through, check-ins with a probation officer, or drug tests. That's why they want to give me another rider, so they can keep me in the system longer and hope that I reoffend. That's how fucked up the system is. They want to give me another rider so they can control me longer, hope I get more charges, and not be free of DOC control as early."

I wasn't sure if he was being paranoid or if he was just an idiot, but part of what he said made sense.

Now I understood why he didn't want to go back. The difference to him was only a few months, with total freedom once he was released without supervision. Was it possible that he was right and the DOC, instead of wanting their inmates to be rehabilitated and return to society, actually wanted us under their control and to keep us in the system? I heard a saying in county that was running through my mind: "Idaho—come on vacation, leave on probation, come back on violation." Maybe that comment had become popular for the sole reason that DOC wanted it that way. I had heard more than my share of horror stories about the overzealous legal system, and I only hoped I was not soon to become yet another story of prosecutors, judges, and correction officials all trying to keep people in the system so they could profit from the federal dollars we brought in. I knew Idaho was a highly religious state built by disgruntled Mormons who came North from Utah when they had some disagreements with Brigham Young. Along with Texas, Utah, and Nevada, Idaho was rumored to have been among the worst states in which to be charged with a drug offense in the entire county.

Not as familiar with the DOC throughout the US as some of these guys were, I wasn't exactly sure as to the truth of most of the things I had heard. Earlier in this year, when Beth had me arrested for missing a court date, I was chain-ganged over from Everett, Washington, all the way to Boise over the course of six days. During that time, I was housed in different facilities along the way, including the King County Regional Justice Center outside of Seattle, Washington; Clark County Jail in Vancouver, Washington; and the inverness transfer station in Multnomah County, Oregon, outside of Portland. Along the way, we would stop at every county jail between Everett and Portland on I-5 and between Portland and Boise on I-84. We were also the transport venue for inmates in any of the Northwest state prisons, going from one facility to the next. These guys were doing years on multiple offenses, and they knew more about the DOC differences from the state in which they were located. According to most who heard my story, the same number of drugs possessed on the first offense in Oregon would be given a thirty-day county sentence and a hefty fine. Idaho wanted to give me three years for the same thing. The flip side was, in Texas, I would have gotten ten years, or possibly the seven-year maximum sentence. It was all relative.

The transport people from the prison were all saying the same things that Dan had just told me about the DOC keeping inmates in the system as long as possible so they could profit from the housing of people, which was the business they were in. If the federal government paid a facility $75 a day for one prisoner and the facility could house that person for $20, the facility was not interested in your rehabilitation and return to society as much as it was in keeping you in the system for profit. Some jails weren't even owned by the counties they served but rather were owned by a corporation subcontracted to run the jail for the county. Rehabilitation was not the corporation's goal in this case. Just profit. That was why they gave you new charges when you violated some of the rules. They could keep you in prison longer and make more money from federal subsidies.

Personally, I had always felt that first-time drug offenders who weren't dealers should all be sentenced to thirty to sixty days inpatient rehab to clinically address their drug addiction and stop the cycle. The legal system, in order to perpetrate itself, found it better to fill the jails and prisons with drug addicts so they could control and profit from their misfortune for years to come. In county, 90 percent of the people who were there were incarcerated because of drug offenses. If some of these people had gone through rehab instead of spending a year in prison, would they have kept coming back through the system in such high number? The reason rehab centers are so profitable and popular these days is that they work. Just thinking of all this through as I strolled back and forth was getting me pissed off, so I sat on my bunk for a while and calmed down by reading my book. Being locked up and having the time to think about so many things was extremely frustrating, and venting was necessary every once in a while. I couldn't let it get to me in here while surrounded by people who did nothing but talk and bitch constantly. Disenchantment becomes a part of almost every discussion inside the walls of a penitentiary and very difficult to avoid.

I read until I had calmed down and then went back to pacing. Nobody joined, thank God, and the solitude was welcoming. In tight quarters, you get a sixth sense about the disposition of the men you are with and begin to sense things about their mood and temper. I learned a lot about certain individuals by observing them while pacing, and by the time I left county, I felt extremely knowledgeable about many of my fellow inmates I had watched over time. Human behavior is interesting, and I filed the observations I had made into my mind to make judgments later.

I was pleasantly surprised on Saturday afternoon when we were told by one of the timers that on weekends there were new movies you could watch that the prison showed at predetermined times, and they also showed us a schedule that was posted on the wall. I hadn't seen anything but regular TV for two months, so the idea of a new release sounded good to all of us. I checked the list and found out that *Batman Begins* and *The Longest Yard* would play all afternoon, all evening, and Sunday at alternating times. We had the option to watch it, and we chose to. Finally, there was a sign that the COs gave a shit and would let us do something cool the whole tier would enjoy. Now, if we could only get some popcorn, nobody would bitch about anything for the rest of the weekend. I had seen ads for both movies and wanted to see them, but I couldn't help but note the irony of watching a prison football team movie while in prison. If all went well, it would make for a decent weekend. If my name was called Sunday night, it would be my last night here. I wasn't really counting on it after what Dan had told me, so once again, plan for the worst and hope for the best.

With only two meals, I was once again starving to death and made a mental note to save half of my breakfast tomorrow so I would no longer have to endure seven hours of hunger before dinner. After the big meal, the guys in the tier decided to watch *Batman Begins*, and we all had a good time. I walked myself into exhaustion after the movie and crashed early, as usual, when my feet started to hurt.

Sunday morning, I was prepared when breakfast showed up, and I saved nearly half of my breakfast and put it into my locker to eat about 1:00 or 2:00 p.m., when I knew I would be hungry. It was comforting to know that while I was keeping an eye on my Seattle Seahawks, who were having a very good year, if I did feel the need to eat, I would be able to do so. Just knowing I had food to eat made me not so hungry, and therefore I didn't even eat it. It was a funny thing how the mind works sometimes. I managed to save some of my dinner that night as well so I could nibble between dinner and bedtime. About eight COs came into the tier and asked us, "Which do you guys want first, the good news or the bad news?"

Almost everybody replied, "Bad news," simultaneously.

CHAPTER

27

"**N**OBODY ON THIS TIER IS slated for transport this week. Each of you will be here at least one more week, maybe more. The consolation prize for not going to Cottonwood this week is, each of you is eligible to receive commissary this week, if you have money on your books. When I call your name, step up and get your commissary sheet, which has your available balance listed on the top right-hand corner. I will be back in one hour to get the sheets, and if they aren't filled out by then, you are burnt." We all laughed at the CO's attempt to use inmate slang words. "Commissary will be delivered sometime tomorrow afternoon. You have one hour." Then he walked off the tier.

It was like Christmas had come, and everybody started talking about what to get for commissary and the fact that we were all stuck here for at least another week. There were no food items available until we reached our final station, except for tea and coffee. Any hygiene items we purchased here, we were allowed to take to Cottonwood, but not any coffee. I ordered all the usual items that were necessities as far as I was concerned, and I was a little pissed that they were making me buy it all again. I had already purchased all the amenities that I now donated to needy friends in Ada. Shower shoes, which were a must, soap and soap dish, deodorant, shampoo, toothbrush, toothpaste, pen, paper, envelopes, and of course, the always-tradable coffee.

After my sheet was filled out, I called home to let them know I would be stuck here at least another week and to see how Sean and Beth were. As usual, at the end of the call, I was emotionally distraught. Talking with them always made me sad. Once I hung up, I felt like I had been hit in the chest with a spare tire. I suddenly realized I had completely forgotten about my property back in Ada County. If I had passed the deadline, my briefcase, cell phone, books, and clothes would be given away to charity. I had two weeks from the day I left to have my stuff picked up, and today was day 10, and time was running out. My briefcase with personal paperwork and my cell phone with all my business contacts' phone numbers in it were very important to me. How I had forgotten about it until now was beyond me. I made a note for myself to call Mark, my lawyer, in the morning and get this taken care of immediately.

This had been my first call home from prison, because until each inmate received a personal identification number (PIN), you were powerless to use the phones. Every time you made a phone call anywhere in the Idaho State prison system, you were required to enter your personal identification number. Your calls were then monitored, recorded, and reviewed by the COs. This prevented other inmates from using your PIN, and they would file new charges on individuals who called people who had restraining orders against them. Just like county, violations led to charges that would keep you in the system longer, which would bring them more money.

I had also heard that once your rider was done, the counselors would listen to your calls to verify the sincerity of your intentions before they let you go home. This seemed like a huge civil rights violation to me, but then this place wasn't on top of the list for civil rights protections, and I wasn't sure if it was even true, anyways. It didn't really matter if they did or didn't; I wasn't planning on violating any rules, and I had no restraining orders against me like some of these guys with domestic violence charges did. It also seemed a little odd that a CO who took one phrase out of context from one phone call and a guy who was dedicated to improving his life could flop his rider over something taken out of context. That kind of power was an open invitation to abuse, so I had to make sure that the opportunity for that kind of stuff didn't happen to me. I paced the rest of the night, worrying about my property. When it came time to bunk up for the night, I was ready to rest my feet from a long, hard day. I was glad to be in my bunk; it had been a long weekend, and I was looking forward to lying down and reading myself to sleep once again.

First thing Monday morning, I called Mark. The amazing thing was, I could never reach him when I was in county, but now he actually answered on the first try. I asked him to pick it up himself if he could do that for me. He assured me it would be handled and to call him Friday to verify that everything was okay. After some small talk, he said he had to get to court, and we said goodbye until Friday. Thursday was my two-week deadline, so the call on Friday would just be for letting me know everything was taken care of. I walked and read the rest of the morning until commissary showed up. Apparently, this was a good-enough reason to get out of bed before noon for the rest of the tier.

I was amazed at how much a cup of coffee did for some people's motivation. This was the first time since I had come to unit 7 that anyone was up before lunch besides me. This kind of sucked, because now the place was just as crowded as in the afternoon. Not only did I lose my morning solitude, but after having no coffee for over a week, the guys would soon be wired as well. Now that coffee was available in the tier, my morning routine could be disrupted by early risers. I wouldn't really know until tomorrow morning. I spent the rest of the day wired from the caffeine, and it really helped me log over twenty miles for the first time since being here.

As I paced, I watched Dan, who didn't seem to be his normal self today. He was withdrawn and kept to himself. He was usually out playing cards and telling his rider stories to anyone who wanted to hear them, but today he just seemed remote. Tomorrow he was to be transferred to another tier, and he told me we would probably all be moved. This was part of the weekly shuffle for RDU, and I assumed that the tier we were moving to was the one vacated by those who had left for Cottonwood this morning. This made sense chronologically, because last week at this time, whoever was in unit 15 began to come to my tier. In a perfect world, I would get shuffled to the transport tier and be on the bus next Monday, but I didn't want to get my hopes up just to be disappointed.

Occasionally, Dan would come up beside me and talk briefly and then wander off on his own. He would say that they couldn't make him go on another rider and that if they did, he would refuse it. Something told me refusing the judge's orders was not the wisest move to make, but nothing was going to change his mind at this point, so I didn't bother trying. Dan already knew my opinion, and I had tried repeatedly to talk to him about his options when we were bunked up at count time. He was hardheaded and stubborn, so rather than piss off the guy I was locked up with, I just let it go. Everyone always says to do your own time, so I let him. It was weird in here; some people cried out for help, and others blocked out their emotions even though the people offering were sincere. The sad thing was, getting the right help in here could mean the difference between serving six months or six years.

Commissary day was always one of high tension with all the coffee and excitement. This also brought back an old feature of jail life for the first time here in prison, and that was gambling. Now there was something at stake, and that could only cause problems in these closed quarters. At least in the dorm you could avoid someone if there was tension between you. It would be pretty hard to do that here. Spades hustlers were teaming up again, frothing at the mouth at the possibility of a quick score.

When I was playing spades, I would just assume that I would win 50 percent of the time and lose 50 percent; I would just take what came with a grain of salt. These arrogant pricks naturally thought they would win 100 percent of the time, and if they lost even one game, it was because someone had cheated them or their partner was an idiot. It's just a card game and shit happens. By the end of the night, there were three or four fights prevented from occurring by cooler heads, and now the stage was set for political maneuvering and playground stupidity. The next step was backstabbing, followed by the rumor mill. Stories became exaggerated along the way, and the next thing you knew, somebody was pissed off and looking for a fight with somebody who had never said anything about him. The main reason I kept to myself and did my own time was to avoid situations like this from happening to me, especially until I got to know them better. All it would take was one fight, and I could flop my rider before it even began.

Dan had almost been in one of the fights, and after that, he went off into the corner to do push-ups and get away from everybody. Something was up with him, and I decided to try to talk to him once we were settled in tonight to see if I could help him. He was the experienced one who knew the ropes and had been through the mill, and yet here I was, trying to help him. It had been the other way around when I first got here, but things change. As it came close to count time, I noticed Dan was acting stranger and stranger. He was talking to himself and mumbling as he walked. He had mentioned something to me about suing the state and how he wasn't ever going back to Cottonwood. His ranting was unusual, and his behavior was beginning to make me nervous.

Finally, it was time to bunk up, and Dan wouldn't even look me in the eyes, keeping his head down, like a child who had just been punished. The COs yelled, "Lock it down!" as they did every time the hydraulic cell doors closed and that was when Dan made his move. He stood next to the sliding cell door, and as it slammed shut, he lifted his hand to let the steel door slam down on it, chopping off his pinky finger in the process. I watched in horror as it fell to the ground outside our cell while what was left of his finger squirted blood. Dan, screaming at the top of his lungs, yelled, "Owwwww! Shit! My finger! My finger!"

"Open the door! Open the door! Medical emergency! Medical emergency!" I yelled down the tier toward the CO. The door slid open, and the CO came running down the tier while everybody stepped out to see what all the fuss was about.

"Bunk up! Everybody back in your cells and on your bunk, NOW!" the CO shouted as he came down to our cell. There was blood all over the walls, on both of our jumpsuits, and on both of Dan's hands as he tried to stop the bleeding. Dan grabbed his towel, and I helped him wrap his wound as best as I could. The CO was on his radio, calling for backup. Once things were stable, he went to the door, leaving out of the tier to let the help in. Dan, who was probably going into shock, was suddenly calm.

The two of us sat at the table when he lifted his head and looked me square in the eyes. "See? I told you I wasn't going back to Cottonwood," he said quietly. *Holy shit,* I thought as I looked down and saw his finger on the floor as the COs gathered him up and took him away. One guard put on surgical gloves and grabbed his finger, while the other one found a spot to hold Dan's arm that didn't have blood on it. They told us all to stay in our cells, except for me. I could stay in the dayroom and wait for the trustee to bring me a new jump-suit to replace my bloody one. everybody asked what had happened, and I told them as I stripped out of the bloody suit and sat at the table, waiting for the CO to come back. A few minutes later, a new CO showed up with another jumpsuit for me, and a trustee went into the cell with a biohazard cleanup kit. I couldn't believe what had just happened, but I was thinking about something else entirely.

At this point, I was almost looking forward to getting to Cottonwood, but now I had to question what was in store for me after what I had just witnessed. If Dan would rather do that to himself than go back there, what was so fucked up about the rider program that I would soon be part of? Could it possibly be that bad? I hoped that it wasn't and that Dan was the problem for whatever reason and he just managed to appear normal even though he definitely had some issues he needed to deal with on a psychological level.

As I sat there, waiting for the blood to be cleaned up, one of the guys blurted out that Dan had told him earlier today that he was planning on hurting himself so he wouldn't have to go back. Once the mess was cleaned up, that guy and I had to give written statements to the COs about the incident, and then it was back to normal. The CO did give me one nice little tidbit of information as he was walking out of the cell: we would all be assigned to the next tier tomorrow after lunch.

That was great news, and once he locked up and walked out, I told everybody in the tier what he had said. Looking back, I should have waited until morning, because now everybody stayed up, talking all night, and after what had happened, I was going to have a hard-enough time going to sleep as it was. Between the trauma and the smell of bleach from the cleanup, dozing off was going to be very difficult.

CHAPTER

28

I N THE MORNING, I THOUGHT I had dreamed the whole episode last night, but once I saw the empty bunk, I realized it was as real as it gets. A guy had chopped off his finger last night to keep from going to Cottonwood.

After breakfast, everyone went back to sleep. I had the tier to myself again, and I walked alone in peace and quiet after my morning cleaning ritual was completed. Once again, I was alone with my thoughts and memories of last night. I concluded that Dan had to have been unstable, and the more I thought about it, the more I began to see the writing on the wall. He was the only one of the people I had ever talked to that had said it was bad at Cottonwood, and with nine good reviews and the one bad one from Dan, I reasoned that he was the problem, not the rider program.

After breakfast, I saved my milk, syrup, and the little pack of sugar they gave us for our oatmeal so I could put it in my coffee later in the morning. It helped to kill my appetite so that I wasn't so hungry and could save more of my lunch and have a little food stashed away for when I wanted it.

After lunch, we were all moved over to another tier, just as a CO had told me we would be. We were all hoping that this was the transport tier, but they wouldn't tell us anything like that. I could only hope and assume that since the tier emptied out Monday from transport, they would move us then, but Tuesday worked just as well for me. At lunch, some of the guys asked the trustee who served us if this was the transport tier, and he said it was. The reason we moved Tuesday instead of Monday was the Veterans Day holiday on Monday. All the transports were one day behind schedule, and so was the shuffle. This meant we were now next in line for transport. As I had learned from experience, I was not going to get my hopes up.

I could be on my way in six days for a total of seventeen in RDU, which, as far as I ever heard, was close to a record. Even if it was one more extra week, which would make it twenty-three, that was still better than the two months I was warned about, so how could I complain? The new tier was identical to the last one, including the same people, but I had a feeling it would be filled in no time. I was given a cell that was empty for now, but the best thing was that I would have a lower bunk, which always was nice. Climbing up to the top wasn't as bad as having to jump down all the time, which hurt my back. Just about the time we had settled into our new home, the COs came in with more guys for our tier, and Scott and Jesus were among them. This was bad news, since I had figured that both of them were one week ahead of me and on their way to Cottonwood already. The flip side was, they would go next week and I would be leaving for Cottonwood the week after, unless the whole tier went at the same time. I was curious how many left each week and how many seats there were on the bus. I suppose the seating didn't really matter, since, as Dan had told me, timers going to Orofino also took seats and the count information as to the split would not be available to inmates. So now it was once again a crapshoot.

As much as I enjoyed living alone, it wasn't quite so bad when the COs assigned Scott to my cell. It was better him than someone I didn't know. After MCU, I knew that at least he was respectful, clean, and quiet. Also, with our history together, I could just tell him to shut up or leave me alone and not have to worry about pissing off some psycho I didn't know. "Looks like I caught up with you after all, huh, Scott?" I told him as he began unpacking his stuff.

"Yeah, but I will be out of here next Monday, and you'll probably have to stay here for Thanksgiving."

"I have a surprise for you, a little housewarming gift," I told him when I showed him the books I had stashed and brought with me from unit 7 and the other tiers. The surprised look on his face said it all. He was a big Patterson fan, and I had managed to hijack two good books by one of our favorite authors. I also brought Hemingway with me, but I doubted that he could appreciate *The Old Man and the Sea* as much as I had. Who was I to judge him? I really had no idea how well-read Scott was, and I found myself making a speculative judgment about someone I didn't know that well, which was wrong of me. I offered it up to see his reaction, and he told me he wanted to read the Patterson book first. I didn't know if it was a stalling tactic or just disinterest. I wasn't quite sure, but I had given him the chance and would now sit back and see if my prediction was accurate. My study of human behavior would continue all week.

When Jesus saw me in here, he looked up and said, "Hey, bunkie, how are you doing?"

"Good, and you? How come you aren't out of here yet?" I asked.

"We leave from this tier. A friend of mine in the other tier knows one of the trustees who serves us lunch, and the word is, we leave here on Monday if there is room for everyone."

This was the best news I had heard all week. Good news from a reputable source who wasn't a CO. The trustees had been working in here for months, or maybe even years, and if they didn't know the system here, then nobody did. I took what he told me optimistically, and even though I knew I shouldn't, I was now counting on being out of here Monday. I was breaking my own rule by hoping for the best, and this was not a good thing to do. I was setting myself up to be let down as I had been so many times before, but after hearing that, I couldn't help it.

The past twenty-four hours had been extremely exciting. The finger, the move, and the information Jesus had given me were all too much for me. Suddenly, I was exhausted and went to lie down and read for a while. The dayroom was packed with seventeen people now in one tier. Moving around freely was becoming more and more difficult, so lying down for a bit was better than trying to fight the crowd. After reading for a bit, I stepped out into the tier and introduced myself to a few of the new guys and found out that two of them had flopped their riders and were being sent to Orofino to do their time. These two had more information than Dan did, and they also had the community model handbook, which was basically the Cottonwood rulebook.

This book contained the eight cardinal rules, eight major rules, and nine house rules, along with other things we would be required to memorize once we arrived. According to these guys, we would be tested after one week on the general rules, so I sat down and wrote the whole handbook down as fast as I could, all thirteen pages. I wanted to make sure I was prepared when I got there, and if these guys got shuffled to a different tier, I wouldn't lose all the information I gathered. It took me a while, but when I was done, I told Scott and Jesus all about the handbook and let them know they could study it if they wanted, so they, too, could be prepared.

The next few days passed uneventfully with my daily cleaning, pacing, and reading routine. I was also memorizing the Cottonwood handbook. I wanted to be sure that I was ahead of the curve and knew everything I was expected to know the first day I arrived. The days were repetitive, and the only reason I even knew what day it was was that I was counting them down until we left. I also heard from Jesus via his trustee friend that the transport would leave on Sunday, not Monday as it usually did, because of the Thanksgiving holiday next week.

Thanksgiving was already here, and I was going to spend it in prison. It was rather depressing when you think about it. On the bright side, time was moving more quickly for me because I was busy. With Jesus's comment about leaving Sunday, my week had just become shorter by one day. Now I only had to wait until Saturday night to find out where I was going to spend the holiday.

I called Mark on Thursday, and he said he had picked up my things from county. He couldn't tell me how long my rider was going to be because that information would be determined by the people at Cottonwood and become available to me during my in-processing there. Other than that, the rest of the week was routine. I had knocked out a few more books and logged around twenty miles a day in a ninety-foot room with sixteen other guys in it and was ready for whatever the weekend and the transport list had in store for me. Even though I was really hoping to go on Sunday, I had once again mentally prepared not to. It took a few days to convince myself so I wouldn't be let down. I was now convinced that I would most likely be here one more week, and that meant I'd spent Thanksgiving in this tiny cement box.

By Saturday, I had stored up so much food from my meals that I didn't care about the two-meal day anymore. Everyone anxiously awaited the transport list, and tensions were high. Those who weren't going to make it would spend Thanksgiving in a shithole, and that would suck, especially with no palatable commissary in here.

After a day that seemed to drag on forever, right after dinner, we were told to gather round for the transport list. The moment of truth was finally here, and the next few minutes would determine where I spent my Thanksgiving and, ultimately, when I got out.

CHAPTER

29

T HE COs HAD COME INTO the tier with ten paper sacks, each
with a name written on the side of it with a black felt pen.
Since there were three guys in here who had already swapped,
this meant seven of us were not going, and I suddenly had a bad
feeling.

"Grab your bag when I call your name," the CO ordered. "Then
fill it with your personal belongings. This is all you will be able to
take with you. No food items such as coffee or tea will be allowed on
the bus. Step up when you hear your name." The COs began calling
off names, and they would turn the bag over so we couldn't see who
was next. Every time they would call out a name, it was echoed with
a triumphant shout of happiness. One by one the possibilities of me
being on the list dwindled. After they had called out seven names,
there were still ten dejected guys gathering around the COs, waiting
to hear if they were next.

"Cline!" the CO yelled out, and Cline stepped forward. Jesus,
Scott, and I were so far staying here, it seemed. Jesus had been here
a week longer than me already, so with only two names left, I had
pretty much given up.

"Villanuevo!" they called out next. Scott and I looked at each
other, knowing we were fucked for one more week. With eight guys
standing there and only one left to be chosen, the CO took advantage of his power and drew the ritual out for dramatic effect.

"And the winner of the last lottery ticket today, the last guy who
won't have to be here for Thanksgiving, is...WALKER!"

Jackpot.

I was out of here.

Relief and anxiety swept through my body until I turned to head back with my bag and almost ran over Scott.

"You motherfucker! You took my seat!" he said in a sad yet humorous way. I knew he wasn't mad at me personally as much as he was disappointed. I felt badly for him and all the others, but my feelings were quickly overcome by learning that I was on my way. It took all of five minutes to pack, and Scott, who had received twenty envelopes from me as we left county, was now the recipient of all the packaged food I had saved from meals, four or five good books he would have gotten from me anyway, and a bag and a half of coffee as well.

The place was electric with the lucky ten talking among ourselves about leaving, while the other seven avoided contact with us, mainly because they were jealous. Maybe they just didn't want us to see how upset they were. I knew I would have been unhappy had I not been picked. I paced and tried to finish the book I had just started reading so I could add one more title to my list before we left, and I occasionally broke out my rule book so I could study. I had already memorized the eight cardinal rules I would be expected to know in one week, and I had most of the major rules and house rules down too.

It was a long night in tier, with all the guys who didn't make it pissing and moaning about how the system had screwed them over and everybody was out to get them. The ones who didn't make it got on the phones to let their loved ones know the bad news. Even a few of the guys who did make it tried to call home, but to no avail, since our PIN was cut off before the CO told us who was on the transport list.

I found myself happy to be gone yet apprehensive at the thought of once again venturing into the unknown. Not truly knowing what was in store for me in the days ahead made me a little anxious even with all the information I had gathered. But the nagging question that overshadowed everything for me was, What was so bad about Cottonwood that made Dan do what he did? The only way to spin that into a positive was to remember that his elevator didn't quite go to the top floor. After what he let me witness so closely, it was a rather difficult scene to erase from my memory. As frightened and curious as I was about my own future, I was happy as hell to be taking the first step toward it tomorrow.

Right after breakfast, we were called out of the tier and told to bring our bags with us. I said goodbye to Scott, and they moved the ten of us back into the holding cell we had been in when we first got off the bus. Sitting in the holding cell, we changed out of rider yellow and put on transport fluorescent orange, complete with shackles, waistband, and handcuffs. They called me and Jesus into the room to change at the same time, and he looked up at me and said, "Bunkie, we are going together. Maybe we can be bunkies at Cottonwood too?" His innocent humor made me happy to be around him. He was sorry for what he had done and the damage it caused his family; he looked forward to whatever it was that lay ahead. That Cottonwood was all about change was what I had been told, and Jesus deep down wanted to change his life. He was the kind of guy I needed to be around. Some of our ten had been on riders before, and it seemed to me that all they really cared about was getting one over on the system and milking Cottonwood for all they could. They didn't want to change, learn, or better themselves in any way, and they were the people I wanted to stay as far away from as possible.

We were given the usual transport sack lunch and loaded onto the bus. As we pulled out of the double-wide perimeter fence and headed back out into the desert on the way to Boise, I was deep in quiet thought. I knew over the past seventeen days I was already changing. Maybe the change had actually started back on Labor Day weekend. I wasn't really sure. I knew I wanted different things in my life than I had over the past few years, and understanding this was like the first step of a twelve-step program. My actions over the past two months had proved to me that I was dedicated to change my life. If I continued to make the best of this bad situation, only good things would come of it.

The first stop we made, twenty minutes into the trip, was the Ada County Jail. We were there to pick up female transports going to Orofino, who rode with us. Of course, they were separated from us and we weren't allowed to talk to them, but after we had been locked up for so long, any female would naturally cause a stir. We headed west on I-84 for an hour or so before turning onto Highway 95 north and farm country. After about three hours, we made a pit stop in Council, Idaho, home to the Adams County Jail. We all got off the bus and were herded into the dayroom of a small jail and told we were not allowed to go upstairs, where local inmates were housed. This stop was nothing more than a twenty-eight-man pit stop to use the toilet. I felt sorry for the poor bastard in Adams County who would have to clean that toilet after we left. It was difficult to use the bathroom with our handcuffs and waistbands on. We loaded back up and continued north through winding, twisting mountain roads that headed into the Idaho wilderness. It was quite scenic and would have been an enjoyable trip, except for its obvious reasons.

Some of the mountains were covered in snow, and the farther we went, the deeper the snow was. I had heard the stories of nonstop snow shoveling the new guys at Cottonwood would be assigned to. Rumors of three or four feet of snow from Halloween until Easter ran wild here, and late fall / early winter meant I should anticipate a snow shovel being in my immediate future. We started to come down on the western side of the Clearwater mountain range and followed along Salmon River until we reached a high plain valley, much of it farmland. Ranches and fenced fields dotted the landscape, and people who knew the area said we were getting close to Cottonwood.

We turned off the main highway and headed northwest and climbed hillsides once again. We were about twenty-five miles east of the Washington/Oregon/Idaho border intersection when we turned off the country road and onto a one-mile-long paved roadway that took us up to the front gate of the North Idaho Correctional Institution in Cottonwood, Idaho. My long-anticipated rider was about to begin.

CHAPTER 30

A S WE LOOPED AROUND THE parking lot at the bottom of the gently sloping hill on which NICI was contained, we passed what appeared to be the administration building, which was the only building outside the perimeter fence. We pulled to a stop in front of another building that was mostly inside the fence except for the one door I assumed we would be going through momentarily. We filed off the bus and into the large holding cell in the segregation building that was bordered on both sides with the perimeter fence that continued around and enclosed the entire compound. We all stood and stressed while waiting to hear our names called so we could move into the next cell two at a time for the same strip search we were given at the pen.

After the strip search, we kept our orange jumpsuits on and lined up along the back wall, which was facing five two-man cells similar to the ones we had just left in unit 7. This was where the guys who flopped or had any disciplinary actions taken against them would end up being housed until the next Tuesday, when they caught a ride back to the pen. This was a place I hoped to never see again. If I did, life as I knew it would be over for the next three years. We walked single file out the back door and up the gentle slope of Main Street to the compound chapel, where I finally got a good look at my new home. The whole place reminded me of Fort Benning, Georgia. It was in fact built for the Army during World War II as a radar station and later converted into the prison and school that it is today. There was one road, Main Street, that ran uphill through the center of the compound. It was ten yards wide and dead-ended about a hundred yards up near the top of the hill. On the right-hand side at the bottom of the hill was unit 4, surrounded by a cyclone fence with razor wire along the top. Directly across the street from unit 4 was a classroom, and next to it was the mess hall. Across from the mess hall, next to unit 4, was the chapel we were all heading toward for our orientation.

We filed into the chapel and each took a seat in the chairs lined up in rows facing the front, where a podium stood as ready as did the man behind it, who began before the last man had even taken a seat. It was more like a medical lecture than an orientation speech, and we were instructed on how to maintain proper hygiene, to not get sick, to brush our teeth, and to wash our hands after going to the bathroom. We were taken one by one off to the side by teachers from the school (as opposed to COs) and asked if we were suicidal, while they took our blood pressure. This had also been done in Ada County. I think it was more for liability reasons than anything else. This way, if we were to drop dead tonight in our sleep, they could always say, "He was fine when he got here." We were also given our long-awaited LSI score. This was determined back in unit 15 in RDU, and we would finally see it in our intake paperwork. I wasn't even sure if a low or high number was better, but mine was 12, whatever that meant.

Once the quick and very uninformative orientation was complete, we were led in a single-file line across the street and around behind the kitchen to the laundry building. This place was about half the size of a basketball court and was divided into two parts. On one side were industrial-size washers and dryers along with huge tables for folding. Scattered about were large laundry baskets with various items in each, waiting to be loaded into the washing machines. The other half was a distribution center with stored clothing waiting for us to receive our allotment of linen and uniforms before we received our bunk and unit assignment. We were each given the standard issue of three pairs of olive-green slacks, one belt, one denim coat, one tie, one stocking cap we called a beanie, four button-down dress shirts (two long and two short-sleeved), three pairs of socks and underwear, one laundry bag, an exercise clothing package with sweatpants, sweatshirt, and a couple of T-shirts, along with one pair of boots and a bunk roll that contained our linen and blankets.

I took my time. As much walking as I had been doing, I wanted to make sure I had a really comfortable, waterproof pair of boots. There were a lot of boots with holes in them or with soles already worn down so much that I was afraid after a week or two with me they would be unusable. After going through five or six pairs, unsatisfactorily, I found a good pair with no holes in the leather, a comfortable fit, and as a bonus, they had already had an old pair of shower shoes inserted into them for extra padding. They were perfect! I was the last to leave the laundry, and I had no idea where everyone had gone. As I was getting ready to head out the door to try to catch up with the group, an old scarecrow of a CO stopped me and said, "Where do you think you're going?"

"I'm going to catch up with everyone, sir." I replied.

"I don't know where you think you are, but here we don't just wander around. We wait until movement is called and everybody has five minutes to get where they are supposed to be. What's your name?"

"Walker, sir," I replied, properly chastised.

"Walker," he said while looking down his list. "Unit 4, bunk number 461A. You better hurry." I had seen the unit 4 sign on the building when we first arrived, so I knew where to go. Looking around as I walked across the compound, I noticed that I was apparently the only one still outside. No one else was on the compound. No inmates or COs were anywhere to be seen. This was not a good sign, and definitely not the way I wanted to begin my rider.

Unit 4 was a long white building identical to the one I was housed in during basic training at Fort Benning, Georgia. The only difference was, in Georgia the building was set up on stilts three feet off the ground, and this one was built on a cement slab. I walked through the door into the ground floor of the unit, and at first, I thought the building was empty. Even though the lights were on, I couldn't hear a thing and feared I was in the wrong place. Looking down the center of the unit from the doorway, all I could see were the foot of the bunks and no people. I walked down the center and slowly began to realize that everyone was sitting on their bunks with their feet on the floor or hanging down if they were on the top bunk. The thing that immediately grabbed my attention was how quiet it was. For a building with 120 men living in it, there was a silence that was quite impressive.

As I walked down the aisle, somebody came up to me and looked at my paperwork and whispered for me to go upstairs. I went back down the hall toward the front door where I had seen the staircase when I came in. I went upstairs and walked down the center once again, looking back and forth from side to side, trying to figure out where I belonged. Halfway down the tier on the left was a mirrored three-sided office that divided the left side of the unit into equal sizes. This was called the bubble, and I found my bunk just on the other side.

I sat down on my bunk and faced away from the bubble while I looked around the quiet room. All the bunks were made in a military fashion, with the second blanket acting as a dust cover and pillowcase. There were two different types of lockers on the tier; some were upright and stood between the bunks, and others were footlockers placed at the end of the bunk. There was no pattern; they probably had just used whatever the Army had left in the barracks when they pulled out. I had a footlocker on the floor next to my bunk, and I put all my belongings from the laundry room on top of it and kept looking around. Everyone was dressed the same in the slacks, dress shirt, tie, and belt we had been issued. The lockers were neat and organized, and the entire tier was spotless, just as they had been during inspection back in basic. There was no garbage anywhere, the floors were shined, and even though the bunks were not hospital cornered, the bunks were all made uniformly.

It was so quiet I could hear footsteps coming up the stairs, even though I couldn't see anything because the bubble blocked my view. Suddenly, the silence was broken by someone over by the stairs yelling out his name and bunk number, followed by another and another. The two COs we're coming around the tier, taking a mandatory headcount, and as they got closer, I was preparing to take my place in the roll call. "George, 458A, sir!" the man three bunks down yelled. "Baker, 459A, sir!" said the man nearest to me. The bunk next to me was empty yet made and ready for inspection, as were all the others. My turn finally came, and I yelled out, "Walker, 461A, sir!" The CO didn't even look at me. He was too busy looking at his paperwork, seeing if the count he had taken matched the number he was supposed to have according to his chart. Glancing about the tier, I noticed the bunk next to me was not the only empty one, so some people were either excused from the count or on a detail somewhere. After the COs finished, they unlocked and entered the bubble. They were totally invisible once inside and the door closed, and I could hear the footsteps of both COs going down a staircase that was inside. I thought that with their departure, the count was over, but I followed suit as everybody stayed where they were and quiet for about ten more minutes. Some of the guys would give a nod hello but said nothing. Finally, I heard over the loudspeaker throughout the compound: "Counts clear."

Everyone got up from their bunks and began to mill around and talk while I started to make my bunk up to match the others as best as I could. I had managed to receive two of the thinnest and oldest sheets I had yet to be given during my incarceration. They were accompanied by to wool horse blankets that surely would irritate my sensitive skin, given the fact that my sheets were almost transparent. While making my bunk, I could hold them up and easily see completely through them. As I went from one side to the other of my bunk, repeatedly, I couldn't help but remember doing the same thing twenty-two years ago in basic training—only now the COs ran my life instead of the drill sergeants. In the middle of the bunk-making process, I was approached by an older man who was obviously coming over to greet me. I stopped what I was doing and turned to shake his outstretched hand.

"Hi, I'm Garrett," I told him. He began to snicker, and then he corrected me with his introduction.

"I'm Mr. Kim. We use *Mr.* and last names here at Cottonwood, and welcome."

"My name is Mr. Walker, then, and thanks."

"I am the assistant senior coordinator, and this is your purple card. You always need to wear this under your ID badge and keep both visible. This lets everybody know you're a barney, and that way, if you break any rules, you will be written up." He handed me the same handbook and rule book that Dan had let me copy back in RDU and helped me put the purple card on my ID badge and continued with his welcome speech. "Memorize all the cardinal rules, house rules, and major rules along with the house philosophy. Keep this handbook with you at all times and do nothing but program, program, and program. I have to tell this to everyone who came in with you." After dumping all this on me in ninety seconds, he ran off down the tier to find another barney and go over it all once again.

I glanced through the handbook he had given me to make sure the one Dan had was not outdated or had been revised. I had no idea how old it was, and this place was constantly revising the format, so I wanted to make sure I wasn't wasting my time. It ended up being pretty much the same as far as I could tell, especially the things that I was required to learn and, for the most part, already had memorized. On the third page were all the privileges that each man gained as he progressed through the different phases of the program. For now, I was a purple card, which meant no visitors, commissary, phone calls, free time, rec, TV, recreational reading, or personal clothing. All I was allowed to do was read self-help books, study the manual, and memorize all the different rules, which was basically called programming. Everybody was a barney or purple card for one week. At the end of the week, everyone who showed up the same day I did would be tested by being asked to recite all the rules we were supposed to be memorizing. Once we passed that test, we would move up to the next phase and receive our orange card. With graduation to the second phase came new privileges, as well as fewer restrictions.

A couple of guys came over and introduced themselves as I continued to organize and square away my things in my locker: Mr. Albert, another assistant senior coordinator, whose bunk was directly across the aisle from mine, and Mr. George, who was in the second bunk down from mine near the bathrooms. I noticed on the empty bunk between Mr. George and me there was a sign that read, "Kitchen Worker." Similar signs were also located on the other empty bunks, and I quickly figured out that they must be getting dinner ready and that was why they weren't here for count.

Mr. George informed me, "We will be getting ready for dinner here in a minute, and we will get you squared away after the evening meeting. Welcome to Cottonwood."

Looking around again, I noticed everybody was putting on their denim coats and squaring away their bunk areas so they would pass any inspection that might occur while they were eating dinner. This was common in basic as well. Many times, upon return from the chow hall, people would find their bunks tossed on the floor by the drill instructors for their personal area not being tidy or the bunks not made up properly. Apparently, the same thing could happen here, so I double-checked my area as the speaker in the unit came on: "Downstairs, go to chow. Upstairs, get on line."

With that, everyone scurried to their bunks and stood in front of them with their backs toward the walls and feet facing the center aisle. Beanies in hand, coats on, with ID badges promptly displayed with the colored card underneath it. Apparently, there was no talking while we were "on line" for chow, because silence reigned supreme. A few minutes later, the CO's voice again came over the speaker: "Upstairs, in bunk order, go to chow."

The man in front of me, Mr. George, turned his head back toward me as we filed down the tier and said, "Do exactly as I do, and you will be fine. Just remember, whatever you do, no matter what, no talking in the chow hall." We walked out in silence, and just as we had in basic, there were to be no hats on inside, yet they were mandatory outside. As I went out the front door, I put on my beanie and headed out into the cold, snowy night. In all the commotion over the last forty-five minutes, I hadn't even looked out the window to see the snow falling heavily around the compound. The upstairs was lined up on Main Street, in single file, quietly being snowed on and standing there, waiting to be called into the chow hall. I was in the highest-numbered bunk in the entire compound, and I wondered if I would be the last one to eat at every meal. Finally, it came time to enter, only to once again wait in line; only now we were out of the cold and falling snow.

We filed into an inside holding area in front of the serving counters, where we lined up in columns of ten, side by side, and waited quietly for the lines to move. When the row next to the wall on my left began to get smaller as the serving line thinned out, all the other columns shifted sideways with one left sideways-shuffle step in unison. The other columns copied the sideways-shuffle routine one after the other until they were next to the wall and ready to move forward. Eventually, after what my stomach deemed an eternity, my column sidestepped over to the wall and began to move forward through the line. I was handed my tray from the two-foot-by-two-foot window that prevented the kitchen workers from seeing whom they were giving the tray to, and I followed Mr. George down the rows of tables and sat down in the chair he had pulled out for me. Following suit, I pulled out the chair for the stragglers who had come in after me, so they could fit into their seats and put down their trays and do the same for the next guy. All we could hear was silverware clanking and background kitchen noises as the five tables with twenty men on each side of them silently ate their meal.

Having completed their meal, men were lining up along the outer wall and waiting for the okay from the CO to be dismissed so they could return to the unit. After a brief eight minutes that were allotted to complete the meal, we were told to get up from the table as our time was up. I stood up and ate as much as I could while standing with my tray in the dishwashing line. Here we scraped off the extra food and dropped off our silverware in a soaking tub, trying to make life a little easier for the dishwashing crew.

I followed Mr. George over to the outer wall and got in line by the back door, waiting for the CO to give us permission to head back to the unit. Standing next to the exit door was my old cellie Jesus from RDU. He must have also been assigned to unit 4, and he nodded to me in recognition, as I did to him, without breaking the no-talking rule. When the CO told us to go, the guy next to Jesus, knowing he was a barney, intentionally guided him out the wrong door, setting off the fire alarm, which drew laughter from half the guy still in the kitchen. Apparently, this was quite a common joke to play on the new guys, and I was just glad it was Jesus instead of me. Things were going quickly here, and I was feeling a little overwhelmed.

To control the inmates and their movements for security reasons, we were supposed to go straight back to the unit in a single-file line with no deviation. This was why we waited inside the chow hall and were dispersed in groups of twenty. As I walked the fifteen yards down Main Street to the unit, I noticed the snow was starting to really pile up quickly. There must have been two or three new inches of snow that had fallen during the brief time I spent in the chow hall. When we first arrived, there was a light dusting as the snowfall slowly began, and by now there had to be at least six inches piled up, and you could no longer see Main Street. Everything was now white. It was much more difficult to enjoy the snow, as I usually did, knowing that tomorrow I would most likely be on the end of a shovel, scooping it up. On the way down the street, Mr. George was telling me about the prank that was just pulled on Jesus and slowly drawing me in closer to him, to hear what he was saying.

"Follow right behind me as we go in, Mr. Walker. I want to pull another joke on one of your buddies," he said to me. The unit was fenced off completely and had a small cyclone fence tunnel that went from the front door out to the street. Wanting to help the guy pulling the prank rather than the victim, I stayed right behind Mr. George, happy to be making friends and getting to be part of the fun crowd right away. As he stepped through the opening that led to the unit, he lifted up his hands and hit the cyclone fencing above the walkway. Looking at what he was doing yet totally unaware as to why, I was too slow in reacting to the landslide of fresh snow that slid off the fence and buried my head in freezing-cold, fresh powder. Jesus had gotten it in the chow hall, and I had gotten it good on the walkway. Always appreciative of a good practical joke, I took it in stride and let them have their laugh and gave them a bow. Nobody likes a sore loser, and he had planned it so masterfully I almost had to admire the man. He had probably been working on the prank since he first noticed the snow coming down. He told me to follow him before we even left the unit for dinner. *Bravo, Mr. George, bravo.* I filed that little trick in the back of my head, knowing full well that in the weeks to come, with winter upon us, there would be many others who would share the same fate as I had. I spent three minutes shaking off all the snow outside and finally stepped into the unit slightly embarrassed and with a cold red face, but I was none the worse for wear. I made my way upstairs and headed for my bunk when I passed Jesus, whose bunk was a couple of bunks down the tier from the stairs on the opposite side of the aisle from mine.

"Hey, bunkie, did you see what happened to me in the chow hall?" he asked me with a big grin on his face. He almost seemed proud that he was chosen—meaning, he had been accepted early in the game by his neighbors.

"I did, but you missed what just happened to me coming into the unit. The guy in front of me dumped a ton of snow on my fucking head from the fence," I replied with the same grin. I could tell from the way things were going that this could be a "fun" place. The jokes so far appeared to be contained to within the confines of those involved in it so as not to draw too much attention to those who caused it. Nobody saw what Mr. George had done to me except the two guys ahead of us going into the unit. What happened to Jesus in the chow hall would be blamed on the new guy not knowing what to do. The biggest issue I could already see coming with how the COs viewed all this was, At what point did they draw the lines between harmless fun, which makes a place like this bearable, and serious offenses, which would bring major consequences with them?

C H A P T E R

31

I WAS SITTING IN THE front row on the aisle, quietly reading the handbook I was never supposed to be without. My head was down, and I was rereading over and over all the things I had yet to memorize for the following week, since I could already pass the test I was going to take next week. Out of nowhere, a man who had quietly stood up and walked up about a foot in front of me yelled at the top of his lungs, "Good evening, community! My name is Mr. Walsh!" When he did this, he scared the living shit out of me since he was standing right next to me while my head was down and I was not paying attention to him but rather my handbook.

The entire community, in unison, responded with an extremely loud "Good evening, Mr. Walsh!" The volume of 120 responding voices was rather impressive. I also realized that I had once again been on the receiving end of the subtle humor that ran through the unit as an undercurrent. Mr. Walsh had been doing his introduction long enough to quietly walk up to the front row and scare the shit out of whoever the lucky new guy in the front row just happened to be. I guess I jumped a little higher than I thought, and again my face was red with embarrassment. If these pranksters were trying to educate the new guys in hopes of perpetuating their pranks, they had chosen the right guy. I was soaking this all up, and these traditions would live on, if I had anything to say about it.

Mr. Walsh continued with his duty by saying, "Welcome to the evening meeting for Sunday, November 20. The evening meeting is meant to bring closure to the day, and we will begin tonight's meeting with the reading of the minutes from the morning meeting. Mr. Feldman, would you please read the morning minutes?"

Mr. Feldman stood and yelled, "Good evening, community! My name is Mr. Feldman." The community responded with the same "Good evening, Mr. Feldman!" He quickly read the minutes from the morning meeting with the skill of a professional auctioneer. The speed with which he did this was entertaining. He had a copy of the minutes in his hand to go by, but the sheer volume of content contained within included everything that happened in the morning meeting with such swiftness and occasional humor I was quite impressed. I assumed that the same outline would be used in the morning and was resigned to the idea that this meeting was going to last a while.

The meeting would last a full hour and resemble an AA meeting or a group therapy meeting in rehab. One of the first things on the agenda tonight was the introduction of new members into the community. One at a time, we were asked to stand up, introduce ourselves, and tell the community what we wanted to get out of the program. Thank God my name wasn't called first, since I had already been laughed at enough for one day. Most people stood up and mumbled their way through their introductions, not really knowing the required procedure or just what to say. By the third introduction, it was more of a scripted response that I followed when my turn finally came.

Every time anyone new began speaking to the community, the proper introduction of standing up and saying, "Good evening, community, my name is…" was mandatory before one began to address the group. This was followed by the group response, "Good evening, Mr.…," so that everyone would learn everyone else's name and we would all get to know one another faster. When my name was called, I was able to avoid the collective group corrections of my predecessors by standing up and introducing myself properly. I then looked out at the community and said, "I would like helping end the destructive decision-making process that got me here, so I can return to my family as soon as possible."

This was followed by the standard round of applause before the next barney spoke. I watched and listened to my fellow purple cards, whom I had gotten to know over the past weeks in unit 7 and who were loud, obnoxious, and very outspoken, wither under the watchful eyes of the community. Public speaking had never been a problem for me, but I could see and hear the terror in the voices of my comrades, whose worst fears had just been met head-on. It was all part of the program here. Learning to overcome the fear of public speaking could only help them when they returned to the world outside.

The rest of the meeting included inspirational readings, rule violation ratings, community business, and other various pieces of information that the coordinators thought the unit needed to know. Toward the end, each coordinator was given a chance to make announcements to the unit and inform the community of the evening rec plans, as well as chapel and library times for the evening. The CO came out of the bubble and made a few comments and then retreated back inside, closing the door, becoming invisible once again. While the door to the bubble was open, I did get a nice view of the office contained within, including the iron spiral staircase leading upstairs and a door to the outside in the back. This way, the COs could discreetly come in to observe anyone in the unit upstairs or downstairs through the one-way mirrored glass, without anyone even knowing they were in the building.

The meeting ended with community reading of the unit philosophy from memory, the group recitation of the Serenity Prayer, and finally, a quote from Mr. Ramirez, the senior coordinator, who was the highest-ranking inmate in the community model system. He was ultimately in charge of the meeting, but the three assistant coordinators each had three crew coordinators to watch over, and they all had designated duties to perform. The whole thing ran like a well-oiled institutional machine. The CO was more of an observer who made sure we did what we were supposed to. He only intervened two or three times throughout the entire hour-long session to make minor corrections concerning the protocol we were required to follow.

It was now 7:00 p.m. by the time we were adjourned. The barneys were all instructed to meet with Mr. Tortelli, the service coordinator, immediately following the meeting. When we did, we were told that we were assigned to the service crew for the first week here and Mr. Tortelli was to be our direct supervisor. The service crew was in charge of the setup and putting away of all the tables used for the meetings and the American and Idaho State flags that flanked the first row of coordinator tables. I had been upstairs during the setup process, after cleaning snow off my head, and didn't make it down in time to help set up the first meeting. I got a pass on this offense from the service crew, Mr. Tortelli, but I was told to "make sure it didn't happen again."

He told me this with a sarcastic tone and a little smirk on his face. I could tell he was a nice guy who was just trying to cover his ass so he would not get in trouble for not informing me. The whole point of this place wasn't so much to tattle on one another as well as to keep one another in check and self-regulate as a community. With fifty rules to follow at all times and 119 people watching you, as well as the COs, you had to make sure you were always compliant, lest you end up going to the pen. From what I could tell so far, nobody here wanted that, least of all me. As I headed upstairs after the cleanup was done, I was stopped by a guy who verified I was Mr. Walker and then took me over by his bunk to have a nice little chat with me.

"I am Mr. Baxter, and I am your mentor. I was supposed to meet you before count, but you came in late, and this is the first chance I have had to talk to you without disturbing another activity." After he said that, it hit me. For the past couple of hours, I had been busy every second and was not allotted any free time whatsoever. We were now on free time for the rest of the night, but technically, free time did not exist for purple cards. We were to be programming from the time we got up until we went to bed at 9:00 p.m.

"Relax," Mr. Baxter told me. "The hardest part is over, and it does get easier. I am here to answer questions and help guide you through your first week here."

"What am I supposed to be doing the rest of the night?" I asked him.

"Read your handbook and memorize the rules you will be tested on next week, so you can get your orange card."

"I already know all the rules. There was a guy in RDU who had a handbook with him, and most of the guys I came in with and I studied for the past week. Can I take the test now?"

"You can't test until you have been here for one week, but I am one of the testers, so I will get with you in a little bit and we can talk more, and I will give you a practice test. Fair enough?"

"Fair enough," I told him. "Thanks, Mr. Baxter."

He seemed like a normal guy, and finally I had met someone whom I could just talk to and go to with questions or problems. If I had run into him before count as I was supposed to when I first walked in, the last couple of hours might not have been so hectic and scary for me. It was my own fault for being late, but having a good pair of boots was more important. Looking around, I could see the shape of some of the other boots the men were wearing, and I knew the extra time I had spent in the laundry room was well worth it. Some of their soles were flopping with each step and almost coming off. Others had holes so big and worn through the leather their feet had to be getting soaked every time they went outside.

Finally, I had a spare moment to catch my breath, so I put away my chair and began to pace back and forth down the center aisle of the tier while reviewing my handbook for my upcoming test. That was when Jesus join me and said, "Hey bunkie, what do you think of this place? Pretty wild, huh?"

"I already like it here. The time here is going to fly by. If they keep us as busy as we have been for the next few months, it will seem as if we have been here for only a short time."

"I didn't like having to get up and talk in front of everybody. Could you tell I was scared?" Jesus asked me.

"Yeah, but over time, you will get used to it and it won't be a problem," I told him. I was right about the public speaking problem some of the guys in here would have. I got over all that in the Army, so it would never be a problem for me, but I felt sorry for Jesus. He was scared to death when he had to give his introduction speech. It was choppy and made him seem intimidated. With his English not being the best, I could only imagine what was going through his mind when his name was called. The coordinator butchered his name first, and then the CO did as well. The CO then let it be known to the whole unit that from now on his title would be Mr. V. The subtle humor behind *bunkie* came from his improper use of the English language and the homosexual undertone it implied. He meant to call me cellie, since we shared a cell, but in his mistake, he inferred that we shared a bunk, which I thought was rather funny, so I just let him keep going with it. Always looking for a way to brighten my day at any cost so that even if only for a moment I could forget I was in prison and smile. Jesus was the first man since county whom I had really connected with, and we got along well. I could call him a friend in a place where, so far, I had very few.

Jesus went off to handle his business, and I memorized more of the handbook. While looking around and going over things in my head, I noticed about one-third of the guys were dressing down into their exercise uniforms and were heading downstairs. After a few more laps of trying to figure out what was going on, I stopped over by Mr. Baxter and asked him.

"Those guys are going to green card rec at the gym."

"I didn't see a gym when I got here," I told him.

"It's behind the baseball field, down the other side of the hill. You can't see it unless you walk out behind the school and go down a path."

"What's in the gym?"

"Basketball and weights is about it, but it is for all the green cards on the whole compound, not just this unit. Everything on compound is done within your unit except for classes and green card rec."

"Thanks," I told him and got back to my pacing, not wanting to be a pest. I would be an orange card in a week, a blue card in one month, and in sixty days, I would be able to go to green card rec. I thought of them as nice stepping stones with which to mark my progress. This would break up the time spent into easier-to-manage pieces and thus hopefully go by faster. With that in mind, I refocused on the task at hand, which was to prove to Mr. Baxter that

I had indeed stepped off the bus as I had planned, totally prepared to take the orange card test one week ahead of schedule. With the green cards gone, the place quieted down a bit, and I kept walking and memorizing, trying to observe and absorb all that I could. Before long, Mr. Baxter came back around and asked me, "Are you ready for your practice test, Mr. Walker?"

"I was ready before I left RDU after you, Mr. Baxter. Let's go."

"Let's go to the back room, and I will give you the test." We went to the storage room, where the cleaning supplies were kept, and he pulled up two chairs and began to test me.

"Recite the eight cardinal rules for me, Mr. Walker," he challenged.

I inhaled deeply and raised my head up as if the answers were printed on the ceiling of the tiny room. It was also some sort of utility room with the furnace in it, and in the middle of a freezing-cold Idaho night, the extra warmth in here felt comforting.

"Number one," I began, "I will not be physically violent, threaten physical violence or intimidation against any person. Number two, I will not steal. Number three, I will not use drugs, alcohol, or any drug or alcohol paraphernalia. Number four, I will not sexually act out, including romantic, sexual physical contact or sexual harassment. Five, I will not have weapons of any kind. Six, I will not display any gang representation of any kind. Seven, I will not destroy any state or NICI property. Eight, I will not refuse to participate in any assigned activities."

"Perfect. Nicely done, Mr. Walker. Push up," said Mr. Baxter with a big smile on his face. "You are going to make being your mentor the easiest job in the world."

"What did you mean when you said 'push up'? I have heard a few people saying that when I was walking."

"Around here, there are two forms of notoriety, good and bad. When you do something above and beyond good, guys will say, 'Push up.' Or possibly even write a push-up and drop it in the box by the bubble. Some of them were read at the meeting tonight. Do you remember hearing any of them? The guys were all raising their hands in the air like they were pushing up."

"I saw them doing it, but I didn't know what it meant. The meeting was a little overwhelming. You are given so much information in such a small amount of time—it's hard to comprehend it all at once," I told him.

"Believe me, I understand completely. Everybody does, because we all get off the bus and have the same kind of day you just had. It does get better. You'll like it here after a week or so. Anyway, the other way to get noticed is with a pull-up. If you see someone doing something wrong or they see you screwing up, they fill out a slip of paper called a pull-up. This means your fellow inmate needs help changing his behavior and he is counting on the other members of the unit to pull him up. These were also read at the evening meeting. Two guys faced each other while the pull-up was read." I had seen both of these things at the meeting and didn't really understand what was going on until now. Mr. Baxter helped me understand the inner working of the community now that I had witnessed it, because then and only then could the new guys comprehend it. If he had had tried to explain that before I had lived through it, I most likely would not have understood what he was trying to tell me.

"You can't just write someone up for an infraction, though. You first have to give them a verbal warning and a chance to change their behavior before you drop the slip on them."

"Drop what slip?"

"When you write someone up, or give them a pull-up, you fill out this form," he said, pulling one from his pocket and showing it to me. "First, you give them a verbal. If they don't alter their behavior, you have no choice but to drop the slip, which means to write them up and drop the pull-up into the same box down by the bubble. Get it, drop the slip?"

"Okay, I get it now. Who is going to explain all this to the other barneys I came in with when some of them aren't the sharpest tool in the shed?"

"Each of them has a mentor, and it is the mentor's job to help them understand what I am telling you. I know two other mentors who are having the same talk with their guys right now on the other side of the tier. Now, you have to be careful not to write people up for stupid things, which will cause you to get into a booking war. This is when two guys just go back and forth, trying to get even with each other by pulling each other up again and again. The COs will see what's going on and bust you both. As a rule of thumb, don't write anybody up for the first week. Just watch and learn, and you'll catch on. It seems hard, but after a day or two, you'll figure it out."

"Hey, before we are done here, what can you tell me about the bubble? My bunk is right next to it. Is that good or bad?"

"The bubble is there so the COs and the counselors can spy on you and watch what goes on in the tier whenever they want. You can't see through the mirrored glass, and walking up and trying to look through it, like having your hands cupped around your eyes, will get you in serious trouble. They have a separate door on the side of the building so they can get in and out and nobody knows. They also have a spiral staircase inside so they can sneak upstairs and watch the second floor just as easily. Always behave as if you are being watched, especially with the bunk you have being so close to it. Oh, by the way, don't count on holding on to that bunk too long. It is probably the best one in the unit, and some green card who requested will be moving into it in no time."

"Thanks for the heads-up," I said. He was getting antsy, and I could tell he had other things to do.

"No problem. That's my job. Let me know if you have anything else you need help with or don't understand." He shook my hand and headed out to the main part of the tier.

I begin pacing once again and looked for Jesus and other barneys to discuss what I had just learned, but apparently, he and the others were still in the middle of their welcome chats with their mentors. This place was a trip. I was trying to take it all in, but the sheer volume of what we were required to learn was overwhelming. I was suddenly paranoid of getting pulled up for a rule violation, so sticking to my pacing and programming routine seemed like a sure-fire way to stay out of trouble. Having proved to Mr. Baxter that I was already capable of passing my first test, I began to focus on the required items I needed to memorize in order to go from orange to blue in thirty days. I didn't see how trying to stay ahead of the game, as I had already done, could possibly hurt. After going back and forth down the aisle for a while, I stopped to ask a couple of quick questions that popped into my head while pacing.

"Mr. Baxter, when do we get to go to bed around here?"

"Not until 9:00 p.m., and don't get caught lying down until then, or you'll get written up."

"And what do I need to do in the morning so I don't have to bug you then? I want to be prepared." I flashed back to basic training when I would have the guy who was on the wake-up shift as the fireguard wake me up fifteen minutes before the rest of the company. This way, I could be dressed, shaved, and have my bunk ready for inspection five minutes after everybody woke up. I was assigned as a squad leader in basic, so I adhered to the rule of leading by example.

"Wake up at 5:00 a.m.," he began. "By five forty-five, you need to be in an ironed shirt, polished boots, and your bunk must be made ready for inspection. Be online for chow at six, count time at seven, and the morning meeting at seven thirty. After that, your day is easy, unless it's snowing. If I were you, I would plan on shoveling a lot of snow tomorrow, Mr. Walker." Having concentrated on the rules I was expected to learn, I hadn't really looked outside to notice the flakes rapidly piling up on the ground, which were easily over a foot deep by now.

"Thanks for the advice," I said and strolled off once again, trying not to be a bother to Mr. Baxter, whose information and candor were greatly appreciated. I was beginning to wonder if I now had two friends in here, which was more than I felt I had when I was a victim of the pranks that were pulled on me.

When the green cards came back from rec, I was confronted by seeing frozen red faces of the victims of the snow-dumping trick that I had fallen for. It was encouraging to know that even green cards, after being here for sixty days, could still be had. I grabbed a couple of shirts from my footlocker and got in line for the iron, so I could be prepared in the morning, just as I had been in basic. While standing there, I met a couple of other guys, mostly orange cards, who were only a week or two ahead of me, for some ideal chitchat about how crowded RDU was and how long we had all spent there. After comparing war stories, I realized that my fears of having about two months' downtime in RDU were all for nothing, and compared to most people, I was in and out in a flash. Some of these guys had been there for six weeks only two weeks ago, and after hearing their side of it, I felt lucky to have breezed through so quickly. Maybe my luck was starting to change.

CHAPTER

32

I WAS READY FOR INSPECTION, and my bunk area was cleaned up and tidy when I looked around to compare my progress to the rest of the unit. It was only five fifteen, and I had thirty extra minutes until inspection when Mr. George came over to me with a smirk on his face. I hadn't really talked to him last night after he dumped all the snow on my head. He went to green card rec, as most green cards did. He offered me a handshake as he approached, and the grin on his face told me he was still laughing about the prank I was victimized by after chow last night.

"I hope you don't take that personally, Mr. Walker. It's sort of a rite of passage around here just as it was for your buddy who hit the fire alarm door in the chow hall. No hard feelings?" He was telling me more than I asked for, but I was a pretty easygoing guy.

"No problem. You just better hope that you never come back from the chow hall behind me on a snowy night," I said while smirking and raising an eyebrow.

"It's good to know you can at least take a joke. So many guys here are wound a little too tight for my taste. Guess I should have asked for better accommodations from my travel agent."

"You and I both," I told him as we went in opposite directions to continue with the morning preparations, thirty minutes ahead of schedule. I headed over to check on Jesus and to give him a hand if he needed one. I noticed others were ironing shirts for their buddies, and some guys who shared bunk beds would make them both together, saving the time it would take to walk back and forth around the bunks repeatedly. Jesus was dressed, shaved, and working on his bunk by himself, so I gave him a hand and told him about the two-man system, so he could work that out with his new bunkie. He and I checked on a couple of other guys we had arrived with, and for the most part, it was good to know that our little group was competent enough to get ready in the morning, which was generally a good sign. The inspection could happen at any time, so of course you had to prepare, or on the one day you didn't prepare for it, it would definitely be the day they would decide to have it.

In all the commotion, I hadn't even looked outside, but when I did, I caught a glimpse of what winter in northern Idaho had in store for the next few months. It looked like it had snowed all night, because there was at least a foot and a half of new snow on the ground. Everything was white, and most of the landmarks, which I wouldn't have recognized anyways, were now humps of fresh powder as far as the eye could see. Main Street was buried except for a few fresh footprints streaking across the grounds, most likely made by whatever CO was now on duty. The call came out at 5:46. All the purple cards had to get their coats on and get to the maintenance shed, check out some shovels, and quickly clear a path from the unit to the chow hall. When we all were ready to go to the shed and get our tools, I made sure I was first in line and Jesus was next to me while I made idle conversation to keep him close. We were told to sign out and head out as a group to the maintenance shed. As we walked out of the cyclone fence tunnel path to Main Street, I jumped up and smacked the fence, dropping a shitload of snow onto Jesus and the guy behind him. We all had a good laugh, and I was sure that from now on, while exiting the unit after snow had fallen, somebody was going to get it dumped on their head daily. I had gone from victim to instigator in less than twelve hours.

Since we had come up one day earlier on transport, the purple cards who had come a week earlier were still purple until tonight at the meeting, when they would receive their orange cards. There were about twenty of us to make the path, and even with the depth of the snow at almost two feet, it only took us about ten minutes to do so. Some of us shoveled the snow sideways into piles, while others swept what was left so the path was almost down to the bare pavement and safe for us to walk on. We returned all the tools to the shed. As we headed back to the unit, a few guys tried my fence trick, but not enough snow had accumulated in such a short time to do any good.

We needed to be ready to eat at 6:00 a.m., and the unit that went first was chosen at random and rotated on some pattern, but essentially, we all just stood "on line," ready to go until our unit was called. We knew we could be told to get on line at any time, so everyone was generally ready, but once the CO announced, "Upstairs or downstairs, get on line," via the speaker, all talking stopped. We were to be dressed in our coats, bunks and area ready for inspection, standing in front of our bunks with no talking. During this five-minute interlude, one-liners were thrown around by green cards, basically giving shit to one another, quietly but humorously. Lack of other ways to blow off steam had turned some of these guys into comedians. Not only was it healthy to laugh at the situation, but I always found it therapeutic, considering our current address.

After what I considered a pretty good breakfast of scrambled eggs, hash browns, toast, sausage patty, juice, half an orange, and as always, not enough milk—God, I missed my milk—before the eight minutes were given to eat was up, we had to line up on the wall and await the okay from the CO to head back to the unit. This was for security reasons, so guys wouldn't wander around the compound by themselves. It was easy for the COs to track groups this way, but they also figured that if someone had a brain fart and tried to escape, the possibility of his buddy stopping him from making this huge mistake would come into play.

Escaping wouldn't be that difficult, from what I had seen in less than twenty-four hours I had spent here. The difficult thing would be to determine why anyone would even do it in the first place. My judge would impose the maximum sentence possible on someone like me, which would mean I'd be in the pen for seven years. I would be charged with an escaped attempt, which carried with it a five-year penalty. I could be home with no more than five months left of my six-month "retained jurisdiction the court gave me" or spend twelve years in the pen. The choice for me was obvious, but that didn't mean all the other geniuses in here had thought it through as well as I had. This place could have no fences at all and it would make no difference to me. My goal was to complete this program as quickly as I could, no matter what. I would sit idly by and let some monster beat the life out of me before I would participate in a fight. One fight in here could cost me three to seven years. I was determined to make sure this would never happen.

After breakfast, we lined up for the 7:00 a.m. count. There were five counts each day, but one was at lights-out, at 9:00 p.m., and another at 2:00 a.m., so only three of them really affected my routine. We were required to be inspection-ready, sitting on our made bunks feet on the floor, with our area clean and no talking out loud. Counts were normally like the one I had walked in on yesterday when I first arrived. Knowing what to expect this time on what would go on and how to act made this count much less horrifying than the last one. The whole process took from ten to twenty minutes, while the entire compound was seated on their bunks. Two COs would walk each tier of each unit and physically count us and verify it against the number of inmates that were supposed to be in the facility at that particular moment.

Once the count was cleared over the wide speaker system, we immediately headed downstairs with our chairs and handbook for the morning meeting. I suddenly remembered I was supposed to help set up the tables and flags as part of my service committee duty. I hurried down to check in with my coordinator, Mr. Tortelli, to make sure I was doing my part, since I hadn't helped last night because no one had told me I was supposed to, which I could only get away with once. Something told me that if I didn't know about the rule I was supposed to, it would be my fault for not knowing the rules in the first place. I helped get the flags in place while my fellow barneys set up the tables for the coordinators to conduct whatever business was going to happen at the morning meeting. Just as last night, we all sat quietly, waiting for the seconds to tick away so we could begin precisely at seven thirty.

There was nobody to scare the shit out of this morning. That wouldn't happen again until next week, when the next batch of purple cards showed up. The evening meeting was all about business, but the morning meeting was intended to set tone for the day and get things started on a positive note. We started with the reading of last night's minutes, which was humorous now, and I understood what Feldman was talking about this time. He gave a brief rundown of what happened and made sure every error, screwup, or oddity that had accidentally happened last night was properly remembered by us all. Reflections from the Bible, thoughts for the day, readings from the Narcotics Anonymous book, headline news from *The Real World*, and even some sports score were read to the group. Activities for the day ahead were also announced, which mostly consisted of snow removal for me, and a few phase changes were read.

Phase changes were a three-page essay written and read in front of the whole unit by individuals giving their personal feelings on one of many possible topics he had previously chosen from the list provided. These forced each member to open up about himself and share his life and past troubles with the community, so we would all know more about one another and be able to help one another to be successful in whatever program we were assigned to. The topics chosen this morning were accountability, forgiveness, and honesty.

Some struggled, while others excelled. When the three of them were done, I felt as though I had gotten to know each of them a little better. Not just what they had to say but how well they could write and how they handled the performance. This could tell you a lot about a person. Where they came from, how educated they were, how outgoing or reclusive they might be were all obvious to me from not only hearing them read it and what the content was but also by watching how they read it. I actually enjoyed hearing each person's take on their chosen topic, particularly because something had happened to them that had made them feel strongly about it. I guess the idea was to get them to think about some of the reasons they were here now. Without having this knowledge and some in-depth background about someone, helping anyone to change their behavior would be extremely difficult. With this bearing of the soul, helping a person find a remedy for their negative behavior would be much easier to accomplish. As a result, you would have 119 men who understood why you did what you did. Admitting the problem existed was always the first step toward solving it.

After hearing the phase changes, I spent the rest of the meeting thinking through the possible topics I might choose. The other thing that kept popping into my head was the question, After all the reading I had been doing, would I be able to write a good essay? Some where more articulate than others? The last guy was intelligent, insightful, and funny, and the crowd came to life as he neared the end of his talk, and he received a long-lasting round of applause. I would make sure that my phase change was so good that everyone there would remember it for the rest of their lives.

When the meeting ended, we completed our service committee duties within two or three minutes. And the compound-wide speaker announced it was time for eight thirty movement. With the authorization from the powers that be, about fifty or sixty men with assorted folders, books, and files all headed out the door and up Main Street, and I assumed they were headed for the schoolhouse or off to do whatever job they had been assigned to. People were allowed only five minutes to get to their destination during movement, and after that, they were required to remain there until the next movement was announced. Anyone caught wandering around the compound without a movement pass, authorized by a CO or teacher, was considered out of area and subjected to disciplinary action or possibly even attempted escape charges, if they happened to be wandering too close to the fences. Not having a clue what to do next, I went downstairs and found Mr. Tortelli so I could get the scoop on what I was supposed to be doing, since by now I had figured out it was apparent that we were all supposed to be doing something almost all the time. I was almost afraid to ask because I knew the answer most likely included a shovel, a broom, and a wheelbarrow.

"Mr. Tortelli, what exactly is it all the purple card should be doing?" I asked him as if I didn't already know the answer.

"I'll tell you, Mr. Walker, exactly what you and all the other purple cards need to do. This week, they should be doing anything I tell them to since I am part of what we call your line of communication. If I can't get it done, then I go to my assistant senior coordinator, Mr. Kim, and he either gets it done or he will go to Mr. Ramirez, the senior coordinator, and if he can't get it done, he and only he will go to the CO, and it will get done. Under no circumstance are you or any other purple card to go directly to any of those people without me telling you to. This system has been designed to handle any problem without bothering them. Understood?"

I nodded.

"Otherwise, Mr. Ramirez or the COs spend all day answering questions that the line of communication was put in place to answer. It also helps that other coordinators do the tasks assigned to them and further their own leadership skills and responsibilities. Now, with your lesson about the line of communication over, I want you to gather up all the purple card buddies that you came here with, get your coats, hats, and gloves, and hit the maintenance shed. Let's get you all out on Main Street, getting that snow out of here before it gets out of control. Also, clear a path all around the unit area, as well as the library next door. That falls under our compound responsibilities. If you have any questions, Mr. Thorne should be out there, and he is the house committee coordinator. If you have any questions, ask him. Do you have any questions for me before you go outside?"

"Yeah. What is it you want me to do?" I said with a blank look on my face, playing stupid just long enough to make him think for about two or three seconds that I was serious. "Consider it done, Mr. Tortelli." Off I went to gather my group of guys and head out into the cold morning so we could get it over with. I glanced back at Tortelli, who had a big grin on his face, and I knew I had made my first friend from the coordinator ranks, the man who would be my boss for the next week.

Mr. Tortelli was a tall older gentleman who had such a deep voice that he did radio and TV commercial advertisement voiceovers for a living. He was brought in on meth charges and ended up on a rider rather than go to prison, so he could be given a chance to change his behavior. He stood a few inches taller than me and was completely gray, with deep, dark skin that told me he had been outside in the Idaho sunshine for many years. He was a no-nonsense guy who was a green card and had only two or three weeks left here, and I was sure by then he was probably pretty sick of being surrounded by the young punks this place seemed to be full of.

After a quick stop at the toolshed, we began clearing the only road in the compound and noticed that all the other guys who had rode the bus up here with us, who had been placed in other units, were out here doing the same. At 9:30 a.m., the speaker announced movement once again, bringing the compound alive with the activity of five minutes while everybody quickly went to the next destination. Some orange cards and even a few blue cards came out and joined us on snow duty, either out of sympathy, because the snowfall was so massive, or the overwhelming need for physical activity. It wasn't too bad, actually. We could talk freely, compare stories, and share information we had gathered in the very long eighteen hours we had been here. The orange and blue cards told us what to expect this first week so we would have a little bit of insight as to what was ahead.

CHAPTER

33

THE COMING WEEK WAS SPENT mostly in processing, orientation, and program placement screening that would randomly fill our three hours in the morning and afternoon, which was when everything around here was done. There were three one-hour classes from eight thirty until eleven thirty each morning, and three more from one thirty until four thirty in the afternoon, with five-minute announced movements in between. The only reason we were allowed on Main Street with such freedom now was that we were performing the snow removal, which was being overseen by the house committee coordinator, whose jurisdiction it fell under. It was your basic "shovel the snow into piles on the side of the road," while others loaded it into wheelbarrows and others continually ran those loads up the street to the baseball field, where it was dumped into a huge pile in the middle of the field. The remaining workers then swept aside the remaining snow with the brooms so the street was bare by the time all this was completed. Northern Idaho snow was unlike any snow I had ever seen or skied on in my lifetime. The snow on the other side of the Cascade Range was wet and heavy, causing it to become unsweepable once it was walked upon. The temperature here was around twenty degrees, and the snow was like sand rather than the snow I was accustomed to. It was much easier to work with since it was lighter, but we had to endure the lower temperatures, which made it so cold it was difficult to breathe while exerting so much energy.

Many hands made it go faster than I had expected it to, and I found out from the blue cards who had been here for at least a month that this was the first big snowfall of the year. That had left the compound speckled with snow patches when I arrived, since it never warmed up enough to melt. Now with two-foot-high drifts blanketing the entire prison, I had no idea if the compound was gravel, dirt, or grass. As we worked through the nine thirty movement, those who walked past us kept saying, "Push up, gentlemen, push up." Around here, a verbal push-up was given to anyone helping the community for the greater good. With all the units helping, Main Street was cleared in a couple of hours. Next, all the men from unit 4 scooped up the snow, revealing the sidewalks. With the snow detail wrapping up, all the purple cards who arrived yesterday were told by Mr. Thorne to be ready at the ten thirty movement so we could attend our first orientation class in the chow hall. We headed back inside to warm up, change into clean, dry shirts, resign out to the chow hall, and be ready to walk to the chow hall when movement was called.

This was going to be the advanced educational screening test. Based on the scores we received on our first educational screening test in RDU, we were each given a more advanced test, depending on everyone's level of completed education and aptitude scores on the previous test. It was your typical number-2-pencil fill-in-the-bubble in the ten minutes allowed, and the whole thing had three or four parts to it. And that was it. As we were finishing the last test, kitchen workers, dressed in their red kitchen shirts, which they could wear while working, came streaming into the chow hall to begin preparing lunch. The background noises were steadily growing, and the teacher who administered the test told us more about the week ahead.

"You will have three or four more gatherings like this one in different buildings throughout the week. Attendance is mandatory, and failure to participate in an assigned activity is a violation of a cardinal rule. It's the obligation of your community members to pull you up for violating it. Since all of you are on the service committee the first week, we make sure the service committee coordinator of each unit knows where you are to be, and when, each day. Even though Thanksgiving is Thursday, we will try to make sure your orientation is complete in one week so we can get you enrolled in whatever programs and classes you need to complete your rider, as stated by your judge in his sentencing guidelines. That is all I have for you. Good luck here at Cottonwood, gentlemen. Line up by units and wait for the eleven thirty movement call to return to your units together."

In all the hustle and bustle of the first day here, I had completely forgotten about the holiday on Thursday, and just hearing about it made me sad that I wasn't going to be with my family to celebrate it. I wouldn't even have any commissary to enjoy, and since sharing commissary around here was against the rules, it would probably be an all-around shitty day. After the eleven thirty movement came count time once again. Quietly studying my handbook, which had now been completely memorized, I made a mental note to myself to ask my mentor, Mr. Baxter, when we were able to go to the library, so I could check out a self-help book, which was the only other thing we could read. The other guys who weren't purple were busy doing homework assignments from classes at school or reading fiction books from the library, and I could only assume we had a specific time or day of the week that we were allowed to go there and get books. Given how much reading had taken over my life since being incarcerated, that time could not come fast enough for me. Reading was all I had done for the past ten weeks, and the thought of an entire library where I could choose what I could read instead of picking through the two or three small shelves of leftovers was sounding like an experience to look forward to.

When count cleared, I walked over to Mr. Baxter and asked him, "When do we get to go to the library, so I can get a self-help book, since I already have the handbook memorized?"

"Unit 4 goes on Tuesday and Thursday nights, but with Thanksgiving, they might change it to Friday."

I was already sick of hearing about the impending holiday, and it was only Monday. Something told me this was going to be a very difficult week for me or anyone to be locked up. We all stood around again, waiting to be called for lunch at any time, and a few guys I hadn't been introduced to yet came over and shook hands and chatted briefly. One of them was Mr. Castro, who was also from Washington, although he had been arrested in Kootenai County.

He lived in Spokane, Washington, which was right across the border from Coeur d'Alene, Idaho, where he was enjoying recreational activities on the huge lake there when his legal troubles began. As most of the guys who were here, meth was his drug of choice, and we seemed to hit it off rather quickly with all the interstate compact issues that were relevant to both of us. Interstate compact meant that once we were done with our riders and placed on probation, we could try to be placed on probation with the state where we lived. Since we were both residents of Washington when we were arrested in Idaho, we were both qualified to return there and fulfill our probation time and requirements in that state. He also had a daughter who lived there and was extremely disappointed to be spending the holiday away from her. He was only an orange card, so I knew he was still going to be here a while longer, and I knew we would have more chances to talk later.

"Upstairs, get on line for chow," said the voice on the speaker. After the usual lineup shuffle sideways, the lunch we were served was a couple of huge peanut butter sandwiches on homemade bread, a handful of potato chips, celery, carrot sticks, and half an orange, more food than I had expected. If it weren't for the rush, the meal would have been pretty decent. On the whole, after sampling breakfast, lunch, and dinner, I would say the meals were, on average, very good. It sure beat the hell out of Ada County oatmeal and two bologna sandwiches. After lunch was the first actual free time we were allowed since we got here, although we were still supposed to be studying the handbook.

I paced as I studied, and several more people came up to me and introduced themselves. I was getting to know quite a few people on the tier. Mr. Castro came up to me and said, "I hear you are looking for a book from the library, Mr. Walker."

"Yeah. Who told you that?" I asked.

"Mr. Baxter said you were asking about library time and told me, because he knows that I work there."

"What can you do for me?" I said with a smile and a friendly tone.

"If you know the title, I can look it up or I can just grab a self-help book randomly for you."

"Just grab any self-help book that looks good, I guess. I will have to trust your judgment. Thanks, I appreciate it."

The time gap in the daily schedule after lunch, I was told, was saved for what were called encounters. This was when a person's behavior had gotten so out of hand and they had received so many pull-ups that they needed to be straightened out by the whole community. Encounters were a bad thing to have happen to you, because it meant that you had not done anything to change your behavior and that the entire unit, the counselors, and the COs needed to get involved to bring your negative behavior to your attention. With no encounter today, there was an AA meeting in one of the dayrooms, prayer group in another, and the rest of the guys were programming, as was always required when you had no classes, unless you were a green card.

I had also learned through the grapevine that everyone here either had school classes to attend or some kind of drug and alcohol or behavior group scheduled. The ones who didn't do well on the educational test were required to take classes at the school to fulfill whatever classes they needed to get their GEDs. The school was state accredited, and they actually had graduations once a month for those who completed their requirements. Other people were in the group therapy sessions, including drug and alcohol classes and anger management classes, each of which lasted a month, and graduations from those groups were also big celebrations here.

Some people who were skilled in certain subjects also worked at the school. They were teacher's assistants and helped with classroom monitoring and tutoring. There was also a computer lab to help the inmates learn basic computer skills. Everyone was also required to complete a portfolio that had about twenty different items that were mandatory for completing their riders. Everything I was hearing about what went on here was encouraging and positive; the only questions I had left were what classes I would be required to take and how soon until I would be able to get into them. The way I figured it, the sooner I could get started, the earlier my chance of going home.

After one thirty movement, the unit again emptied out, with everyone heading off to group and classes. Some of the guys who stayed in the unit were already done with their programming and were just waiting for their names to be called so they could go home. All their program requirements were fulfilled, but there was only so much room on each bus for those going back to the county jails. We didn't have to return to the prison but instead went directly to the county from which we were sentenced. We waited for a week or so to go in front of our judge and be told we had received probation and our fixed sentence or were to be sent back to Cottonwood one more time to do it right.

At two o'clock, Mr. Tortelli gathered all the new purple cards and gave us new duties we were to undertake. They included passing out the bags that had just come back from the laundry room. All the laundry bags were dropped off in the dayroom, and it was our job to get the bag number when the owner came up to the door and told us what his was. Unfortunately, half of the guys would just barge in and take their bag, because guys had a way of distinguishing their bags from everyone else's. This created a total clusterfuck in the dayroom, since none of the green or blue cards would listen to any purple card that showed up yesterday. It wasn't my system, but I was required to work with it for the time being at least. For the next couple of hours, the dayroom was a constant flow of people coming in and out, bitching about which bags were whose, opening bags and items that were missing because they hadn't tied their bags properly. Since there was absolutely nothing I or even Mr. Tortelli could do about it, we just sat there and took it. Just as in the kitchen, there was a whole group of guys that worked in the laundry facility who I was sure would have been better at dealing with the problems than we were.

Some guys took the wrong bag, so others were missing theirs, while others grabbed what they thought were there bunkies' bags and got the wrong ones by mistake. The whole process sucked, and I began to analyze the situation and try to figure out a way to keep this nightmare from repeating itself on Thursday or whenever it was laundry day next. Once the mad rush started to slow down and we had slack time, I took Mr. Tortelli aside and asked him if we could talk about improving the system he was ultimately in charge of. I had no idea how long he had been service committee coordinator, but whatever was going on here with laundry distribution was not working as well as it could in a place as organized as I had seen so far. The snow-removal operation, even for the first major snow, was a well-oiled machine. I saw no reason that people getting their laundry couldn't be as efficient as well.

Mr. Tortelli and I left the dayroom and went over to his bunk area so we could talk privately. If I accidentally said anything that offended him, I didn't want to do it in front of all the other guys. I knew that in the military, if you went up the chain of command, you did it privately, and I was trying to use the same discretion here, whether I needed to or not. Better safe than sorry.

"I hope I'm not overstepping my boundaries here, but there has to be a better way to get that laundry passed out than the way we're doing it. How long have you been the service coordinator, and how long has the laundry been done the way we did today?" I asked him so politely, smiling the whole time so that he couldn't have gotten mad at me if he wanted to.

"I have been service coordinator for three weeks, and the laundry has been done this way since the day I got here three months ago. I have heard stories of laundry being passed out to the bunks, but that was before I got here."

"What if I and the rest of the barneys came up with a new system where the bags are passed out by us next time, since we have nothing else to do anyways? Anything must be better than the clusterfuck I just witnessed. Would you support us if we came up with a plan and ran it by you for approval before implementing it on Thursday?"

"With the short weekend because of Thanksgiving, we will have laundry again tomorrow. Think you guys can come up with something by then?"

"We can try. If we run it by you and it sounds good, will you let us try it? You are the service coordinator, so it's your call, right? We don't have to go through the COs and get approved or anything?"

"Nope, it's up to me. You figure it out, and I will back you up, Mr. Walker. Push up," he said as he walked away.

I went back to the dayroom and began brainstorming with guys who were pretty frazzled from the hectic bullshit we had just endured. I shared with them what I had just asked Mr. Tortelli, and everyone agreed that if we could come up with a better plan, they were all for it. After about half an hour of throwing ideas back and forth, we came up with something that might actually work. The real challenge we had was getting it all set up by tomorrow. I went back to Mr. Tortelli, and he sat down to hear what we had come up with.

"We divide the unit into four sections," I began to explain. "The north wall and south wall, upstairs and down. As we speak, four people are each personally going around the rest of the night, asking the thirty bunks in their section what their laundry bag numbers are. They are also going to introduce themselves and tell people what we are trying to do. We compile a master list, and when the laundry comes in, we keep everyone out of the dayroom except for the service committee guys. We just take a couple of bags at a time and look up whom they belong to on the list and set it on their bunk so it's there by four thirty count. That gives us a couple of hours to pass it out, and we avoid chaos in the dayroom. Laundry gets delivered to all the orange, blue, and green cards, while the purple cards get to meet all their neighbors. What do you think?"

"I like it, Mr. Walker. Well done. Push up to you and all the purple cards. We can try it tomorrow. Just make sure the list gets completed tonight."

With this, four thirty movement was called, and that meant once again it was count time. I had been here twenty-four hours, and things were already getting better. Before I got to my bunk, Mr. Castro came up to me and handed me a book called *Addictive Thinking*. I thanked him for it, and he said "No problem" as he headed to his bunk.

I read my new book through the count and a bit longer while pacing and waiting to go to chow. I also had to gather bag numbers for my side of the upstairs area, and right before chow was a good time to do that since everyone was fairly close to their bunks and waiting for the speaker to call us out. I was almost done except for a few people. One was my neighbor Eldrin, so I could get his at lights-out, and a couple of other kitchen workers who had already gone to get dinner started before we began this little project. We would be ready for tomorrow as planned.

After another big meal, I was sort of looking forward to the evening meeting, so I could figure out what exactly had happened last night, now that I had a little better understanding of how this place worked. We all sat in silence, waiting for the clock to strike six o'clock so we could begin. This time, the CO was in the bubble with the door open, so he could easily hear and see what was going on. The minutes from the morning meeting were followed by a few announcements, and then it was time for the push-ups and pull-ups to be read. Now that I knew that pull-ups were when someone wrote you up for doing something wrong, I could tell who was in trouble and who was being praised. Also, knowing more people made the whole deal more personal, since I had met twenty or thirty guys today. I wanted to know whom to work with and whom to stay away from during my stay so I wouldn't get into trouble. First were the pull-ups, and the expediter coordinator, Mr. Walsh, read them to the whole unit. During the reading, if your name was called, you were required to stand up and face the person who pulled you up and maintain eye contact.

"Mr. Jones, pulling up Mr. Smith for not helping to shovel snow when asked to do so," Mr. Walsh read. Followed by the required assignment for the offense. These were handed out by the COs but tracked and marked completely by the expediter committee. "A two-page essay on why everyone in the community needed to help the community, due in three days." The party in question now had three days to complete the assignment or the punishment would be more severe. The next punishment was a sanction for talking during the meeting, and you were not allowed to talk for two days. The punishments were known to the entire unit, so if anyone broke them, they become more severe with each repeated violation. Some guys lost their commissary for a week for sharing, others lost rec privileges, but most received essay assignment of two to three pages apologizing for their offense to the community.

Mr. Walsh then read the push-ups, so we could focus on the positive.

"Mr. Smith, pushing up Mr. Anderson for helping him with his computer lab work during his free time." Everyone applauded, and the two guys had to face each other. After a couple more were read, I was shocked to hear my name called by Mr. Walsh.

"Mr. Baxter, pushing up Mr. Walker for knowing everything to pass the orange card test within three hours of getting off the bus. Way to start your rider. Push up!" I was finally figuring out what all that "Push up, gentlemen" stuff was all about. It was saying, "Way to go, guys, you're doing good. Keep it up." It felt good to be recognized on my first day here for a good reason and not something bad. The expediter committee kept track of every write-up on a sheet with your name on it so the COs and counselors could go through your record to look at your behavior history from day 1 until the day you got on the bus to go home. If you got too many pull-ups, you were a likely candidate for an encounter, so my goal was to not get any for the whole time I was here. This way, the judge would have no choice but to give me probation, and I could go home. Too many pull-ups or encounters, and I would be coming back for another rider. I was going to do everything I could to keep that from happening.

CO Wiley came out of the bubble and introduced himself. "Good evening, community. My name is CO Wiley."

"Good evening, CO Wiley," 120 men responded in unison. Apparently, even the guys goofing off in the back rows began to respond when he was involved.

"For you, new guys, my name is CO Wiley, and with the departure of CO Gherkin, who is taking a medical leave, I am now the head CO for this unit." His comment drew a nice round of applause, which signified to me that he was one of the better COs to have. "I just have one quick announcement tonight, and that is, when you are piling up all the snow from Main Street, it is not okay to make a huge ramp up against the fence so everyone can just walk out of here. Is that understood?"

"Yes, sir," said all 120 of us once again, followed by a lot of laughter from the group after we painted ourselves a mental picture of what he described. The afternoon shovel crew had been piling the snow, so all someone had to do within a couple of days would be walk right over the fence. Whether or not it was intentional or humorous, I had no idea, but his comment made us all laugh. Then he went back into the bubble with a crooked little grin on his face, shaking his head as he closed the door.

The new twist for the night was all the going-home riders were dressed in the Cheetos orange jumpsuit I had arrived in yesterday. Even though we were one day early, they had been camped out in the dayroom upstairs, waiting until tomorrow to catch the bus back home. Each of them got up and gave a short goodbye speech and thanked a few close buddies they were going to miss. All of them told the new guys to enjoy it here because before you knew it, you'd be saying goodbye and it would happen much too quickly. Most loved their stay here and popped a few one-liners to a few buddies, and some even started to cry. It was all overwhelming, and it let me know that some people got pretty attached to this place in the short time they were here. But all seemed to enjoy their stay and got something valuable out of it, and that was what was important. It was all about change. Change in attitude, change in behavior, and change in the thought process that led to the behavior that had brought them here in the first place.

After the meeting, I was walking and reading once again, thanks to Mr. Castro, and enjoying the book he brought me from the library. On his way out to rec, Mr. Albert stopped me and gave me a bit of information that might be helpful in the future.

"Mr. Walker," he told me, "don't just read the self-help books. Take notes as you read them, so you can prove that you've read them. This lets your counselors and the judges know that you just didn't say you'd read twenty books, because this is proof. I will show you my notes when I get back from rec."

"Thanks, Mr. Albert. Have fun for me while you're there," I told him as he headed downstairs to line up for rec.

And the unit then quieted down with the departure of the senior members of the community, who had endured and complied with the rules. After the meeting tonight, I seemed to be observing the green cards that lost the rec privileges, and it appeared that sanction, above all, was one of the most devastating things to be handed out. Not only did you lose the rec, but you also were missing out on social time with green cards from other units.

I was a stranger to most of the things that happened around here from the minute I turned myself in on Labor Day weekend eleven or twelve weeks ago. It seemed like it had been another lifetime. Most of these guys had been in and out of jail and on the streets, doing God knows what with so many others who were here. Once they arrived here, it was like a high school reunion. They all knew twenty or thirty friends from the outside, and green card rec was the only place they could catch up on their bullshit stories. Taking that away was painful to them, and the funny thing was, the COs knew it, or the guys had not changed their behavior with the essay writing and previous sanctions, which meant the COs were left with no choice but to start hitting them where it hurt. Maybe now the offender would get an idea of what this place was about. It was not acceptable to disobey the rules of our society, which was why they were sent here. Sadly, something told me that more than a few of these guys were headed back here at least one more time, or maybe even prison.

I continued to pace repeatedly, up and down the center aisle, reading the book that Castro had somehow acquired for me from the library, stopping only to write down important passages on a sheet of paper I had managed to get from the education committee coordinator, Mr. Erickson. Since I had no commissary yet, he was obligated to hand out paper and pencils to anyone who would need it or had not yet received their commissary. Phrases I thought were interesting, important, or insightful made it onto a list, which was on yellow notebook paper. Before Mr. Albert and the rest of the green cards came back from rec, I had more than two pages of notes taken from the twenty pages of the book I had read so far. After reading nothing but fiction for the past couple of months, I found it interesting to read about how the mind processes addictive behavior and rationalizes it. Many of the symptoms and conditions the doctor talked about were dead on as far as the things I had done, as well as the reasoning behind it. I felt that in order to completely and permanently solve my problem, the best way to do so was to understand it so I could change it. I had five days left until I would be allowed to read fiction again, so I might as well learn as much as I could about my addictive behavior until then.

People would approach me occasionally about laundry bag assignments, asking for help, and by eight thirty, when the green cards finally returned, the list was 99 percent complete. I put my book down and began to compile a master list of the four sections from the unit, using a regular pen for the bunk numbers and a pencil for the laundry bag number. This way, when we all moved next week, the bag numbers of those who left could be erased and filled in with new ones, and the new purple cards could carry on the laundry bag distribution system. We had even set it up within the allotted time, as instructed by Mr. Tortelli. The only question left to be answered tomorrow was if it would work.

CHAPTER

34

FTER HE HAD SHOWERED, MR. Albert came over and showed me the notes he had taken and compared them to the ones I had already written for myself. We were on the same sheet of music, and I was on the right track according to him. I thanked him for the advice, which I vowed to continue to use with all the self-help books I intended to read as long as I was in Cottonwood. As long as I had an assistant senior coordinator sitting here, talking to me, I decided I would jump the chain of command just this once and see if I could get some information from Mr. Albert about that imminent phase change seminar. Mr. Albert anticipated me and, out of the blue, asked me, "Have you got yourself a word yet?"

"What word are you talking about?" I asked, just to be sure. I had a feeling he was talking about the phase change word from the list I had yet to see.

"You need to choose a word from the community values list that Mr. Kim has. Look them over good because the word you choose will be one you will be required to write a three-page essay on and then read it to the entire community during the morning meeting. You have seen the other guys read their phase changes, haven't you?"

"Yeah, and it's one of my favorite parts of the meeting."

"Me too! That's why you want to choose a good word that you can write a meaningful and inspirational presentation for. It's basically your coming-out party to the community. It's the first chance the whole community will have to hear a bit of your personal story and get to know your public speaking style and ability to educate others based on your own experience."

"So I just pick a word, write three pages, and stand up and read it. That's it?"

"Yeah. First, you must get Mr. Kim to okay your word, so we don't have ten people giving a phase change on the same subject. Then you need to submit to your committee coordinator for your first week. It's Mr. Tortelli, right? Then he signs off on it to make sure you understand the meaning of the phase change seminar. Some of these guys with a poor background in school just don't understand even after hearing two or three of them each night. He also checks it for language, content, and relevance to the subject matter. Then he passes it on to his assistant senior coordinator, who has to sign off on it, and then he passes it on to the senior coordinator, Mr. Ramirez. This way, if some guy gets up in front of the group and reads a bad phase change, the COs can look at the sign-off sheet and blame the coordinators for not getting some help for the new guy. If you don't get what the phase change is all about and you need help, ask your mentor, or your coordinator, and they will either help you or find you a tutor. The first thing you need to do is get with Mr. Kim and get a meaningful word before your buddies get the ones that are important to you before you do. Which will make the whole process easier on you."

"I get it. Thanks, Mr. Albert."

"Anytime. That's what I'm here for. Use your line of communication, usually, but I came to you tonight to talk about the book note thing, so don't worry about it tonight."

Now I completely understood the importance of getting to Mr. Kim to get a word before any other purple cards did. I checked the clock, and there were still ten minutes until lights-out, so I went to find out if it was too late to get a look at the list of words we were to choose from.

"Mr. Kim," I asked as I stuck out my hand to shake his. "What does a fellow have to do around here to be able to look at the list of words he can choose from for his phase change seminar?"

"Ask me to show you the list."

"That was easy. May I please look at the list, Mr. Kim?"

"You sure may, Mr. Walker. Hey, I heard what you guys are doing," he told me as he began to dig through his bin box to find the list. "The laundry thing has been a mess forever. I'm eager to see what you guys came up with." I gave him the brief rundown with the master list in pen and the bag numbers in pencil that we had made throughout the day, as well as the reasoning behind it. Personally, I felt that it was a good way for the new guys to meet the rest of the community and it served a much-needed purpose. He agreed whole-heartedly with my mission statement and then turned around with the list in his hand.

"Can I look it over at lights-out and give it back first thing in the morning?"

"I am not really supposed to, but you're only a few bunks down and you seem to have your act together, so I will let you do that. Just don't give it to anyone or let anything happen to it, okay?"

"No problem. Thank you, Mr. Kim. I appreciate this."

Now I could look over the list and pick a word to write an impressive phase change about, with no pressure to just pick one quickly in the morning. I organized my bunk area for 9:00 p.m. count time and got the last four or five missing laundry bag numbers for the master list, since by now everyone was back in the unit. With the laundry bag project now complete, I dropped it off to Mr. Tortelli and jokingly asked if he needed to be tucked in tonight before I hurried back upstairs to get into bed. My first full day here had been fairly productive, and I was feeling pretty good about it. Knowing that I wouldn't be able to sleep right away, I kept my book out along with my pen and paper, so I could take notes as instructed, and read until I was ready to sleep. Little did I know how far off sleep was actually going to be for me tonight.

CHAPTER

35

J UST LOOKING AT THE WORDS to choose from was inspiring. Words like *discipline, respect, commitment, honesty, change, family, truth,* and *principles* were among the many choices. I briefly looked at each word and decided whether it would be a suitable topic for me to write about or not. I instantly made up a short seminar in my head on each subject title and determined how I would write a phase change for it on that particular subject. As quickly as I attempted one in my head, I would dismiss it and move on to the next word on the list. I could have written about any of the subjects had I been forced to, but I wanted to let the whole community know who I was and give a phase change that would not soon be forgotten. I made a short list of the three or four possible topics, and I had it narrowed down to three and then put the list away for the night and picked up my book. Clearing my mind of the phase change and addressing it again in the morning would give me a fresh perspective. With all the information I had now been given on the phase change seminar, a strange thought popped into my head. Some guys who had language problems were shy to begin with and didn't perform well in crowded rooms. They would really struggle with this assignment.

I suddenly felt an overwhelming sense of nervousness for my buddy Jesus. He would hate to do this. He had a hard-enough time with English as it was and was extremely shy. Just the thought of this would probably make him quite anxious, let alone actually having to do it. He was a good friend, and I vowed to myself to help him with this project since I knew he was going to need help more than any of the others. I was beginning to obsess on the phase change. To keep my mind off this, I grabbed my book and began to absorb all the addictive thinking information from this very informative book that I could.

It was now nine fifteen, and all was quiet on tier, except for the house crew busily cleaning the tier. Suddenly, I heard a loud screeching alarm echoing throughout the unit at ear-piercing-decibel levels. Beeping nonstop. "Fire drill! Everybody get out to Main Street, right now!" said the coordinators all at nearly the same time. I got out of bed and threw on my slacks, boots, and coat before heading down the back stairway we were only allowed to use for emergencies and ran out the back door. It was colder than shit outside; it couldn't have been more than fifteen degrees out. I was one of the last ones to make it all the way around the building, as most people had come out the front. It wasn't that I was slow; it was just that from my bunk, in the center of the unit, going out the back door and then having to go around the building to get to Main Street, where everyone was assembling, made me the last one to get there.

The scene on Main Street was total chaos. Guys with no military experience were trying to teach others with no clue as to how to line up in four straight rows so the COs could count us to make sure everyone was out of the building safely and accounted for. Some people were shouting instructions to help get everyone in line; others were telling them to shut up so the COs wouldn't get pissed off at the noise level. It was a complete joke. Looking around, I noticed that some guys were completely dressed in proper uniforms from head to toe, most likely the house crew, who were cleaning. Some were dressed like me, and there were even some people with their boxers, boots, and a blanket wrapped around them and nothing else.

I overheard one of the COs tell another one of them this wasn't a drill and that the fire alarm was real. *Great,* I thought to myself, *this is going to take forever.* And most of us were already freezing our asses off after just five minutes. Finally, the situation began to settle down as the COs had their important count straightened out and everyone was finally accounted for. Since they didn't do this intentionally, the next thing to happen was that the COs had to make sure it wasn't an alarm malfunction and the building wasn't really on fire.

The whole process by now had taken at least fifteen minutes, and the frigid night's temperature was beginning to take its toll on people. We could see the COs running in and out of the building, trying to figure everything out. If the place was slowly smoldering and they sent us back inside, where someone could get hurt, it would bring a class-action lawsuit with lots of zeros at the end of it.

The crowd was definitely getting restless, and it seemed as if the danger had passed. Most of us wondered why we couldn't go back in. The guys in their boxers and blankets only were in the early stages of hypothermia. Their nonstop chattering was a testament to the bone-chilling temperatures. I gave my coat to one of them, trying to help him last a little bit longer, and I noticed others doing the same. We had now been outside for at least twenty-five minutes, and some of us wouldn't last much longer. Even though we were told to be quiet, the complaining and disgruntled mumbling grew louder and louder. The COs were still running around like they had no clue as to what the hell was going on. Finally, a few minutes later, we were given the all-clear to return to the building.

According to the clock on the second floor, we had been outside a total of twenty-seven minutes. It was fifteen degrees outside, and nobody had a clue as to what we were supposed to do, and most of the inmates were clueless as to how to do whatever it was we were supposed to be doing. It was a complete US Army regulation-style clusterfuck. It took about ten minutes for everyone to calm down and get back into bed so we could warm up.

At about 9:50 p.m., things were finally quiet, and I was reading my book with the covers pulled up all around me, still trying to get my bones to unthaw. The guys who were one week ahead of me on the house committee were busy getting the tier cleaned and scrubbed from the day's events when I heard a steady beeping sound. Oh my god, the fire alarm was going off again! This time, we began getting dressed for the long haul. I quickly threw on my slacks, boots, shirt, coat, and this time, I grabbed my blanket as well. I was still one of the first ones to leave the upstairs and head out the back door onto

Main Street. The COs were yelling at us to get out and telling us we were taking too long, but nobody was in a hurry to be stuck outside, freezing their ass off again. I was trying to help line people up on Main Street but was told to quit talking. If people didn't know how to do it and we couldn't talk to get ourselves organized, how could we ever line up and be counted? None of this made much sense to me, but so many things the COs did rarely seem to be logical, so why was I surprised that this would be any different? Lives were potentially at stake in this kind of situation, so I guess I was just hopeful that somehow that might be different this time. But I was wrong.

I quit trying to help and just took my place in the lineup and listened to the COs contradict themselves and what they had told us earlier. The coordinators who were supposed to be in charge were again clueless as to what was expected, and the whole scenario played itself out again. We might have gotten in trouble for taking too long, but 99 percent of the guys were warm this time, and so how long it took us to get out didn't really matter once the minutes began to tick away. It didn't matter to us, but the COs were extremely pissed off for some reason. Apparently, it took seven minutes for everyone to get out of the building, and I'm sure six of those had been spent getting dressed after the previous twenty-seven-minute nightmare we spent on Main Street. I wasn't really sure if this drill was planned just to see if we could improve our time, because they were so upset over how long it took us to evacuate the first time.

Whatever their motive, the result was the same, and by the time we settled down and the all-clear was given, we were allowed back inside after twenty-two minutes this time. Guys were still freezing their asses off, even fully dressed. Twenty-two minutes in the fifteen-degree weather still bordered on exposure. The clothing we had been issued would keep us warm during movement and if we were outside, shoveling snow or performing other physical labor, at daytime temperatures of around twenty-five or thirty degrees. Standing in formation in the middle of the night for half an hour was not what the state had in mind when the clothing issued was chosen for Cottonwood.

The pissing and moaning from the tier took much longer to dissipate this time, and rightfully so. We had just spent forty-nine of the last fifty-four minutes standing in the frigid Idaho winter night. We were doing something nobody in charge had taught us how to do properly. We were getting our asses chewed out for not doing it according to the standards they expected, even though they never let us know what was expected of us.

This place was starting to remind me of the Army big-time. The Army would do things like that just to see how we adapted and solved the problem. We would be told to do something one way by one drill instructor and then told it was wrong and to do it another way by a different DI, just to see how well we would make the adjustment.

Eventually, I faded into oblivion, and I woke up at 2:00 a.m. with my book on my chest. When I got up to go to the bathroom, I noticed I wasn't the only nocturnal creature on the tier. There must have been seven or eight others who had difficulty sleeping around here. They were all reading and keeping to themselves as I glanced out of the window and noticed the snow was once again falling all around the silent compound. I quickly got back in bed in anticipation of a long day ahead with a shovel or a room in my hand.

CHAPTER

36

B Y 5:01 TUESDAY MORNING, I had already learned that in order not to be held up by the line waiting to shave, I had to go directly to the sinks once I woke up. After that, I could work at my own pace and was ready to go at 5:10. I took the phase change list back to Mr. Kim and thanked him for letting me look it over, then I went downstairs to check in with Mr. Tortelli, to see what I could do for him or the service committee.

"Go see Mr. Thorne and see about shoveling all that new snow out there. I can't wait till you get some coffee on commissary." He sarcastically smirked. He was still in his underwear, unshaven, and in the middle of making his bunk.

"I am just a morning person," I said as I headed off to find Mr. Thorne and see if I could help blaze a trail to the chow hall before breakfast and lead by example. I was already hoping to be a coordinator someday, and it would be much easier to send guys out to shovel snow all day with a clear conscience, knowing that when I was a purple card, I had done more than my fair share. Not being able to walk as much as I had been in RDU and county, and not being able to go to rec for another fifty-seven days, I also figured I could use the exercise. Off I went with a couple of other guys, out in the morning cold to set a good example and lay the groundwork for a future leadership role in the community. The five of us shoveled, swept, and hauled for forty-five minutes, and by the time we headed back in, I was ready for a nice, big breakfast and some heat. I was even offered another opportunity to drop last night's fresh snow on my unexpecting coworker on the way back inside, thanks to the large amounts of fresh snow that fell overnight. Every cloud has a silver lining, right? I figured, if you didn't know someone well enough to dump snow on their head after forty-five minutes of hard labor, then you were never going to.

I calmed down and changed out of my sweat-soaked shirts into a fresh, clean one and went downstairs to make sure Mr. Tortelli knew where I had been so that on his clear, safe path to breakfast, he appreciated my hard work. I also wanted to make sure we were on the same sheet of music and there were no problems with the laundry bag delivery program, which we had spent so much time working on yesterday. Everything according to him was ready to go, so when downstairs was told to get online for chow, I went back upstairs to be ready to do the same in five minutes when we went. With the routine of the day already etched in my mind on only the third day here, we had cleared a spot in the snow on Main Street right in front of the kitchen, for half the unit to stand, while waiting to go into the chow hall, so our feet didn't get cold and wet. After the usual chow hall shuffle and quick meal, I went back upstairs and took out my book and notepad, so I was being productive during count time.

I wasn't trying to kiss ass, but you never knew when the COs or the counselors were in the bubble and watched you for twenty or thirty minutes before calling you into their office for introductions. That way, if you sat there and bullshitted your way through your first meeting with them, they know you were a lying piece of shit and your work here was a constant uphill battle. Whether this rumor was true or not, I wanted to make sure it made no difference by constantly working on trying to improve myself and setting a good example for others to do so as well. It beat going to prison for three years, and who knew, maybe something good would come of it. I also wanted to give the book back to Mr. Castro by eight thirty movement when he left. The motive behind all this was the hope he would get me another one today while he was at work. I was dutifully jotting down notes from my self-help book when the COs came by and I shouted out my name and bunk number, hardly even looking at them while continuing with my studies.

During the morning meeting, I heard a couple more phase changes, which, with all the laundry bag and fire drill excitement,

I had almost forgotten about. For being in prison, I found myself extremely busy, and I had not even been here three full days yet. Looking out the window during the meeting, I could tell it was going to be a sunny, clear, and beautiful day even if it was only twenty degrees. It sure beat the cloudy, wet, and drizzly weather I was forced to endure all winter long in Seattle.

Today, Mr. Castro got up in the morning meeting as we were wrapping it up and gave his version of David Letterman's top 10 list with a Cottonwood twist, and the whole unit was laughing so hard when he was done—some of the men even had tears in their eyes. The guy made fun of the chow hall line, the bubble, and even the fire drill last night, all under the guise of good humor and with preapproval from the COs before the meeting started. It was good to know that a smile on everybody's face to start the day was more important than taking themselves too seriously and letting us have a little fun in the process. Castro seemed really comfortable in front of the group, and I only hoped that I, too, would be when it came time for my phase change seminar.

After the meeting, Mr. Tortelli gathered all the new guys around when we were done putting away the flags and tables, and he said, "You purples only have one thing to do today. It is a meeting at the school to get your portfolio information package. Other than that, be ready to pass out laundry when it shows up, study your handbook, or shovel snow." I checked with Jesus to see what he was doing, and he was still working on his rules in the handbook, so I let him be while I went up to Mr. Thorne, who said I was his favorite purple card due to all the hard work I had been volunteering to help take from his overworked house committee. While his guys worked on cleaning up Main Street, I was told to go around the unit yard and clear the walkway. That didn't sound too difficult, even though it was a pretty long walk away. I came up with a good idea, though, and went to get Jesus to come out and help me, and in return, I would also help him.

"Hey, bunkie," I said to him as I put on my coat and the gloves Mr. Thorne gave all the shovelers. "Come outside and shovel snow around the unit with me. We can go over the rules as we work. It will get you some fresh air, and I know you miss me." I walked up next to him and put my arm on his shoulders.

"Okay, bunkie, let me get dressed. It's probably freezing out there."

"Don't be a big baby. It's nice and sunny just like back home in Guadalajara."

"Si, but in Guadalajara it's like ninety-five degrees and sunny." He had a good point, but I didn't feel like arguing over something as trivial as seventy-five degrees. We went out and began to shovel and sweep the walkway between the unit and the chapel. We had to find it as we went since neither of us had ever seen any part of it besides what was closest to the building. There was a cement sidewalk that went down the entire length of the building; that much I had known from getting out during the fire drills. It was about three feet from the building and wide enough for two people to walk side by side and stay on the cement.

We shoveled and swept all the snow up against the building in the two- to three-foot gravel area that surrounded the building. Then as I begin to ask Jesus his cardinal rules and helped him when he struggled, we started to discover and follow the path slowly up the hill toward the chapel. In the front of the building only a fence away from Main Street, a sidewalk slowly crept uphill until it butted against the chapel wall and another fence. On the back of the unit, it was a flat walkway for about ten yards, and then there were about fifteen cement stairs that went up the embankment to the same chapel wall. Jesus was getting better at his rules, and we worked up such a sweat that we took off our coats outside, which you were only allowed to do while on work detail.

The path that connected the two walkways on top of the hill running next to the chapel was gravel, so we just swept it as best as we could and hoped it would be good enough. It was nice to see I could now continue my pacing outside when allowed to without having to go up and down the center aisle inside the unit.

Jesus was spouting off the rules and had pretty much memorized them by the time we were done with the sidewalk, so we headed out to Main Street to see if we could be of any help out there. Only about fifteen minutes with the house committee, we noticed a huge laundry bin being wheeled toward our unit, and I knew that the decisive moment with our little project was about to be upon us. We checked in our broom and shovel and went inside to get Mr. Tortelli and try to see if all the time we spent on the laundry delivery system was worth it.

"All right, you purple cards," Mr. Tortelli said in his ultradeep baritone. "You guys want to make this a better place, you came up with a good idea, and now let's see if it actually works."

"Sorry to interrupt," I said, "but if we don't put a sign up on the door to keep people from coming in and screwing up whatever we are doing, we will never know if it works or not."

"Mr. Walker," he said as he took a firm stance, folded his arms, and squared up in front of me. "You live with 119 roommates in a place like this. Yesterday you guys went around and got everybody's bunk number matched up with their personal laundry bag number. Your list was very thorough, and you have 120 names and numbers on your list. I ask you, Is there anybody in this unit who doesn't know what the hell we are trying to do?"

"If they don't, then they are complete idiots, Mr. Tortelli. So my guess is yes, there are probably a few."

"Point taken, Mr. Walker. You guys do whatever it is you're going to do now, and I'll make sure nobody comes in here."

"You want one of us to do it?"

"I better do it. Nobody will listen to a purple card, but they know better than to mess with me."

Over the course of the next forty-five minutes or so, Mr. Tortelli was true to his word and kept everybody out of the dayroom so that we could work out magic. I think he saw it more like a train wreck that he would enjoy being a witness to, since on more than one occasion, I heard him tell people that the barneys had started this fiasco and we could now sit back and enjoy the show. Apparently, in the past, when this was tried, everyone got the wrong bags and inmates had their personal clothing and purchases from the commissary stolen. Other unfortunate episodes occurred, and finally, the unit leadership demanded delivery be stopped because it caused more problems than it solved.

With this past history, the scuttlebutt around the unit was to let us find out for ourselves just how badly we could fuck this up and then put the idea back on the shelf. I felt, with proper organization and supervision, all the previous problems that plagued us, they could be avoided if addressed properly before they began.

"Okay, guys, this is our chance to make a mark here, so let me explain some things I have heard about in the tiers. They all think this is a joke and we are going to fuck things up. I guess the people who had tried this before were complete morons, because they stopped after two or three days. I believe we have a good system ready, and if we put out a little extra, it will show them that we are an awesome group of purple cards, unlike any they've seen before."

If the new routines take too long, people will get pissed off. They want their clean clothes right away. If anything comes up missing, the guy who delivers the bag will be blamed and searched by COs. "Don't just drop off the bag. First, introduce yourself so we will get to know everyone. We want to do this right, quickly, and socially, so in six months, when we are gone, they will look back and say, 'Those guys did it. Why can't you?' They all laughed at us, looking forward to our failure. Even Mr. Tortelli thought this would blow up in our faces. Now is our chance to prove them all wrong."

During the next forty-five minutes, everything went according to plan. Everybody received their bags in an orderly way. We pulled it off without a hitch. Before lunch, the word on the tier was verbal thumbs-up; the entire unit had nothing but praise for the job we had done. After lunch, we all headed to the school for our portfolio class and our lesson of the day.

CHAPTER

37

THE PORTFOLIO WAS A PACKET of information we were required to assemble about ourselves to help us find employment once we returned to the real world. It contained job résumé, educational background, employment history, sample budgets, including allocation for the court cost, recitation, and cost of supervision, which all of us would most certainly have once released. Some of the stuff we were supposed to do for the portfolio was only available in the computer lab in the library. It was there for those who didn't have everything in their packets; this meant we would learn some basic computer skills before leaving. This included me. There was also a goal worksheet to help us plan. Patient information was included, but we were told there would be a whole other class specifically on probation, most likely on Friday after Thanksgiving. With the short week for the holiday, they were trying to cram all our orientation stuff into one week. We were also given the educational class assignments required to complete our riders. Some of us were required to earn GED while incarcerated. We were all expected to learn how to think clearly for a change. Behavior classes needed to be completed before some could be returned to living among others.

How many classes we took, how full they were, and when they started were all determining factors for establishing the date of our release. If the required class was full for two months and took a month to complete, we would be held longer. We could be stuck inside the walls of Cottonwood for up to four more months than we would be otherwise, including however long it took to be transported, once all the requirements were fully met. When I was to hand in the file that was to contain my information, there was nothing under the heading—NONE. We were told that if none was listed, that meant we were required to join the compound education workforce and assist the guys who needed help. Those who had skills in math or computers, were bilingual, or had educational background in any subject needed to get their GED were to work in the school as teacher's aides. Some would be kitchen workers or help out in the laundry room. With my construction background, I would be happy almost anywhere except the kitchen. Maybe it was my military history that gave me an advantage, but I had a good hunch that I wanted to avoid the kitchen at all cost. These guys left for the chow hall two hours before each meal and returned about an hour after and came into the morning and evening meetings asking for permission to join the meeting already in progress. Usually, they started you with dishwashing. When I had worked at a buffet restaurant at sixteen, I had absolutely hated scrubbing the pots and pans. I would volunteer for anything but the kitchen work. *Anything.*

After the class ended and we had everything we needed to get to work on our portfolios, I began to ask around about what jobs on the compound were the best to have, and most people agreed with me that staying as far away from the kitchen as possible was a good idea. It did have some advantages, like being able to sleep during the day at times to make up for getting up at 4:00 a.m. to get breakfast ready. I am sure, even though it was strictly against the rules to take food out of the chow hall or help yourself as you worked, people were figuring out a way to eat well if they worked in the kitchen.

Maybe laundry was the way to go. Nice and warm coats, new and dry boots, socks with no holes in them, and nice, thick sheets and blankets for your bed. Although from what I had seen so far of the laundry CO when I was late getting my supplies the first day, I wasn't sure if I wanted to work for the compound's biggest prick for the next few months. I had to choose wisely and go for a good job, since whatever I chose or persuaded for would most likely be where I would be stuck for at least six hours a day, five to seven days a week, for the foreseeable future. I had no special educational skills and had actually hoped to take a computer class while incarcerated, so helping to teach one was definitely out of the question. The school jobs were nice because they only held five classes five days a week and you had the weekend off. The kitchen and laundry guys worked seven days a week. I decided to do more investigating and become well-informed before jumping into a shitty job and getting stuck with some CO I hated. It would make the rest of my time here unbearable.

We also learned in the class that we had weekends off. For around here, school and classes, at least. We also had the added bonus of Thursday off this week for the holiday. A day off was great, but that also meant we would only have two meals. With no commissary yet and the no-sharing policy, this meant I was destined to spend the Thanksgiving holiday hungry. Having to watch everyone else stuffing their faces while catching the occasional glimpse of food on TV. With the Seahawks in first place in the NFC west, the football season was actually becoming interesting. Knowing my luck, the Seahawks would probably win their first Super Bowl this year. Instead of being at home for the victory, I would be stuck in here. I really wanted to be able to see the games. I knew there was a way to do it; I just had to figure it out quickly and in a way that wouldn't get me into trouble.

I spent the rest of the beautiful Sunday afternoon gathering information from anybody who would give it and pacing around the outside walkway Jesus and I had cleared off earlier. The sunshine was enjoyable, and it felt good to put some miles on my old legs; I hadn't been able to get out of the building and stretch for a while. Inmates would come out and join me for a little while, introduce themselves, and chat for ten or fifteen minutes and then give up and go back inside. In between conversations, I would go over the possible topics for my phase change seminar, and as the temperature quickly dropped late in the afternoon, I had chosen my word. I had a good start on my presentation. As Castro came back into the dorm for the four thirty count, he handed me another book from the library called *The 7 Habits of Highly Effective People*. Mr. Albert had asked him to get that one for me because he had already read it and said it was an impressive book.

"What job is it that you do in the library?" I asked Castro. I thought the library might be the perfect place for an avid reader like me to happily occupy his time at the Cottonwood Hilton. Tonight, I would actually get to go to the library for the first time, and since we couldn't go to rec, this was going to be the highlight of my entire stay here until now.

"I have the best job on compound," he told me. "I work in multimedia, but my office is inside the library, so I have total access to the shelves all day long."

"What is it you actually do?"

"We make movies and PowerPoint presentations for safety classes and whatever else Mr. Walters wants us to do. We have access to computers, music, and even some movies we can watch on the VCR. It's pretty cool. We do what we want all day and sometimes even take a nap."

"How do I get a job there?"

"You can't right now. We are fully staffed with four people, and our office is only the size of about three bunks."

"When does the next green card leave so I can get a job in there?" I asked him. The job sounded like the perfect one for me.

"Not for over a month, and unless somebody gets fired, you will be scrubbing dishes in the kitchen by the time there's another opening in here," he said, laughing at my predicament. "I sit in there and make up top 10 list, write letters home to my daughter, and work on my portfolio whenever I want. It's the best job on the compound."

"What qualifications do I need?"

"You need to prove you're proficient with Movie Maker software and able to use PowerPoint and video imaging programs to make, edit, and add some bites to presentations and videos we make for the school and for the safety classes. I can show you tonight if you are going to the library." I was zero for four as far as matching the requirements, and since getting fired could get you in big trouble here, jumping into something I was totally unqualified to do might not be a wise move. Castro had sparked my curiosity about his job, though, and I told him I would see him tonight in the library. What else did I have to do?

After dinner at the meeting, all the purple cards were pushed up two or three times for the beautiful job we did with the new laundry delivery, including its impact on the community. CO Wiley even commented on our achievement when he came out of the bubble for his evening ritual.

"These new barneys have grasped what this place is about quickly, and their ideas and actions were beneficial to the community as a whole. The more we all get to know one another, the more comfortable everyone is about opening up, sharing, and trying to make this place better for all of us. This is the only way the program works. If you hide in the back row and never comment, don't join in and participate like some do not, and you know who you are, then we all suffer."

He looked over the rows of the chairs all the way to the back while the rest of us were laughing.

"Then you don't get the benefit of the community model we are trying to achieve. Well done, purple cards. Push up." When he said this, he was looking right at me, and I couldn't help but wonder if it was by coincidence or if he had any idea of the effort I had personally put into this or if he knew the role I had played. Maybe he was tipped off by Mr. Tortelli, or even Mr. Albert, who was a senior assistant and ranked high enough up to have the ear of the COs. Whatever the reason, it was good to be recognized by the COs so early in my stay. Or maybe it wasn't and I was better off keeping a low profile, doing my time, and moving on. At this point, it was too late to stress out over it. The deed was done. He also gave us a brief rundown on the fire drill protocol, so we had some idea what to expect of us. Hopefully, last night's problem wouldn't become a pattern.

CHAPTER 38

AFTER THE MEETING, THOSE WHO wanted to could go to the library for one hour. You had to stay at the library the entire hour and come back as a group, but it was still the first trip I'd take to any library since I became an avid reader. I could check it all out and see what titles would await me when I could read. I also was hoping to check out Mr. Castro's little workplace just in case I was somehow able to get my foot in the door of his cushy job. As usual, we signed out to the library and headed over as a group. I was startled when I got there by how many books there were to choose from. It was a small building, but considering I had been getting books from a small cart at county and RDU, it was good to see such a large selection. I started checking for my favorite authors to see how many of their books I had yet to read. I was specifically looking for a few titles I had heard through the grapevine were exceptional readings. I liked to mix up my reading list with a little Western fiction so I wasn't stuck in a rut. Too much of a good thing always seems to ruin one's enjoyment eventually.

I was limited to what was available in the dorms or what was sent to me and my friends, but now for the first time, I was staring at a thousand titles, and it was truly wonderful to have more of a selection. It was liberating and exciting. I hadn't read much before being locked up. It made me realize just how much being incarcerated can change a man. To be excited to be in a library was new to me.

The library itself had only three walls of books and three free-standing rows of shelves between them. It was long and narrow and quite confined, but the twenty-five of us who were there managed to move around without crowding the others while looking for books.

Choice was one of the few luxuries we had during our incarceration. Nearly everything else was chosen for: what was included in the meals we ate, when we could eat, what we could buy on commissary, how much we could spend each week, what we wore, what time to get up, and when we went to bed. It was a very controlled existence for a group of men who, for the most part, had been in control of their own lives for years. We managed to get drugs, survive, and even profit from the transactions with other inmates quite well, though.

I went over to the self-help section to see if Castro and Albert were doing me any favors with their choice of books for me to read; I was pleasantly surprised to find out they were giving me good advice. The self-help section was rather large, but considering why we were here, it was appropriate. Castro would likely continue his little deal with me if I couldn't get a job in the library. I would be able to just tell him what books to get for me instead of recommending whatever he liked. I could read it, take notes, and give it back to him to return as soon as I was done.

The hour flew by, and before I knew it, it was time to go back. I checked out two books, which was our limit, both from the self-help section, which I was still limited to. I also had a nice list to choose from for the rest of the week, so I was feeling pretty good. When you are locked up, you don't have much to look forward to, but with the list of books to read, with titles that actually intrigued me, it meant a lot to me. These books were like Christmas presents that I had yet to open. The longer it took to open them, the longer the holiday would last.

That night, while lying in bed, I wondered if I could keep from being thrown into the kitchen worker pool long enough to get the media production job with Castro, which I now wanted more than ever. The library was the place for me. I could even try to be a librarian but would have to work nights like tonight during free time so people could check out books. Once I became a green card, that would suck, because I would miss rec. After I had gotten up at 5:00 a.m. the past few days, sleep was a welcome thought at 9:00 p.m. Just as that thought crossed my mind, the fucking fire alarm went off. Again. This was going to get old real fast.

We followed CO Wiley's advice during the meeting, and within five minutes, we were lined up and accounted for, waiting to go inside. With three fire drills thus far in two nights, anyone might think that the time it took us to do it might be even less. But for 120 guys, it was pretty good. The sky was clear all day, but it was colder at night. The COs must have learned something yesterday, because after only about ten minutes, we were given the all-clear to go back inside. Once inside, the COs began messing around with the fan in the back stairway, which wasn't venting the steam from all the showers after rec. A lot of guys showered from eight thirty to nine, and the humidity level was setting off the fire alarm again and again. They had to figure out how to solve the problem, or we would end up doing this every night, which didn't sound like much fun to me. I suggested to Mr. Albert that he or someone else tell CO Wiley that we could turn on the fan manually each night from eight thirty until lights-out, and it would most likely solve the fire drill problem until maintenance could fix it permanently. I was already sick and tired of this, and what the hell did I have to lose by suggesting it? I hoped my idea would trickle up the line of command to someone who would listen and we could actually go to bed at nine o'clock instead of nine thirty or ten o'clock each night.

Wednesday, as with most days when you got up at 5:00 a.m., came all too early again. It was the usual morning routine, except today I didn't have to shovel snow for a change. Killing time before breakfast, I went downstairs to get the scoop on what was in store for us today from Mr. Tortelli, who was not a morning person. I was inspection ready at 5:10 a.m., and he looked like he hadn't done anything yet.

"I have a question, Mr. Tortelli."

"Well, hopefully I have an answer for you, Mr. Walker."

"Since your bunk is in front of the bubble, how do you stay in bed until five fifteen without getting into trouble?"

"Fuck you, Mr. Walker" was his answer to my question, which also got a good laugh from his neighbors, who were almost ready too.

"Mr. Tortelli, I am verbally pulling you up for using offensive language."

"Thank you, Mr. Walker. I will get on top of that."

That was a community-handbook-authorized verbal pull-up, to help modify a man's behavior without giving him a written pull-up, which would get him in trouble. He gave me the community-hand-book-authorized response, and that way, I wouldn't get pulled up for not verbally pulling him up, which technically I was supposed to do, but most people let small things slide. Not wanting to comply so close to bubble was a bad idea, so we both got a good laugh and set good example of "proper behavior and proper response" for those around us.

"What five minutes of important information will the state of Idaho force us to sit through in a two-hour class to receive today?" I asked Mr. Tortelli.

"You have this place figured out already, don't you, Mr. Walker? I think you go see Ms. Robertson for your probation orientation class. I am not quite sure. They usually tell me what's up before the morning meeting. Probation review and library are all you have left, I think."

"I'll check back with you when you're done putting stuff away after the meeting. Thanks anyways."

It was good to know the orientation was almost complete. For me, orientation stuff was like my classes during basic training. They have to teach you things at a slow pace to make sure even the dumbest guys can figure it out. That translates to five or six guys being bored for two hours, while fifteen or twenty guys go over the easiest instructions ten times. In prison, some of the tools in the shed aren't very sharp.

At breakfast, two guys a few seats down from me from the next unit in the chow line had a little problem with their meal. They started to argue quietly at first, since there was no talking in the chow hall, but before you knew it, they were throwing food at each other, which turned into a fistfight right over the table. Everybody who was close enough cleared away while the COs separated them and then handcuffed the combatants and hauled them off to segregation. I never found out what happened since they were from a different unit, but I did find out how fast a rider could end. The answer was three seconds, because that was how long they were fighting before being cuffed. Instead of three or four months here, they would be going to the yard for three or four years. Whatever it was, I doubt it was worth it. What particularly sucked was that it was likely there was one person who was the aggressor and one guy who was just defending himself, and for doing so, he would go to prison for three or more years. It didn't seem fair, but it was very likely.

I listened intently to the phase change seminars at the morning meeting since to go from purple to orange, on Sunday we had to submit and read our papers by then or we wouldn't move up. It was a way to force everyone to participate, or else they would stay purple and continue to comply with all the restrictions that came with it. I had heard of people completing their rider as a purple card, but it would really suck to go through the whole program with purple card restrictions. Having put no effort into the program, they probably would be sentenced to a second rider by a judge.

I spent the better part of the morning walking the loop outside and occasionally stopping at the tables provided to jot down ideas for my phase change as they popped into my head. I also explained the concept to Jesus so he could begin preparation for his, which might take him a little longer than most. He was smart, but his translation skills needed a little work. He probably needed even more work on his public speaking skills. He even admitted he would be scared to death when his time came. The first night when we all stood up and introduced ourselves, he was a stuttering, sweaty, nervous wreck. I was hoping to help him with the translation issues so that his phase change presentation would come out smoothly. I also asked him to read it to me out loud until he became comfortable reading it so that by the time he went up in front of the whole unit, it would be a piece of cake for him.

After lunch, our group went down to Ms. Robinson's class, called prep for probation. Here we were given a brief insight into what would be expected of us once we received probation. In today's class, we began the lengthy process of bureaucratic paperwork that, if we were lucky, would be completed by the time we left. Today, I had more questions than usual since my situation was more complicated than those of all the guys from Idaho, because I was from out of state. I needed to apply for an interstate compact so my probation could be shifted to Washington, since I was a resident of that state when I was arrested. After I questioned the first four or five things she had to say, Ms. Robinson told me to ignore the class and see her after everybody else left to avoid any confusion.

The average intelligence level of the guys in this room was simply amazing. She would tell them line by line what piece of personal information to put in each base, and still 40 percent of these clowns still had to ask her what they should put down given their situation, which had no relevance to the answer they were told to give. After about an hour, she was finally fed up and told them to quit asking questions since this class was almost an hour behind schedule. And I had thought the guys in basic training were slow. These guys had done so many drugs that their last flickering brain cell was too busy keeping their bodies alive to allow them to think properly.

Finally, after three hours in a two-hour class, she let everybody go back to the unit except me. I had a whole other set of papers to fill out, given my situation. It took me only fifteen minutes. By this time, it was count time and she had to radio into the COs that I was with her and accounted for, and then I had to stay there until count was cleared. When I strolled into the unit after missing count, everybody thought I was in deep shit, until I told them what had happened.

I read and worked on my phase change for the rest of the day and into the night. I was getting close to having my first rough draft complete. Then all I needed was to rewrite it with some careful editing and turn it in to Mr. Tortelli for approval. I knew I would be the first of our group to read one, and I wanted to show them and the rest of the unit how it was supposed to be done. At eight thirty, when the green cards started to shower after rec, the COs manually started the exhaust fan in order to vent the steam from the showers and keep the humidity down. My idea worked at lights-out, when, for the first time in three nights, we were granted the luxury of not having a fire drill. Being mentally exhausted from all the activity but getting up at 5:00 a.m. was becoming a little easier each day. I looked forward to getting lots of rest because I had a feeling that tomorrow's holiday was going to be a tough day for everyone here.

The public tends to get a little edgy during the holidays, and this often leads to a lot of people doing stupid things that get them into all sorts of trouble. It is probably worse when you are serving time with people who are a bit unstable to begin with. I had a funny feeling about tomorrow, and as far as I was concerned, Thanksgiving would not be over soon enough for me.

CHAPTER

39

AKING UP FROM A DREAM and realizing you are still behind bars is sometimes the hardest part of any inmate's day. Waking up on Thanksgiving in prison isn't any easier. The Thanksgiving holiday was finally here, and as far as the state of Idaho was concerned, today was just another day of programming for us riders. This was my first day with a holiday/weekend schedule, and I was curious to learn if we got to sleep in or if we could skip the meeting, but I was wrong on both counts. We were awakened at 5:00 a.m. as usual, but with a late breakfast, we had nothing to do but program until the seven o'clock count, followed by the morning meeting. Then we ate a huge breakfast, not because of the holiday, but because we would not get a lunch, and dinner was still at the same time. This meant it had to be huge or those of us with no commissary would have a rough time making it until dinner was served. It was around 9:00 a.m. when the CO's voice came over the speaker and delivered a brief announcement.

"Because of Thanksgiving, we will skip the superclean and move right into free time. Enjoy, gentlemen."

This brought a round of applause from the entire unit, and I could only assume that we had been granted a reprieve from whatever horror superclean involved and the rest of the day was ours to do as we pleased. A lot of guys headed for the dayroom to watch the football game, others headed for the recreation committee coordinator's bunk to check out games to play, while others headed straight for their bunks and were fast asleep before I could even get downstairs to ask Mr. Tortelli what free time meant for purple cards.

"Well, Mr. Walker, it means absolutely nothing for you and your unfortunate group. You are required to be programming at all times during your first week here, and as a purple card, you do not get any free time even on Thanksgiving. You can't watch TV until you are a blue or green, so even the orange cards miss out on the football games today. I will help you out, though, Mr. Walker, because of all you guys have done this week and the success of your laundry system. I want you all to come with me."

He got off his bunk and waved his arm for me and the other barneys downstairs to follow him and see what joy we would be allowed to experience on this particular holiday. By now, I was curious to learn what he had in store for us, but I had a feeling this was going to be a good thing.

We went upstairs, and Mr. Tortelli started barking orders at us to follow him. We had set up two folding tables where we could work on our handbooks, read self-help books, and take notes or work on our phase changes together and help one another out as a group. We had been instructed by our coordinator to be at this specific location and do as he said, so if anybody had a problem with it, they could take it up with him. Mr. Tortelli had taken care of us and made the holiday nice for all of us by setting up the tables right in front of the dayroom so as we did our work, we could also see the TV, as long as we were discreet about it and didn't make it too obvious what we were really up to. For the rest of the morning, we all sat at our tables and looked over into the dayroom and got to see some football, all while we compared ideas about our phase changes and bragged about how well the laundry delivery had gone. All of us had been praised at the meeting, but most of us had also made friends while doing it, and this had helped us to make social connections. If one of the guys you met while delivering laundry helped you with the rules, or your phase change, then not only did we accomplish our goal with the laundry, but we also made a new friend that could help throughout the rider.

Most people here were friends with the guys that they came in with, since they had spent time at RDU together, just as I was pretty close with my fellow purple cards, especially Jesus, who was my cellmate in RDU. That left 118 guys in the unit to get to know. And by the time I left, most of these guys would already be gone and there would be 118 new guys to meet. It was impossible to know everyone, but I had a feeling that the more friends I made in a place like this, the better off I would be in the long run.

Even though we had free time all day, at 10:55, everyone turned off the TVs and put away the games, and we folded up our tables and put them back in the dayroom up against the wall. The guys who were asleep had to wake up and be fully dressed and inspection ready for the eleven o'clock count time. I used the lid to my bin box on my lap as a table to write notes in my book while the fifteen minutes it took to count the entire compound slowly ticked by. After count was cleared, all activities resumed as usual, and I decided to go out and pace for a bit to stretch my legs. Within fifteen minutes, the compound-wide speaker came on and everyone was told to remain inside the unit until further notice. This was something new. I went in and asked Mr. Tortelli what was going on.

"Visitors are coming through the gates, and nobody can be outside until they are safely inside the chow hall, where the visits take place." He also told us we could look out the upstairs window to see the visitors but not to get caught doing it or we would get written up. Forced back inside, I couldn't believe what was going on by the microwave next to my bunk. There were probably eight or nine people in line for the microwave all with Tupperware items full of water, ready to make their spreads just like back in county. By now, I was beginning to get hungry, and the aroma of the food cooking was difficult to handle, knowing I couldn't have any of it. I went over to the tables that the guys had set up again, and we all kept working on our phase change presentations.

Between everybody eating their commissary and the banquets being advertised on the TV, I knew it was only going to get worse throughout the day. Not knowing anybody well enough yet to get a ramen from without them thinking they would get into trouble, I wasn't about to ask any of them for food no matter how hungry I was. All this on the traditional stuff-your-face-until-you-fall-asleep holiday. I thought about life back in Everett and the spreads going on at home, complete with cold beer, maybe a Bloody Mary, or even something I had really missed, milk. What I would give just to be able to chug a half-gallon of milk! It was those small items that we were denied that made it so difficult in here. The small things added up. Just knowing what was going on all across the country and not being able to be a part of it was hard to deal with, but this is what happens when you break the law.

It only took about twenty minutes of commercials and spreads to make me want to go back outside, but I wasn't sure if we were stuck inside until the visitors went into the chow hall or until visit was over, and that might take hours. I went to find Mr. Tortelli and used the line of communication like I was supposed to to get an answer, but he was asleep. So was Mr. Kim, my assistant senior. So I was forced to go into the TV room and ask Mr. Albert. He went down to the bubble at the next commercial, and shortly thereafter, an announcement came over the compound speaker that it was clear to go outside.

Pacing and thinking seemed to go hand in hand for me. Walk for a while, jot down the good ideas in my head, and repeat the process. Healthy as well as productive, it was better than smelling all the food people were eating inside.

A young kid who was a green card came out and joined me while I was doing laps. His name was Mr. Strahm, and at twenty years old, he was already a convicted felon with a year in prison under his belt. Not the best way to start your life off, but it was what it was. We exchanged stories and chatted about Cottonwood for a bit, and I found out he was an IV drug user with a bad history since he was a teenager.

"I have been slamming dope since I was in junior high, and I really needed this place. It was the best thing that ever happened to me." He was telling me this, and I could hear the sadness in his voice. "I go home in a couple of weeks, and I don't know what I'm going to do."

"What do you do for a living?" I asked him.

"I've been making meth or dealing drugs my whole life. I don't even know if I can get a job, let alone keep it. Nobody hires ex-cons anyways, do they?"

"There has to be programs and services for guys like us. Otherwise, we just go back to drugs, and that's just what they don't want us to do."

"I heard you talking with some other guys. You are from Washington State, right?"

"Yeah. I go back to do my probation in Seattle if my interstate compact goes through. Ms. Robinson said it would be the case since that was where I was living when I got arrested."

"I was thinking of moving up there to get away from all the drugs and bad influences in Boise. I have done a little framing. Are there any construction jobs up there?"

"Dude, you could get a framing job in Seattle in fifteen minutes. The economy is much better, and the probation people are on your side. Around Boise, I heard that they actually want you to fail so they can throw your ass back in jail."

"Maybe I will do that. I know if I stay in Boise, I am going to get in trouble. I have too many friends that are into drugs. It's just a matter of time before something bad happens. I'll either start selling or using or both. I just know it's a matter of time before I screw up my life again."

"Then do this: kiss your probation officer's ass for five months, and when I get out, I can set you up with a job so they can authorize you moving to Washington. If you have a job for fifteen or twenty an hour, how can he not let you move if you have a good history and you are moving up in the business world?"

"I don't know. They are such assholes they might want to keep me here because they know I will be back. It's a revolving door in Idaho," he said. "Thanks for talking to me. I am going back inside. It's too cold out here."

We shook hands, and off he went.

I felt sorry for the guy. He was in a tough spot, but at least he was aware of his predicament and he was trying to do something about it. It also invited me to the position of many of those who were here faced. They were usually running from the law and surviving by illegal means, and now that their punishment was winding down and it was time to return to the real world, where did that leave them? I had overheard some conversations here, and I knew that some guys thought this was a joke. They wanted nothing more than to get out and go straight back to the lifestyle that brought them here. Others like Mr. Strahm were sincere about changing their lives so as not to return to this place or, worse yet, receive their total sentence due to continued drug use or sales, ending up in prison for years to come. The underworld was all some of these guys had ever known, and avoiding it would be one of the most difficult things that they ever attempted in their lives.

I, too, was getting cold, and shortly after he went back in, so did I. The warmth was comforting, but the food smells and commercials once I rejoined my group at the table were instantly disturbing. I began to get sad at the situation I was in and for the decisions that I had made that had put me in this place. I wasn't wallowing in self-pity but more reflecting on things that I could have done differently that would have put me at home with my family on this holiday as I should be. All of us should be, but here we were.

I continued to work on my phase change and found myself making editorial changes, rewording sentences, and generally going over it time and again to make sure it was as perfect as possible. We all helped one another or anyone who had trouble while bouncing ideas around the table to avoid embarrassment when the time came to perform for the whole unit. Nothing worse than looking like an idiot on your first phase change and having everyone think less of you the rest of your stay. We wanted the support we were giving one another with our phase change seminars to make a statement about how working together was better than doing it alone. Just like the work we did as a group with the laundry had benefited our group as well as the whole community.

By the time everyone started to clean up and wake up for count time, my stomach was growling. I was starving to death and just about at the end of my rope. Everybody was talking about the upcoming meal and if it would be bigger because of Thanksgiving, but I highly doubted it. It should at least be bigger than the usual dinners because it was a two-meal day, same as they were at RDU. Rumor around the tier from the kitchen guys was, the meal would be just like going to Grandma's house for Thanksgiving, complete with pumpkin pie. I didn't want to get my hopes up and believe the rumor mill, but with the appetite I was developing, it was already too late. Hopefully, it would be a good meal, and I knew nobody would appreciate it as much as our little group would. None of us had any commissary, and until we were around a little longer, nobody would be stupid enough to take a chance on giving us any food.

The sanction usually given out for getting caught sharing commissary was loss of commissary for one week. The COs would give you a huge bin box, put all your stuff in it, and lock it up in the administration building until your sanction was up. If you violated again, during your sanction, it was extended. Nobody was willing to help us out, because if they did, they could possibly go without as well. Purple cards were just too new to the program and weren't likely to take that kind of risk. I completely understood the logic of not helping us out, and I am sure I would have done and would do the same when I reached green card status. I was never so happy to hear "Upstairs, get on line" over the speaker as I was on that afternoon. I was curious if, along with the bigger meal, we were allowed extra time, but since no one here now had been here for a previous holiday, none of them could really answer with any certainty. We lined up outside the chow hall, and the aroma was extremely enticing. The kitchen workers were right; it smelled just like Grandma's house. I was sure that part of the reason it was so much more appealing tonight was that I hadn't eaten anything in over seven hours.

The meal itself was awesome and met or exceeded everyone's expectations: turkey with cranberry sauce, mashed potatoes and gravy, green salad, a huge homemade dinner roll, and a nice slice of pumpkin pie made for a very fine meal indeed. I decided to break the no-food taken out of the chow hall rule just this once and saved my roll for later. The only reason this could possibly work was that I was on the end of the table, and if it was timed properly, nobody would be able to see me do it. After the guy across from me got up and left, I took a quick look around and slid my roll into my coat pocket without anyone seeing. Now, all I had to do was get it back into the unit without anyone noticing the lump in my coat pocket.

When I stood up, I moved my beanie over on top of the roll so it looked like the lump was from my hat and therefore not so noticeable while still in the chow hall with all the COs around. Once out in the dark night, I would be in the clear. We exited quickly out the back when the CO cut us loose and we began the stroll back down the hill to the unit. As we came out onto Main Street, CO Wiley came out the front door and started counting off the guys walking back.

"One, two, three, four, five, six, seven, eight, nine, and, Mr. Walker, you are number ten. Line up here on the street, facing the chow hall, and no talking."

My heart stopped for a couple of beats, and I had a feeling one of the COs had seen me take the roll. For the first time in all my eleven or twelve meals here, I was being searched on the way back from the chow hall. I had never ever seen this happen to anyone else on the entire compound so far, and to have it happen during the same meal I chose to take something from the first time seemed just a little too coincidental for me. I was busted red-handed taking food from the chow hall, and now my rider could be over before I even got through one week.

CHAPTER

40

A S HE SLOWLY WORKED HIS way up the lineup, searching each man as he went, I watched CO Wiley like a hawk to familiarize myself with his search pattern and routine with each man. He would stand behind a person and do the basic, cop-like pat-down and then do the left arm and leg, followed by the right arm and leg. I decided to make my move when he was bent down, facing the other direction, frisking the right leg of the next individual, before he got too close to me at the end of the line. When the time came, I put my hand into my pocket and tossed the roll up Main Street and into the snowbank piled up on the edge of the street. I had pulled it off without some green card screaming that they had seen me and what I had done.

CO Wiley had dismissed each guy as they passed inspection and sent them back to the unit. By the time he came to me, it was just him and me out on Main Street for my search and pat-down.

"Did you enjoy the meal, Mr. Walker?" He surprised me by even knowing my name as he did when he called it out for the lineup. I was nervous and tried to hide it as best as I could and play it cool.

"It was very good, sir, better than most expected, but probably not as good as the one you had, sir."

"In case you didn't notice, Mr. Walker," he continued as he was finishing up patting me down, "I ate my Thanksgiving dinner a couple of tables away from you, so they were probably about the same, wouldn't you guess?"

"Yes, sir."

"We are done here. Get back inside and get ready for the meeting."

"Thank you, sir, and happy Thanksgiving."

I turned and quickly walked down the hill and turned into the unit when I saw CO Wiley stop near the snowbank where I had thrown the roll. Before I could see what happened, I quickly went inside and went upstairs. Even if he did find the roll, it would be difficult to prove whom it belonged to. As much as I could figure, I was in the clear.

As we began to congregate downstairs for the meeting, everybody was talking about how good the meal was and how much it reminded us that we weren't at home. I was just happy to be full and not locked up in segregation or headed back to the yard. I made a mental note to myself to never take food from the chow hall ever again! No matter how hungry I was from now on, as far as I was concerned, the risk just wasn't worth the reward. There was a holiday atmosphere in the air, and I could tell from the way the coordinators were looking forward to their ball games and rec time more than usual tonight. Comments were kept brief, and the pace of each segment that was mandatory was done with extreme efficiency. At the end, CO Wiley came out of the bubble to give us a few words of fatherly advice and made a couple of announcements.

"First of all, gentlemen, I would like to wish you all a happy Thanksgiving. I know it's hard to be here on a holiday and away from your families, but let this be a reminder to you when you get out to not practice whatever behavior brought you here, and you will be able to spend the rest of your holidays with your family. I am sure right now you all agree with me, and I am sure your families do as well. Second of all, I think we should give a round of applause to the kitchen staff, who, as I was telling Mr. Walker out on Main Street earlier, made an awesome dinner not only for you all but for the staff as well."

A loud standing ovation erupted. The effort made to make it seemed just like home, and we let them know they had succeeded.

"The staff on duty today was not at the bottom of the seniority list and forced to work the holiday. We came in today to be with you

251

and help you guys so that hopefully you will not return. We, too, are away from our families because we believe in this program, and our dedication, I think, reflects that. It sure isn't the money, I'll tell you that."

We all started to laugh at that one.

"Okay, on to business. Do any of the ten guys I pulled out and searched on Main Street want to take responsibility for this tonight?" With that, he stepped back into the bubble with the roll I had tossed into the snowbank and set it on the front coordinator table. My heart stopped for the second time that day, and I thought for sure I was busted. If this was to continue as it did in the military, the whole unit would probably sit there until the guilty party confessed to the crime. If nobody came forward, then we would be there all night and all day tomorrow if necessary until the guilty person stepped forward and took responsibility for his action. The biggest problem I had was a guilty conscience since the guilty party in this situation was me.

The units sat in silence, with only a few chuckles here and there, but Wiley was the best CO on compound, and out of respect, the room was silent. He slowly looked one at a time at those of us he had searched, and I looked at him square in the eyes when my turn came, hoping I had a good-enough poker face to pull it off. I was getting ready to stand up and take whatever became of it like a man. He would probably have more respect for a guy who copped to it than a man who would make the whole unit suffer. As I shifted my legs to stand up, he quickly picked up the roll and put it on his desk in the bubble and said, "I didn't think anybody would. After a meal like that, what did you need to steal a roll from the chow hall for? I was stuffed. Anyway, due to the Thanksgiving holiday, everyone who wants to go to rec is invited, even the orange and purple cards. Carry on."

Applause ripped through the unit, followed by yet another standing ovation, complete with yelling and shouts of joy. Not only had I escaped being convicted of my first major violation, but the punishment was not exacted on the unit as well. I was never implicated or suspected, and I even got to go to rec. With that, he closed the door to the bubble while we finished the meeting as quickly as possible so we could go to rec. One time a week on Thursday, it was unit 4's rec night, and everyone was allowed to go except the purple cards. The daily green card rec was compound-wide only after one had been here for sixty days, so any extra rec time was greatly appreciated by all.

The unit lined up on Main Street, and we walked two by two up the hill toward the school, continuing past on a sidewalk around the baseball field, and eventually down some stairs and into an old gymnasium. It was an old barreled-roof gym that was probably built during World War II and appeared to have had no renovation sense. It was basically a basketball court, and on the far side, running the entire length of the gym, was a weight training area about twenty-five feet wide, with all kinds of barbells and weight lifting gear for training. I had wanted to stretch my legs and run for a while, and this was exactly what I chose to do. I did laps around the basketball court at a crisp pace and basically observed the rest of the unit doing their thing. I hadn't played basketball in years and didn't want to risk the social embarrassment if I joined a game and didn't measure up. The aggressiveness of the sport could get anyone playing against the wrong guy into a fight in no time. I wasn't willing to take that chance until I knew a little more about whom I would be playing with.

There were four or five guys running along with me, and we were respectful of the two five-on-five games being played on each side of the court. The weight area was crowded, with most of the unit there, and there were lines waiting to get to each machine. It felt good to finally get out and stretch my legs. I couldn't even remember the last time I had gone running. I was also glad I had spent the extra five minutes in the laundry room that first day, because my boots felt like Nikes on the hard gymnasium floor after forty-five minutes. I knew I was going to be sore tomorrow, but what the hell! I had no major plans. I walked the last fifteen minutes to cool down and stretch out the stiffness as I went. I watched a few minor altercations on the court, but nothing that seemed to upset CO Wiley to the point of involving himself in it. Apparently, he was willing to let them play and work it out themselves, but I was sure there was a line that was not crossed today, or he would have let it be known. He spent the hour in another bubble that gave him a view of the entire gym, and he spent most of his time reading some hunting or fishing magazine in between glances around the gym to be sure everything was okay. We cleaned up when our time was up and took a head count before walking two by two up the stairs between the ball field and the school and then down Main Street to the unit. We immediately turned on the exhaust fan to make sure we didn't spend the night doing fire drills, and it seemed like nearly the whole unit took showers in the next thirty minutes before bedtime.

I wasn't too happy knowing that I couldn't call home, since we weren't allowed to use the phone until we got our orange cards. I wondered if Beth and Sean would be upset about not hearing from me on the holiday or if they would understand I was under purple card rules still. I had been thinking about them most of the day. How they would spend the day having fun and eating made me sad, because I wasn't with them. Between the good meals and going to rec, it had been a decent day here, since I felt sad as I got into bed just knowing I couldn't even say "Happy Thanksgiving" to either of them. What even made me more upset was that in a month, I would be forced to do this all again when Sean's birthday and Christmas came, on the same day.

I was glad to have Thanksgiving behind me, and I was exhausted from all the running I had done. I only read for about ten minutes before I put down my book and fell into a deep, relaxing sleep.

CHAPTER 41

WHEN I WAS SENTENCED a month ago in October, I instantly knew that there would be two really hard days ahead of me. Finally, one of them was behind me. Since the state had given all the teachers and counselors a four-day weekend, there were not going to be any classes or groups until Monday, and this meant we basically had Friday, Saturday, and Sunday off. Today, we were back on our regular schedule with three meals, which was good, but over the weekend, we would go back to two.

After the morning meeting, I was fortunate enough to get my first look at "superclean." Each committee was given a rotating cleanup job from the list, and all twelve members of that crew worked on that particular task until it was complete and passed inspection. Free time would not begin until all the chores were checked off. The quicker we finished, the sooner it would be playtime for the whole unit. Sacrificing the quality of the cleaning for speed was the worst thing we could do, since when inspection time came and something was to fail, it would be an even longer wait until free time. Obviously, there was some sequence of events that was necessary to complete, like mopping, that couldn't be done until the sweeping was finished and until all the windows, railings, and other nooks were all attended to. Once your assigned task was checked off, you were to remain sitting upright on your bunk and be busy programming until the entire unit was done. Today, it took about forty-five minutes before we heard the free time announcement we had all been waiting for.

The first thing I did today was turn my phase change in to Mr. Tortelli so he could proofread it, sign it off, and pass it up the line of communication to Mr. Kim, and eventually to Mr. Ramirez. If all approved it, I could then read it sometime over the weekend and be ready for my orange card on Sunday night. As far as I knew from the guys at the tables again today, nobody else had turn theirs in yet. So as I expected, I would be the first in our group to speak. I also helped Jesus make a few minor adjustments to his presentation and made him read it to me four times to make sure he was getting more comfortable with the speech part of the task and, by sheer repetition, was slowly losing his fear.

We had to distribute laundry again in the middle of the morning. Now, after five times, the laundry distribution system our little group had put into action was now a well-oiled machine. We had set up a new system, nobody had anything missing, and we proved that it could work. While we were running laundry bags back and forth, Mr. Tortelli asked me to come over to his bunk when we were done so he could talk to me about my phase change. This had me worried that something was wrong and it would have to be redone. As I finished my last couple of bags, I kept worrying that I had missed the concept of the phase change and that when we spoke, he would straighten me out. This was upsetting, since I was hoping to go first, and after all the help I had given the guys, they, too, would likely be headed in the wrong direction if they had listened to anything I had said.

"Mr. Walker," he questioned me with the deep voice that only two packs of Camel Straights a day could give you, "who helped you with your phase change seminar?"

"Are you accusing me of plagiarism? Nobody, Mr. Tortelli. I have been working on it for three days now. I might have listened to a few suggestions from the tables. Why?"

"I have been here almost four months now, and this is by far some of the best writing I have ever had the privilege of reading. I hope all the purple cards are using whatever advice you have been giving them at the tables upstairs, because seminars like this are what make people listen up and pay attention during the meetings. I am very proud of you, Mr. Walker. Keep up the good work."

"Thank you. I will. How many days will it be until I will be able to read it at a meeting?"

"Hopefully tonight. I'll pass it on to Misters. Kim and Ramirez, and I'm even going to tell them not to bother reading it, so they can experience it firsthand with the rest of the unit."

I walked away from Mr. Tortelli feeling proud of my work and slightly eager to read it tonight if I was cleared to do it. It was the first time since high school that I had written anything that was critiqued or, for that matter, even read by anyone else. It felt really good to know that after I had read around forty books since Labor Day, some of the authors' writing skills had rubbed off on me.

We had a normal lunch today, and then we were free the rest of the afternoon. I spent a lot of time walking around outside and reading over a copy of my phase change that had only a few minor corrections, so I could practice it before reading it to the entire unit tonight. Jesus joined me, and we took turns reading to each other. We went back and forth so many times that I could have just as easily read his or vice versa. He was still too nervous to read his tonight, and he was planning on doing it tomorrow, which for him was still pretty good. As long as we had them read by Monday, we would get our orange cards at the end of the meeting Monday night. We could take the test that I had already passed with Mr. Baxter and would receive the orange card on the following night after the test results were approved by the COs.

Midway through the afternoon, Mr. Tortelli came outside and yelled, "Hey, you two! Get your butts in here! You're not going to want to miss this!"

Something told me this was good news, from the tone of Tortelli's voice, and we immediately stopped pacing and went back inside. As all the barneys gathered around, I could tell by the computerized bubble sheets that he had in his hand that this was about commissary. I had totally forgotten that I had been told a couple of days ago that Friday was the day commissary would show up.

"These are the commissary order forms that need to be filled out in the next couple of hours. If the commissary lady does not have them in her possession when she is done delivering our commissary, you are burnt. I have two or three order books here. Set up your table, fill out the order forms, and fill them out properly, or you will not get what you ordered. Also, for the holiday weeks, you can order $75 worth instead of the usual $50, and that goes from now until Christmas. Technically, you are not supposed to have commissary until you are an orange card, so pay attention to this next part very carefully. If you think you might fail the test on Sunday night, do not order any commissary. You will have it taken away, and you will be pulled up by the entire unit for ordering commissary as a purple card. You guys are granted an unspoken pass for purple cards to order the first week you are here, but trust me, you do not want to fail and then have your name called by the commissary lady. She gets here around 3:00 p.m., and the senior coordinator gives her all the commissary sheets when our unit is called. Just because we are unit 4 does not mean we will be called last. It all depends on how the truck was loaded and what unit is on top when they are done unloading, so you have them ready by 3:00 p.m. to be safe. After that, I don't want to hear about your problems. You have all been warned."

We all scurried upstairs to look at the available options and do a little budgeting to make sure we got as much as we possibly could without wasting one penny of available purchases. I wasn't exactly sure how to plan for this one, because I didn't want to get into trouble for running store up here, since the consequences could be severe. I decided to get what I wanted and not worry about store until I had the system figured out a little better and made a few more friends. The commissary options here consisted of the entire prison list instead of the condensed version we were limited to in RDU. I could do a perfect rider, but if I got caught running store or was pulled up so many times for sharing commissary, not only could I lose my own commissary, but I could also get sent to prison as well. The stakes were too high, and it wasn't worth the risk. Not yet, anyways. There was also a bonus list for the holidays with Spritz cookies, summer sausages, and other holiday goodies not usually available. They even had powdered milk available, but I could never stand the stuff and would never contemplate trying it as a substitute for the real thing.

God, I missed my milk. Before long, I had my list filled out and was back outside, walking and practicing my phase change seminar out loud for the hundredth time, with thoughts of next week's commissary dancing in my head.

From the 4:30 p.m. count time and all the way through dinner, I found myself getting slightly nervous about my reading. Maybe it was more excitement than nerves, because I had spoken in front of crowds many times and public speaking had never really bothered me when I had done it before. I had even chanted cadence in the Oregon Army National Guard for a battalion of men marching down the avenue. We were in Coronado, California, at the Navy amphibious assault training course the day the *Columbia* space shuttle blew up. As a corporal, I was the NCO who sang the cadence as we marched to and from training that day over 1,200 men. Reading three pages to these 119 guys was a piece of cake to me.

For Jesus, it would be a different story. I doubt if he had ever said one paragraph in front of more than three friends in his whole life. I decided it was more excitement and now, with what Mr. Tortelli told me, a little bit of pressure since his expectations were so high. What he had said was fine, but it was only one man's opinion. What if the other 118 people didn't like it as much as he and I did? Maybe it would be a hit, or maybe not. I would find out in a couple of hours. I knew it was better than half the crap I had already heard, so now all I needed to know was if the rest of the unit agreed with Mr. Tortelli. If so, then great. Maybe all the books I had read had taught me a thing or two; if not, at least I would still be able to become orange. Mr. Tortelli handed my phase change speech back to me before the meeting that night and told me it was approved for reading. I let Mr. Albert know that I intended to read mine tonight, since he was the assistant senior coordinator in charge of tonight's events. When the time came for phase changes, Mr. Albert didn't even ask if there were any. He just stated, "Mr. Walker will now come up to the front of the unit and read his phase change seminar for us."

"Good evening, community. My name is Mr. Walker."

"Good evening, Mr. Walker."

"My phase change is on the word *challenge*." I paused and looked out over the unit, making eye contact with a select few.

"*Challenge*, as defined by the dictionary, is called to engage in a competition, a demand for an explanation, to summon action or stimulate. To me, a challenge is someone questioning my skills, abilities, and resolve. They do not think I can accomplish the task put before me. We are all challenged constantly on a day-to-day basis, from the simple challenge of making it to work on time or completing a project on schedule, to the more difficult challenges of staying sober and repairing the damage we have caused our families and loved ones with our addiction.

"I personally look forward to these challenges as an opportunity to show my friends and family just what I have learned from my mistakes and also how capable I am. I want to show them I can accomplish any task that demands it. Although most of us enjoy winning, I personally find the challenge lies more in the effort one puts into the competition than the outcome. I find it is the discipline needed to prepare for the challenge that is more admirable than winning or losing. All of us have challenged our own natural instincts with addictive behavior and the problem it causes for most of our adult lives, and we have lost the battle. Our problems continually got worse and led to challenges with the cops, and we also have lost that battle. Then we challenged the justice system, and if you are hearing me read this, then you lost that challenge, just as I did. This means all of us here at Cottonwood have no wins and at least three losses, gentlemen.

"Here at NICI, we are once again being challenged by the justice system to prove that we deserve another chance at freedom rather than go to prison for a few years. It is up to us, while we are at Cottonwood, to prove that we are smarter now and care more about ourselves, our freedom, and our families than the timers at the yard who don't. Anyone can do time. That's the easy way out. We have all accepted the challenge of completing the rider program and all the 5:00 a.m. wake-up calls. The house major and cardinal rules must be followed as well. By doing this, we have stepped up to the plate and taken a swing at having a say about what becomes of us. We are the ones who control our own future, rather than the state of Idaho. We are also being given the tools and the knowledge to help us succeed when we get out. How productive we are while we are here will help determine if we have disciplined ourselves sufficiently to prepare for the challenge of returning to our families as changed men.

"With all the bad memories they have of us and a proven track record of lies and deceit, it will now be up to us to prove to them that we met the challenge at NICI and made positive changes in our lives. We owe it to them to be the husbands, fathers, and sons that they once looked up to and respected. We need to prove to them, with our changed behavior, that things will be different this time.

"Society loves a challenge so much that even when we have nobody to test our abilities against, we still look for a good challenge. We will play games against a computer, time ourselves running around a track in circles, measure if we can jump higher and higher, and even play one of the hundreds of versions of Solitaire against a deck of cards. Who among us hasn't recently challenged one of our peers to a friendly game of spades, three-on-three basketball game, or bet on our home team to win a game? We have lost our battle with addiction, have lost our attempts to outrun the cops, and lost our battle with the justice system. Now it is time to separate the men from the boys. This is game 7 of the World Series for most of us. You are down by three runs, it is already the bottom of the ninth, and the bases are loaded. There are two outs and a full count. I challenge each and every one of you to step up to the plate and hit a grand slam to win it all, because basically, gentlemen, we are out of options. Thank you."

The entire unit stood up and clapped for at least thirty seconds. My face was red, not from what I had said, but from the length of the applause I received. I had never been so proud of anything I had written in my life. Mr. Tortelli was right. It was pretty good. At the least, all the books I was reading weren't just a waste of time; I was actually learning something from them. I like to think that this was something teaching me how to write.

Even CO Wiley came out of the bubble, clapping his hands, at the end and said, "If anybody needs any help with their phase change seminar, go see Mr. Walker. That is what phase change seminars are all about. Well done, Mr. Walker."

Mr. Tortelli was nodding and had a big grin on his face, just as if he were a proud father.

CHAPTER

42

I WAS FEELING PRETTY GOOD after the meeting, and people kept coming up and telling me how much they enjoyed listening to my phase change. A couple of people even followed CO Wiley's advice and asked me for a few pointers, which was more difficult for me to do than it sounded. To do that, I would have had to live their lives and write their seminar for them, because that was all I did for mine. Friday night was our unit's other library night of the week, so I decided once again to go there for the hour instead of wasting the opportunity. I checked out two more self-help books so I could read and take notes all weekend, which I hoped would fully impress my judge and counselor, as Mr. Albert had informed me it would. When I was done, I checked out the fiction section that had impressed me so much the first time I was here. By Tuesday night, I would be able to check out real books for the first time since I had become an avid reader, and I think I was almost looking forward to that as much as getting my orange card. Saturday and Sunday were almost identical to Thanksgiving, except that we did superclean on both days and a new snowstorm dumped about a foot of snow everywhere. Instead of being at the table all day, we would shovel falling snow. Some guys bitched about it, but I didn't mind. It was almost as if the others were forced to exercise with me and keep me company. By now, I had gotten to know most of the group pretty well, and with the exception of Jesus, none of the others and I had really hit it off.

I was making other friends throughout the unit, like Mr. Castro, Mr. Albert, and Mr. Tortelli. Not that I was trying to be a kiss-ass or work my way up the ladder, but each of these guys had something to offer as far as helping me here, and that was helpful to my comfort level while staying here. The books from Castro, the advice from Albert, and the guidance from Tortelli all helped to form my first week here in a focused, productive time. Apparently, no green card had requested my bunk this week, so I was safe in my one-level Hilton for now. Once the new purple cards arrived and another group became green, who knew what might happen? All in all, this place wasn't too bad. They kept us busy all day every day, and you could be as productive and helpful to others as you chose to be. The other option was, you could do as little as you wanted and "slide under the radar," as the COs called it. However, if you slid too far under, it would yield negative reviews of your performance, which could possibly bring you back for a second round. With only four meals all weekend, I was complaining about my hunger when Mr. Albert offered some good advice that might actually work.

Immediately after breakfast, I drank a ton of water all day until dinner, and I wouldn't be so hungry. I wasn't a huge water fan, but at least out here it was good, clean water and the fountain served it ice-cold. The water was actually pretty good, and his suggestion helped. I was still hungry, but the empty feeling that nagged at my gut all day was missing, and I was thankful for the tip.

At the Saturday-night meeting, Jesus did a great job reading his phase change, and I couldn't help thinking I had a big part in his doing so well. I sat in the front row that night and told him to just read it and look at me as he had done so many times the last few days, and everything went well. I could tell he was a nervous wreck, but to the rest of the unit, he probably looked just fine, even though his face was beet red the whole time. He let out a big sigh when it was over, and only then did everyone else fully understand just how hard it must have been for him not only from a language standpoint but from a personal one as well. Some people don't like to open up to their best friends or even their wives. Being forced to do so in front of 119 guys in prison is extremely difficult, but once completed, looking back at what has been done, you'll realize it is a truly amazing accomplishment.

Sunday night after the meeting, we were tested for orange cards, and every one of us passed. Nobody was going to be in trouble for ordering commissary, and the speech Mr. Tortelli gave us most likely was what made it happen. Nothing is as motivating to an inmate as having a few treats and luxuries after being denied them for over a month. Although we still wouldn't get our cards until tomorrow night, it was nice to know we would all only be purple cards for one more day.

It felt good to have what I had foreseen as the worst part of my stay over and done with. The downtime in county after sentencing, RDU, the first week with no commissary, and Thanksgiving while purple to boot grated on us ever since sentencing. I had dreaded this last month after all the rumors I had heard about this place, and now all my anxiety was behind me. Tomorrow I would be an orange card, with book and phone privileges, and commissary was ordered and on its way next Friday. Life was as good as it could get in prison. I was hoping it would stay that way until I left.

With Monday morning came the usual Cottonwood workweek. Up at 5:00 a.m., breakfast at 6:00 a.m., count time at 7:00 a.m., the morning meeting at 7:30 a.m. Castro entertained us with yet another one of his top 10 lists, which put smiles on everybody's face to start the day. You had to admire the guy, who, all on his own, took it upon himself to create, write, and read in front of the whole unit these lists, which, if they weren't funny, would have brought ridicule and repercussions from the whole unit.

Also, in the morning meetings, we were occasionally forced to do what we called around here image breakers. These were stupid, humiliating things that, either individually or in small groups, forced people to participate. We crab-walked, skipped or danced down the center aisle, told short stories about ourselves or others, made animal noises, or did other embarrassing things to get guys to come out of their shells and become active members of our group dynamic. Often, the coordinators would intentionally pick on the group of recursive slackers that always hid in the back rows, hoping to never be called on. Some mornings, we even did the hokeypokey, so nobody would ever feel stupid doing anything at all after that. If you can do the hokeypokey in front of somebody, what would you ever be embarrassed to do in front of them? Most of the time, the answer was nothing, and that was the idea behind the image breakers. The cool thing was, they actually worked.

Monday morning, we were hanging around the unit when the last laundry delivery we purple cards were going to have to make arrived. Once this was again successfully completed, Mr. Tortelli informed us that our last orientation class would be today. It was in the library with Mr. Raymon, who was the teacher in charge of what was called workforce development. We were to go to the library at the nine thirty movement to get the information from him, and after that, our purple card orientation week would be over.

As our little group of barneys gathered in the library, it dawned on me that somewhere along I-84, the next group of purple cards shackled in the Cheetos jumpsuits were on the bus, slowly making their way toward replacing us as we moved up the ladder one small notch. The poor bastards didn't have a clue as to what was in store for them today, and for some reason, that put a big smile on my face.

Mr. Raymon was a tall, slightly balding, dark-haired gentleman with thick-rimmed glasses who oversaw workforce development at Cottonwood. He also taught the occupational safety classes that we would take to receive a vocational safety certificate. He explained how the judges liked to see more certificates in your portfolio other than the ones you were required to do, since it showed them that you were applying yourself and striving for self-improvement rather than flying under the radar.

He informed the class that some people would be so busy around here with classes and groups required by their judges that there was no way possible to be involved with workforce, while others like me would be on the opposite end of the spectrum and have nothing to do but work. The thing that bothered me about this was that my judge had requested I get drug and alcohol counseling while here, yet the powers that be decided it would be better to give my seat in a drug and alcohol class to someone who needed it more than I did. I just hoped the judge wouldn't send me back here since the NICI administration was the one who didn't follow his recommendations.

Those who had a specific job in mind for themselves would be required to fill out an application, including job history and specific qualifications for the particular job they wanted. He or Mr. Walter would then hire them for the job, and they would be required to fulfill all requirements of the job by filling out a weekly timesheet and job skills handbook that would be checked off by the CO or teacher, who was also your boss. Everyone who was involved with workforce development would also be required to attend and complete the occupational safety course that he was in charge of from 1:30 p.m. to 2:30 p.m., Monday through Thursday, each day school was in session, to receive a safety certificate that would go into their portfolio. He also stressed the importance of these certificates to the judge. The more certificates you had when you went in front of the judge, the more it looked to him like you had applied yourself up here. These certificates would go into your portfolio, and when you went to court, the judge might ask to look at it while you were there for your rider review hearing. It was the only thing you could take with you from here to the county jail that did not get put on your property. If you had received your GED, safety certificate, job skills certificate, and preparation for probation certificate, your judge would see all this and be less likely to send you back to us, or to the yard, because you did not apply yourself.

"Gentlemen, I have seen so many people come through here two or three times before they go home. Probation is not the foregone conclusion to your stay here," the instructor told us. We spent the next fifteen minutes filling out job applications and qualifications, to be turned in later in the week, so we could start our jobs as soon as possible.

We still had ten minutes until movement, so we were released early. But we were told to remain in the library until movement was announced. As I was standing near the library door, waiting for the word to go, Mr. Castro stuck his head out of the media production room, where he worked, and said, "Hey, Walker, what are you doing in the library?"

"We just got out of Mr. Raymon's workforce development class from orientation week. Is this the media production closet you were telling me about?"

"Yeah. Come on in here and close the door. Did Mr. Raymon go back up to the school yet?" he asked me.

"Yeah. He left when the class was over."

"Good, check it out. You want to listen to some music?"

I hadn't heard any music since before Labor Day, and the thought of rocking out for even one song sounded really good to me.

"Hell yes!" I said as I crowded into the small room.

I took a seat while Castro was getting something ready for me to listen to. He turned and handed me a set of headphones and told me, "Put these on and hold them tight to your ear so nobody outside hears the music. I don't want to get either of us in trouble." I put the headphones on, held them tight to my ears, and was totally ecstatic to hear Lynyrd Skynyrd's "Free Bird" blasting away in my ears. It had been so long that I went without a radio that I hadn't even realized that I was being deprived of the joy of listening to music for almost three months now. It sounded awesome, and I didn't want it to end, but he suddenly came over and grabbed the headphones from me.

"Time to go, Walker. Movement is in one minute, and the COs and teachers come through here during movement, so you get out or we will all get in trouble for having guys in here that don't work in the office. It is called being out of area."

"I understand, and thanks for letting me listen. It was awesome, even for just a little bit. I appreciate it."

I left the small room amid some snickering from the guys who worked there and went back out into the foyer of the library and waited for movement to be called. I headed back to the unit, where we had all decided to work on our portfolios until lunch, since our orientation week was now complete and we had nothing to do until lunch.

Most of us had read our phase changes over the weekend, but there were still a few people who had until tonight to do it if they

wanted to get their orange cards with the rest of us. I couldn't figure out what was going on, but I could tell something was amiss
between the looks I was getting and the snickering I heard before I
left the media production room. I took off my coat and looked for a
sign or sticker or something that Castro might have put on my coat
while I was listening to music. I didn't really think he would stoop to
something so childish, and by now I had expected a slightly higher
caliber of prank from these seasoned veterans. I couldn't figure it out
as I walked into the unit, so I decided to face the music and went
straight to Mr. Tortelli to see what I could do next, if anything, for
the service committee. His laughter told me the whole story without
the need to say the word, and I immediately went to the bathroom
to look into the mirror to see what the hell was going on. If my
admiration for Castro and his sense of humor was relatively high
after I heard his top 10 list this morning, after I had seen his latest
trick, it was higher still. He had colored the headphone padding
with a black felt-tip pen so heavily that I had left the media production room with two huge black circles around my ears. He even had
suckered me into helping him by "pushing the headphones tight to
make sure nobody else outside would hear the music." I had been
set up once again.

I spent the next fifteen minutes scrubbing black ink off my
ears, which only made the side of my head turn darker and redder
from all the scraping I was doing. Now it was almost worse than
when I started, and I needed to get into the shower to clean up, but
that wasn't allowed until eight thirty, so I just kept scrubbing away.
By the time the ink was all off, it was almost count time and the
sides of my head were bright red. I looked like I was sunburned or
just got slapped upside the head. I was sitting on my bunk, waiting
for count time, when Castro walked past me coming back from
the library. He couldn't keep a straight face long enough to get two
steps past the bubble before bursting out laughing until his face was
red and he collapsed on his bunk, still laughing hard. The men in
the tier filled him in about the struggle I had in the bathroom over
the last thirty minutes, and that just seemed to make him laugh
even harder.

"I figured we all owe you a good laugh after the top 10 list, Mr. Castro!" I yelled over to him. "Just my small way of saying thank you, Castro," I told him.

During count, a CO Edlund, whom I wasn't familiar with, looked at me when I yelled out my number. He stopped, looked at my red cheeks, and said, "Are you okay, Mr. Walker? What happened to you?" Not wanting to get Castro in trouble, I gave the only reply possible.

"I slipped on a bar of soap, sir."

Without another thought, he walked off while everyone on the tier laughed. We probably all could have gotten in deep shit if the CO hadn't been so cool about it. I shouldn't have been disrespectful, especially during count, in front of everybody, and with no talking protocol in place during count, everyone else could have been in trouble for laughing. But apparently, he was in a good mood, so that was the end of it. I also earned some respect from the guys for the joke and not for throwing Castro under the bus and getting him in trouble by having to explain the situation to the COs. From that moment on, Castro and I were pretty tight, and with him only one week ahead of me, I knew I had made a good friend for the rest of my stay.

We spent our last afternoon as purple cards working together at our table upstairs on our portfolios. The portfolio was all about getting organized and preparing for a job search once released. Since I had a job waiting for me and had never been unemployed or filled out a résumé my whole life, I highly doubted that I would need one once I was released from here. Some of these other guys were a different story. Someone copied the résumé they were making, and it would probably be the only one they passed out for the next few years. Others were completely unemployable, and I doubted their drug dealer would even look at the résumé or job qualification sheet before giving them their old job back, anyways.

I went outside around three thirty to pace and get some fresh air. I had already passed my test, but we were still required to be programming all the time, and there was yet another test coming up in three weeks to get my blue card, so I decided to get a head start. All this sounded so dedicated and proper, but the real reason to be outside was a whole different story. True, I loved the fresh air, and with the on-and-off snowstorms, I had to walk when the weather allowed me to. But my true motive was the arrival of the barneys on the transport bus this afternoon. My timing couldn't have been better, since I could see the bus was already here, and a row of heads in the segregation window kept popping up and down from their first view of the compound.

Within minutes, with their strip searches complete, they were walking single file up Main Street and headed for the chapel and their first orientation meeting. As they strolled up the street, I saw that good old Scott had made it out of RDU and was now one week behind me as far as going home, provided we were sentenced to riders for the same length of time. Some were on 90-day, 120-day, and even 180-day riders, depending on the judge they had, but nobody really knew until they talked to their counselor sometime during the second week. This gave them a little bit of time to observe you and see if you were getting good reviews with push-ups or bad reviews with pull-ups before they sat down and talked with you about your stay here. My appointment would be sometime this week, but these were announced at the morning meeting by the CO each day, so all I had to do was wait to hear when mine was, and I would have my last question answered.

About 4:00 p.m., give or take, since nobody out here had a watch, the Cheetos made their way down to the laundry room to get out of their orange transport jumpsuit and receive their uniforms. I had seen what I wanted to see and went back inside. With four other units, the odds were that Scott wouldn't be in this one with me, so I just wanted to see if he made it this week or not. Without contact with other units, I had only seen some of the guys from RDU who were in other units during orientation classes for purple card, so I most likely wouldn't be able to talk to Scott for a month or so, if even then. It was possible the next time we spoke would be during green card rec after he turned green, which was what made getting and keeping our green card and rec privileges so valuable.

As I walked through the entryway, there was a white poster board on the wall that had the names of every man in the unit written on it with erasable pen. Each committee was listed, coordinator on top and all the members below, along with assistant senior and senior coordinator listed in the slots they occupied. On the board were the names of the new guys who were coming in today, and Scott's name was not among them. I also noticed that our group was no longer part of the service committee but had been moved up one row to the house committee now. This meant that Mr. Tortelli was no longer my line of communication but rather Mr. Thorne. After I got my orange card, I had the feeling that people here would open up and be easier to get along with. I had not gotten into trouble during the first week, and I had proved to all these ahead of me that I wasn't a complete idiot.

About half the guys in our group had been pulled up for one stupid thing or another, and they had been socially isolated because of it. Associating yourself with people who were in trouble would only lead you to getting in more trouble at some point, and for that reason, any purple card found it hard to make friends in their first week. Guilt by association could get you three years at the yard, and that was a risk many people were not willing to take.

At four thirty, I felt sorry for the new barneys as they came straggling in one by one. They were at least fortunate enough to be greeted and talked to for five minutes before count time, so they knew what was going on instead of just walking into a silent unit with everyone staring at them, as I had last week. During dinner that night, somebody set up one of the new guys to trigger the fire alarm on the chow hall exit door, just as they had done to Jesus earlier. Mr. Walsh scared the shit out of one of the new guys when he crept up and yelled, "Good evening, community! My name is Mr. Walsh," just as he had done to me. Ironically, this week both things were hilarious when viewed from a different standpoint, and I could appreciate the humor much more than I had a week ago.

We were introduced to the new guys, and we heard the going-home riders give their farewells. Finally, after enduring the dreaded weeklong purple card restrictions, we all finally received our orange cards.

CHAPTER

43

FTER THE EVENING MEETING, WE still couldn't go to rec, but we could sit around and read regular books and not have to be programming constantly. I wasn't as relaxed as I had been at free time last weekend and over the holiday, but it still felt pretty good. One of the first things I did was call home and let Beth and Sean know why I hadn't been able to call earlier and tell them as much as I could about the last week without boring them or going into too many details that I knew they wouldn't understand anyways. With my restrictions no longer an issue, I let them know that I could now call whenever I wanted or whenever they wanted me to, since it was costing $15 each call. Each call was ended after only fifteen minutes at a dollar a minute. I knew money was tight and I wouldn't be able to contribute until I got out, and wintertime was always hard in the roofing industry, so the frequency of the call was a financial concern more so than a matter of convenience.

The monopolization of the prison calls to families and the rates they charged were a travesty to the justice system. What it would cost to call home with a calling card as opposed to the collect rates at a dollar a minute was just as criminal as some of the things people had done to get sent here. Why the prison system or the state felt it was okay to take advantage of those who were locked up was beyond me. It seemed to me that in a free market, there had to be a better way to make a buck than off the incarcerated, but when you're locked up, you really don't have too many choices to make or the means to affect any change.

When everybody came back from green card rec, I found Mr. Thorne to figure out what was expected of us at lights-out. I knew

274

the house committee oversaw cleaning up the unit after the 9:00 p.m. count, but I wanted to know the schedule ahead of time, so I didn't get in trouble and we didn't end up working until 10:00 p.m. to get the job done.

"We all gather in the supply room after the nine o'clock count clears, and I will go over everything," Mr. Thorne said. "You need to stay in uniform, and, Mr. Walker, if you could tell all the others in your group, I would appreciate it. Mr. Tortelli told me you were the go-to guy in the group."

"No problem, Mr. Thorne. Anything to help the community run a little smoother," I told him as I went off to spread the word. It took a while to find everyone since I think they were enjoying not having to program as much as I was, but eventually, everyone got the message. I stopped by to see Mr. Tortelli and told him, "If you need any help with laundry delivery and your new guys can't pull it off, just let me know. I will be upstairs."

"I can handle it, Mr. Walker," he replied with a grin. "But thanks for the offer. I know where you live if I need you." With that, I went back upstairs and looked out the window to the snow starting to fall in huge flakes. The house committee oversaw snow removal with the help of the purple cards, so I could tell tomorrow was going to be a long day.

We all met in the supply room to get our cleaning assignments from Mr. Thorne, who gave us the skinny on what the job entailed.

"You must stay in uniform for the 9:00 p.m. count, but as soon as it is cleared, you can take off your tie and dress shirt just like when you are shoveling snow, because you are on work detail. This is basically like superclean, but we do it every night and you can shower afterward, if you so desire." He then showed us a list of the jobs that had to be done and asked us to figure out who would do what among ourselves. "There are a couple of options, so listen up. Everybody does one thing, and they do it all week long until the barneys get their orange cards and take over next Monday night or everyone does one different thing each night for the week and we spread the shit work around. You guys decide." After a brief discussion, we decided to just accept one job, figure it out, and stick with it all week instead of having to learn something new each night. This way, all we had to do was tough it out for one week no matter how bad the job was and be done with it. Trying to figure out something new each night would not only be a pain in the ass but would also ultimately get us to bed later, and nobody wanted that. I volunteered to mop, which nobody else wanted to do because it was the last thing that needed to be done and everyone wanted to get to bed early.

"Mr. Thorne, if I am the mop guy, can I read in my bunk until it is time to mop, since I will be mopping when all these guys will be in their bunk, sleeping?"

"No problem. I don't care what you do or how long it takes, as long as the unit is clean and it passes the CO's inspection should he decide to inspect after I tell him it's complete."

We all had our assignments, and with nothing to do for fifteen minutes until everyone else was done, I went to my bunk to begin some recreational reading for the first time since leaving RDU. After only five minutes, I heard the clicking noise that came before the fire alarm last week and leaned over to my neighbor Edlund and said, "Fire alarm." Sure enough, one second later, the alarm was wailing as the unit grumbled out of bed and onto Main Street. As we piled out, I was trying to recall if anyone had turned on the exhaust fan tonight, and to the best of my recollection, I couldn't remember it being on at all. The seven inches of fresh snow quickly accumulated on Main Street, which would now be packed down under all the footprints and thus harder to clean up tomorrow morning. The new guys were just as clueless as the whole unit had been last week. It took longer than it should have but was still quicker than last week, thanks to the numerous rehearsals we had been required to carry out.

Once back inside, I returned to my bunk and my book while my buddies began redoing everything the fire drill had ruined. I had a clear conscience, knowing full well that they would all be in their bunks, going to sleep, while I was still mopping the tier. I only had to do the upstairs, which was still a chore with over sixty bunk spaces, lockers, and the center aisle. Somebody else did the lower tier since we had divided the unit in half right off the bat. While I was mopping, most of the other guys took advantage of the extended shower time given to us, which I would surely use once I was done with my task. Some of the guys who were still up would engage me quietly in some small talk as I mopped around their area, and some of the new guys wanted to know what lay ahead for them. I calmed their nerves and told them it wasn't too bad here, to just give it a couple of days to calm down and everything would be all right. I remembered how my thirst for information had been at this time last week. I wanted to help them out as much as possible.

The tier was quiet as I finished up, and there was a calming effect in the serenity of my chore. It was actually good to meet a few more people, most of whom were reading. I made a mental note as to who was reading what, so I could either trade or ask for their opinion later if that book was good or if they read many books by one particular author. I had my favorites, but with a broader selection to choose from now, I was open to reading new authors if they came highly recommended from someone who had similar taste to mine. I only read for a little longer after my shower. I knew tomorrow I would have a shovel in my hand most of the day since it hadn't stopped snowing since the fire drill. Even if I didn't have to shovel snow all day, I needed to find a job before I was drafted into the kitchen pool, which would pretty much ruin the rest of my stay here.

Tuesday morning, there was over a foot of snow on the ground, and the minute I woke up, I resigned myself to working outside most of the day. As soon as I was dressed and inspection ready, I went to see if Mr. Tortelli was out of bed yet and to find Mr. Thorne so I could go outside and start shoveling snow. Once we had our usual path cleared from the unit to the chow hall, the five or six of us went back inside, where I quickly changed into a dry shirt and threw my dirty clothes into my laundry bag and then threw the bag into the bin. I was curious about how the new guys would handle the delivery system without our help, which would give me the opportunity to give Mr. Tortelli a hard time. I also wanted to see if he or his crew had any problems, since none of us who devised the system would be there to troubleshoot.

After the morning meeting, which included the new guys doing some funny image breakers, everyone on the house committee bundled up and headed outside for a long morning of snow removal in the cold, bright, clear mountain air. I was beginning to enjoy the shoveling as a new form of exercise. It was rather difficult to walk with the weather conditions being what they were. Even if we did clear the snow off the path, it was twenty degrees outside, and the path was usually ice or slick. When I would jerk myself from slipping, it would hurt my back, and going from a steel slab to the mushy hospital spring bed I was on now was already making it difficult to get around. The best thing I could do for my back was to strengthen my stomach as I had in county, but around here, you were not allowed to exercise except during authorized and highly organized rec times. If you were caught doing push-ups or sit-ups anywhere other than rec, they could actually charge you with "conditioning for escape." The threat of the charges was more a deterrent than anything else, but you were surely going to get pulled up by anyone who saw you doing them.

After shoveling for a while, I switched to hauling the wheelbarrows uphill to the baseball field for a while. It only took me three or four trips to run into Cottonwood's newest member, my buddy Scott, who was happily wheeling snow from across the street over at unit 2.

"So happy you could join us up here at Club Med! Did you enjoy that extra week in RDU?" I asked him sarcastically.

"Mr. Walker, how are you doing? What's it really like up here, I've heard all the rumors but nobody really talked to me last night and I just want to know what to expect." He sounded frustrated and almost concerned that the unit he was in wasn't addressing his concerns.

"Doesn't your unit give you guys mentors, to help you through the first week?"

"Yeah, but mine is a real tool. I just sat on my bed and memorized the handbook all night while he went to rec."

"It's pretty mellow the first week, all you do is go to one class each day and then help with the snow and memorize the rules. It's not too bad." We had dumped our loads and without wanting to get in trouble, we each headed back to our respective work areas to fill up again knowing we could chat some more on the next trip. When we met up again, he was all excited and a smile broke out on his face.

"Hey, I forgot to tell you Jay showed up after you and your group left on transport. He is probably going to be here next week."

"Yeah, I was pretty hard to leave you there when I left. How was Thanksgiving by the way?"

"Fuck you, it sucked locked up in that cement slab with no commissary."

"Yeah, well don't feel like the Lone Ranger, it wasn't the best up here either. At least nobody in RDU has commissary, we had to smell and watch all day while everyone else stuffed their face with commissary. Plus, they do the two meal a day thing up here on holidays and on weekends. I was starving the whole day and nearly got busted taking a dinner roll out of the chow hall. Don't mess around in the chow hall up here or you will be screwed." We parted ways once again and a few minutes later they called for all the new guys from our unit, who were helping with the snow to go to their first orientation class. I knew Scott would not be coming back with his wheelbarrow since he would be heading to that class as well. It was good to see him and hear that Jay would soon join us. Hopefully he would be in my unit, odds were against it so I didn't get my hopes up.

We all went back in around 11:00 to get cleaned up, dry and warm from the morning full of work and during the movement before count time. Mr. Castro and one of the guys he worked with were having a huge problem. As they made their way through the unit it would eventually escalate into something that would not be good for either of them. I separated Castro from the other guy, not physically but by calling him over to my bunk so they could cool down before things got out of hand.

"Whatever is going on, it's not worth it. Just let it go," I told him so he could get a fresh perspective and clear his head.

He was pissed, "That guy just sits there in that tiny little room we all have to work in and farts 3-4 times today without the common courtesy to get up and go outside so the rest of us can breathe. What an inconsiderate asshole! No pun intended."

"Some of these immature punks think farting is still funny, which it can be if you're not in a phone booth with three other people. Living with so many other dudes can break up a man's personal space on a level most people don't get. We are forced to be confined and out up with things we normally wouldn't have to on the outside, and sometimes people don't understand when that personal boundary has been crossed. "Look around this place Castro, most of these kids never got out of high school, let alone had a job."

"That's no excuse to think we wanted to be forced to stay in that room for three hours with his stinky ass! What a rude disgusting pig!"

It's probably just how he was raised and doesn't know better. I'm sure he does now though. Forget about it and get ready for count time."

Castro had a point, but I thought he was also being a little too sensitive. You can't blame a guy for how he was raised, and now he knew how the others felt he should be more considerate. Such is the way of life when you are locked up with 460 other guys for the better part of the winter. If you can't live in harmony, there was no way you would be able to do it when you got out. Getting along within society and following the rules that govern it was a big part of what they were trying to help us learn while we were in here.

I understood exactly how Castro felt about his situation since I myself had been dealing with the same sort of immature bullshit that half the punks in jail or prison seem to think is acceptable behavior these days. Half these guys referred to their girlfriends as bitches, chewed with their mouth open and had np respect for the guy sitting with them. In a normal social situation, none of this would be acceptable. I pretty much felt that half the problem was the fact that most had never been in what most people would consider a normal social setting, therefore excusing them due to their ignorance.

The other half just flat out didn't give a shit and most likely never would. No amount of classes, behavior modification or time behind bars would change their attitude toward other human beings. I found that disturbing. It's not that I was expecting a bunch of charm school graduates in this place, but society as a whole, seemed had taken a downward spiral since I was subjected to a similar environment in basic training. It seemed to me that the younger generation just wasn't as disciplined or motivated as they used to be. I had also noticed this type of behavior in guys that had worked for me over the years. The availability of quality, hardworking and dependable people had slowly dwindled over the past few years. I strongly believed the next generation just flat out wasn't raised properly and didn't give a rat's ass about anyone but themselves.

With nothing else to do all afternoon I decided to take on a new project to keep myself busy and spent the time after lunch recruiting as any people as I could to help me. I wouldn't be the easiest thing in the world to accomplish and I might take us all afternoon, but once completed it would benefit the entire compound. I was once again taking initiative, just like I did with the laundry delivery. I slowly began to separate myself as a future coordinator by developing a reputation for getting things done. Leaders who could not successfully change what was wrong had no business being in the leadership role. I had learned at a young age in the Army to lead by example and always be prepared to accomplish whatever it was you were going to ask of your men. That was why I always had a broom or shovel in my hand and ready for inspection at 5:15. If I could do it, there was no reason everyone else couldn't do it too.

When the 1:30 movement was announced I headed out with my recruits to the tool shed together whatever supplies we could for our task, then we headed up to the ball field to begin. There was 7-8 of us and we broke into 2 groups and began to work our way around the jogging path that circled the baseball field. Mr. Bradley had told me how I the summertime 20-30 men would be running laps when it was 105vdegrees outside during their rec tie. For the life of me with two feet of snow on the ground and 20 degrees out right now, I just couldn't picture it. Our goal was to clear off the path as Jose and I did around the unit area so joggers could once again jog if they so desired. Half of us went one way and the other half went the other direction so we would eventually meet up on the far side of the field with a running path behind us for everyone on compound to use. Of course, it might need some touching up from time to time but nobody had done anything in over a week and my thought was once we did the hard part, maintaining it would be a piece of cake.

Two men working side by side would begin and forge the trail by following the path they uncovered with their shovels and the rest would come behind and widen, clean and groom the trail so runners would be able to use it. Had this been done in Washington we could have just rolled the snow like snowmen into balls and pushed them aside leaving a clear path. The snow here was so dry and powdery that it would have been impossible. We worked for over an hour before some of the guys decided they had done their fair share and headed inside. Others had somewhere to be at 2:30 movement and that I understood. There was now just a few of us left and that made what we had left to complete that more difficult.

We literally plowed on ahead throughout the afternoon, slow but steady. We made it halfway around the path I was originally working on ad realized we were completely isolated from the rest of the compound. For a week now we'd been piling snow into the middle of the field and there was a gradual ramp from the street to the center of the field where we dumped our wheelbarrows. The pile had become a small mountain and where we were working, we were unseen from any angle.

"All we have to do is jump the fence and we could be out of here in no time," said Mr. Wells. He was a huge green card and finished with the program, so he was just waiting for his name to be on the transport list. "They wouldn't even miss up until 4:30 count tie and by then we could be halfway to Boise."

"You can't be serious. In these clothes and this weather, I would give us 30 minutes before someone spotted us, a local or a CO coming into work. We'd be put in seg before we got a free trip to Boise for the next 7 to 9 years. I don't think so." The smile on his face told me he was joking, and he tried to play it off as a test for the new guys.

"I was kidding! As a green car and senior member of the community, it is y obligation to make sure none of you new guys get the notion in your head that even if presented, the possibility of escape is at best, a futile effort." He sounded like a news anchor who had spoken the same monologue a hundred times and he did it with such deadpan accuracy. If I hadn't already seen this guy act like such a clown during the last week, I would have believed him myself.

"Has anyone ever escaped from here?" I asked him as we slowly started to come back around the mountain of snow and into the view of the compound once again.

"I've heard of 11 escapes and 11 recaptures in the years this place has been used as a prison. These CO's hunt and fish and would probably look forward to an escape just so they can have the opportunity to have a challenging chase on their hands. This is their backyard, with all this snow an escapee would be tracked down in 30 minutes tops just by following the footprints," It was getting late in the day and the temperature was beginning to drop quickly and the cloudy sky was turning darker with each passing moment. I wasn't sure if we could finish today without killing ourselves, so we decided to come back out tomorrow. We would be here anyway and neither of us really had any other plans on our social calendar. That way if it snowed tonight, we would touch that up too.

I was sitting around reading my self-help book when Castro came in right before movement was announced. He was wearing a Media Production badge on his coat. He headed over to his bunk, just a couple past mine and grabbed something before coming straight over to me. Movement was in 10 minutes, so I knew instantly something was either very wrong or very good.

"Walker," he kneeled next to me and spoke quietly, "How would you like me to hand you the best job on the compound on a silver platter?"

What did he think I was? A complete idiot? I wasn't about to let him get the best of me again.

CHAPTER

44

"NO THANKS," I SAID. "I think I would rather scrub pots and pans for the next few months than scrubbing ink off my ears." He knew I had enough and was onto his game.

"You dish it as well as you take it and I need someone like that in media productions with me, Mr. Walter just fired a guy so there's an opening that will fill up quickly. I figured I would be better off with someone I knew I cold get along with rather than some anal-retentive prick that wouldn't let me do what I please."

"What do I have to do?" I asked him.

"Do you have your resume done from portfolio yet?"

"No, we don't have computer lab until tomorrow at 10:30, then I have to get it printed and they said it takes at least a couple days for that."

"Don't worry about printing. I got to get back to the library right now, but I will talk to you later tonight and tell you what you need to know. Don't go to the library after the meeting and we can talk in private." With that, he took off leaving me with a million questions and an optimistic attitude toward y impending employment. It sounded to me like I had the inside track, thanks to Castro, on one of the best jobs around and if he needed me to do something to make sure I got the job, I would do it.

My mind was racing all through count tie, dinner and the evening meeting and I could hardly wait until rec time. Castro and I headed toward the back of the room where the study area was located. Right where Mr. Best had given me my rules test on my first night here. We grabbed a table and set up in the alcove to make it look like we were studying. That would give us as much privacy as one could hope for in a place like this. For a little while anyway.

"What is it you need me to do?" I asked him once we got settled in. I had pen and paper handy so I could write down everything he told me. I didn't want to forget something and screw this up. Failure meant scrubbing pots and pans and I didn't want to risk that, especially since the best job on the compound, according to him, was right within my grasp. I sat, pen at the ready and waiting for him to begin.

"Tomorrow when you go to computer lab, type out your resume and then come to the media production room before you take it to the library to have it printed. I'm going to add some stuff to your qualifications so that Mr. Walter will want to hire you on the spot," he explained to me.

"But dude, I don't know squat about computers and I, don't want to flop if they found out I totally bullshitted my resume," I came back.

"Don't worry about that, I will teach you everything you need to know while you're working there. I need something to do anyway." This was looking pretty good to me since I was hoping to get some compute skills while I was in here. I would rather learn firsthand than from some lame classroom full of self-absorbed people who asked the same stupid questions over, and over again.

I began writing as he continued with his instructions, "Once I get your resume printed out at the library I want you to head over to Mr. Walter's office and wait in line, resume in hand. Tell him you want to work in media productions and that you know how to use Power Point, Windows, Movie Maker and that you are familiar with all sorts of editing and dubbing software from making home movies of your kids."

"I only have one kid,"

"He doesn't know that and believe me he doesn't give a shit. Tell him you have worked with computers for 10 years and that you have some good ideas for occupational safety videos from your construction background that would make you a perfect fit for our department. He likes people who know what they want, he can't stand these clowns who straddle the fence or let hi decide what they should do with their life. If you take charge with him, he will respect you and you will own him until you leave. Any questions?"

"Yeah, will my complete and thorough line of bullshit in any way shape or form get me I trouble if he finds out I falsified my application? I just don't want to be sailing along with no problems and then get fired because Mr. Raymon comes in one day and gives me one of the job skills tests he was talking about last week during orientation."

"No problem, I am the one who gives you the test, so I have a feeling you're going to pass with a 98%, not bad Mr. Walker. Not bad. Congratulations. He gives that speech so most people get the job they are qualified for, otherwise this place would fall apart. What we do doesn't matter. We do what we want. I mean I can lean against the office door and take a nap. The door wakes me up of someone comes in so I don't get busted. We play games on the computer all day and listen to music we can even do pushups without getting pulled up. It's the best job here. We can be running this place for the next few months. What do you say, Mr. Walker? You in?"

"Am I? Hell, yes, I'm in. I'd be a fool not to be."

"Okay then, do what I instructed you to do and knock on my door as soon as you finish your resume. Now I'm going to go call y daughter before everybody comes back, and I can hear what she is saying. I'll see you in the library, Walker. We can own this place if you don't let me down."

"I haven't yet, and I'm not going to start now. See you in the library." We bumped knuckles, a common prison handshake and he headed to the phone booths while I grabbed my notes. This is the break I'd been waiting for. A way to stay out of the kitchen, have weekends off, learn my way around a computer and best of all, I would get to working the library. Castro had been able to get me books at will, so that must be one of the perks.

All night I was fired up because of our chat. When my mind gets going it makes it extremely hard to sleep. I ended up reading until well past midnight. This was after mopping the upper tier and a late shower. Even though I was slowly getting used to the 5:00am wakeup time, when you stay up as late as I did it was always hard. I couldn't wait until commissary got here on Friday, so id have some coffee to help kick start my day. Once I got moving, I was fine but that first 5-10 minutes was brutal. Not to mention, I was pretty damn sore from all the shoveling I did yesterday. In all the excitement about the job, I had forgot about my jogging path project with Mr. Wells. I always finish what I start, so there was no question I would finish complete before the unit came out at the 9:30 rec time.

No shoveling was needed before breakfast since we didn't get any snow last night, so I began to work on my resume at 5:15am. I was hoping to have it ready to be typed up when I went to computer lab later this morning. I could hardly wait for the day to get started because I was so stoked about everything I had ahead of me. I was starting to keep busy with a lot of things I had an interest in, it was almost as if I wasn't in prison. Almost as if I were in the free world working on a project in my backyard, then seeing my friends' on the ball field followed up with a job interview. It felt good to have things to look forward to, and I wondered if that was a bad sign. I hoped not, I was just trying to be productive with the time I had.

After the morning meeting, Wells and I resumed our mission with renewed enthusiasm and only a short distance to cover. We finished the loop in 30 minutes, giving is plenty of time to go around the whole thing one last time and touch it up. When unit 4 came out for rec time the path was 3-4 feet across and bare down to the frozen ground that went all the way around the ball field just waiting to be jogged on. Neither one of us had mentioned our project to anyone and it seemed even the guys who went in early yesterday afternoon said anything either. The few runners who noticed, were shocked to see what we had done and appreciated the effort we put into it.

"Is this what you guys were doing late yesterday when I saw you on the far side of the field?" one asked.

"Anything we can do to make our fellow community members time here more enjoyable is what Mr. Walker and I are all about!"

Wells said with a surprisingly straight face. I couldn't help but smile. The man had deadpan humor down to an art.

We had completed our mission, and no one could take that away from us. I could almost picture a week or two after I was gone and somebody saying to the new guy, that back in November Walker and Wells cleared the entire path with two feet of snow on the ground so we owe it to the to keep this path cleared off.

I watched the guys take off jogging and feeling good I went in to make sure I was ready for my next task, my showdown with Mr. Walter.

I changed my shirt and went over my resume and notes to make sure I had everything down. The last thing I wanted was to make a fool of myself by saying the wrong thing and not get the job Mr. Castro had gone to all the trouble to line up for me the ball was in my hands and I didn't want to fumble this close to the goal line. I kept repeating the words Castro had told me to tell Mr. Walter, Windows, Movie Maker, Power Point and editing software over and over. I wanted the words to flow from my mouth as easily as my phase change seminar had just a few days ago. The main reason I had been able to read it out loud so successfully was from sheer repetition.

Now that I was an orange card, the group I was part of had about 20-30 guys in it. Those of us in the new group who weren't headed to class at the moment, headed to the library at the 10:30 movement to work on our portfolios. Just as the rules test and the phase change both needed to be complete before we could move up to blue. Even though that was still a way away, with orientation complete and not yet employed, now was the time to get it done.

Today there were 15 of us and 12 available computers, that wasn't as bad as some of the stories I'd heard when all 30 orange cards went at the same time. I was able to grab a computer the minute I walked in the door and began typing up my resume as quickly as I could hunt and peck the letters on the screen. The only thing I had done in the past 20 years was roofing, but I managed to squeeze in the computer skills that Castro told me to use by listing them as skills I had acquired while running my own company. Most self-employed business owners need some computer skills in order to conduct day to day operations in this day. I was hoping by stating so, Mr. Walter would draw the conclusion that I should be qualified for a job that I totally was not.

Castro came over just as I was wrapping up and he went to get my resume printed out by using his obvious library connections. In no time I was all set to go stand in line at Mr. Walter's door to present my sales pitch for a job I knew nothing about. If Castro was yanking my chain, as he did with the headphones I was going to be in deep in a matter of minutes. I didn't think that was the case, it was one thing to pull pranks but it was a whole different level of fucked up to make a guy do something that would cause him to flop his RIDER and a possible three year prison sentence. I had seen nothing of that sort since I arrived here and hoped I was not to be the first.

Mr. Walter wasn't even in his office and there were 5-6 of us in line waiting for him to arrive. After a few minutes, Castro came over and started talking to one of the guys.

"Hey Williams," he said quietly, "Do you want to come in here and listen to some music?" I smirked and just shook my head as Castro winked at me. I knew shortly his catch of the day would soon be scrubbing ink off his ears, just as I had a few days earlier. I really am hoping to have a blast working with this guy.

Sure enough, a few minutes later, Williams emerged from the media room with big black circles around his ears and started heading toward the computer lab. He was completely unaware of the laughter being at his expense. Once again seeing this happen, and from a different perspective I found it was pretty funny. Castro sure did enjoy himself inside these walls. I was thinking how I couldn't wait to be a part of this little world just as Mr. Walter showed up.

"Well good morning gentlemen," he said as he snaked his way through the crowded hallway. Stopping at the first guy in line he asked, "So, what sort of job are you looking for?"

"I'm not really sure. I've worked in restaurants before and I've done some landscaping. So maybe kitchen duty or maintenance."

"Next, how about you?" he moved to the next guy in line and waited for his response.

"Whatever job you give me Mr. Walter."

"Your turn, what do you want to do here in the work force?" He was working his way down the line and I was next.

"I am not too sure, Mr. Walter. I have never had a job before, so I don't really know what I'm qualified for." Now it was my turn. He moved down the line one more spot, turned to me, and asked me the same thing he had asked the others without hesitation. I responded like if he didn't give me this job that was perfect for me, he would regret it for the rest of his life.

"My name is Mr. Walker, and I want to work in media productions. I have experience with Windows Movie Maker, PowerPoint, and dubbing and editing software. I have shot and edited tons of home videos and would like nothing more than to be able to use my extensive background to improve the occupational safety presentations for Mr. Raymon's safety classes." I nailed it. It wouldn't have turned out better if I had read it word for word from my crib sheet.

"Did you, other gentlemen, hear that?" he asked as he was looking up and down the roadmen. "That is what you say when you go in for a job interview. You tell them what you want, what your qualifications are, and how you could be an asset to the office. You don't go in and say, 'I don't know,' or 'You tell me.' If you do, you'll sound pathetic. Mr. Walker, may I have your résumé? You can start on Monday. At eight thirty movement, come to this room."

Bingo. With a lot of help from Castro, I had pulled a rabbit out of my hat and landed myself the best job on compound. Now, if I could just pull it off without getting caught lying, things could be looking up for me during the rest of my time here.

When Mr. Walter went into his office, I figured it was time for Castro to get a little taste of his own medicine. I stuck my head in to the media production room and had a little fun with the man who had it coming.

"I don't think I got it," I told him while straining to keep a straight face.

"What happened?" he asked me.

"He already has someone else in mind for the job, but he said he would let me know."

"Great. We will probably get some by-the-book, anal-retentive prick who will write us up for everything we do that's questionable, and believe me, that list is extremely long."

"Yeah, that's what Mr. Franz just told me. I'll see you back at the unit." I left his small office and went back into the computer lab to find someone I knew well enough to volunteer for the other half of my payback with Castro.

Mr. Irwin was a fellow orange card now. He had come on the bus with me and was probably up for what I had in mind without being offended. I had to find someone Castro wouldn't want in there without being pissed at me for using him as a setup. It was a tricky situation, but Irwin was a guy who could pull it off. He and I had worked together on the laundry thing last week, and we knew each other well enough to do it without getting offended.

"Irwin," I began after sitting down next to him while he was still at the computer, "can you help me get back at Castro for the black-ink-on-my-ears incident?"

"Sure. Anything I can do to help a member of my community and a fellow orange card. What do you have in mind?"

"Castro and I have gotten to know each other in the short time we've been here, and he was trying to get me a job in the media productions. I went to see Mr. Walter today, and he gave me the job, but I want him to think Mr. Walter gave you the job and not me. The only reason I want him to think that is that the size of the office and you. Except for Mr. Harper, you are probably the biggest guy on compound." With him standing six foot four and 250 pounds, just the idea of having to maneuver around in the office with Irwin working there would be enough to send Castro over the edge, with me standing there, waving as he went by. Payback sucks, doesn't it?

"Don't do anything until after lunch," I told Mr. Irwin. "If I rush him with it at eleven thirty movement, he will know it's a setup. I will come get you between lunch and one thirty movement to spring it on him." It felt good to be the instigator instead of the victim for a change, and I was just hoping that Irwin wouldn't fold.

Wednesday was sub sandwich day, which was one of the best lunches this place had to offer. Fresh, homemade hoagie roll, cold cuts, chips, and the usual carrot and/or celery sticks made for a pleasant meal. The problem was, with the allotted time and the chewy bread and the fact that we had to put it all together, there was very little time left to eat it. Every Wednesday, you could see guys stuffing their pockets or see faces with as much as they had room for on the way out of the chow hall. I would just stuff as much as I could in my mouth, having learned my lesson on Thanksgiving.

Around one o'clock, I went downstairs to have Irwin go upstairs to talk to Castro about the new job Mr. Walter had given him earlier today, and Irwin actually seemed excited to be on the better end of a prank than he had been lately. He waited two minutes for me to go back upstairs, and then he came wandering through the tier, looking around like he was lost. Strolling up to the bunk next to Castro, he asked somebody, "Where can I find Mr. Castro?"

Being only two bunks away, Castro overheard the question, looked up when he heard his name, and curiously replied, "I am Mr. Castro. What do you want me for?" I watched from my bunk down the tier as they stood face-to-face and Irwin dropped the news to Castro.

"Mr. Walter just hired me to work in media productions, and my name is Mr. Irwin. He said, since you were also in unit 4, you could be my mentor and kind of show me the ropes."

The look on Mr. Castro's face was priceless. He looked like a twelve-year-old kid who had just realized his bicycle was stolen as he came out of the 7-Eleven. I turned away from the scene in case he looked over at me, because this was too sweet to end now.

"Okay, Irwin," Castro said with a blank look on his face. "I will see you in the library after one thirty movement. Nice to meet you." They bumped knuckles, and Irwin headed back downstairs, stomping his 250 pounds with every step and giving me a wink as he went. He should have received an Oscar for his perfect performance. He never broke down, never smiled, and never gave any impression that he was not on the up and up. Castro began sulking, and then he headed over to me to let me know about his newfound good fortune.

"Mr. Walter hired Irwin to work in media productions instead of you. Now I have to train the big guy, who is going to have a hard-enough time just fitting in that room with the rest of us, and I don't even know the guy. How did you fuck up your interview and not get the job, Walker?"

"I did everything you told me to a tee. I pulled it off perfectly, and since you colored my ears with black ink, I felt compelled to have Mr. Irwin help me get even with you after Mr. Walter gave me the job this morning."

"You son of a bitch!" he said, smiling from ear to ear. "So that's how it's going to be from now on, huh? Are you sure you want to go there? You want to go toe-to-toe with me pulling pranks from now on until we go home?" His comment was almost scary, knowing the collaboration of prank this man was capable of.

"I would rather team up and work together, pulling our creative resources and going after whoever crosses our path or deserves it the most."

"That sounds better than having to watch my back all the time. Deal?"

"Sounds good to me," I said as we knuckled on it. "Mr. Walter told me not to come in until Monday morning, so now I have the rest of the week off and, thanks to you, the best job on compound to look forward to at the beginning of the week. Nice job on Franz, by the way. Aren't you worried about getting in trouble for having other people in the office?"

"I knew him from county, and he is a stand-up guy. He wouldn't get me in trouble just like you didn't, but yeah, we do have to be careful. We get caught with anyone in there who doesn't work there, and we could lose our job. Mr. Walter caught somebody once, and that's why he got fired in the first place, and you wouldn't even be around."

I wasn't planning on inviting the compound into the office so I could color their ears, so it didn't really matter to me.

I was spending the afternoon working on my portfolio in the unit when I was introduced to a different approach to the portfolio project. Some of the guys who had been here a while and were proficient on the computer had figured out a way to capitalize on the free market economy while locked up in prison in a cashless society, as I had done while running store back in county. The difference was the risk factor involved. You had 119 eyes on you at all times plus the bubble.

These individuals had already had their portfolio graded or reviewed. This gave them the advantage of already knowing just what to do and what not to do to make sure you passed without drawing attention to yourself or getting in trouble for copying. I actually thought some of these guys worked as teacher's aides in the school and helped to put on the portfolio workshop class that finalized and checked off the portfolio on your to-do list. Some of the other orange cards who happened to have money on their books were more eager to share this information with the new guys in the group because the broke individuals who would offer this service would be watching for us to come back inside on commissary day and see if we wanted to trade. Apparently, the going rate for getting your portfolio completed to workshop specification was $10 worth of commissary. For a guy like me with $600 to $700 on my books, as opposed to eight or nine hours' worth of work that I realistically didn't need to do, it wasn't a trade at all. It was a steal. However, if getting caught doing this somehow could cause me to flop my rider, then it would definitely not be worth it, and this weighed heavily on my mind. Since at this point I had no commissary to trade yet anyways, I continued to work on mine to the best of my limited abilities. I never liked these kinds of assignments in school and had no reason to believe this particular one would be any different, so I just plowed away, doing all the easy stuff.

Some other guys were working on answering questions out of a variety of colored pamphlets. After completing the reading assignment, you then had to answer twenty or twenty-five questions on the back couple of pages that were a chapter review quiz. Your answers were mailed in locally to be graded, and the essay questions were evaluated by the area's prison ministry service. Once you completed all twelve, you received a framed certificate stating you had successfully completed the home Bible studies course, a series in four parts. This was yet another way to impress your judge, by showing that you had not necessarily found God while incarcerated but had begun to look into the Bible to guide you through your current struggle. A lot of the inmates had the certificate and believed it would help them when going in front of the judge in this extremely religious state. Idaho was said to have been the runner-up among all fifty states in terms of religious extremism, a close second to Utah.

What the hell! I might as well get all the certificates I could get. When I came to a slow spot in my portfolio, I went around, gathering more information about the Bible course, so I could show my judge that even if they wouldn't give me the classes he wanted me to have, I still had kept busy and applied myself as best as I could. This way, he would have absolutely no possible reason to send me back here for a second rider. I already knew a few individuals who were on their second rider right now, and it worried me. The thought of that happening to me was unacceptable, and I was prepared to do anything to prevent it. You were required to get the pamphlets for the course from the chaplain, who was usually in his office in the chapel. You could also get them on Sunday after church services, which I had no intention of attending. My neighbor, Mr. Edlund, overheard me asking about the Bible study courses while he was lying in bed with his kitchen worker uniform, which allowed him to nap periodically throughout the day.

"Walker, come here," he ordered me over, and naturally I went to see what he had for me. "Are you talking about these pamphlets?" He held three or four different chapters in his hand, including the first and second, along with chapters 4 and 7.

"This is exactly what I'm looking for, Mr. Edlund."

"You can have these if you want them. I will grab some more when I go to band practice in the chapel this afternoon."

"Band practice? They have a church band here at Cottonwood?"

"Yeah. Didn't you hear all that music coming out of the church last Sunday morning?"

"Yeah, I guess I did, but I just figured it was a tape or some kind of sound system cranked up for the service."

"We have two guitars, piano, bass, and drums. You should come see the service and hear us play. We are pretty good."

"I think I'll just open my window and listen, but thanks for the pamphlets. I appreciate it."

"No problem. I will get you the rest of them in the next few days."

It was nice of him to help me out. I think it was partly because he knew how around the second or third week, you would want to keep busy getting things done before you got hired. After you got your job, I had been told, you didn't really have much time for anything else while you waited, with all the daily requirements they piled on here. Now I had two projects to keep me busy all weekend between the Bible course and the portfolio. I could jump back and forth without getting burned out on either and still be able to do both with the appropriate amount of effort they each required. Being raised in a Lutheran family and attending church and Sunday school every week until I was fourteen, I realized the pamphlets were basically a refresher course on what I had been exposed to while growing up. It wasn't a difficult quiz, one I possibly could do well on without even reading the pamphlet, but with all the reading I had been doing, it only took ten minutes to buzz through.

I had chapters 1 and 2 completed in less than an hour, but I couldn't mail them off until I received my commissary on Friday. I was in desperate need of stamps to affix to my still-unused collection of county envelopes I had acquired while running store back in county. With an hour until the four thirty count time, I figured, Why not just get chapters 4 and 7 out of the way early? So I did both even if I wasn't doing it in the proper sequence.

After dinner, at the meeting, Mr. Albert had a nice little surprise in store for a couple of hardworking community members. During the push-ups, read by Mr. Walsh, I was pleasantly surprised to find out that Harper's efforts and mine had not gone unnoticed.

"Mr. Albert, pushing up Mr. Walker and Mr. Harper," Walsh read from the push-up slips, while Harper and I stood before the unit, facing Albert. "For going above and beyond community ideals and taking it upon themselves to clear the snow off the jogging path so others may exercise safely." We were given a nice round of applause, followed by a few scattered "Push ups" incessantly shouted in between the round of applause. CO Wiley even came out of the bubble and graced us with a few of his wisely chosen words of wisdom.

"Good evening, community. My name is CO Wiley."

"Good evening, CO Wiley."

"Am I to understand that Walker and Harper cleared the entire jogging path around the ball field with two feet of snow on it?"

"Good evening, community. My name is Mr. Harper," he said as he stood up.

"Good evening, Mr. Harper."

"Yes, sir, Co Wiley. It took us a day and a half," Harper blurted out.

"The amazing thing," CO Wiley replied, "is that I saw Walker run about five miles on Thanksgiving in the gym, but he can't even use the track for a few more weeks, and you would probably have had heart attacks after you rounded the first corner if someone hadn't cleared the snow." Laughter erupted from the unit while he sat up front, enjoying the fact that most of us got his jokes. "Why did you do it?"

I stood up to put in my two cents' worth. "Good evening, community. My name is Mr. Walker."

"Good evening, Mr. Walker."

"Just planning ahead, sir, so that when I can go to rec in twenty-four days, running around the track will still be an option if the new barneys continue the tradition Mr. Harper and I hoped to start. I was just trying to help out my fellow community members who are trying to maintain the physical requirements of recovery, as well as the psychological." I sat down to a round of applause and a few "Push up, Mr. Walkers" that were blurted out.

"Well done, gentlemen," CO Wiley said as he nodded to me and Mr. Harper before heading back into the bubble.

I was again being recognized in a positive manner, in front of the whole unit, for doing something for the common good without being told. I wasn't doing it for recognition but just to keep busy, and I didn't want to get a reputation as a kiss-ass either.

Mr. Edlund was true to his word, and after dinner, he gave me the missing chapters from the Bible study pamphlets that he managed to get from the chaplain earlier. I was hoping that if all went well this weekend, I would be done with the Bible certificate requirements and well on my way to completing my portfolio as well. Since even during free time all weekend you couldn't sleep or watch TV unless you were a blue or green card, I figured I might as well make the most of the next couple of weekends and get as much done as possible, so I could relax later if I wanted to. The way things were going, I had no idea what I would be doing by then.

While the unit emptied out for rec, I broke out the table in front of my bunk and began working on two more chapters of the Bible study while shooting the breeze and helping whoever came by, asking for help. My having the closest bunk to the only microwave on the upper tier meant there would be a constant flow of people coming by with commissary, but with only forty hours left until I received mine, it didn't seem to bother me as much as it had during the last twenty-nine days I was forced to go without. People would slowly come by and introduce themselves while their water heated up. Occasionally, a small group of two or three would stop and chat about one thing or another. I was slowly getting to know almost everybody in the unit on some level, and I liked to think it was because of all the hard work and extra effort I was putting into the program. Maybe that was just the way it was here, or it could have been the microwave. Eventually, I would know the real reason, but for now, it was just nice to be recognized and feel at home.

CHAPTER

45

THURSDAY AND FRIDAY WERE BOTH about the most boring and slow two days I had at Cottonwood. With orientation completed and no need to search for a job, all I had to do was work on my portfolio, work on the Bible study chapters, and watch the seconds tick away until my month without commissary was behind me. I was back to reading fiction from the library now instead of my handbook, which I had completely memorized. Between sessions at the table in front of my bunk, I would go shovel snow or pace to get some exercise. The purple cards would be asking questions about the place, just as we did last week, so I tried to help as many of them to relax and get going on their phase changes as early as possible. Since I had already been to basic and completed twenty-eight days of rehab, I felt this place was a unique combination of the two, and I personally found adjusting to life here very easy. I could only imagine what was going through the minds of most of the guys who rolled into this place without a clue as to what to expect. I am sure it was all pretty overwhelming. Then on Friday afternoon, just about the time I had given up, the commissary truck pulled in, and suddenly life seemed just about as good as it could get in prison.

While incarcerated, a person has so little to enjoy or look forward to that commissary day becomes the one time of the week that everyone looks forward to. Even those who have no money or commissary ordered look forward to it, because even though it doesn't work for the average citizen, trickle-down economics works perfectly well for the incarcerated. It was very difficult in county to open your bin box and make your third or fourth cup of coffee while the guy next to you, whose wife was cheating on him and had a restraining order not to see her or her kids, was drinking hot water and had been for weeks now. There always seemed to be an overwhelming feeling to help those less fortunate than you, especially when you were locked up and had a full locker or bin box. If you were locked up and there were people who were still less fortunate than you, then you felt for the guy and tried to help him in even the smallest way to make his existence just a little more bearable. Even though it was strictly against the rules, I had not written up anyone for trading commissary, and only rarely heard about it. The bottom line was just not to be obvious about it, or else people in this kind of program would literally be forced to write you up for it or they themselves would be written up for turning a blind eye, and then get in just as much trouble. It was a fine line we were constantly walking. Balancing charity with survival was growing more difficult every day. Now that my commissary would soon be in my possession, I had to quickly figure out just how to juggle all the options that lay before me.

I anxiously watched out the window as each unit was called down to the classroom across Main Street from the unit. They would line up and wait for their names to be called. It took about twenty minutes for the first unit to get all their stuff, and then there were the usual two or three guys who were left out in the cold with nothing they had been anticipating showing up for them. Computer glitches, money not deposited in time, or even a lost commissary sheet would mean they were burnt until next week. Not only the psychological letdown after a long wait was factored in, but they had also spent the last half an hour out in the cold for nothing. If your stuff wasn't there, that was it. There was not a customer service department to expedite an overnight box for you. You were burnt. End of story. See you next week, maybe. I had heard about the commissary truck going off the road only a few weeks back, killing the driver. That week, Cottonwood and the prison up at Orofino had to go without because the truck was carrying commissary for both prisons when the accident happened. I had to go without commissary since I left county almost a month ago. It reminded me of how agonizing it was to wait for the first twelve days or so in county and how I felt when my commissary finally did show up.

As I went through all the possible scenarios, it crossed my mind as I watched these guys walk back up Main Street, heads hung low and empty-handed. I knew it was possible that I, too, might not get mine after all the waiting. Not wanting to be too let down, I tried to go into my "plan for the worst, hope for the best" mode, but I had to be honest with myself too. I was way past planning on the worst. I had waited a long time, and today should have been my day.

Around 4:00 p.m., they finally called for our unit to line up outside, and I knew, good or bad, I would have my answer shortly.

I stood in the persistent snowfall for twenty minutes, listening to names being called, only to be disappointed at not hearing mine and figuring out there was no system at all to the distribution process period. With only ten or so left freezing our asses off, the commissary lady came out of the building, and my heart sank. The burnt inmate I had witnessed earlier was now me. Things had been good for a while for the most part. In and out of RDU, nice bunk again, best job on compound—hey, I was due for some sort of letdown. Why did it have to be commissary? In my haste to dwell on the negative, I barely even heard the sweetest thing since I arrived as I began to head back to the unit.

"The rest of you, gentlemen, will have to come back after count."

Thank God I still had a chance! The thought of commissary so consumed me that I had no idea we only had five minutes to get to our bunks and be ready for count. Could they possibly drag this out any longer? I seriously began to wonder if I had filled out my form properly, or maybe Mr. Tortelli never turned it in on purpose just to mess with me. There were too many options to consider, so I grabbed my book and made the best of the longest count I could remember. Since we still had to finish with commissary, we would be last for chow, and when count finally cleared, the ten of us that still had hope quickly went back outside to resume our places in the continuing snowstorm to wait for our names to be called. I knew it wasn't an orange-card-restriction thing, because I had seen others I had arrived with already receiving their commissary. For some reason, it came as no surprise to me to be the last guy standing outside when the reality of going without for one more week was closer and closer to becoming a reality. When my name was finally called, a wave of relief passed through me. Now I was free from the monotonous meals and hungry weekends I had endured for so long. It appeared at that moment that I had come over the crest of my journey and it would be all downhill from here. The only bad thing left was getting through Christmas, but at least I would have the things that made life comfortable for me. I would never be without again.

Since I was the last guy on compound to receive my stuff, when I went back into the unit, everyone was standing around, waiting to go on line for chow, as I walked through with my huge bag of commissary. Now everyone knew I had tons of stuff and probably would for the duration of my stay here. Now I would be hassled constantly. Green cards could enjoy commissary whenever they wanted. Blue and orange cards had time restrictions as to when they could partake. An hour in the morning, after the evening meeting, and on weekends were all I was allowed for now, so I couldn't even have a bite of a candy bar until the meeting was over later tonight without the risk of getting pulled up. Friday, Saturday, and Sunday were CO Wiley's days off also, and that meant that we were at the mercy of whatever power-tripping CO was destined to take his place. Depending on who it was would determine how our evenings would be spent. Some of the COs were different as night and day. While some were helpful, respectful, and genuinely concerned with rehabilitation of each individual here, others had absolutely no place working in a program like this with a clear conscience.

These COs had chips on their shoulders and were out to prove how superior they were to all of us. They made our lives a living hell. Mr. Reemer was one of those types, and as soon as we headed down for the meeting, I knew it was going to be a long weekend. He was a scrawny little guy with a Napoleon complex. He was getting his CO start here so he could work his way up to maximum security at the yard, where all the badasses were. Maybe that was where the real money was if you were a career CO. I assumed they got hazard pay. I wasn't sure, but that was where all the asshole COs wanted to be assigned. Apparently, messing with the riders for a year or so was part of their training program.

As we came down for the meeting, Mr. Reemer was standing outside the bubble with a hand folded across his chest, waiting for somebody to talk or get out of line so he could jump their ass. We all filed in and took our seats, but it was inevitable that to prove what a hard-ass he was, it was necessary for him to get at least one person in trouble, even for nothing. And so he did. The meeting was like any other except for the fact that we missed out on CO Wiley's words of wisdom, which all of us had come to appreciate and take to heart. When the meeting was over, Mr. Reemer made us sit quietly in our chairs for ten minutes because of all the disruptiveness before and during the meeting, which was truly nonexistent on our part and a childish control trip for him. He was worse than most drug addicts who are waiting for a fix. His addiction was to power and control, and he found it amusing to inflict pain on others. Once ten minutes were up, he told us to place all our belongings on our bunks and be prepared for property inspection in five minutes. This reminded me of superexchange in county, where the COs would go through the unit after we received commissary to match all the receipts with what we had, mainly to get guys in trouble or filing new charges for the sole benefit of the dollars that brought in to keep us there longer.

Being my first commissary day and having not unpacked it yet, all I did was take out my receipt and my bag, and I was ready for inspection. He spent the next two hours going through everybody's commissary and the receipts that went with it, along with a locker and a bunk inspection, during which time he found fifteen or twenty different people who had managed to collect, over time, extra items that they should not have had in their possession. Two pillows stuffed in one pillowcase, extra blankets, shower shoes, or thermal underwear without receipt. These were simple luxuries that had been handed down to guys by departing community members that hadn't been purchased on their own commissary, so the CO confiscated them. It was technically a rule violation that could possibly lead to severe punishment or at least sanction. The bigger problem was, he was also holding neighbors of the offenders responsible for not writing the offender up for the violation, and then the coordinator for not keeping a close eye on his crew. It was all bullshit. He was looking to make a name for himself as hard-ass CO and, in the process, was ruining lives of some good men who deserved nothing more than having to write a two-page essay on how it was detrimental to the community.

Some of the offenders had notations put in their chronology report that went to the judges. If the judges felt it was a severe-enough infraction, these guys could end up in prison for a couple of years just for acquiring some extra underwear because they didn't want to freeze to death during the fire drills. Most COs didn't care about the little things, but this guy did. Before it was all over, twenty-five or thirty people were in trouble, and if you had one of the few particularly strict judges, you might be coming back for another rider because of what had happened tonight. It seemed to me that it was too much power for one asshole to have, and since the COs worked alone in the units, there was nobody to hold him in check. So after missing rec because of the inspection and the disciplinary action and paperwork that followed, we were pretty much confined to our bunks for the rest of the night and told to program until 9:00 p.m. This meant no consumption of commissary until tomorrow. After waiting so long, I was now forced to wait even longer. At this point, I didn't really care. At least it was in my bin box, and that in itself gave me peace of mind. Mr. Reemer would go home eventually, and the unit would be back to normal. The guy had single-handedly, and for no good reason, ruined a perfectly good Friday night for the 120 of us in unit 4 just to prove he could.

Mr. Thorne warned us to clean extragood tonight before we started our house duties and to keep the shower short, for obvious reasons. We all understood completely, and I was never happier to finally get into bed and read my book as I was tonight. Just when I started to get used to this place, CO Reemer came along with his degrading treatment of us. It reminded me of basic training again.

The COs worked twelve-hour shifts, so we only had two to deal with each day, but more than likely, Reemer would be back again tomorrow to see how much more he could mess with us. The only good thing was that he wouldn't be here for superclean in the morning, and for that, I was grateful.

Saturday morning at five o'clock, I was finally allowed to partake of my commissary without violating any of the rules set forth in the handbook. People were sneaking some of their food items last night while we were programming as per CO Reemer, but after waiting over a month to receive it, I wasn't about to test fate or a possible sanction with mine. It felt good to wake up and get a cup of coffee with a ton of hot cocoa in it. One of the benefits of having the closest bunk to the microwave was that nobody could get out of bed faster than I could, which meant I would be the first one to heat up my water every morning and until some green card took my bunk from me. Going without since RDU lowered my tolerance once again, and by the time we were lined up for chow, I was wired.

Weekend breakfasts were always bigger and quite filling by jail standards. This would be my first weekend not on purple card restrictions and to be able to enjoy the pleasure of commissary. Knowing that I had all the food I wanted until dinner gave me the peace of mind and allowed me to enjoy the weekend for the first time since arriving at Cottonwood. Now that we were on the house committee and cleaning the unit all week, superclean on Saturday morning didn't really seem too bad either. With each committee taking on the task of thoroughly doing what twelve of us had done daily all week long, this week all we did was sit around and wait until everyone else was done so we could mop half the unit. I had mopped half the unit each night this week alone while everyone else slept, and today I had three guys helping.

Since there were only four mops in the unit, two upstairs and two downstairs on each floor, one was only used for the bathrooms and one was only used for the tier floor. Everyone was on their bunks with their feet up, waiting for me and my helpers to finish so the senior coordinator could inspect the unit with the CO and we could begin our free time. I almost felt rushed with all the eyes on me. I rather enjoyed the time to myself at night, the peace and quiet, and the short discussions with people as I would work in their area quietly. With ball games to watch and fatigue from a long week setting in, there was a sense of urgency to get the mopping done and use my free time to read or exercise before shift change and the uncertainty that came with it. Free time only lasted until 3:00 p.m. today if CO Reemer showed up and began messing with us as he did yesterday. Having only been here thirteen days, I wasn't really sure if what he pulled last night was normal or not. Judging by the reaction of the unit as a whole, it appeared not, and I could only hope that was the case. I continued to mop as fast as I could without missing any spots that might cause a whole unit to fail inspection.

Free time couldn't have come early enough for the blue and green cards, who were fortunate enough to have TV and sleeping privileges. They immediately scrambled for the best seats in the dayroom as the college football season was beginning to get interesting. Others, like me, grabbed a folding table as quickly as possible and set it up in front of Jesus's bunk, which just happened to have a view of the dayroom TV. Since Mr. Edlund had brought me a few more Bible study chapters to work on, I figured this would be as good a place as any to start my weekend. Jesus and a couple of other guys from our arrival group pulled up our chairs. We began to watch the game—I mean, we worked on our portfolios or Bible certificates while talking back and forth. I also noticed that since we had all been together last weekend, many more of us had discovered the Bible study pamphlets from one another or other neighbors in the unit. I guess everyone wanted to have more certificates in their portfolios to show the judge. And who could blame them?

Before long, Mr. Irwin came up to join us and sat down across from me with some interesting information on the Bible study certificate. "Good morning, gentlemen. Can I join your work table?" he asked us in a very formal tone. Everybody welcomed him, and he revealed his new information. "Did you know you can become a minister while you are in here? I have seen five guys downstairs to

306

have a certificate of ministry from the New Life Church." He jumped up to go downstairs as he yelled back to us, "I will grab you guys one and show you!"

"Jesus," I said, "do you want to be a minister in the New Life Church?"

"No, thank you. I am strictly Catholic, and I have no desire to become a priest. My wife wouldn't like it much either."

When Irwin came back upstairs, we all looked at the certificate he had in his hands. It said so and so "has been ordained on this day and has all the rights and privileges to perform all the duties of the ministry." It came from the Universal Life Church in Modesto, California.

"What do you have to do to become a minister for this church?" I asked.

"It is much easier than the Bible study course. All you have to do is send them $5 and your name and address, and they send you one of these certificates. Pretty easy, I'd say."

"Yeah, it's easy, but if the judges know it's that easy as well, Mr. Irwin, what's the point? If they think or they know the only reason you did it was to get another certificate, it might actually offend some of the religious right-wing judges in Boise."

"Another certificate is another certificate," Irwin told me.

He had a point, and there were a lot of fellows around who, later that day, I would discover, were ministers in the Universal Life Church. Strength in numbers, I always say, and if it was a bad thing, then most people wouldn't be signing up. The more people I'd talked to throughout the day, the more it seemed that almost everybody in here was a minister, so I decided to go with the flow. What could it hurt? If the judge wanted to see change, I'd make sure he saw change. Five bucks, three hundred inmates, four or five times a year, and the Universal Life Church made $7,500 off this facility this year alone, times how many prisoners in the country? Nice little business they had going. For extra monetary contributions, they would even send you certificates with a title to them. I could be a deacon, bishop, or cardinal in their church if the price was right. Five bucks was all they were going to get out of me, as I was reluctant to send them even that much.

CHAPTER

46

ITH A GOOD CHUNK OF my portfolio done and two-thirds of the Bible study course complete, I was looking for another project to help occupy my time until I was a blue card and was able to enjoy the weekend as much as some of the others did. My Seahawks were on a roll and dominating the NFC west and had a good winning streak going. Most of the guys here were big Denver NFL football fans, and the Broncos were doing okay as well. No new snow had fallen lately, and it was really cramping my exercise routine, so I was again back to pacing in between chapters and reading some fiction I had checked out from the library. After the reception I got from my phase change seminar, I was contemplating doing some writing with all the free time I had. I had read over forty books by now and was pretty sure I could write something better than some of the books I had read, but with no real experience or training, it could be a waste of time. When you think about it, though, time was the one thing I had plenty of, so what did I have to lose? I also had about fifteen pages of notes I had taken from the self-help books I read during the first week, not to mention some interesting quotes from the fiction books as well. Combine that with four or five pages of Proverbs and words of wisdom from the Bible, and the notes I had accumulated were becoming rather extensive.

The other thing I noticed from all this was the fact that I had actually enjoyed writing the phase change, and I think it showed. My buddy Scott was always writing in his journal back in county, and the Vietnam vet had written some pretty good short stories about his adventures in the war. I had kept a journal during my stay in rehab, but those entries were for feelings about sobriety more than a story.

I was considering keeping a journal of what was happening to me in prison, which might not be exciting enough to become a story, but I wouldn't know the answer until it was finished, and by then it would be too hard to go back and remember everything that happened.

I decided to keep track of the major events that took place during the rider so if anything interesting did happen, I would be able to tell the story from my notes. This would also be a cleansing process, as it had when I had written down my drug history in rehab. We had to read to the groups the stories of what had transpired in our lives, and I read my story to the group and was told both times how interesting it was to hear. Maybe I have a gift for storytelling, and with nothing else to do and a lot of spare time on my hands, what a better way to be productive than to find out once and for all if I had the ability to write something others would want to read.

The thought of doing this was inspiring and motivational. This place was a perfect setting to accomplish something that I had kept only in the back of my mind until now. If I could leave here with a book or a movie idea, then maybe my time here would not have been in vain. All things happen for a reason, and maybe this was mine.

I went outside to pace and gather ideas, as I had with the phase change. The fresh air and solitude were extremely useful for clearing my head.

The only thing I knew for certain about writing was that I would need discipline and a time schedule allowing for a certain amount each day to be spent writing, and sure as the sun came up, eventually I would have a manuscript. With all the different assignments to carry out and with COs who could ruin your day at the drop of a hat, it would be difficult. There was only one thing certain, time that I could always count on each day and a location to make writing possible. Three times each day, we sat on our bunks and tried for thirty minutes not to be bored. If I could turn the downtime into productive writing time for that long, three times a day, seven days a week, until I left, I would be as productive as I possibly could during count time. I took some paper and a pen with me to jot down notes and keep things in order, and before too long, I would be well on my way to an outline of what I needed to do. It felt good to have another project to work on, and this one would last me the rest of my time here. Maybe even longer. I went back inside for the eleven thirty count and put my plan into action. I took out some paper, pulled my bin box on my lap, and began as I had planned. It was all strange to me, but it also came more easily than expected. In the next twenty minutes, I had already written three pages. Once count was over, I did a little math and figured out that with three counts, seven days a week, for four or five months, I would easily have over a thousand pages done before I left. I knew that was far too much for a book or a movie, but they weren't actual pages; they were more like notes to work from when the time came to actually do the writing.

Handwritten pages on notebook paper were different from the same pages in a book, and I knew that, but it was a start, and I was having a good time in the process.

It was also great to be able to enjoy some lunch from my commissary on the weekend for the first time. I went downstairs when I had eaten to chat with Mr. Tortelli and tell him about my new project. He had no money on his books, and I knew he was indigent, so if there was anything I could do to alleviate his hunger, I would be more than happy to help him out. He was leaving on Tuesday, and I wanted to thank him for helping me during the first week and for letting us manage the laundry the way we did. His positive response to my phase change was also a catalyst for the writing I had begun, and I just wanted to say thanks and goodbye before things got too hectic at the beginning of the week.

"Congratulations, Mr. Tortelli," I told him. "You made it, and you get to go home on Tuesday. I am totally jealous."

"Why, thank you, Mr. Walker. I see you got your commissary finally."

"Yeah, and just between you and me," I said, lowering my voice and looking around to see that no one was nearby, "if there's anything I can do for you food-wise, don't be afraid to ask. You were good to me my first week, and I appreciate that more than you will ever know."

"Well, thanks. I might take you up on your offer tomorrow, but I am good for now. You will do fine here. I could tell it from the first day I saw you."

"I hope so. Three years in prison doesn't exactly sound like fun to me. I am actually starting to enjoy this program, if you can believe that."

"A lot of people do after they settle in. Have you found yourself a job yet?"

"Castro hooked me up with an opening in the media production. Says it's the best job on compound. And I start Monday."

"Good for you. That is a good job, inside the library, playing on computers all day. You should have a good time the rest of your stay."

"I'm also starting to write about what is happening to me here since my phase change was so well-received. Some of the things you said stuck in my mind, and I just wanted you to know before you left that it helped me to become motivated and productive here, and I have to thank you for that. Or possibly blame. We'll see how it turns out."

"Good for you, Mr. Walker. I hope it all turns out well. This is a good place, despite what happened last night. The COs care about us, and most of them are here to help. CO Wiley is a good man. Unit 4 is the best unit on compound, and he is a big part of the reason."

"Just wanted to say thanks and good luck. Take care, if I don't get a chance to say goodbye again."

"Good luck to you too, Mr. Walker."

With that, we shook hands and I headed back upstairs to join my group at the table and began getting some things done. If I was going to be stuck here for a few months, I might as well have something to show for it.

I spent the rest of the afternoon working on the last couple of bible chapters I had the books for, and then I went back to outlining my notes for the past two weeks so I wouldn't forget what had happened before I had time to write about it. I also asked around and found out that the number of ministers here from the Universal Life Church was 75 to 80 percent of the prison population, and that spoke volumes for the value of the certificate. I sent my application in this afternoon so I could be part of the majority and add one more certificate to my portfolio as soon as possible.

Since I was able to eat lunch for the first time since I began the two-meal system, dinner was almost too big. Without my starving all day, the meal now appeared to be extremely large, and for the first time since I arrived, I left some food on my tray that wasn't particularly to my liking. I noticed a few guys who coincidentally happened to have a well-stocked locker who wouldn't eat any bread or potato products at any meal. By cutting out hash browns, mashed potatoes, rolls, and such, you could effectively reduce your starch and carbs intake dramatically and replace it with beef jerky and tuna packages from commissary. These guys were usually green cards who were on six-month riders, and with all the weight lifting and running to be done at rec, a person could actually have a pretty good makeover going on by the time they went home. Therein lay the catch-22 with your rider length. If you stay that long, it sucks, but if you go home after ninety days, you only get weights and lots of rec for thirty days before you leave, which isn't enough time to accomplish much. Ada County meals were essentially a starvation diet, but some county jails load you up on starch and bread before you're sent here. Some guys put on a lot of weight over the course of their incarceration, and what you ate needed to be paid attention to, or you could put on the pounds really easy.

I didn't even notice before dinner that we were lucky enough to not get CO Reemer tonight, which everyone was talking about before we went down to the meeting. During the meeting, all the pull-ups from the inspection that Reemer did last night were read, along with all the essays and sanctions that came with them. It usually took a few minutes to do this, but tonight it took ten. When all was said and done, over twenty people were pulled up, and most likely, only three or four deserved to be. This was all part of the program, I understood, but clogging the system with trivial bullshit as he had done would be detrimental to the good of the unit as a whole. The next few days, the meetings would be overloaded with trivial essays for things most COs didn't care about, and this would then take time away from other important issues we needed to attend to daily.

Without Reemer to ruin our evening, all was well in the prison world, and we enjoyed a relaxing evening doing whatever we wanted—within allowed restrictions, of course. During my short stay here, we had to deal with four COs each week. One CO would be in the unit from morning until 3:00 p.m., and another until 3:00 a.m., Monday through Thursday. The other three days a week, we would sometimes get the same two for all three days, and other times it would just be a random selection. I still wasn't sure if this was the normal way things were done or if CO Gherkin and her medical leave had thrown the unit into a more sporadic schedule than the other units, but I would find out in due time. Since the attitude and demeanor of the CO could greatly affect the comfort level in the unit, which CO was going to be with us on a given day was of major concern. The only constant presence so far had been CO Wiley, Monday through Thursday, on the evening shift, which was inherently more important than the day shift, when almost everyone was at work or in classes. Having the wrong CO on duty in the evening would take away from our free time after the evening meeting until bedtime, and this was something most of us looked forward to daily.

Sunday was a repeat of Saturday, except that I got a shitload of writing done while watching the NFL game through the dayroom window. Watching football and writing went very well together. I had time to write in between plays, while gathering my thoughts. Before I knew it, it was dinnertime, and I realized I had been at the table all afternoon, getting over twenty pages down on paper and out of my head. The only thing I noticed was that it came so naturally to me it was almost startling. Now I only had to find out if what I was writing was interesting and marketable or just a waste of time. But I wouldn't know that until I was out of prison, and by then, the time I had put in would already be spent.

CHAPTER 47

ONDAYS WERE ALWAYS BUSY AT Cottonwood with all the going-home riders packing up to leave and the new arrival showing up from RDU. This particular Monday was even busier since I now had to report to the library and begin my job in the media production room with Mr. Castro. When the morning meeting was finished, I signed out and walked with him up to the library during the eight thirty movement and eagerly awaited the beginning of my new job. He introduced me to the two other guys who would be working with us while I shook their hands and tried to size them up. Mr. McGladrey was a tall, dark-haired, late-twenties guy from unit 2, and Mr. Cobbs was a short, stocky, and very tattooed kid from unit 3. Along with Castro, the two of them settled into the seat in front of their computers in the long skinny room and begin to tell me the way things worked.

"The objective, Mr. Walker," McGladrey began to explain to me, "is to get as little done as possible while looking like you are busier than shit. Think you can handle that?"

"I think so? Since I really don't know how to do any of the things I put on my résumé, anyways," I replied.

"How did you get the job, then? This is the best job on compound," said Mr. McGladrey.

"Castro told me what to write on my résumé and what to say to Mr. Walter, or I would probably be scrubbing pots and pans with a red kitchen shirt on right now."

"Walker here owes me big-time, don't you, Mr. Walker?" Castro interjected with a big grin on his face. He reached over and put his hand on my shoulder, squeezing it to make sure I understood.

"I guess I do, Mr. Castro. Is this going to get expensive, or am I your bitch until the day you leave?"

Everybody started laughing, and with that I was accepted by the office staff. They showed me the music selections that had been smuggled in by groups before us. It was the same music that had been used to lure me into the office while my tormentor circled my ears with black ink last week. Now it was my turn to return the favor. Once the whole unit saw someone scrubbing his ears, you were pretty much burnt with that joke until a new batch showed up next week. With four units on the compound, sometimes you could get two people from each unit before word got around.

The main rule in Cottonwood was that no one could be any place where they were not permitted to be. No one other than the inmates who worked there could enter the kitchen or the media production center. We needed to be very careful about whom we invited into the room, or we could be in trouble with the two teachers who oversaw our work: Mr. Walter and Mr. Raymon. These guys had already figured out their schedules and pretty much knew when it was safe to let someone in and when it wasn't. Word spread fast that we had music in our office, and all morning long, people would stick their heads in to listen to music for the first time in months, only to be told they couldn't come in.

Occasionally, we would invite a friend in, but these visits were few and far between. During these moments, one of us would stand guard outside the door to alert the others if the teachers came back unannounced. If this happened, we had to slip that person out in a two- or three-second window of opportunity, or we would all be in deep shit. Losing your job was a major infraction that your judge would not look upon favorably. Getting caught with guest in media production room would definitely get one fired.

They showed me the games that were available on the computer. It turned out most of the time here was spent gaming. Playing solitaire, pinball, and FreeCell was the most popular, but not as played according to the rules. If you were going to play, one person needed to have a chair up against the door, so if a teacher or CO tried to get in, the game could quickly be erased before the chair blocking the door could be moved. This, too, was a violation that could get you fired, and for the good of the group, the game playing had to be kept secret; the records of the wins and losses had to be erased each time we left the office. We never knew when our hard drives would be scanned or searched for contraband, and the last thing we wanted was a score posted on the game site. Something as simple as racing stats could cause you to lose all the perks that came with the job.

They also showed me a few videos made by previous groups in the office and then let me in on one of the perks that would benefit me personally: total access to the library. That was how Castro was getting me the books when I first got here. All we had to do was go out to the library to pick up a book and bring it back into the office. Once movement was called, we put it in our pocket and take it back to the unit. It was better than the librarian job.

Instead of one hour twice a week, we could browse anytime the teachers weren't around, take any book without checking it out, and just switch it for a new one once we were done. We obviously had to be careful about it, but just as I had gathered my own private book-store in county, I now had the whole library at my disposal. I wasn't planning on abusing the opportunity, but it did raise my comfort level, knowing I had unlimited fiction choices available until the day I left. I could also search the library for interesting books and my favorite authors in my spare time. I could read the back of the jackets, all in the name of research, for whatever project I was sup-posedly working on in the office. Time flew by. Before I knew it, it was time for eleven thirty movement. The morning seemed to zip by, and that was exactly what I was hoping for by getting a job as soon as I could. I had found out in county that the busier a man kept himself, the quicker each day went, and then suddenly, one day they let you out. I was applying that theory to my time here so the time I would be here would go by as fast as possible. I still had not met with my counselor yet, which was when you found out just how long of a rider you were on and the one important question I still had no answers to.

Kim, Ramirez, Albert, and Strahm all were on six-month riders, along with many others, and if that was the case for me, I wouldn't get home until sometime in early April. I was sick to death of basic training after one month, and the thought of being here for six months was overwhelming. While it was slowly turning from scary to tolerable, even productive to some degree, the sooner I got home to my family, the better.

The afternoon went even more quickly than the morning; only this time I was briefed as to what was really expected of me instead of what I could get away with. We were basically at the disposal of Mr. Walter and Mr. Raymon, making videos, movies, or safety PowerPoint presentations for the occupational safety course. During our downtime, we could invent and persuade any project we chose if it had staff approval, and we or a partner was able to complete it before we left. Castro had just finished something the guys before him had not finished and let me know we should come up with a project to begin once he was done with the old one.

McGladrey and Cobbs were working on some safety PowerPoint presentation for Mr. Raymon, and they would be done in two or three weeks. I was on my own killing time until somebody else was done, and that gave me time to brainstorm. Once an idea was conceived, we then had to outline it and present it on paper and verbally to Mr. Walter for staff approval before getting the go-ahead to persuade it. We needed to show some kind of progress each week and document it on our job skills booklet, so the staff would see what was being accomplished.

With all this to think about, I was also watching McGladrey, who was working on a PowerPoint, so I would at least know what it was I claimed I was capable of doing on my job application. Being more of a hands-on type of guy, I found it difficult to just watch and learn. I probably would have understood it better if I actually had done it as he talked me through, but this was his baby, and I think he was afraid I might really screw up if I did something wrong. If I were him, I wouldn't want some idiot erasing a month's worth of work with the wrong keystroke, so I just sat back and observed while trying to come up with a good idea for a project. I also discovered one of the benefits of working in the library was one that Castro hadn't even bothered to mention. We had access to our own private bathroom with a door and only one toilet in it. We weren't given the privilege of having a lock on it, but considering the five toilets side by side in the unit, this was agreeable. Having access to newspapers as well, we could go in the restroom with the paper and have some privacy for the first time in three months. The small things that you find enjoyable while locked up always amaze me.

During movement, with nowhere to go and the library empty, I would read book jackets that looked interesting and slowly begin to compile a list of possible reading choices. Already having chosen a few favorite authors, I felt it was also necessary to expand my reading genres and make sure that some new authors I hadn't read yet were included on my list. The broader my horizons were while reading would only help my situation should I decide to do any kind of writing now or in the future. I also introduced myself to some of the librarians, none of whom were from unit 4. Keeping them on my side could only enhance my situation. As long as I was working in the same building, in desperate need of their cooperation, they would allow me to move about freely in their domain. If one of them chose to be an uptight prick and write me up for not checking out books as I was supposed to, I could get in serious trouble and even lose my job. I decided to tread lightly at first in order to feel things out before doing anything that could possibly have serious repercussions.

Just as in the morning, before I knew it, four thirty movement had come and the day was over. On my way back to the unit, Main Street was crawling with new barneys heading from the laundry room with their new uniforms and bag stuffed with linen and exercise clothing, each branching off and heading to their units for count. I looked them over for familiar faces as they went by, and who should I see but my good old Jay, my late-night reading buddy from county, who was now two weeks behind me. Without getting in trouble, we gave each other a quick nod of recognition and I flashed him the number 4 with my fingers and nodded toward my unit. He shook his head no, flashed me the number 2 with his fingers, and we continued in our separate ways.

Except during work details, no talking in the chow hall or on Main Street was the most strictly enforced rule COs enforced. Each movement, one or two of them would sit quietly, back in a doorway, watching and listening, just so they could bust you for a rule violation and then tell your buddies to be sure to pull you up. The COs would then check the daily pull-ups and punish violators' friends for not pulling up the violators. It was difficult to stay out of trouble in the prison environment. Turning a blind eye and being caught doing it was more severe violation than the original violation. This was especially true for the green cards and coordinators, who were expected to lead the unit by example and help educate the newer members regarding how things worked. We basically governed ourselves, but the COs could always be in the bubble or in the control room that housed the monitors connected to the security cameras placed in the unit or in various places on compound. It wasn't uncommon for the COs to pull you up for something they had seen even when no one else was nearby. You never knew when you were being watched, and the fact that there was no camera in the media production room was something I was extremely grateful for.

In the beginning, I thought the coordinators had made it up, but after I observed the way it really was for a couple of weeks, I found out the truth. Not only did they have to have their act together, but they had to keep all those below them in the chain of command in line as well. On more than one occasion, the coordinator had been punished for something someone in his crew had done and the coordinator truly had no knowledge of, but that was the way it was. Once you were pulled up, there was no fighting it or arguing about it; it was a done deal, and you had to accept it. Making excuses or blaming someone else was called flipping the indictment, and that was not allowed here. These were the rules you lived by in Cottonwood, and bitching about them or trying to manipulate them was a complete waste of time. That was the way it was.

CHAPTER

48

A S I SAT ON MY bunk, writing, during count, my mind kept drifting, and I found myself actually looking forward to the meeting tonight. Instead of nameless faces saying good-bye with a few choice words, I would actually know some of them, including Mr. Tortelli. I was also curious to see what the new batch of barneys were all about, since the unit was always changing. If the unit had some good guys and everyone was well-behaved, it was much easier when Mr. Reemer was on duty and came down hard on us. If ten good men left and ten schmucks showed up, it would only take a few weeks before the whole unit would suffer, and that made it more difficult to be here. By now, I could read a man just by the way he introduced himself the first night, and if not then, definitely by the end of his first week, when he had to read his first phase change to the unit. When count cleared, the assistant senior coordinator, Mr. Albert, came across the aisle with his chair and sat down at the end of my bunk to talk to me.

"Mr. Walker, what are you doing over here? I see you constantly writing, but I haven't seen any books that you're taking notes on. Talk to me."

"I have decided to journal my experiences here, so I am documenting the events of my rider chronologically until I get caught up to the present day, when it will become easier to keep track daily. Maybe I will turn it into a book someday."

"Good for you. Are you starting to get a feel for the place now that you have been here a little while?"

"Yeah. I am working with Castro in media productions, and it seems like a cool job. I just started today. This place is starting to grow on me, and I definitely feel better than I did the first two weeks."

"Yeah, it's all pretty overwhelming at first. That's why I didn't come over right away to talk to you. I usually give new guys about ten days to settle in and see how they react before associating with them. Around here, the wrong type of guy can pull you down with him. Just look at the guys who sit in the back rows at every meeting."

"I know what you mean, and I try to stay away from most of them. Guilt by association has a high price in this place. Thanks for the note-taking idea. It helped me to come up with the journal idea, and who knows, maybe someday it will result in a book or a movie. It doesn't cost a thing if I have all this time to kill anyway, right?"

"Good for you, Mr. Walker, good for you."

With that, upstairs was called for chow, and Mr. Albert went back across the aisle with his chair and we all put on our coats so we could quietly stand in front of our bunks until it was time to eat. Naturally, on Monday night, someone was always able to set up a barney to trip the emergency exit in the chow hall, and it seemed to be getting funnier each week, or maybe I was just able to appreciate it a little more. Either way, it was another small moment to look forward to each week. The same thing went for the petrified-looking new guy that the new service coordinator set up in the front seat so Mr. Walsh could freak him out. A few of the barneys stumbled through their introduction speeches, but overall, it seemed to be a pretty able group. Finally, it was time to hear some goodbyes. For the first time, this actually meant something to me now.

Mr. Tortelli even mentioned me in his remarks, telling everyone to pay attention to my next phase change if they really wanted to learn something. He mentioned how fast the time here went by and how much they would miss the safe and protective fences. Some guys came to tears as they said goodbye to friends they had made, the kind that only come from shared experience. It was inspirational to see that guys could learn and grow together in a positive environment, even in prison, and I knew that eventually my turn to say goodbye would come. The only question I still had was when.

With the beginning of the third week, I had totally forgotten about the big board. Last week's service crew was now the H-Committee, and I was moved up a row to the creative energy committee. There wasn't much for the crew to do on this committee, and also, I could go to bed at 9:00 p.m. instead of staying up until nine thirty or ten, mopping the floors. Service and house were the two hardest-working crews, and everyone was assigned to them for their first two weeks here. After that, things mellowed out and the coordinator did most of the work, only occasionally asking for some help from his crew. By then, most people were assigned a job, as I had been, or starting to take classes either at the school or in behavior modification sessions held in various rooms around the compound.

I also checked the board for names of the new service committee members but didn't recognize any of them. Unless some guy from county whom I might recognize down the line showed up here, I pretty much had figured all the guys I knew that were coming, and they were all here by now. I was the exception, as most guys with extensive criminal histories and street connections would always wait at a window on Monday to see which one or two of their friends would show up on any given transport. Some days, someone would go to a friend and say, "Oh my god, you are never going to believe who just showed up!" This was more common than I thought possible, but I wasn't a career criminal. If this had happened in Snohomish County, Washington, it might be a different story.

As soon as the evening meeting was over, the going-home riders headed over to the laundry to put on an orange "Cheetos" jumpsuit for transport tomorrow morning. Once they got back to their units, the real goofing off began, because even if they were pulled up five times tonight, they wouldn't be read, and punishment didn't dish out until tomorrow night's meeting. By then, they would be back in county. Some saw this as a ticket to raise hell, but you were still on your rider until you were in front of your judge, so you needed to be careful. You could have a perfect rider and gotten into a fight on the way to court and would end up at the yard for a few years if the judge wasn't too happy about it.

Tonight was mellow, and the Cheetos were running around, saying goodbye and getting phone numbers from friends. Even though probation rules strictly prohibited felons to contact other felons, this was my third week of witnessing this happening. I said goodbye to Mr. Tortelli again and then left him to his packing. I was still the new guy to him, and I was sure he had friends here he would rather deal with than me. You had to know your place, or you would piss people off, and that was the last thing I wanted to do to a man like him.

Since I was no longer on the house committee, I was forced to shower with the herd at 8:30 p.m. instead of being the only guy in there, as I had all last week. The extra hour of sleep was enjoyable, since I still wasn't allowed to sleep on weekends and the grind was slowly beginning to take its toll. If I was restless in the evening and couldn't go right to sleep, I would end up reading. If that happened here, I couldn't take a nap to make up for it like in county, and over the last couple of weeks, it was catching up to me. I found myself actually missing my reading time, which calmed me down before going to sleep. Sometimes, if the book was particularly intriguing, I couldn't keep myself from continuing. But before I knew it, exhaustion overtook my mental stimulation and I was out like a light.

One of the worst things about prison life was its sheer repetition, the same faces, the same food, the same schedule over and over, day in and day out. From the time I was sentenced until now, I had been exempted from that headache. Things were different for me almost every day. Getting settled in and sitting through orientation, I found my life had been one of indifference.

As I walked into the media production office for my second day of work, I came to the realization that wild things had been thrown at me a mile a minute, but at least they weren't repetitive. There was something new to deal with almost every day. I was afraid this was all about to change.

Lucky for me, the guys I was working with were all pretty cool, and so were the librarians. Over the next couple of days, I was welcomed as the new guy, and with the title came all the care and respect every trainee got from the drill sergeants during basic train-ing. I rightfully took my place doing all the mundane daily tasks they could pawn off on me, and even a few that were probably added just to see how far they could go. I still had plenty of free time to explore the library, play computer games, and even take a small nap or two while sitting against the door in case the staff tried to come in. Between accounts, writing, reading, meetings, and my new job, the week flew by. I was busy all day from the minute I woke up until the minute I fell asleep. Suddenly, I was in front of the library on Friday afternoon, talking with Castro and McGladrey about possible projects for three or four of us when we saw the commissary truck pull in. This was the minute I realized just how much faster the time went by when you were busy. I spent the whole week trying to come up with a worthwhile idea for media production, knowing whatever it was would most likely dominate the rest of my time here. It was three o'clock Friday afternoon when a guy from our unit came up toward the library, saying he wanted to talk to me.

"Mr. Walker?" he asked as I nodded in confirmation. "You are wanted in Mr. Kennison's office for your initial counselor's meeting right away."

Finally, after forty-nine stressful days, my last rider question would finally be answered. I was about to be told when I would be going home.

CHAPTER 49

I CHECKED OUT FROM WORK with Mr. Walter and headed back to my unit. I grabbed my portfolio from my locker and stood in front of the counselor's office door, waiting as instructed. This was the meeting I had been waiting for since my lawyer, Mark, told me I wouldn't know how long my rider was until I got here. Councilors had all the court paperwork and legal information as to just what kind of rider you had been sentenced to. This was the moment of truth, and I would soon find out if I was to be here for 90, 120, or 180 days. The answer was three months of my life, and when that thought went through my brain, I immediately found myself getting nervous, just as I had been in the courtroom before sentencing. Trying to stay positive and not be disappointed no matter what he told me, I was again hoping for the best but planning for the worst. I was already in the mind-set I would be here until April, so if I was going home any earlier, great.

Mr. Kennison was a portly fellow with gray hair, mustache, and beard who could easily have worked at the mall at Christmastime and needed nothing more than the red suit to play Santa Claus. This meeting was basically a get-to-see-the-man-face-to-face thing, in case he or I had any questions at this point in the rider. After looking over my paperwork, he answered the only question that was left for me to ask by telling me I was on a ninety-day rider and would receive my end-case statement on or about January 25, 2006. Awesome! I was on a ninety-day rider and would not be stuck here until April. Technically, you could go home anytime after your end-case statement was given to you. It was merely a statement of the counselor's recommendations of probation or prison, based on your rider evaluation. The judges could follow the advice, or as I had already seen firsthand, he could toss out the expert's opinion and do whatever he wanted. A good end-case evaluation was the only obstacle standing between me and freedom.

I had my job, end-case date, commissary in my bin box and even more in the truck parked outside. I wasn't stuck here until April, as I had feared. I had two months at least to work on my writing, and incarceration wasn't looking too bad, all things considered. If I was to be here for a couple of months, I was sure going to make them as productive as I possibly could. I left Mr. Kennison's office with a big smile on my face, relieved to know my rider length once and for all. After hearing the horror stories from some of the six-month riders about how boring things got around here after their programming was finished, I was grateful to have a judge who wasn't rider-happy. All the six-month riders did once programming was done was sit around and get into trouble. How could that possibly speak well of the program?

There was also talk of not sending us back to county jail once our riders were done. This would be counterproductive to all the programming we had absorbed at Cottonwood. Back in county, we would be susceptible to a negative environment, surrounded by those in county who had not learned what we had learned here. That could do nothing but destroy all we had worked for, and rumor had it that some counties were going to start releasing you from county jail the day you got back from Cottonwood. Then a week or two later, you would go to court as a civilian and receive your rider review hearing. Of course, everyone here wanted this to be the case, so we could go home two weeks earlier. Since we weren't in charge, it didn't matter that there was 100 percent of us in favor of the idea. There was some basis to the rumors. The idea had even been mentioned at more than one of the meetings by more than one of the COs. If they had brought it up, then it was proved positive that it wasn't just the prison rumor mill running amok, as was often the case. Walking back to the library, I was overcome with relief and ready to get into a nice group. I had my commissary, my few friends, and a busy routine to help time go by quickly. What more could a guy ask for while incarcerated?

Unit 4 was called second to receive commissary this week, and by 4:00 p.m., I already had my name called and was upstairs, putting all my stuff away before the crowd could see just how much I had. I still hadn't had anything ripped off that I knew about, but others had, and that made me nervous. Maybe being so close to the bubble and the microwave had its advantages. I was also always waiting for that inevitable bunk move, which I knew would come but hoped would not. So far, everyone that turned green didn't want to be so close to the bubble or just wanted to stay close to the area they were in already. They just wanted to move to a lower bunk, and that was fine with me. I don't know what I would have done if I didn't have a hospital bed with nobody above me. I was getting used to the comfort, and going back to the metal slab and two-inch mattress just wasn't going to cut it anymore.

Just as most people look forward to the weekend, so do prisoners. The only difference is that the weekends begin on Thursday and they aren't over until Tuesday morning. This helped us to get through some rough times. Thursday night was when CO Wiley read off the list of who was going home. Those lucky few would begin the roll-up process, which took a few days, and they also began to say their goodbyes. Friday, we got our commissary, and Saturday and Sunday, we had free time, but only two meals. Monday, the new guys showed up and promotions were listed on the board and new coordinators were named, and Tuesday morning, the Cheetos all physically left sometime around the morning meeting.

By looking at the program this way, it was clear that the only day that nothing really went on was Wednesday, giving us something to look forward to every day. The little things like that were what got you by in prison, so we took what we could get. The downside of this was that we didn't have CO Wiley on Friday, Saturday, and Sunday, so when we got a shitty CO, it could ruin the entire weekend in a hurry. This always left us a little apprehensive on Friday afternoon, because even though it was commissary day, it was also when we found out which CO would most likely be in control of our lives for the next three days.

CO Dupea was the answer to the "Who will it be?" question, and all in all, everyone was pretty happy about it. He was an even-tempered man and was also fair. As with most of the COs, you could get along with him as long as you didn't get on his bad side. If that happened, all hell was going to break loose. He had a good sense of humor and always appreciated a good joke. At least we weren't stuck with CO Reemer yet again, which allowed us to breathe a big sigh of relief. After that, we were on free time until Monday morning, except for meetings, meals, and superclean.

This particular weekend, though, I began to discreetly run store as I had in county. Even though I was completely aware of the consequences if I were caught, I was extremely quiet about it and only talked about it with those whom I trusted or came highly recommended by others. I wasn't looking for trouble, and everyone involved was fully aware of what would happen, so we all had something at stake to protect. I wasn't trying to be a profiteer, but remembering my first two weeks of hunger pangs, I had developed a soft spot for purple cards with no commissary as of yet. Better that they buy store from me than get caught stealing food from the chow hall, as I almost had on Thanksgiving.

The word was out to all my friends, and by Saturday at lunchtime, when they should have been initiated into Cottonwood by the right of having endured a starvation weekend, many of the new guys were hiding out somewhere, one at a time, enjoying an uncooked Top Ramen sprinkled with the seasoning, or what we knew as prison pizza. Using the microwave or even being seen eating anything would have raised some eyebrows, so along with the food I stored out to them, they were also given the knowledge of how to eat it without getting caught. Most of them gathered this information and the ramen while pacing with me, for it gave us some privacy to exchange the necessary information, and I even got to know a few of them a little better.

It was a sunny and crisp weekend, so I spent a lot of time outside. Trying to stay on top of my walking and stay somewhat physically active in here, I felt, was as good for my mind as it was for my body. Midafternoon, Mr. Strahm came out to join me for a mile or two, and I was amazed to hear some of the things this poor, troubled kid had to tell me.

"You are from Washington, right, Mr. Walker?" I had heard this line of questioning before and immediately knew exactly where it was headed.

"Yeah. I live in Everett, which is a suburb of Seattle."

"How is the construction business going over there? I have done some framing, and if I don't get a real job and get away from all my drug-fiend friends, I know I will end up back in prison."

"Good for you. Seeing the problem before it becomes one and taking the initiative to prevent it from happening shows you're getting ready to go home."

"Yeah, my name was called Thursday night, and I am out of here on Tuesday morning. My girl called the county to see if there was any truth about the book-and-release rumor, and she says it's not happening yet."

"That's too bad, but at least you're going home, so you can't complain too much. I just got my end-case appointment for late January, so I won't be home sometime until March. When was your end case, so I know about how long in between getting an end case and going home?"

"It was about a week, maybe ten days. Most guys are gone within a couple of weeks of the end case. Can I tell you something I haven't told anybody else, Mr. Walker?"

"Sure, your secret is safe with me. I hardly know anyone, anyways, and all my friends are back in Washington."

"I know this may sound crazy, but I don't want to leave here. I am safe, am comfortable, and don't have to worry about staying clean. I wish I could stay another month or two, because I know I'm going to go home and get in trouble. It's just a matter of time. That's why I want to move to Seattle and get a real job. Can you help me?"

"I can't do anything for a few months until I get out, but once I'm home, I can hook you up with a job, a place to live, and anything else you need. I have been roofing there for sixteen years. I know all kinds of people in the construction world, and the probation people in Washington want you to succeed so they can cut you loose. In Idaho, from all the stories I have heard, I think they truly want you to fail so you end up back in their system. The best advice I can give anybody is to get the hell out of Idaho. Check in with your probation officer, pass all your pee test, report when and where you are supposed to, so he has absolutely no reason to want you on his caseload. After a few months, they will realize you are a waste of their time, and that's when you tell them you have a job offer from Seattle and you want to move to Washington. They can't put you back in prison, so they might as well cut you loose."

"I'm actually scared to leave this place. When I got here, I couldn't wait to go home, and now I'm afraid to leave. How messed up is that?"

"It's not. It just says a lot about this program. The things you have learned here have given you the insight to recognize the uphill battle that you face. It has also given you something a few short months ago you never would have thought. You are thinking for a change. You should be proud of yourself. You're making the right choices, and your future will be better for it."

"I hope so, Mr. Walker, and thanks. I'm going inside for a bit. It's getting cold out. I can get your contact information." Mr. Strahm went back inside, leaving me alone with some strange thoughts. He was scared to go home because he was afraid of screwing up. Yeah, he had been given all the tools to recognize his problem, but apparently, he didn't think he was capable of becoming sober. I felt sorry for him and admired his foresight at the same time. I continued walking for a long time after Strahm went back inside. I fancied myself a fairly intelligent guy, but it took hearing a few things like that to send me deep into thoughts of prison, sobriety, and adjusting to life back in the real world. He was right to some extent. It was safe in here. The battle with addiction never begins behind bars or in a rehab facility; anyone can stay sober under those conditions. The real battle begins the day you leave.

Sunday was a repeat of Saturday. I spent a lot of time outside, walking between writing sessions. The two complemented each other about as well as milk and cookies. The fresh air outside, along with the exercise, was the perfect environment to get things straight in my head before putting it down on paper. Alternating between the two also kept either of them from getting too monotonous throughout the day. It also gave me some time to think about what to write next when I return to my bunk. Sunday night, at the meeting, one of the guys stood up and made an announcement to the unit that none of us ever expected to hear. One of the guys who had left before I had arrived had friends among the guys who were still here. His wife was friends with the wife of Mr. Zeek, who was still here. Zeek stood up and addressed the unit without the enthusiasm required to make 119 prisoners pay attention to you.

"Good evening, community. My name is Mr. Zeek."

"Good evening, Mr. Zeek."

"I spoke to my wife this afternoon. She is a friend of Jane Knistler. Mr. Knistler, for those of you who are new, was with us for a few months and was sent home to Ada County less than a month ago. Apparently, after his release on probation, he was hanging out with some of his old friends and there was some kind of altercation. She wasn't sure if Mr. Knistler had relapsed or just happened to be in the wrong place at the wrong time. In any case, he received a bullet wound because of being around the wrong people. This morning, he died in the hospital from the gunshot wound. He was a good man with a wife and two kids, and I would ask that we have a moment of silence in his memory."

The unit was silent as well as shocked while this information was digested. A man who apparently a lot of these guys here knew pretty well. I figured he must have left the week before I got here and possibly even gave his goodbye speech the day after I got here, because I had not seen his name on the board or heard anyone talk about him until now. Whatever the case, it was a sad situation that could happen to anyone who returned to the old lifestyle that most of us had shared before we ended up behind bars. It would have been even more sad if he had been staying sober and had just been a victim of poor timing.

After the silence, I noticed some of the guys were teary-eyed and made absolutely no effort to hide it. The meeting was adjourned shortly after, and a small group of his closest friends gathered in the dayroom for a small memorial to their fallen comrade. Others were in tears because they said he had worked so hard in here and was a changed man. It couldn't have happened at a worse time since he had put a lot of effort into his rider and was looking forward to beginning his new life free from the drugs that had control his life for so many years. It also told me a lot about the men here, who cared so deeply for one another that this experience would affect them so dramatically. Life is hard, and when you suffer as most of us have, to have your life tragically taken away just as you are beginning to turn it around is hard to accept. It was also the risk all of us knew and accepted every time we chose to use. The drug world is a hazardous place, and you never know when an episode of lunacy would occur. This doesn't make it any easier to accept. Somewhere, there was a grieving wife with no husband, a child without a father, and a mother with one less son. Our crimes were definitely not victimless.

It was a somber night, and tensions were high. Grief does strange things to men in a place like this. I think the similarities in our checkered past brought us closer, and this made grief even harder to deal with. Some saw it as a sign that no matter what you did, things would still end up bad, and tonight's news was a harsh reality check for them. Just as we got in bed, I heard the high beeping sound that preceded the fire alarm just before it was sounded. It always happened after we were all out of uniform and just getting comfortable in bed. We were getting better at it, and the COs were as well. After ten drills in my first three weeks, how could we not?

With the clear weather came cold nights, and it was again down in the *teens* when we were all outside. This was getting old, and obviously maintenance wasn't going to fix it, so something had to be done. Being proactive, as I had with laundry and the baseball path, I figured it all out. It was amazing how clearly a man thinks in the frigid, fresh mountain air, wrapped in a horse blanket, a pair of boxers, T-shirt, and wearing shower shoes. I almost forgot about the eight-degree temperature and impending hypothermia while coming up with a media production project that would soon consume my life as the drugs that brought me here once did.

CHAPTER

50

JUST AS I HAD ENJOYED silently dissecting human nature during booking at Ada County Jail, checking out the new guys and how they handled drills like this made me question the direction society was headed in. It was funny to see what they had chosen to wear on Main Street tonight. There were always the complete idiots who were standing in their boxers, shower shoes, and a blanket. I had to wonder if that was Castro's doing. We were back inside after only eight minutes, but still, when it was this cold out, eight minutes could be an eternity. Absorbing the heat from the building for a moment, I asked Castro a couple of questions and quickly got in bed to get warm. I always had my pen and paper handy, so I wrote down a few notes for myself so tomorrow I wouldn't forget what I had come up with before reading myself to sleep.

At breakfast, I found myself contemplating the low-carb, low-starch diet that others had opted for. With green card rec still five weeks away and my locker full of commissary, the need to eat all the hash browns and bread with each meal was not quite as mandatory as it had been a couple of weeks ago. I had seen more than a few men pack on the weight in county, and the meals there were half of what we got here. Of course, they had not eaten any solid food during the four-year drug binge before their arrest, and this probably had its effects. Remembering my three-hundred-something triglyceride level in RDU, I had an even stronger argument for a low-starch diet. My walking had decreased dramatically, except for this last weekend, and I didn't want to leave here with twenty extra pounds due to lack of physical activity.

By introducing this new program into my eating regime, I accidentally stumbled across a new problem I would be forced to deal with that I hadn't even thought about.

"Hey, Walker, are you going to eat that?" The question sprung up from two or three directions when others saw me leave food on my plate for the first time since Labor Day. It did make me realize I would soon be as popular as the others who had extra, and giving it away was an extremely dangerous move. It was hard to deprive the hungry, but getting caught sharing food was a major rule violation and also difficult to do in the chow hall without being seen. Even if the COs didn't see you, all the witnesses in the chow hall could give you a pull-up, and some kind of sanction or essay to read to the unit would ensue. Pull-ups were bad, and so far, I had not received one and had no intention of getting any. It would really suck for generosity to ruin a perfect rider.

The one good thing I did have in my favor was that I was the last guy in the unit bunk order, which usually meant the guy next to me was quite often from another unit. It was easiest to give the guy next to you your extra food, and this immediately cut my problem in half. Occasionally, upstairs would go first, but usually I was one of the last guys in the unit and/or compound to sit down. If I was last, then nobody sat between the COs in my open side.

I went up to the library during the eight thirty movement and walked in like I owned the place. My week of being the grunt was over, and I didn't have to stand out, but I did have to stand up. I was one of the elite, do-what-we-want crowd, and I was envied compound-wide. I quickly took a spot in front of one of the computers to let them all know that initiation week was over and I wasn't going to be their gopher for the next couple of months. Cobbs had begun his D&A class this week, so he would not be here until later. That meant a computer for each of us, and I settled in for a morning of FreeCell solitaire, pinball, and hearts. Trade the uniform for a bathrobe and slippers and I could be home.

"Gentlemen, I came up with a brilliant idea for our next project, if anyone is looking for a new one," I blurted out to McGladrey and Castro.

"They aren't really group projects, Walker. I think you misunderstood. You get your own and lead it, and everyone else gives you support and helps you in their free time, keeping everyone busy. You write up an outline and description for Mr. Walter to approve, and since I am almost done with my last one, I can help on and off. I have to start the D&A class like Cobbs this week, but mine starts in the afternoon. It worked out good that we don't have it at the same time, so there will be some room in here."

"What time is yours, Castro?" McGladrey asked.

"My class is at one thirty. Why? Don't tell me you're in my class."

"Nope. Mine starts at two thirty. Looks like Walker is going to be the only one here full-time while all of us are coming and going for a while. Can you hold down the fort without us?"

"I'll manage. I just hope I don't get caught doing anything I'm not supposed to be doing, like work."

Not wanting to get in trouble at work, I began to outline the idea I had for my new project. I spent the rest of the day trying to figure out just how to do that. I truly was computer illiterate, but I believed in my idea and felt it would be good for the entire compound, including the COs.

After only three weeks on compound, I couldn't fly under the radar at this point even if I wanted to. I was already so involved with every minute of every day that at this point, I decided that somehow, someway, I would leave my mark on this place. A piece of me would always stay on compound for the future riders to have it a little easier than the 2005 holiday riders. Eventually, I would leave, and when I finally did get to go home, people here would look back, laugh, and tell stories of some of the things the crazy riders did years ago. Those riders would not be myths or folklore but rather true stories about us. Scattered around the unit, there were drawings, phrases, and motivational quotes that were artistically made and framed on the wall. The names of the men who made them were also there for all to see, and though that wasn't what I was going to do, I still wanted to be known after I was gone in some positive way. I hoped that my new project would do just that.

The guys came and went all day at the office, but with one of them gone all the time, there was room for me to work and also a computer for each of us to use all day. With the privacy we had in our tiny office, I realized I would also be able to write or do whatever I wanted, as long as I put my chair up against the door, and I could delete the screen instantly if need be. I stood outside when the new guys showed up, and as expected, no faces were recognizable to me until the very last man came out of the holding area in segregation. A huge smile spread across my face and his when my good friend Monopoly came strolling up Main Street. I was shocked and sad for him, because I thought he was getting out, but his sentencing must have gone about as well as mine had, and his next few months were not going to be what he had hoped. While I had hope for his sake that he had been released, I was also glad to have him around, even if *around* meant he was in prison.

I flashed him four fingers so he knew what unit I was in, but until he came out of the chapel, he wouldn't even know which unit he was in. All I could do now was hope he strolled in before count, but so far, no one I knew from county was in unit 4 with me.

That night, the fears and thoughts Mr. Strahm had shared with me while pacing, he recited to the entire unit during his goodbye speech. Another guy broke into tears remembering his friend who had died, and said how good it was here in Cottonwood and how safe we all were. CO Wiley even came out of the bubble and said how devastated the staff was hearing what had happened and how the COs really wanted us to succeed and that they took it as a personal failure when we failed. His view was that the staff hadn't diagnosed and solved the issue that they needed to for those who failed and that the program was geared toward success, not failure.

I talked with Strahm for a long time that night, and I really worried about the guy. Once you get deeply involved in a drug lifestyle, it becomes all you know, and getting out of it is very hard. Even if you do, it is only a matter of time before something or somebody tries to lure you back in. Your friends, income, fellow workers, and sometimes family members can all lead you toward going back to the old ways. And that is when the tools and knowledge we were given here are tested the most, and he was worried that when the time came, he would stumble. I sincerely hoped for his sake that he was wrong.

Tuesday morning, bright and early at 5:00 a.m., I was lucky enough to witness something I had never thought I would, but it was again something I was glad to have seen firsthand. One of the new guys who showed up yesterday, Mr. Chavez, was either misinformed about what kind of program was going on up here or suddenly had a serious change of heart about participating in it. He refused to get up and started going off in Spanish to one of his buddies about how he wasn't going to do all the bullshit required here daily. His mentor, coordinator, and a couple of assistant seniors all tried talking to him, but the only thing I could make out in English was "Fuck this bullshit! Take me to the yard." The guy actually wanted to go to prison for two years rather than follow the program and be home in a few months. His attitude and situation, I would soon find out, was similar to Dan's in RDU. Some guys, just as in basic training, were not wired correctly to handle a disciplined environment, and no matter how hard anybody tried to help this man, they were beating a dead horse. The way Chavez saw it, all his friends were at the yard, and in two years, he would be free and not required to comply with probation regulations for six years once he got out.

It only took about ten minutes for the CO to find out about what was happening and come upstairs to solve the problem. Chavez was stubborn and determined to go back to Boise and lose twenty months of his life for the freedoms you get at the yard instead of participating in the program offered at Cottonwood. The CO told him to stand up and put his uniform on, which he took his sweet time doing. Needless to say, the knot in his tie left a little to be desired. He was patted down, handcuffed, and taken back to segregation, where he could go back to sleep and wait until next week to be transported back to Boise.

After all the excitement, the scuttlebutt around the unit was that all his buddies and fellow gang members were all at the yard, and two years with his friends, lifting weights and shooting pool, would go by much faster for him than remaining here, knowing a guy with his attitude would eventually fail if not here definitely on probation. If you didn't play ball here, it would be a miserable six months for anyone. Some people just didn't care if they were locked up that long, and Chavez evidently was one of them.

I said goodbye to Strahm after breakfast, since the going-home riders were usually called out sometime during the morning meeting, and I had his phone number and contact information needed to reach him already written down. Tuesday and Wednesday were always the two slowest days on compound with not much going on. I saw Monopoly at lunch, and he flashed me two fingers to let me know he was in unit 2, I suddenly felt left out with Scott, Jay, and now Monopoly all over there. The next thing I had to worry about was the weekly bunk moves that came with the weekly blue cards becoming green. I could survive at least one more week in my luxurious accommodations, and as in all the previous weeks, no one would want to be next to the bubble or the microwave.

Everyone came and went all day from the media production office. I stayed for three hours every morning and three in the afternoon. I was slowly beginning to learn how to do the things my résumé claimed I could. I also learned where all the games and music were stashed. We had some music on file to use for background with the videos we made, but most of it was big-band music and WWII stuff. There were, however, countless files already on the hard drive that we could look up and find out what those who came before us had managed to put in the computers when they were here.

The only other people who had computer access on the compound worked in the school office. Interaction between us was strictly regulated, and having contraband on your computer was strictly prohibited and could cost you your rider. I had heard stories of former counselors or other outsourced staff who would bring in music or porn on a disk, but so far, I had not seen any sign of that happening now. That didn't mean it wasn't already here, and believe me, McGladrey and Castro spent a lot of their time going through each folder, one by one, trying to find prohibited media.

We did have a decent music selection we could access, but most of it was new stuff, including lots of rap, which I didn't particularly care for. I liked classic rock from the sixties and seventies, so the choices for me were few. Beggars can't be choosers, and I was still happy to listen to almost anything, just to keep the peace in the office. With everyone gone, I was the go-to guy if Mr. Walter or Raymon needed anything done. With no other choice available but me, I was given a nice little Christmas bonus when Mr. Walter walked in and asked me a question.

"Mr. Walker, do you have off-compound status?" I nodded. "Good. I have a project for you and four or five of your friends that I will need help with later this week. Make sure they are all done programming and have off-compound status, and tell them Wednesday and/or Thursday."

"Can I tell them why they are needed?'

"Trust me, they will want to do this. I can't tell you exactly what it is you will be doing until the day I need them, for security reasons. I do know it will be better than sitting around the unit all day, trying to not get into trouble."

Mr. Walter was a pretty nice guy, and for the job he had to do, he made things fairly tolerable for us. I didn't have seniority in the office, but it was now my project by default, and I would score some points with those I offered this project to. Anything to break up the routine was always a good thing here, and one less day of boredom was one day closer to home.

CHAPTER

51

THAT NIGHT AFTER DINNER, I told Mr. Albert about what Mr. Walter had asked me to do and figured he would want in on it. Mr. McGladrey, Castro, and Cobb all had programming, so they were definitely out, but Albert knew who was cool, had off-compound status, and was done programming, which limited my choice to only about 50 out of 120 people in unit 4 right away. Albert was in, and he suggested Mr. Kim, another assistant senior, and Willis, who had come up with me, was still waiting to get a job, so he had nothing to do yet. Mr. Lindbergh was another assistant senior, and Albert picked out a few more to complete the group. Everyone was excited, even though we had no clue what was in store for us, but something different was always better than the same old routine.

No green cards wanted my bunk yet another week, even though I was told by my neighbors not to get too comfortable. No coordinators left this week, so the leadership on the board stayed the same, and now I was moved up to the information committee. We were responsible for news and sports scores at the morning meeting, and since I worked in the library, I was the delegated information gatherer.

Funny news clips always got a laugh when read at the meeting. Stupid crime and drug-related scores from Boise or Coeur d'Alene that we could all relate to or learn from were also popular. This gave me an excuse to read the paper during movement without getting in trouble. Each day, a different man from the committee would read these stories, and that would help them with their public speaking and group participation. Word around the unit was that next week would be huge as far as leadership positions went, with four or five coordinators expected to go home. We wouldn't know for sure until Thursday night, when CO Wiley read the list at the meeting.

During my chats with Albert, I had decided not to fly under the radar and to actively participate and help lead the unit. I wanted to be a coordinator, or maybe even assistant senior, which would also help the judge to see that I was actually accomplishing something up here, so I could avoid coming back. My greatest fear now was a pissed-off judge who didn't think I devoted myself to the program and would make me do it again, as others had been required to do. Mr. Kennison had told me to do more than they required of me, so the judge would see my willingness to participate in the program; anything else risked your freedom. If a bunch of coordinators was leaving next week, that meant everyone would move up. I wasn't even sure if you could be a senior coordinator until you wear a blue card, but for me that was only a week away now. When that thought popped into my head, it made me realize that with all the stuff I had been doing, I had totally forgotten about my second phase change, and I needed to complete it in order to move from orange to blue.

While talking with Mr. Kim about the job for Mr. Walter, I decided to go through the second list of words to choose from for my second phase change. I wanted to do as good a job as I had on the first one. By now, I had caught up chronologically to the current date with my writing journal, so I did have some time to work on the seminar, and I was sure Jesus could use all the help he could get once again. I hadn't seen much of him lately since he had begun classes at the school and was working on his GED. With one week remaining until we were allowed to watch TV at night, I decided to pull out the table and gather the old group to check everyone's progress on their phase changes. The holiday was quickly approaching, and we all were missing our families, so we made do by keeping our group tight as kind of a surrogate family. We were all working the program, being productive, and getting by rather well, all things considered. It was enjoyable to compare stories with the old group, since lately we had all gone our separate ways, although we still helped one another out one-on-one when necessary. I couldn't help but wonder if eventually we would all be sitting at the tables in front of the meetings, running the show.

The next morning, we made Jesus read the news to the unit to help him get used to talking in front of everyone, and even though he stumbled a few times, he quickly recovered and added a little humor into the mix as well. I felt like a proud father knowing that I had, in some small way, helped him become more comfortable about speaking. Those who didn't participate were often picked on for stumbling over questions, the opinions they offered, and other comments they made in order to embarrass them. The coordinators knew who was goofing off and not paying attention, so they would deliberately make them answer a question or do a task, hoping to embarrass them into paying attention next time.

When I got to work, Mr. Walter asked me if I had all the guys lined up for him, and I told him yes. He still wouldn't tell me what he wanted us to do, but he did say it would be happening tomorrow and to let everyone know they should be ready. With my curiosity aroused, I was looking forward to tomorrow and spent the day working on my phase change while playing computer games in the office. The outline for my media production project was done, but I needed Castro or McGladrey to format it for me so everything looked like I knew what I was doing when Mr. Walter looked it over.

The next day, we all showed up as instructed at eight thirty movement, and finally, Mr. Walter told us what it was we had all volunteered for.

"Each year," he said, "NICI participates in the Cottonwood Christmas parade that marches through downtown Cottonwood. Up in the maintenance building, we have a 1945 fire truck that some inmates from NICI decorate with lights and tinsel so we can give the appearance of community participation in local events. Mr. Walker here has chosen you, gentlemen, to help decorate the truck today, so it will be ready for the parade this weekend. Anybody have a problem with that? Any religious issues that would prevent you from doing this?" We all shook our heads no, and he said to be ready in five minutes while he went into his office to prepare to leave.

We all agreed that decorating the truck was as much Christmas as we were going to get, but even a little taste of the holiday was better than none. As we walked up the hill and out through the back fence, Mr. Walter said that Mr. Castro would be coming up later to take some pictures of what we were doing. Mr. Walter would then email the pictures to the local newspaper, and we might have our picture in the paper. Having your picture in the paper was one thing, but in a situation like this, it was a completely different story. Being asked to smile for the camera in your prison uniform was not too appealing to a couple of us, and they were told they could hide their faces or not be in the picture at all if that was their preference. I was three hundred miles from home, so I couldn't care less. I did, however, understand their point of view and thought that if I was doing this in Everett, would I be taking their position or not? I would at first, as they were, be a little apprehensive and might need a little time to decide. It was a good thing they had until this afternoon, when Castro would get out of his D&A. Since they did this every year, the boxes of decorations were all huge, and I knew that this was going to be a fun day. They had a Santa sleigh with reindeer, tinsel, lights, and all kinds of Christmas stuff. The cool thing about this detail was, it was up to us how we wanted to decorate the truck.

We quickly came up with a game plan and went to work trying to be as creative and colorful as we could. This was much better than hanging out in the little office all day long, talking with Albert and Kim about what coordinators really did. It had its perks, but it also came with some responsibility and headaches as well.

Wanting us to get back to work quickly so we could finish the truck in one day, Mr. Walter sent us to the front of the chow line at lunch. Then he told us to head back to the library to get him at 1:00 p.m. instead of the on thirty movement like everyone else. We finished the decorating about three thirty, just as Castro showed up with the camera, and that gave us almost an hour to get some pictures to send to the paper. It turned out to be pretty cool, and we posed for forty-five minutes in different poses to make sure we all were happy with the choice of which one was sent to the newspaper. In the end, everybody decided to be in the picture, but two of them, and understandably, didn't want their names printed under it.

Mr. Walter said that all of us in the group would also receive a copy of the picture to keep and take home, a surprise bonus. The only pictures you were allowed to keep in here were from your group graduation or other pictures authorized by staff. Being in possession of a picture you were not authorized to have was a major offense, and since they could search us at any time, it wasn't such a good idea to be in possession of an unauthorized one. People were constantly asking Castro to slide them one so they could send it home. In order for us to print it, the picture had to go to the school and be released by multimedia-staff-authorized work order, which prevented us doing it for them. No inmate on compound had internet access, and I wasn't sure if anyone in the penal system did, and I knew exactly why. Convicts always would try to get away with as much as they could, and making the internet available to us could only cause somebody to get into some serious trouble, given the opportunity.

The next day was Thursday, and with it came the list of going-home riders. The list today would dramatically change the unit. Five coordinators were going home, including Senior Coordinator Ramirez, Assistant Senior Kim, and three of the committee leaders. They were ecstatic to finally get the news, but the changes around here would be dramatic and cut deep into the core of the unit. Since we pretty much ran ourselves, the new leadership could greatly affect the well-being of the entire unit with just a few minor changes. Losing so many high-ranking prisoners was very unusual, but once you were appointed, you stayed in office for the duration of your stay, until you were promoted or got fired, whichever came first. Albert would become senior coordinator based on seniority, two coordinators would become assistants, and there would be five new coordinators come Monday night. Since I wanted to be one, this was actually good news but also scary at the same time.

I had heard in the library that other units were in the middle of a booking war, where guys constantly wrote each other up for stupid shit, and I didn't want that juvenile stuff to happen with us. Life in here was hard enough without the COs breathing down your neck, making your life miserable. Some units were on "tight house." This meant no free time, no phone calls, nothing but programming all day, every day, even on the weekends. It was like the whole unit was back to purple card status until the tight house status was lifted.

Friday came, and for the first time since being locked up, my commissary was screwed up beyond compare. I thought I had done something wrong on the order form or some other stupid thing, but once back in the unit, I found out it wasn't just me. Apparently, the medium-security prison in Orofino was allowed to buy double orders for Christmas, and by them doing that, commissary ran short on half the stuff we had ordered for our holiday. Everybody was missing coffee, candy bars, ramens, and other popular items, so the guys in Orofino could stock up, and we were burned. Good thing I was well stocked and running store, so I had plenty and those who got jacked would soon be coming to see me. I went back up to the office after putting away my commissary, and Mr. Walter told me the picture was going to be in the paper next week along with a little article about NICI decorating each year. The paper came out only once a week, but still, it was something to share with the family, and I hoped they could see it online. I was also glad to have at least one picture, since I wasn't in any classes or groups that would allow me to have one.

On Saturday during free time, the man who dumped snow on my head the first day, Mr. George, showed me how to make slushies with the coffee or Tang out of snow. The right combination made a perfect Slurpee, and if you didn't get caught bringing the snow into the unit, it made for a nice drink. With Christmas a week away and us being stuck in prison, it was a pretty sad weekend. Something told me that next weekend would be even more depressing. If it weren't for the Seahawks being on a winning streak and looking really good for the playoffs, the weekend would have downright sucked. The weather was blizzard-like. I didn't even think about going outside, and everyone cooped up inside had cabin fever. I took some time off from writing and went back to reading for a change.

After a long, boring weekend, I couldn't wait to get to work on Monday and keep busy in the office. Weekdays always seemed to fly by, but the weekends would drag on and on. Monday also meant the board was going to change, and that usually happened when CO Wiley showed up. I wasn't really disappointed when it finally did happen, since there were a lot of people ahead of me and I wasn't even blue yet. All the coordinators were green cards, but that didn't mean you had to be. Since Albert was the new senior coordinator, when he approached me to talk before dinner, I was curious about what he had in store for me.

"Mr. Walker, do you think you can handle being the tenth coordinator?"

"The tenth coordinator? What the hell is that?"

"I want you to be my minutes reader, since Mr. Feldman is leaving tomorrow with everybody else. Can you handle that?"

"No problem. When do I start? Tonight?"

"No. Let Feldman read them one last time and you take notes. Tomorrow morning, I will have a minutes taker and you can read from then on. Fair enough?"

"I will sit up front at the meeting, then. Are you nervous about taking over tonight?"

"Hell no! I was born to be senior coordinator. So are you, someday." With that, he walked away to get his act together for tonight. He might not have acted like it, or said it, but I knew he was eager. I could see it in his manner. He would make a great senior, and I was glad to have him available to me at any time for any reason. He also had a wife and a two-year-old at home and his own company to work for when he got home, so we had a lot in common. Once I started thinking about it, I was a little nervous. It was a step up, which was what I wanted, but I hoped not to get stuck doing the minutes for too long. I wanted to be a coordinator. I didn't even care about which committee. I just wanted to sit at the big tables with the leaders of the unit. I wanted to have a say about what was going on, and until you were a coordinator, that wasn't going to happen.

At the meeting, I was sitting up front with the big boys. True, I wasn't a coordinator, but I was still an orange card, and all the rest of the men up front were blue or green. That in itself made a pretty strong statement as to my leadership capabilities. Maybe others wanted to fly under the radar, but that was not my business. But I wasn't willing to risk having to come back here by not participating in the program. Albert and Kim had pretty much told me it was an easy duty while we were decorating the fire truck, and since then, I pretty much wanted to be a coordinator.

I had learned in the Army that it is better to lead than follow, because at least that way you are kept in the loop about what is happening instead of blindly marching over the cliff. I liked to know what was going on around me and have my voice heard. Many times, in the Oregon Army National Guard, I had volunteered to go to classes for two weeks at a time to learn leadership, demolition, and other weapon skills. The two-week classes in the winter paid me four times what I would have made even if I could find roofing work at that time of year. I would then come back and be in charge of the weekend drill, where I would pass the information I had gathered on to the entire battalion. Instead of riding in a cold deuce-and-a-half from Eugene, Oregon, to the Yakima firing range in Washington for seven hours on Friday night, I would ride up in a jeep Friday morning with three or four others and help set up and run the drills for the weekend. This way, I was released from the herd and all the bullshit the Army piled on. I didn't want to be part of this herd either, knowing that with responsibility came privilege.

I received some strange looks from my buddies who were surprised to see me up front tonight, but I was glad to be among the leadership of the community at such an early stage. For tonight and tonight only, I was required to keep track of the meeting, write down everything that happened, who read their seminars, who got pulled up and pushed up, so that tomorrow morning, I could read the whole thing to the unit as Mr. Fisher had done for the month since I arrived. The idea was to keep it fast, direct, and humorous so that we could get on with the meeting. The minutes were basically a backup written log of the events that night or the morning before, just in case there were any discrepancies later on. If the expediter coordinator missed an entry, we could go back to the minutes and see that Mr. Jones did in fact read his apology to the unit, and then he would not get in serious trouble for not having completed it, as the expediter might have thought. We were self-governed, and the expeditor coordinator was basically the attorney general for the unit, which made the minutes taker the court recorder.

After doing this for so long, Mr. Feldman had developed quite a knack for doing it, and when he finished reading tonight, he bade the unit goodbye and received a standing ovation. He then helped me for the rest of the meeting to make sure I knew what I was doing, so I could teach the next guy in the morning when I started reading. It was a job that was pretty much self-explanatory if you followed the form they gave you, and all I really had to do was fill in the blanks. The hard part wouldn't come until the morning, when I had to read the minutes to the unit in under two minutes, as Feldman had done so smoothly for such a long while. The few times in the last month when he had stumbled, he had quickly picked himself up. The minutes taker would mention his mistake the next day, which would always get a good laugh.

The last entry I made at the end of the meeting was a quote from the new senior coordinator, Mr. Albert. It read, "If you think the problem is out there, that's the problem." I had never noticed the quotes I had heard at the end of each meeting, but for some reason, now I was paying close attention to them. Had I not even heard the last twenty-eight quotes at the end of every meeting since I had arrived? While reading throughout my incarceration, I would frequently stop and write down good one-liners, quotes, and words to live by that I found interesting. I had accumulated twenty or twenty-five pages of them so far, and I made a mental note to pay attention to these quotes from now on. The worst part of the meeting was all the going-home speeches, which took forever. These guys were all leadership, had been here on 180-day riders, were done programming months ago, were bored to death, and couldn't wait to get home. Needless to say, when it came time for their goodbyes, they took their sweet-ass time and the meeting went fifteen minutes long because of it.

The expediter coordinator would normally get in trouble for this, but with all the coordinator moves tonight and the long good-byes, CO Wiley let it slide and even had some good things to say about those who were leaving.

"It's now up to unit 4 to prove it is the best unit on compound by stepping up, filling the leadership gaps, and working as a unit to keep the integrity of the unit intact. I have seen units completely fall apart with less change than this, and you guys don't want all the problems that are going on in the other units right now. Unit 2 is on tight house with no privileges. Unit 3 has a no-talking sanction on the entire unit for a few days, except for meetings and programming.

"Leadership is about keeping this kind of crap from happening, and you guys have a good senior and some good assistant seniors, who I hope won't let that happen here. Good luck to all of you men going home. It's been great working with you. Don't let me see you come back."

He got a standing ovation and went back into the bubble. He always seemed to know just what to say without being long-winded or repetitive, as some of the COs could be here. Hearing what he said about units 2 and 3 made me not miss being with Scott, Jay, and Monopoly, since they probably hated their lives right now. I knew CO Reemer was up there, and I couldn't help but wonder if he had something to do with this or if another CO did. But either way, I was glad to be in unit 4.

CHAPTER

52

M Y THIRTIETH DAY ON COMPOUND was tomorrow, and I needed to read my next phase change and take the test tomorrow night, so I could get my blue card the next night at the meeting. The only difference would be some extra free time and being able to eat commissary at lunchtime as well. Other than that, all the good perks came with the green card, and that was now only a month away. I had been here thirty days, and it had gone by rather quickly. I knew the right people, had the best bunk, had the best job, and I was quietly contemplating when my streak of good fortune was going to end.

Mr. Albert was so jacked up to be the new senior coordinator that it showed in every movement he made. He was determined not to let the unit fall apart, along with the string of good fortune we had going and all the changes that were taking place. I spent the night working on my phase change and studying for the blue card test, because I was planning on doing both tomorrow night. The test wasn't as much of a problem as the phase change. Giving it my all on the first one, I worked on it almost the entire first week I was here, trying to make a name for myself, which I did. This one, I wasn't into as much as I should have been and basically just wrote it out as it came. I knew it would be acceptable, but I was a little disappointed with myself for not putting as much effort into it as I had on the first one.

I found myself a little nervous before the morning meeting, since today would be my first time reading the minutes. The weird thing was, I didn't know why I was nervous, since public speaking had never really bothered me, and I figured I just wanted to do as well as Mr. Fisher had done. Maybe it was just doing something new that was the problem, and I also knew that after the first or second time, it wouldn't be a problem anymore. I pulled it off flawlessly and, after that, began to show the minute taker, Mr. Salazar, what Mr. Fisher had shown me just the night before. Salazar had come up in our group, and I knew him fairly well, so now there were two orange cards up front, at least until tomorrow night.

In media production that day, Mr. Castro helped me format my project outline so I could get it approved and move forward. He was done with his other project finally and wanted to help me or even turn it into our project. That was okay with me, since I would probably need his help on it anyways, and two heads are always superior to one. We waited in the office, playing games and trying not to get in trouble, when Mr. Walter popped in and surprised the hell out of us.

"I know you two aren't playing card games on that computer. That would be a violation of the rules and would get you fired," he said as he walked in and busted us. We instantly cleared the screens, realizing that neither of us was in front of the door. Castro just turned to face the music since I had yet to have a confrontation with the man. I hoped he knew how to save our asses.

"Why, no, Mr. Walter. We would never even attempt something like that. I was familiarizing Mr. Walker with the defragmentation process, and we were trying to erase all unnecessary crap, so we had more space in the hard drive for our new project."

"Good save, Mr. Castro. I will accept that. Here is your outline back and my stamp of approval. I think this is a great idea, but it crosses some lines with teachers, the staff, and the CO regarding jurisdiction, so you need to figure that out on your own. I hope it turns out well. Oh, and by the way, don't let me catch you defragging any more. There should be plenty of room on there. Fair enough?"

"We won't, sir, and thank you," Castro told him as he left the office and closed the door. We just looked at each other and let out a huge sigh of relief. We had just dodged a major bullet, and Mr. Walter was totally cool about it. If that had been a CO, we would have been fired and/or failed.

"Good thing that wasn't CO Reemer," I told Castro. "We would have both been on our way to seg right now."

"I never thought I would say this, but we need more people in here to block the door," he said as we started laughing. That was too close for my comfort, and my heart was still pounding.

Our new project was approved, and all we had to do was gather a ton of information and get the pictures that went with it. This project would give us carte blanche to run around the compound at our convenience, all in the name of work. Mr. Walter would give us movement passes, and we would have the freedom to roam around at will anywhere in the compound. We could go into unit 2 and talk to anybody we wanted if we told the staff it was for the project. This kind of freedom only came with careful planning to make sure it fit within the guidelines of the outline we had given Mr. Walter. After that, we could make it up as we go along and do whatever we wanted for the next month or two. Life was as good as it could get in here, even with Christmas quickly approaching. The key was to keep busy, and I was definitely doing that.

The next night, I read my shitty phase change and aced my test to get my blue card. I wouldn't receive it until tomorrow night, but the hard part was over. Now all there was left was getting my green card and going home. My rider was moving along just as everybody said it would. It was much better to be here than in county because of all the things we did to make time fly. I didn't know what I would have done in county for six months besides read and walk. I never would have thought to start writing, so maybe coming here was actually a good thing in the long run.

I got my blue card the next night, and even though I should be happy, I found myself growing sadder by the day with Christmas only a few days away. Knowing I would be here instead of home had an effect on me. I wasn't really sure if it was because I was here or because I wasn't there for them. I felt bad for Sean, who had his birthday on Christmas and, I was sure, was probably more than a little disappointed about where Dad was this year. I vowed to someday, somehow, make it up to him. When you completed the Bible study course I was working on, they sent you a Bible with your name embossed on it, and I had seen some of them that other men had received. They were nicely bound, and I decided to have mine sent home to Sean and to have his name put on it instead of mine. It wasn't much of a Christmas present, but it was the best I could do under the circumstances. I finished the last four chapters of the study course over the next couple of days and sent all the information in so I could receive my certificate and he would receive the Bible.

Toward the end of the week, an older guy who was the oldest and most-liked man in the unit, Mr. Knight, gave a voluntary seminar reading to the unit. Mr. Knight was an exception to the rule here, and he probably didn't even deserve to be sent on a rider. He probably never broke the law in his life except for the DUI he received that got him sent here. He was a white-collar guy who didn't really fit in with this crowd, but he made the necessary adjustments and helped teach at the school. He also spent many weekends of his free time helping others study for their GED test or doing anything else that was asked of him. In his seminar, he stated that his parents were deceased, his wife had left him, and he had no children. Those of us who were feeling down because of the holiday and not being close to our family should be happy that at least we had families. He wasn't looking for pity but rather trying to make a positive out of a negative. To look on the bright side of going home to them as changed men and to make sure we didn't repeat the mistakes that sent us here. It was moving to listen to, and he got a standing ovation as he wiped the tears from his eyes when he finished.

CO Wiley commented that Mr. Knight bared his soul and opened himself up so some of us would learn something and make different choices in the future. If everybody did things like this, those of us that were paying attention would learn from him and keep us out of trouble. Mr. Knight was right, and instead of being sad about being here, I should have been happy not to have gotten three years and to know that Beth and Sean would still be there when I got out. Some people are just not optimistic and always see the negative instead of looking for the positive in any situation. Albert and I were both optimists, and that was why it was so good to talk with him. He always had good things to say instead of the same old prison and drug talk.

I survived one more week of bunk moves, but my number was soon to be up. I had been told by a few people that when they turned green next week, they were going to request my bunk and my cushy ride would be over. I was still happy to have made it as long as I had and was surprised I had kept my bunk for over a month. Making for an extralong weekend, the commissary truck showed up a day early this week, bringing everything we ordered for the holiday, including $25 extra to spend on holiday packages. Christmas cookies, snacks, and other onetime-only items available to us for the holiday still didn't make up for getting screwed last week, but it was better than what we usually had, and that made all the difference in here.

That night, Albert's bunkie, Mr. Brand, read a letter he got from his daughter in the morning mail.

"My daughter wrote me this, and for those of you who think your family doesn't miss you or care about you, listen to this. 'Dear Dad, I love you, Dad, and I love you very much. You are the best dad ever. I wish I could be with you this Christmas, even if it means I have to be in jail with you. I wish you could be home right now, so I could be with you. Dad, I care about you very much.'" Mr. Brand paused here, took a few deep breaths, and tried to hold back the tears in his eyes, but it was no use. "'I am about to start crying just writing this letter to you. I miss you so much. I love you, Dad. Merry Christmas! Love, Melody.'"

Brand was a fountain of tears, and so were many others I saw while looking around. Most of the men who got emotional about the letter, I knew, had young kids of their own. I was even a little watery-eyed, thinking of Sean at home and wondering if he missed me that much. Brand received a standing ovation that seemed to go on forever. It took a lot of guts to read something like that out loud, and even though I think he made all of us miss home a little bit more, it was still important to realize that the loved ones we left at home had just as tough a time dealing with our incarceration as we did.

There was a Christmas celebration in the gym over the weekend, with a church service and Christmas music for those who wanted to attend. Thinking it would just make me miss home even more, I opted not to go and stayed in the unit and read to keep my mind off things. That proved more difficult than I thought, and I found myself not paying attention to what I was reading and having to reread some pages, just as I had the night before sentencing. While everybody was down in the gym, celebrating Christmas, I stayed in the unit with a few other guys, quietly contemplating what tomorrow would bring. Ever since I had been sentenced, I knew that on Thanksgiving and Christmas, I would be away from my family for the first time on the holidays, locked up in prison. I could only hope that Sean's birthday and Christmas would not be as hard for me to deal with as Thanksgiving had been. I had been dreading this day for over two months, and when I opened my eyes next, that day would be here.

CHAPTER

53

THE ONLY THING WORSE THAN waking up in prison to start your day is doing it on Christmas morning. We all awoke at 5:00 a.m. to a small paper bag next to our bunk filled with candy. The sergeant of the guards had done this with a little help from one of the local churches in Cottonwood so every inmate in here would have a little something for the holiday. It was a nice thought, and everyone really appreciated not being as forgotten as we thought we were. The indigent men really appreciated it, and since it was okay to be in possession of this candy, everyone was trading with the others to get the kind they liked the most. This was the first candy some guys had in three or four months, and they appreciated it.

We still had our morning meeting, but it was kept light and brief, followed by not having to superclean for the first time on any day off. Our Christmas present from the CO, and now I was a blue card. Now I was able to watch TV all weekend, and instead of setting up my table in the aisle and sneaking peeks at the game, I set one up in the dayroom with the other blue and green cards. Rather than sitting around, feeling sorry for ourselves today, we tried to laugh and joke around to break the tension that was as deep as the snow outside. Nobody talked about it, but we all missed home and wanted to be there instead of here. I called home later that night and talked to Sean and Beth, but not for too long. I was getting more upset by the second on the phone, and I kept it short so I wouldn't lose my composure. It was a long, drawn-out day, and I was glad when it finally came to an end. I vowed to never spend another Christmas away from my family ever again. I really wasn't sure how the rest of the world treated the Monday after Christmas, but around here, it was a three-day weekend, and none of the teachers or counselors came in on that day, so we ended up with another day of free time. This was awesome news, since it meant that we were most likely going to get the same treatment the day after New Year's Day as well. Although we did have to superclean, we still enjoyed another day of no programming, lots of football, and for some reason, Mondays off always seemed better than Fridays. This was especially true when you hadn't expected it. The transport bus, though, didn't bother to make it a holiday, which meant the leadership board was going to note the changes. According to the two or three vultures hovering over my one-man Hilton, my comfy hospital bunk would soon belong to someone else. Albert was busy all day, shuffling in and out of the dayroom and talking with CO Wiley in the afternoon when he showed up for the night shift. Shortly after their chat in the bubble, Albert came back into the dayroom and asked me to talk to him over by my bunk for a minute.

"Walker, you have been doing a great job as minute reader, and I wanted to double-check with you before I confirmed something with CO Wiley. Mr. Walsh is being bumped up to assistant senior coordinator, so how would you like to be the new expeditor coordinator?"

"Are you kidding me? Hell yes!" I responded without hesitation.

"It is the toughest coordinator spot on the board, but I think you can handle it. Everyone thinks you're the dickhead who passes out sanctions, but the COs tell you what punishment to hand out. All you do is read them and keep track of who has completed them and make sure they do it on time. If they don't, then you, as expeditor coordinator, are required to pull them up, or else you get pulled up by the CO for not doing your job. I was expeditor for three weeks, and if you do, you will be the assistant coordinator in no time."

"I will be any coordinator as long as I am up at the big table."

"The expediter runs the meetings and keeps everything moving on the proper schedule. If the meeting goes long, it's your fault. All you do is start it and turn it over to the assistant, who runs it. Follow the procedure and fill in the blanks."

"When do I start?"

"Tonight, at the meeting. Can you handle it?"

"I will be ready."

"I will have Mr. Walsh come see you, and he can sit by you tonight to make sure all goes well. You'll do fine." With that, he headed down to the bubble to talk to CO Wiley and start adjusting the leadership board for the meeting tonight and the new guys who were coming in.

Shortly afterward, Mr. Walsh came up and told me basically the same thing Albert had, since Albert was the one who trained Walsh. I had gotten my wish, and I was now a coordinator. The question now was, Would I be happy after getting what I wanted, or was this just a nightmare waiting to happen? If it were any other coordinator but expeditor, I wouldn't be concerned at all, but now I was in the hot seat. But at least I was in.

Mr. Walsh also showed me how to log entries into the big book. This was a three-ring binder that only the expediter, counselors, and COs were allowed to see. It had pages of entries for each man in the unit that detailed every push-up, pull-up, sanction, apology, or essay that was given to them as punishment. Each entry was dated, and names of the person who offended or the person who wrote them up were entered as well. This way, when staff reviewed an individual's record, all they had to do was look up his name and see his entry history since arriving at Cottonwood.

There was also a smaller book where the sanctions, essays, and apologies were listed by date to make sure each individual completed it on time, as required. Failure to do so would mean that I, as expeditor coordinator, would have to pull them up for noncompliance. This made me look like the bad guy to the new people who didn't know the system, but it was the COs who checked on me, so it was either them or me, and I wasn't going to let it be me. Mr. Walsh, as it happened, was two or three days behind on his entries, so that meant I now had the task of catching up all on the work he had let slide. Knowing who was leaving each week, he probably figured out when he was going to become an assistant and let it slide for a few days, knowing he could dump it on whoever took over for him. I could let the men on my committee help with the entries, but I was determined to do it myself, so I could learn the process before I began to delegate. I was responsible if anything was wrong, so I wanted firsthand knowledge of exactly what was going on. I also wanted to know how long it took to do these things, so I knew what I could expect from my guys when they were helping me. I was always taught to lead by example, and if I didn't do this myself for at least a little while, that would not be possible. I had gotten what I wished for, and I was already wondering if I was going to regret it.

That night at the meeting, I picked out one of the new guys who wasn't paying attention, just as had happened to me. I watched the clock as I crept up in front of him, and on the stroke of the clock, I yelled as loud as I could, "Good evening, community! My name is Mr. Walker." This guy practically jumped out of his chair while I shattered the silence with a huge grin on my face. It was much funnier when it happened to somebody else than it had been when it happened to me on my first day, and I was proud to have passed on the tradition. After this, all I did was pass the meeting to the assistant senior coordinator, and he took over from there. After ten or fifteen minutes, it was passed back to me to read the push-ups and pull-ups. CO Wiley had handed me the actual slips to read to the unit, complete with the required assignment that he had already written on the back. I read the names slowly, so the two men could stand and face each other, then the violation was stated, followed by the punishment.

"Mr. Johnson, pulling up Mr. Smith for sharing commissary. Sanction: three days forfeit of commissary privileges. Mr. Sanchez, pulling up Mr. Andrews for talking while on line for chow. Two-page apology to the community, due in three days." On and on it went for roughly five minutes. Wanting to end on a good note, we did the push-ups last. Same scenario, only with positive result and praise for good deeds. When I was done with my duties, I passed the meeting back to the assistant senior once again, and I was almost done. At the end of the meeting, I was the one who dismissed the unit.

It was after the meeting when my work really began. Now it was time to enter all the sanctions into the small book and date them. Since Walsh left me so far behind, I decided to start where he stopped, so it would be completed chronologically when I got done. I spent the rest of the night making big-book entries and didn't even come close to catching up, let alone on what had happened today. With each entry having to go into two individual log sheets and ten to fifteen pull-ups and push-ups each day, I had 120 entries to make in the big book and another 60 or so in the small one. The book was alphabetized, and the slips that were written on were chronological, which was how they were supposed to be entered. This made it a slow and tedious process. It had to be done one day at a time, so the staff could follow how each person had changed throughout their rider.

They kept track of the person who wrote you up to see if everyone was participating in the program or just flying under the radar. Not writing anyone up was almost as bad as getting written up, since that meant you weren't actively participating in the spirit of the program. It was quite amazing how the whole process worked, and until tonight, I really had no idea just how complex the community model program really was or how much work I had just taken on. Poor Mr. Walsh had been doing all this since the day I got here, and because he lived downstairs, I never saw any of the work he had to do as it happened. What had I gotten myself into? I spent the rest of the night making entries, and by bedtime, I was exhausted from two and a half hours of paperwork.

During the morning meetings, all I had to do was start them and end them, since all the slips were read at the evening meeting. Going to work turned out to be a break from all my work as coordinator, but I also knew I would be caught up in a few days, and it wouldn't be as hard after that. I couldn't do the expediter stuff during the day because the big book was not allowed to leave the bubble, unless I came and got it. The COs knew I had a job, so that wouldn't fly. Even if one of the guys on my committee wanted to work on it in the day, I still had to get it for them. The big book was the rider history for each man in the unit, and the CO kept careful track of it so everyone wasn't messing with it. I actually had the power to make things disappear from the book if I wanted to, but the consequences for that would be me appearing at the yard, and that was not an option I cared to exercise. Walsh had told me people who had figured the system out would try to bribe me to do just that but the punishment was way more severe than the crime and to not even think about it.

Work became the most enjoyable part of my day after I became coordinator. Morning, noon, and night, I was answering questions, writing in the big book, and attending coordinator meetings that were held after bedtime. At least at work I could relax and do whatever the hell I wanted. Tuesday, it was my turn to put the headphones on one of the new guys, and it was always funnier when it happened to another guy. The guy I did it to had the bunk across the aisle from me, and he had no clue for three or four hours that dark stuff was on his ears and people were snickering behind his back until late in the afternoon. Nobody told him, and if he hadn't looked in the mirror before dinner to pop a zit, it could have gone on all night. Humor was what kept Castro, McGladrey, and me going. I couldn't imagine this place without the two of them and Albert. They helped make life in here at least bearable. When it came time for Tuesday's bunk moves, my luck had finally run out. The two or three guys who wanted my bunk were now green, and I was going to get bumped tonight for sure. When CO Wiley called me down to the bubble to get the big book, he let me know how he ran things with his coordinators.

"Mr. Walker, there are four requests from green cards for your bunk. Did you know that?"

"No, sir. It's too close to the microwave and the bubble for most people."

"Well, I will tell you what I'm going to do. All of them are going to have to choose another bunk so nobody gets it."

"Not even me, sir? I don't understand."

"I have some guidelines when it comes to bunk moves, and one of them is, even if a green card wants your bunk, I won't move my coordinators. They work hard for the unit, and even though you are barely blue, I won't make you move from that single hospital bed you have managed to somehow keep since day 1."

"Thank you, sir. I appreciate that."

"You have earned it. Now, get out of here while I figure out how to tell these guys they need to make another choice."

I was so stoked as I walked out of the board. So I was coordinator until I left, which meant I got to keep my killer bunk until I went home. That was the best Christmas present I could have gotten.

Castro and I spent the short week brainstorming how to put our project together and the sequence of events that would need to take place for it to happen. We needed to talk to the COs, make diagrams of the units, and take a bunch of pictures for the PowerPoint presentation we were to make. This would give us reasons to go all over the compound and recruit people to be in the pictures, so we could show as well as describe what it was we were trying to convey in the presentation. Since CO Wiley was cool and it was always good to be on his good side, we decided to start by interviewing him and letting him be our liaison between the COs and staff, as Mr. Walter had told us to do.

He gave us thirty minutes one afternoon and liked what we were doing and how we were going about it. He also informed us that the CO we really needed to talk to with was CO Edlund, with the same name as the guy in the bunk next to me. By Thursday, we had managed to do the same with CO Edlund, only to find out that he needed to go to the lieutenant whose jurisdiction our project technically would fall under. This was turning into a complete bureaucratic clusterfuck, and we hadn't even been able to get started yet.

CO Edlund's ability to move quickly regarding the task at hand was truly amazing. By Friday, he had come to us in the office, which was never a good idea, to let us know he had the information we wanted and when would be a good time to get together and go over it. He was one of the COs who worked Friday through Sunday, so Castro and I got permission from Mr. Walter to work the weekend to access CO Edlund no matter what unit he was assigned to. Once again, we had managed to manipulate the staff into giving us movement passes—for the weekend, no less—and now we could do as we pleased all weekend long.

It took me until Friday to catch up in the big book, and by now I was ready to let my crew members on the committee help me keep up, which was much easier to do than catch up. I was now comfortable in my new job as expeditor, and even though some took it personally, I knew eventually they would understand I had no choice but to do what I did. It fell under the job description of expeditor, and failure to comply on my part could get me sanctioned in a second.

Friday afternoon came with a couple of nice bonuses. Around 2:00 p.m., Mr. Walter asked McGladrey and me to go to the chapel and photograph the GED graduation ceremony for media productions. One of our jobs in between our project was to periodically take group pictures for the members of D&A classes. Each class or group member who graduated received what he would take of the group. No bunny ears, gang signs, or other goofing off was allowed, and if it occurred, the group picture would be denied to everyone, so everybody had to be careful. It was great to see the happy faces of the men who got their GED, as well as the pride that some of their families took when they received them. Spouses and parents could attend the ceremony, and some of these men were in tears while hugging their families after their noteworthy achievement. If you ever thought good things never happened in prison, this afternoon would definitely change your mind. It was a wonderful afternoon, and I was glad to be there to see the pride these men had in their accomplishment, and I was proud of every one of them. Instead of taking the hard road and doing nothing about their future, they decided to be productive, and this was exactly what Cottonwood was about.

The pictures turned out well, and everybody got a copy to take home. If it weren't for these pictures, most people would have nothing to show anyone what this place was like. Everyone asked for extras, but printing them was out of our hands. Castro and I worked all weekend and got the project off the ground. CO Edlund was very cooperative, and we had the foundation for a great presentation. The whole idea was to get a fire drill procedure that was identical for the whole compound and to train each inmate the same way on the first day they arrived. After what happened to unit 4 the first few days I had been here, I wanted to make sure that everyone was on the same sheet of music and knew what to do. It was better than standing outside and freezing our asses off for twenty minutes because nobody had ever instructed us on what we were supposed to do. CO Edlund had to clarify some of the stuff with the lieutenant to make sure that what we were teaching was approved by the fire marshal and approved by the staff. Giving out false information would probably do more harm than good and maybe even get somebody killed. We wanted it to be just like any of the safety PowerPoints that Mr. Raymon showed in the vocational safety classes that were required for the certificate he gave out. These were professionally made and viewed by hundreds of people each month. We could only hope ours turned out as well and then given to new guys on the day they showed up so there would not be a problem ever again.

To be honest, I was surprised that this wasn't required already, since most places had fire codes and regulations that were strictly enforced. When I first arrived, we were told not to use the fire extinguishers. Only the COs were authorized to operate them. That way, if someone needed it, it was operational, not having been messed with by anyone who was inexperienced in their proper use. CO Edlund contradicted this rule and said, "If I am on fire and you don't grab the fire extinguisher and put it out, you are going to be in deep shit with me." Obviously, we needed some clarification so that no one acted inappropriately or got in trouble for doing something they weren't supposed to. Things like this were what he needed to check with the fire guy about so the advice he gave us to base our presentation on would all be accurate legally, as well as practical. CO Edlund was happy we were doing this, because the COs got their ass chewed for the fire drill taking so long the first few nights when I first got here, and they were also trying to figure out a solution for the problem.

We didn't work all weekend, but we put down five or six hours each day, which might have been a little generous, but Mr. Walter didn't work weekends, so he would never know. It was possible that the quicker we got our required hours for the workforce development certificate, the quicker we could go home, but Castro and I didn't know for sure. With no required classes, that was my main certificate to acquire before departure could occur, so anything I could do to speed up that process was top of my to-do list.

Maybe my hours had a bearing on my departure, and maybe it was all about the ninety days, but I figured it was better to be safe than sorry. With the holidays almost behind us, I was now looking toward my green card, then going home. The worst was over for me psychologically—getting sentenced, downtime in RDU, Thanksgiving, and Christmas. So now I had to make sure I did everything properly for the judge to make 100 percent sure that I was going home. I had only been here around thirty-five days, but life was finally predictable, comfortable, and because of my new job, almost relaxing. There was always something to do, and I found myself enjoying more and more. Even when I watched a ball game, I would have paper out and write between plays. I was constantly multitasking eighteen hours a day, nonstop, keeping as busy as I could.

Just as I had hoped, my first phase change seminar really reached people. It took until mid-January for someone else's to really hit me. Mr. Jameson was two weeks behind me, and when he read his second phase change, it struck me like a dagger. He told us how, as a child, he was always on one side of the door while his parents were doing drugs on the other side. It hurt him because they wouldn't include him, but once he got old enough to know what was really going on, he understood why. Later, he was in the room, doing drugs with his father, and eventually he was keeping his child on the other side of the door. His message was to quit doing the drugs and to open the door to your children and involve them in your life. Don't ignore them, because it hurts the kids and they blame themselves. They are too young to understand that they are not the problem—you are. Apparently, it hit home with a large percentage of the men here, and he received a standing ovation that lasted for several minutes.

It hurt to hear him say that because that was exactly what I had done to my son for way too long. I knew I was hurting him, but addiction is a fucked-up disease that makes you do stupid things. I guess for me to process what I had done, I needed to hear it from someone else. I was glad Mr. Jameson had been man enough to share what he had done with the unit. It also made me wonder how he had overcome his addiction, and I prayed that I could do the same for Sean. I was stubborn and had to live through my mistakes. I hadn't been willing to listen to anyone, and now I was in Idaho prison. I hoped Sean would learn from my mistakes and not follow in my footsteps. I would never forgive myself if he did.

CHAPTER

54

EACH WEEK, I SCARED THE shit out of someone new at their first meeting. Someone would find themselves walking around the unit with big black circles around their ears. Every Monday night, the alarm would go off in the chow hall at dinner. I was still running store and had so much stuff I had to get a bigger locker from one of the going-home riders so I would have enough space to keep it all. After the first week of January, when McGladrey finished his "thinking for a change" class, he was moved into unit 4 right across the aisle from me, and that was when the pranks really started to get rolling. Castro and I were holding our own, but now with the trifecta going, nobody was safe.

The three of us would sit in the media production office for hours, working on top 10 lists for Castro to read in the morning meeting. We would run guys all over the compound with some bullshit story and our movement pass so they wouldn't get in trouble; they handed them off to one another at a different point just so we could watch them. We did this with the barneys after their one-hour orientation class was finished for the day, telling them they needed to get something from somebody else who didn't exist. We had guys all over the compound in on it, so the guy would go to the laundry, be told to go to the school, then be told to go to the kitchen, and so on. We would start the wheels in motion and sit back in front of the media production office, watching these guys go up and down Main Street for two or three hours and laughing our asses off. Some days my stomach would ache because we were having so much fun, laughing so hard that it hurt.

We still were making progress on our project, but we could have finished much faster. We took our time. Once it was done, all the privileges that came with the project disappeared like Cinderella's pumpkin coach. For now, we could do almost anything we wanted. The pranks were becoming so frequent that in order to get anything done in the office, we were constantly double-checking with Mr. Walter to verify that some assignments were authorized by the staff and it wasn't just someone messing with you.

Castro, McGladrey, and I also began to take the vocational safety courses Mr. Raymon gave every day from one thirty to two thirty. On Fridays, those who had completed the course took a test to earn their vocational safety certificate. Most of the information covered was pretty basic, but every now and then, he would throw something difficult at us, so I took notes in every class, so I could pass them on to the next guy when I left. It was helpful to sit through these PowerPoint presentations because this was exactly what we were trying to do with the fire drills, and we wanted ours to come out as good as the ones Mr. Raymon was using.

While looking through the computer directories one day, McGladrey found the safety test that we needed to take at the end of the course. It was one of three tests that was used randomly. He had found it accidentally while trying to find us some music. We copied it down so we could study it before we took the test. The answers were all pretty much the same for all the safety test, only differently worded or in different order. It made a good study aid, and of course, it would be passed onto the next guy we favored who was still in the class when we were done.

Castro and I were already friends with McGladrey, who fit right in with the rest of the unit but was indigent. Since he was teaching me the job skills I claimed to have known in order to work in media productions, and he covered my ass when Walter or Raymon gave me an assignment, I owed him. Since he knew about all my commissary and the store I had built up, I became responsible for feeding his coffee habit every day and provided him with any other goodies he might want.

"What's in this for me?" I asked him after he had already consumed about $25 or $30 worth of my commissary.

"What do you want?"

"I need a laptop when we get out. Do you have a spare one you can give me?"

"What do you think I'm in here for? I can get you a laptop no problem."

"I have fifteen or twenty of them in a storage unit. I will give you one when we get out. Now, quit your sniveling and hook me up."

You are never supposed to trust anyone you meet in prison, but we had grown closer than most inmates did in here, and I had never heard him contradict himself when telling stories, so I had no reason to doubt him. I had enough coffee for both of us anyways, and if I actually got the laptop out of it, great. If not, oh well. I shared my commissary with a lot of people anyways. It was not like I was stingy. Getting taken advantage of was a completely different story. Some guys were just moochers and didn't even talk to you until they wanted something. They had no way to pay you back, and that got tiring real fast. McGladrey and I were friends before I started giving him coffee. And the gift of laughter he brought more than compensated for the food items I had given him.

Once he was done with his current project, he instantly latched on to Castro and me to help us get the fire drill PowerPoint done now that we had decided to try to take it to a whole new level. Not only were we going to create it, but we also wanted to teach it to all the new guys on the day they arrived. In three or four months, the entire compound would be on the same page just by participating in a fifteen-minute class that was conceived, produced, taught, and passed on to the next group by the three of us. It would be a way for us to leave this place a little better than when we got here, and if it kept 461 men from freezing their asses off or save somebody's life, it was time well spent.

Of course, the three of us put a picture of us, along with our names, at the end, giving us all the credit we deserved, and then some, for being intelligent enough to conceive the project in the first place. The final credits, giving the COs who helped a small line in black and white with their names printed so tiny that you could barely read them. Of course, our names were flashing, bold, colorful, huge, and accompanied by some good music. It wasn't meant to demean the COs, and they knew that. We were just trying to get them to laugh in a place where a lot of them did not.

To move from blue card to green, there was one last test to take, and your portfolio had to be cleared and completed through the verification class. This was a Saturday class that was held once or twice a month in the morning, so the teachers and their helpers could check you off the list and give you your portfolio certificate. Those who still needed work on theirs would have to complete it before enjoying the privileges that came with the green card: commissary any time you weren't programming, sleeping most of the weekends, green card rec every night, and the most TV time for anyone here. One of the assistant seniors was Mr. Steele. He and I were talking one day, and he offered to look over my portfolio before I took it to the class this weekend to make sure it was acceptable.

"Mr. Walker," he told me, "if you were to turn your portfolio in like this tomorrow, you would not get a passing grade, and you wouldn't be able to turn green on time. However, for a nominal fee, I can fix the few things that are wrong with it and make sure you pass with flying colors."

"How *nominal* would that particular fee be exactly?"

"Keep me in coffee until I leave in a few weeks. Sounds fair?"

"I am not sure. How much coffee do you drink in a day?"

"Just a cup each morning, maybe two once in a while, but I could go home any day now and you would be off the hook. Are you a gambling man?"

"Yeah, but I already have a couple of people I am sponsoring upstairs. How about I just give you one bag and we call it even?"

"That sounds fair to me."

"I just want to run it by Mr. McCracken, who also happens to be in the computer lab as a teacher's assistant, just to make sure you're not working me."

I took the portfolio over to Mr. McCracken, an openly gay African American who was as smart as they come. He was sort of an outcast in the environment, but he lived right across from me upstairs and we had seemed to get along fairly well under the circumstances and had a few intense discussions on current events and historical ones as well. He didn't flaunt his sexual orientation in here because that would get him in trouble with everyone, not just the CO and staff. This was something he really didn't want to have happen. He didn't deny his orientation or his feelings, and he had no problem talking openly and honestly with those of us who befriended him. I knew I could get a straight answer from him, and his opinion in this matter might make the difference between turning green on time or having to wait until the next class for my portfolio to pass muster. He, as was the case with most people in here, had succumbed to the evils of meth, and even though he was highly intelligent, the addictive nature of the drug had ruined his life.

He told me the same thing Mr. Steele had and confirmed that on the whole, this was pretty much how it was done. There were a few things that needed to be fixed, and those small items would keep me from getting my green card, and until my portfolio was approved in two weeks, when the class was held again, this meant I would not get to be green for two extra weeks. And no matter what it was going to cost me, I wanted to make sure my portfolio passed the first time around. At least Mr. Steele was being honest, and for that, I was appreciative, but it never hurt to get a second opinion, especially when it came to things I didn't know much about. And the portfolio definitely fell into that category.

I gave my portfolio to Mr. Steele and told him when I received my completion certificate that I would give him a bag of coffee, and the deal was struck. There were a lot of guys who paid to have the whole portfolio done by someone else, but their price was much higher. The portfolio was basically designed to help people get jobs once they were released, and since that wouldn't be the case for me, I felt it was okay to fudge a little bit on this one assignment.

That weekend, my portfolio passed, and I also received my Bible study certificate in the mail, giving me two certificates to put in my folder. I was halfway through the safety class and workforce development, not to mention being the minute reader and now expeditor coordinator. The judge would see these things when I went in front of him. It would be obvious to him that I was applying myself, but just when I thought this would be the case, my whole world was rocked on Monday, when the new guys who were showing up had to have their names put on the board by the expeditor committee.

Four weeks ago, we had said goodbye to Mr. Wells. He was here on a 180-day rider and was one of the guys who made few changes in his behavior while here and definitely was flying under the radar. He was a green card for my first month or so, and we had talked a few times since his bunk was just down the aisle from mine. One of the names I was writing on the board was Mr. Wells, and I couldn't help but wonder if he was the same one who recently left us. CO Wiley confirmed to me that this was indeed the same Mr. Wells that had only a few weeks earlier given his goodbye speech and left us.

"He was sentenced to another rider," CO Wiley told me. "The judge must have not thought he got it right the first time."

"How often have you seen that happen, sir?"

"It is more common than you think. I see the same people come back on back-to-back riders, or some come through two or three times years apart. It's a revolving door up here, and even though we do our best to keep it from happening, some people just don't care."

I felt bad for Mr. Wells, but if you didn't apply yourself to the program, then you took your chances. Most people just assumed they would leave here and be put on probation. Some were sentenced to the yard for their full time, and yet others wound up in county for another six months. I knew all too well that it was up to the judge and his take on what you accomplished up here. Nothing was a given in the justice system, and I had to start preparing mentally for any possibility. When you go in front of the judge, you never know what you are going to get. The last time I was in front of a judge, I was planning to go home that night, and here I was, months later, beginning to worry about going back in front of the same judge. When would this end?

I was almost beginning to understand the guys who said, "Screw it, send me to the yard." You jumped through hoops for six months, got sent back for six more, and then faced years of meeting probation requirements. You violated while on probation, and they sent you back here again. With two years at the yard, you did what you wanted and you were free after that. Without more hoops to jump through, the DOC didn't seem so out of line after seeing how the system actually worked. If you had no wife or kids, I could see the logic in it, but still, the rider program wasn't that bad, and at this point, I was kind of getting into it. Mr. Wells gave an interesting comeback speech and informed us that probation was not a given, as he obviously found out the hard way. He warned us all to apply ourselves or what happened to him could easily happen to any of us.

We finished our project that week and turned it in for staff approval. Since they had helped us with the information we put into it, approval was pretty much a given. Once they approved it, we had to give a sample oral presentation to CO Edlund and CO Wiley to make sure it was okay to give to the men. Mr. Raymon sat in on our first presentation so he could grade it for the safety class as well. Everyone was satisfied and it went off without a hitch. We were to give it in the safety class this week and to the new guys next Monday if all went well. In no time, the whole compound would be doing fire drills efficiently, and that was what the whole project was about.

Albert was supposed to leave next week, so he and I spent a lot of time talking and trying to see if we could make any money together when we got out. He had the worst judge in Ada County and was concerned that he might end up at the yard even after completing a flawless rider. He definitely was not flying under the radar, but just as Wells came back, so could just about anybody. He was pretty nervous since the judge could still send him to the yard if the mood struck him.

On Wednesday that week, I finally made it to the last stage of this nightmare and received my green card on my sixtieth day on compound. Well, I passed the test and qualified but would not get it until tomorrow, my sixty-first day, but I was still happy about it. Now there were no more hurdles to overcome or goals to attain, except for getting my end-case statement and going home, but even that wasn't a sure thing. Albert told me when he left that I would be getting bumped up to assistant senior coordinator and would no longer be the expeditor coordinator. That was the best thing I had heard; of all the coordinators, the expeditor was the hardest assignment, and even the senior coordinator didn't have as difficult a task as I currently did. Becoming assistant senior would be a nice break, and I could hardly wait for it to happen. I would miss Albert quite a bit. He was an outgoing, motivated, and positive individual in a place where most people weren't, and it was good to have him around.

The one constant thing in the universe is change. Things were changing around here, and maybe it was the old group of guys, and maybe it was just me, but the unit seemed to be going downhill and there was nothing that could be done to stop it. Each week the guys seemed to be younger and more immature. They reminded me more and more of the punks in county, as opposed to caring, dedicated guys who were here when I first arrived. Maybe it was up to the senior members to bring the new guys around, but I wasn't sure we could. The men in the unit didn't seem to care about helping one another as much as we did when I was a purple card. Whatever the case, things needed to be set right or we would all suffer severe consequences in the long run.

The COs implemented a new toilet paper distribution system this week, which constantly left guys stranded on the toilet without paper in a place, where cleanliness was important every day. To save money, only a limited number of rolls were distributed to each tier in each unit, and whatever system they had come up with to determine how much to allow us each day was completely off base. We never had enough, and it was beginning to be a pain in the ass—no pun intended.

That Tuesday, Castro, McGladrey, and I gave our first PowerPoint presentation to the new guys after their first orientation class was over. Mr. Raymon sat in just to be sure all went well, and yet the alarm went off that night as well. CO Edwards said things had gone amazingly well compared to before and he thought the class we had given each unit before we gave it to the new guys was part of the reason. He was really into the whole deal we had going, and I wasn't sure if it was because he was the designated fire CO or it was just us trying to do some good while here. Either way, he was behind us, and the effort we had put in to make it a reality was all our own. He said it showed true concern for the common good of the community.

The week also marked the return of CO Gherkin. Gherkin was a heavyset female CO who had worked at Cottonwood for ten or eleven years. She was familiar with the system and was in the unit Friday through Sunday in the mornings, and now Gherkin or Wiley was there every day. They were our two main Cos, and the rest of the time, we took whoever was on rotation. Edwards was there a lot, and since he was pretty cool, everything ran fairly smoothly most of the time.

On Thursday night, when CO Wiley read the going-home names, he didn't call out Albert for two minutes after he was done with the rest. The look on Albert's face for those two minutes was priceless, and it was good to see the COs had a sense of humor. After he had been here for over 168 days, I could only imagine Albert's disappointment in not being called to go home. Then again, the look on his face when Wiley stuck his head out of the bubble and said, "Oh, yeah, Albert, you're going home too," was amazing. The man smiled as only he could and let out a jubilant yell, which was out of order but well received. Albert was told by his judge to pull a perfect rider or he would end up in prison for at least a year, and Mr. Albert had done exactly that. He had completed all his counseling and group classes as well as the Bible certificate, served as a senior coordinator, and had some other church group participation certificate. If he didn't get probation, nobody could.

It was a long and boring weekend even with a green card. I was now allowed to sleep during free time, and between writing, football, and reading, a nap was a welcome luxury, one I hadn't had in quite some time. I lay back in between writing a number of pages, and before I knew it, I was out like a light. I awoke to CO Gherkin tapping the end of my bed and asking, "What are you doing asleep, Mr. Walker?" I awoke in a daze and scared to death I was in big trouble. There went my perfect rider. She had a mean glare on her face, and everyone around was looking at me. It always takes a second or two to realize where you are when you wake up in a strange place, and even though I had been in the same bunk for sixty-some odd days, it still seemed like a strange place. I woke up in fear, thinking I was in deep shit, until I realized, slowly, that it was okay for me to be napping as a green card. When I glanced over to Castro and McGladrey, their laughter told me instantly that they had put the CO up to this on my first weekend I was able to sleep more often. Even sixty days in, I was still a choice victim whenever they could pull it off. My heart was racing for a while after that, and I decided that if that was how they wanted to play, then it was game on.

That afternoon, the Seahawks won the NFC title game, and since I was not going to be there, I had no doubt they would win the Superbowl, and the only one to miss that party would be me. They were on an eight- or nine-game winning streak and looking really good to possibly beat the Steelers in two weeks at the Superbowl in Detroit. The biggest event in Seahawks history was about to occur, and I was going to miss it and all the exciting events that came with it.

On Monday, I said goodbye to Albert and was promoted to assistant senior coordinator. All the assistants had to do was run the three coordinators underneath them and the meetings. The meetings were on rotation with three men, so about every other day, it was my turn. All we had to do was introduce who was doing what next. It was much harder than most of the coordinator jobs but much easier than the expeditor coordinators by a long shot. I also had to teach the new expeditor how to use the big book, but since he was one of the guys on my committee who had already been helping me, that was easy too. Besides, I didn't leave him back-logged by four days like I had been when I took over for Mr. Walsh, who, as it turned out, was now the new senior coordinator. Before Albert left, he told me I was in line as he and Walsh had been for the senior slot, but with two other men at assistant who had more seniority than I did, the chances were slim I would ever make it before I left.

One of them was Mr. Steele, who was still here and would have been milking me dry of coffee had I not switched the deal with him to one bag. He was a die-hard Pittsburg fan, and we had a little banter going on about the upcoming game and were trying to figure out how to bet on the game in a place where gambling was not allowed. Both of us could get in serious trouble. We had to be especially careful because we were in our visible leadership slots. Mr. Steele was indigent, which was why he wanted the coffee so badly, and since he had nothing to bet commissary-wise, we had to figure out a way to keep it interesting without betting commissary items. We settled on the loser making the other guy's bunk for a week, with each of us wagering on our team to win outright with no point spread at all. I think Pittsburg was a two- or three-point favorite, but we both just went for the victory since a Superbowl win was still a championship, whether it was by 1 point or 50.

Tuesday night at the meeting, I was in charge, and after the new expeditor turned the meeting over to me, I decided to make a stand on behalf of the men, knowing what was going on upstairs at this particular moment. After I was introduced to the community, I was out of order as far as protocol went, but I and the rest of the guys had finally had enough of the new toilet paper rationing.

"I would like to break from protocol for just a second to ask by a show of hands really quick. Who thinks this toilet paper situation needs to be resolved immediately?" Every hand in the unit went up, and when I turned to look at the coordinators' table, half of them were up too. CO Wiley came out of the bubble and had a tone in his voice that I had never heard before. He sounded pissed, and I wondered if I had just crossed a line.

"Mr. Steele, would you please take over the meeting? Mr. Walker, would you please step into my office?" He wasn't asking; he was demanding. And he wasn't too happy with what I had done.

Once I was in the bubble and the door was closed, he looked up at me and shook his head.

"Mr. Walker, do you have any idea how disrespectful to the system what you just did was?"

"I meant no disrespect, sir. I was just trying to get the point across to everyone concerned that something needed to be done right away. What is happening now is not working, sir, and I can prove it."

"What do you mean you can prove it?"

"Right now, as we speak, there are two men who are on the toilet, missing the meeting, because they are not going to get up until they get some toilet paper. And I don't blame them at all."

"Are you serious? Why don't they have any toilet paper?"

"I am not sure, sir. That's between the house coordinator, his assistant, the senior, and the COs, but it has been going on for over a week, and the guys are getting frustrated because it happens every day. A man has the right to be able to wipe his ass, sir. Believe me, I meant no disrespect to the COs or Mr. Walsh, but something needs to happen quickly to remedy this situation. I was just looking out for my men, sir. Isn't that what leadership is about, sir?"

He told me to join the meeting while he locked up the bubble and went upstairs to see what the hell was going on. He did have a roll of toilet paper in his hand as he went up the stairs, and I was glad that he was going to handle it and not some asshole CO. The system was broken, and when it came to toilet paper issues, that needed to get fixed yesterday. The two men came down shortly, and before the end of the meeting, CO Wiley came back out and addressed the whole unit concerning the situation.

"Mr. Walker, although he should have gone about it a different way, has brought to my attention that the TP distribution system is not working out as it was designed to. I was unaware of the urgency of the problem until I went upstairs and found two men on the toilet, waiting for some paper. After the meeting, I want to see the house coordinator, Mr. Walsh, and a laundry worker in my office right away, and we will get this thing taken care of tonight." Laundry workers had access to supplies. He received a standing ovation. Since I was back in charge at that point, I stood up and introduced myself once again, interrupting the meeting.

"I would like to ask forgiveness from the community for the disrespectful way I brought the issue to the unit. It was certainly not my intention, and I also meant no insult to the house coordinator, Mr. Salazar, or to Mr. Walsh. Will you please accept my apology?"

"Apology accepted" came back from the whole unit.

I might have ruffled a few feathers, but apparently, that was what it took to get the job done. Within twenty minutes of the meeting dispersing, we had plenty of toilet paper both upstairs and down, and we had no TP problem after that night. I was developing a reputation for getting things done, and in a place where the line of communication worked slowly, this meant I was now the go-to guy for just about everything. I was now going to green card rec every night, playing basketball and running. I had lifted some weights, but the lines for the machines and dumbbells were hoarded by the hard-core guys. All I needed was some cardio to help burn off some excess energy, and I would be able to sleep soundly. I found it extremely difficult to run on the frozen snow. The path I had dug out when I first arrived was still maintained, but the constant slipping jolted my back, and after a few attempts of running the ball field loop, I decided it wasn't for me. Besides, I was supposed to be working during the morning rec time, and I had sneaked out a few times when I was new. Now if I pulled something like that, too many people knew me, and that could easily ruin my perfect rider.

CHAPTER

55

F INALLY, AFTER ALL THE REQUIREMENTS had been met and after enduring a long winter at Cottonwood, I had my end-case appointment with Mr. Kennison. I was getting my port-folio ready to show him, along with all the notes from self-help books I had read while here. I had over fifty pages of notes from over fifteen books, complete with a separate list of titles and authors to show him. We were also required to prepare our own handwritten end-case statements on one page to present to the counselor. This was to state, specifically, what you had learned here that made you less likely to reoffend and what changes you had made to your behavior that would now make you an asset to the community instead of a problem. I listed my active participation in the program and all the self-help books I'd read, and even the fire drill class and laundry delivery service projects, both of which I had conceived, outlined, got an approval for, and implemented while here. My coordinator status was also a plus in my appointment while still an orange card, which proved that I was actively participating in the program and living up to its ideals rather than flying under the radar as so many did. I might not have received the drug and alcohol counseling my judge thought I would, but that was not my fault and I shouldn't be sent back here if the staff here didn't do what my judge had asked.

Wednesday night, one of the new guys had a slight accident that I thought I would never see in a place like this. Mr. Simons was a blue card who was lucky enough to be on a bottom bunk, but he woke up this morning covered in piss from the guy above him wet-ting the bed last night. The new man above him, Mr. Plains, obvi-ously had a bladder problem at his age, and instead of bringing it to the attention of the COs, he thought he could hide it or handle it, but apparently, he was wrong. Mr. Simon's was extremely pissed, no pun intended, and rightfully so. Plains had absolutely no respect for his fellow community members if he was going to pull this crap, and it made me wonder why this apparent medical condition hadn't been addressed or identified during his time in county or RDU. This was only his second night, which meant he was doing this so far at a 50 percent ratio, and that was not going to fly at Cottonwood.

He was moved to a bottom bunk, but the next night, it happened again. What kind of screening was actually getting done in RDU that something like this was getting by without being addressed? I felt sorry for Plains because he was immediately shunned by most members of the community, and I personally thought he should have not tried to hide this condition and the problem should have been solved before he arrived here. NICI was forced to order him some Depends, and the COs had to wake him every two hours to use the restroom, which solved the problem, but the social damage was already done.

Another one of the new guys who showed up that week was Mr. Edgar. He was a sixty-seven-year-old man who was quite out of place here. He was having a hard time adjusting to the boot camp lifestyle and being forced to deal with all the young punks who seemed to be taking over the whole compound. He, too, was getting up every two hours to pee on his own. He was sentenced to a rider for his drinking problem, just like Mr. Knight, and I doubted he had ever broken any other law in his entire life. He reminded me of my grandfather, and I tried to help him as much as possible, which for the first week was extremely difficult without both of us getting in trouble.

The man couldn't function without his morning cup of coffee and would bring down the wrath of the unit and get him pulled up at this early stage of his rider. I had been making prison taffy since my first order of commissary showed up, which was made by mixing Chick-O-Stick candy with moon pies in the microwave and stirring them together. I would alter the flavor with some Tang or cocoa to vary the taste. By substituting coffee into the mix, I figured I could help the old guy out and not get him in trouble. If I made him a few strong batches of taffy, he could discreetly eat some each morning to help get him going.

My idea worked, and Mr. Edgar was a changed man after that. He rose from his bunk smiling, helped out others, and made a complete 180-degree change. All it took was a small infusion of caffeine to make the difference. I thought it tasted like shit, but the old guy loved it, and I had made his day with a small gesture. I had made so much "prison money" from running store I decided I should probably give some back to the community, and this was one way to do it.

While most of the unit shied away from Mr. McCracken, he and I had formed a bond I had never expected to have with a gay man in prison. He was very interesting to talk to and knowledgeable on many subjects. His sexual orientation was not a problem but rather just another venue for his knowledge to be shared with me. I had never had the opportunity to get to know a guy like him before, and with his honesty and candor, I would do it again if ever the situation arose. He was getting harassed by some in the unit who were patronizing and rude. Those who didn't accept his lifestyle shouldn't have judged him until they got to know him and what he was truly all about. The same guys were also causing some bad moments for the men in unit 1, which housed inmates who had committed sexual crimes, including child molesters and sexual deviants.

One of the reasons we weren't supposed to associate with other units was to protect the unit 1 population from the harassment so common in correctional facilities. Those who were incarcerated for sex crimes, especially against minors or other males, were often victims of violence and segregated from the general prison population for their own safety. In here, violence of any kind would get you sent to the yard, but far too many one-liners and inappropriate comments were thrown about at the expense of the men who were housed at the top of the hill in unit 1.

Thursday night, Mr. McCracken read his phase change from a word he had picked out that wasn't on the list but that I had received prior approval from CO Wiley for him to use. The word was *tolerance*. He stated point-blank that he was a gay man and how, even though most of us might not approve of his sexual orientation, this country was founded on each individual's right to do as he pleased without fear of persecution from others if he wasn't hurting anyone else. He was not harassing us or putting us down for not liking females, and he deserved the same respect for his life choice whether we agreed with them or not.

Putting another man down for his sexual orientation was against the ideals of the program, and continuing to be disrespectful of others' choices proved that you had not learned anything from being here. Mr. McCracken said he would make sure that we were pulled up just as if we had broken any other rule if we disrespected him, which so many guys here were constantly doing.

He was a good man, but he had reached his limit. This was the entire unit's verbal warning to respect him as we would any other inmate or suffer the consequences. He was direct, honest, and correct in the way he went about it and received a standing ovation. Even CO Wiley came out of the bubble, clapping, and had a few thoughts to add about sexual harassment.

"If I hear of disrespectful comments, jokes, or harassment of any kind toward this man, who has the balls to stand up here and discuss his sexual orientation with a crowd like this, they are going to have to answer to me. Do you men realize what it took for Mr. McCracken to stand up here and say the things he just said? If you had no respect for him before he did that, you should now, just for the man doing what he did. Good for you, McCracken. What you did took a lot of guts. You should be proud of yourself. Another thing, gentlemen, before you go thinking about how much better you are than the men in unit 1, just think about a thing or two. I want you to raise your hand if, when you were eighteen, nineteen, or twenty, you were sleeping with sixteen- or seventeen-year-old girls."

Most hands went up in the air, including CO Wiley's.

"That's what I thought. The only difference between you and most of the guys who are housed up on the hill is that the parents of the girls you guys were with weren't such assholes. Most of the guys just happened to hook up with girls whose parents are pricks and decided to prosecute them to protect their Susie's reputation. Most likely, those parents did it for themselves, more than for poor little Susie, who I am sure was just as into what happened as most of the girls I knew when I was that age were. Now true, some of those guys are sick, perverted, messed-up individuals who are in desperate need of serious therapy, but 95 percent of them are here because of overprotective parents who were looking out for their own social reputation and took it out on those men. They don't even deserve to be here, in my opinion, but my opinion doesn't really matter. The judge's is the one that counts. Reading some of your files, I am convinced that many of you really don't deserve to be here. But you are here, making the best of a bad situation, and for that you should be proud. Don't judge people so easily, gentlemen. Things are not always as they appear, and most likely, you don't have a clue as to what the real story is in many cases. Carry on, gentlemen."

As usual, he received a standing ovation for his words of wisdom, but this short speech seemed to go on longer than most. The man wasn't afraid to tell it like it was, whether he was bucking the same system he was part of or not. He made an extremely valid point, and his comments changed the way I looked at the men from unit 1 from that day on. I was guilty of the same thing that had brought many of those men here. Most of us were. Judging them so harshly up until this point wasn't right for me or anyone to have done. If I ever thought I got the short end of the stick here, I could only imagine what it was like to be sent here for six months and labeled a sex offender for sleeping with a seventeen-year-old when I was nineteen. If I had heard the same argument from anyone here other than him, I might have still been skeptical. That the statement came from a man who had the information on a computer in front of him and had been here long enough to absorb it and share his true opinion about the hypocrisy he saw made it more poignant than ever. I was grateful to have this man as my CO, and some of the things he had said over the months were truly words of wisdom. I considered myself fortunate to be able to hear them. He was a man of few words, but the words he spoke were worth listening to.

That weekend, after superclean, and with nothing to do, I sat on my bunk, waiting for the all-clear, and relaxed until free time began. I somehow got just a little too comfortable, and before I knew it, Mr. Walsh was waking me up.

"Mr. Walker, as assistant senior coordinator, you are not setting a good example of what to do while waiting to be cleared for free time."

"Sorry, Mr. Walsh. I must have dozed off."

"I need to meet with all the coordinators in the upstairs dayroom for ten minutes after we are cleared. Can you let everyone upstairs who needs to be there know?"

"No problem."

I was flat-out busted just as I had been by CO Gherkin last week as a joke. This time, it was real, and I knew right away that my perfect rider was over. Witnessed by half the upstairs, Mr. Walsh would have no choice but to pull me up even if I was an assistant senior coordinator. If he didn't do it, he would be pulled up for showing favoritism and not enforcing the rules. Until we were cleared for free time, and everybody upstairs knew it, I shouldn't have been sleeping. I couldn't have dozed off for too long, or my neighbors would have looked out for me and would have woken me up. There would be no excuses and no playing favorites. I knew without a doubt that I would be pulled up at the meeting tonight, and that was the way it was.

The thing that bothered me the most about it was that it was natural. Many guys would lie down on their bunks with their neighbors watching out for them and never get in trouble. Mr. Kim was the master of doing that. My offense was purely accidental, but that made no difference; breaking the rules meant you paid the price. I was fairly lucky it hadn't happened until now. With all the rules I had broken, I sort of figured it was just a matter of time before my luck ran out, and it finally did.

Later that night, just as I expected, I heard the words from the expeditor that I had been waiting for all day.

"Mr. Walsh, pulling up Mr. Walker for sleeping during super-clean. Two-page apology, due in three days."

It was about what I expected for my first offense, and as I was standing there, facing Mr. Walsh, we both couldn't help but smile because we both knew he was just doing what he had to do. I would set a good example and have it done by tomorrow, and like all the other apologies I had heard over the last couple of months, I wasn't going to make excuses or explain my behavior. I was going to apologize and say why what I did was wrong and how, as a leader, it would set a bad example for the new members of the community to see me do this. If my motto had always been "Lead by example," then what kind of picture was I painting for the purple and orange cards by sleeping before we were cleared? I kept asking myself why I had been stupid enough to lie down in the first place and got comfortable enough to let it happen. That was my biggest mistake, because I should have known better than to put myself in a position to let this occur at all. I should have been particularly careful as an assistant senior coordinator, knowing everybody was watching me. How Kim managed to get away with it, I would never know. My perfect rider was shot, but I still didn't get into any serious trouble, and for all practical purposes, I should be on track to go back to county in two or three weeks and most likely get probation once there.

I had done my time and done it well. I was eager to get out of here and go home. My only worry now was whether or not the judge agreed with me or not.

I met with Mr. Kennison on Monday, and my end-case statement according to him stated that I should receive probation as I had hoped. The judge didn't have to follow the recommendation from the counselor, but in most cases, they did. Now all I had to do was not get in any serious trouble between now and the time I appeared in front of the judge, and I was probably home free. Castro was hoping to have his name on the list this Thursday so he could go home in a week, and he really had his hopes up for getting his name called. Last week, at the last minute, they pulled two guys off the list after they were told to pack up, and the look of disappointment on their faces was obvious when they came out of the bubble after being told they were staying put for one more week. Nothing is worse than getting your hopes up for something as big as going home only to have the rug pulled out from under you at the last minute.

Just as Castro had been expecting to be called, I was also hopeful but not really anticipating it quite yet. Next week maybe, and the week after that for sure, but I wasn't in any hurry to have my hopes shattered just yet. Usually, two weeks or more after their end case, most people were on transport, but nothing was a given, and it seemed the more you wanted it or were anticipating your departure, the longer you ended up waiting. There was no telling how long a person was going to sit at county, waiting to go before a judge. On that day, if all went well, you would be released from county jail. What really sucked was that your dreams could easily be shattered by the judge. There was no sense in looking forward to your beliefs, because until you got to court, no one knew what their future held. Look at Mr. Wells. He thought he was going home, only to be sent back on a second rider. That was what made me constantly nervous about planning ahead. Until the judge made it official, you never knew exactly what was in store for you.

One of the new guys this week was Mr. Chang. He showed up with an attitude and demeanor that made most of us sick. He was pulled up five or six times in the first couple of days, and he couldn't comprehend the reasons why. I was just waiting for the guy to get in a fight, and the list of people willing to fight him was fairly long for such a short stay. My fear was that the fight would get someone who didn't deserve it in trouble. Chang had pissed off a lot of people in a short time, and the list of the pissed-off seemed to be getting longer every day. This was not a place to make enemies right away, and at this rate, he was going to be as popular as Mr. Plains in no time, if he wasn't already.

I was now going to green card rec every night, playing basket-ball, and running. I had lifted some weights, but the lines for the machines and dumbbells were hoarded by the hard-core guys. All I needed was some cardio to help burn off some excess energy, and I would be able to sleep soundly. I found it extremely difficult to run on the frozen snow. The path I had dug out when I first arrived was still maintained, but the constant slipping jolted my back, and after a few attempts of running the ball field loop, I decided it wasn't for me. Besides, I was supposed to be working during the morning rec time, and I had sneaked out a few times when I was new. Now, if I pulled something like that, too many people knew me, and that could easily ruin my perfect rider. With Castro scheduled to leave, and McGladrey and me shortly after, we began to look for replace-ments to fill our spots in the media production office, so they could be educated before all of us left and would have at least some clue as to what they were supposed to be doing. Mr. Walter was starting up a new project that the state had asked him to initiate, describing how the rider program worked. It would chronologically follow an inmate through the rider process from arrival to departure. I think it was meant for prison authorities to see more than inmates so that states could decide whether to implement similar programs in their states, using riders as guidelines.

We also had to train one of these guys to take over the fire drill class, to teach the class as soon as we were gone. After all the research and information we had gathered creating it, teaching the class was pretty much second nature to the three of us. We had gone over the information so many times we could probably give the class without the help of the PowerPoint. The three of us also completed the safety course and began studying for the test that we already had the answers to. The test was on Friday, and by then we would know who was going home on Monday and who was staying another week. Castro was counting on going home so much that if his name wasn't called, I was afraid he might have a nervous breakdown.

When Thursday night finally came, CO Wiley did the same thing he had done with Albert a few weeks earlier and held back Castro's name. For these few minutes, I felt bad for the guy because

I believed he wasn't going home. After getting me a job and working with me five hours a day for two and a half months, he was the first guy I had known this well to get his walking papers. Albert came close, but Castro and I had bonded during my first or second week, and along with all the time spent in the office together, we had really gotten to know each other. He was serious about his sobriety, spending time with his daughter, and maybe even patching things up with his ex-wife and putting his family back together. Cottonwood would be a different place with him gone, and I was going to miss his sense of humor every day until I left, and for many more days after that. He was responsible for more pranks and laughter here than any ten people combined, and he had personally gotten the best of me more times than I could remember. McGladrey and I had no intention of just letting him walk out the door; we had one more surprise in store for him before he left so we would leave here knowing who the master pranksters in Cottonwood really were.

CHAPTER 56

I T WAS SUPER BOWL WEEKEND, and I was fired up about my Seahawks, who had an excellent chance at winning it all. It was probably more of a diversion, subconsciously leading me to not think about all my friends back home getting together for the big game without me. I was the only one here from Seattle, but the Idaho football crowd, having no NFL team to root for, was evenly divided between Seattle and Denver fans. Of course, they only cared about pro ball when they weren't rooting for the Boise State football team, whose season was over.

On Sunday, everyone was glued to the game. My Seahawks outplayed the Steelers and, in my opinion, were the better team that day. When it came down to the final quarter and things were just getting interesting, we all had to bunk up for count, and by the time it was cleared, we went to chow. When I ran up to the dayroom after dinner, the game was over and the Seahawks had lost. Apparently, there were some bad calls by the referee that affected the outcome, but I never got to see what all the controversy was about. All I knew was that the Seahawks should have won, and now I would have to make up Mr. Steele's bunk for the next week, since I lost our bet.

On Monday, McGladrey and I tried our best to stick it to Castro one last time. When we got to the office that morning, we started spreading rumors to everyone who would listen that three or four people were getting pulled off transport tonight, with the hope of having the rumor get back to Castro from anybody but us. If he heard it from us, he would know we were messing with him, but if it came from an outside source, the rumor would have credibility. CO Wiley was even in on it, and we had talked to him last week about helping us. After all the jokes Castro had pulled on so many people around here, he said he would help us.

When CO Wiley showed up that afternoon, he came to the media productions office and asked me to come down to the unit and see him in the bubble for a few minutes. I was nervous on my way down and wondering what kind of trouble I was about to get into. I went in through his open door, and when he told me to close it and sit down, my anxiety level quadrupled. I was desperately trying to figure out what I could possibly be in trouble for.

"Mr. Walker," he said while looking directly at me, "CO Gherkin and I have been talking, and with Mr. Walsh leaving tomorrow, this unit is in need of a new senior coordinator. Mr. Steele is technically the senior assistant coordinator, but we have talked it over and decided to make you the new senior. Is that going to be a problem for you or create a problem with you and Steele that you can't deal with?"

"No, sir, not as far as I'm concerned."

"Good. Then I will talk to Mr. Steele to take the pressure off you, and you will be the new senior coordinator at the meeting tonight."

"Thank you, sir." With that, I left the bubble and went back to the office. I didn't say a word to anyone about becoming senior coordinator; I just told McGladrey everything was set for tonight with Castro.

After dinner, Castro came up to me and asked if I had heard about people being pulled off transport this week. I could hear the nervousness in his tone, and I knew the groundwork McGladrey and I had put in place for Castro was functioning perfectly. The look on everyone's face when they learned I was the new senior coordinator was priceless. Steele had talked to me earlier in the evening and said he was okay with it since he was going home next week. Being the senior was easier than any other coordinator job, as long as all the other coordinators did their jobs. All I had to do was manage the three assistants and make sure they managed their three coordinators, and everything would be fine. I also had the privilege of giving the final quote at the end of the meeting and picking the guys from the unit to lead the Serenity Prayer. Of course, I picked the shiest, most reclusive individual I could think of, my old buddy Jesus. When I called on him, he nodded in acknowledgment with a smile as if he almost expected me to pick on him.

When the meeting ended, CO Wiley called Castro down to the bubble before all the going-home guys went to the laundry to change into orange jumpsuits for transport. While in the bubble, Wiley was telling him that he was one of the unfortunate men who got bumped off transport and he would have to stay for one more week. Wiley apologized for the mix-up sympathetically, and Castro left the bubble obviously dejected and headed back upstairs. The look on his face said it all to the rest of us, and he stopped and told a few friends about the unfortunate luck that had been dumped on him. By the time he got upstairs, where his close friends were, he was watery-eyed and on the verge of tears. He had cried before while reading a seminar about his daughter, and I knew he was an emotional guy, but I didn't count on the three- or four-minute delay to converse with the guys downstairs. When he made it up to his buddies on our tier, he was visibly shaken up and about ready to lose it.

While all this was happening, CO Wiley had come up the spiral staircase inside the bubble and was watching through the one-way mirror until the time was right. As Castro passed the bubble and could finally see my bunk, he noticed ten or fifteen of his closest buddies all hiding around my bunk. When he looked up and saw us, we all yelled, "GOTCHA!" just as Wiley opened the door to the bubble with a smile and a comment.

"Walker and McGladrey figured you got everybody around here at some time or another, so they just wanted to get you one last time." Wiley went back in with a smile on his face, and the look on Castro's face was worth all the time I had spent setting him up. He breathed out a huge sigh of relief, and he, McGladrey, and I gathered for a happy embrace. The man was in tears by now, but tears of happiness rather than disappointment. I looked up at him and let him know we never intended for it to go this far.

"I am sorry, dude," I apologized. "I didn't count on you stopping downstairs. We didn't want this to go so long that you got upset."

He smiled while wiping away his tears and began shaking his head. "You motherfuckers got me good," he said as a smile came back across his face. "The only reason I was so upset was that I talked to my daughter over the weekend and told her I was coming home. I had disappointed her for so long it was tearing me up that this would disappoint her yet again. I deserved every minute of that." Deep down, I think he was almost appreciative of the complexity and cooperative effort that took to pull off a prank like ours and also for keeping it brief. There was a fine line between humorous and cruel that we tried not to cross and hoped we hadn't.

"Tell me one thing?" he asked. "Was there any truth to the rumor that two or three guys were getting pulled off transport?"

"McGladrey and I started that rumor this morning in the library, knowing that it would get back to you," I confessed.

"You guys played it brilliantly, because that was what made the whole thing in the bubble so believable. I had been worried all day that I would be one of them. You motherfuckers! I have never been set up like that in my life. My hat's off to you guys."

We spent the rest of the night reminiscing about the stunts we had pulled and all the guys we had messed with over the last few months. We also told Castro how much his sense of humor was appreciated and how much he would be missed.

The next morning, we said our goodbyes and the office seemed a little less enjoyable from the first minute I walked in. Knowing that I didn't have to watch my back constantly made it not as fun, and that was when I realized just how sorely Castro would be missed. I couldn't imagine what the past few months would have been like without Castro to lighten my anxiety level each day.

Life as the senior coordinator was, for the most part, a piece of cake. I was definitely the go-to guy, but now I had the title that went along with it. The week went by slowly, and even though I tried not to get my hopes up for having my name called for transport this week, I couldn't help but want to get out of here as soon as possible. All the cool guys were gone, the men who replaced them were not of the same caliber, the unit was changing for the worse, and there wasn't much anybody could do about it. It was filling up with young punks with no respect for anyone, and I could only hope that I was out of here before the shit hit the fan.

Mr. Chang was up to his antics once again, and this time he was messing with other people's riders and not just his own. Telling the old guy Mr. Edgar that he was indigent, Chang had Edgar's wife send money to put on Chang's books for commissary purchases. He basically intimidated the old guy into doing it, and his bullying was not going to be tolerated by any means by the men of this unit once they heard what was going on. By Thursday night, I was more than ready to get out of here. I wanted no part of the crumbling of unit 4 that was happening around me. When CO Wiley called my name for transport, I was actually surprised that things were finally going my way. It was the best news I had heard since being locked up over five months ago, and Mr. McGladrey was on the bus with me. He was going to Canyon County in Caldwell, but we would be on the same bus home on Tuesday, and neither of us could wait.

On Friday, my commissary was held back, which was normal for those going home, and with only three days left, I was well stocked for the weekend and didn't really need more stuff anyway. Since Chang had commissary this week, the word got out about what had happened last week between him and Mr. Edgar. Finally, Edgar confessed the truth to CO Wiley, in my presence, and technically, Chang had not broken any rules. What happened between two men with the cooperation of people on the outside was not Cottonwood's business and therefore not punishable. True, what he did was ethically wrong and taking advantage of the old man's naivety could not be excused, but it fell under none of the many rules established here by the powers that be.

Chang was proud of his accomplishment and had no problem letting everyone know how badly he had screwed the guy over. One of my duties as senior coordinator was to turn in the commissary sheets before the truck left the compound. McGladrey and I decided that since Chang was such a dick and there was nothing anyone could do about it, we thought we would take the matters into our own hands one last time. We set things right with Chang before the commissary truck left, and my only regret was McGladrey and I would not be here next week to witness our handiwork.

Over the weekend, the going-home riders were busy packing up and out-processing in preparation for going home. We were only allowed to take one brown paper sack filled with personal items and legal paperwork along with our portfolio. Whatever we took with us, there was no guarantee that the facility we were headed to would let us keep these things. This place was run by the state, and we were all headed to county jails. They didn't let you bring in anything to the dorms that they didn't sell you from their commissary, and I wasn't sure if it was for profit or security reasons. I knew once again I would have to wait seven to ten days to get back into my comfort zone once I got back to county. The weekend went extremely slow and seemed to drag on forever, but that is usually the case when you have something that you've anticipated for so long happen to you. Going home had seemed like a dream, and I had been waiting for this for months, but the reality hadn't quite sunk in yet. It most likely wouldn't until I was heading out through the door of the Ada County Jail and was headed back into the real world. I suddenly remembered the money I had left by the railroad tracks, thinking I would be back for it in a few weeks. It was six months by the time I got to it, and I wondered if the Boise winter or some bum had made the cash disappear since I had left it there.

They cleared my books with the state and sent my $132 back home to Beth in the form of a check. That would mean when I arrived at county, I would have no money on my books for commissary and I would have to have some sent to me by her. When I talked to her, I needed to let her know I was on transport. She seemed happy to hear it, and I knew it had been a tough road to go for her just as it had been for me. She said she would send the money and even a book for me to read so they would both be there by Wednesday, the day after my arrival. With my luck, I would be one day behind commissary day, forcing me to wait another week for any luxuries.

Monday night, I was relieved of my senior coordinator duties and gave my short goodbye speech. Basically, I told the new guys to apply themselves and that they would get out of this program as much as they put into it. I thanked a few guys, especially McGladrey, and reminded the men in the unit to work with one another for the common good. I thanked CO Wiley for his words of wisdom, and when it was over, we headed back to laundry to change into orange Cheetos for transport in the morning.

I took my bin box down to CO Wiley when he called my name, so we could bag up my personal belongings for transport. I now had given my entire commissary away to needy individuals and my laundered thermal underwear to Mr. Edgar, who told me he was constantly freezing his ass off. CO Wiley was going through the pile of things I was taking with me when he looked up and asked me a question.

"Mr. Walker, I have been doing count four days a week, month after month, in unit 4. Every time I came to the end of the compound, there you were with your paper and pen each time. You hardly even looked up after a while, and I got to know, what were you writing all that time, day after day?"

I pulled my expanding file off my lap and held it in my hand so I could show him the answer to his question.

"I decided, after my first week, to journal my experiences here, and I hoped to write a book about them once I got out. I would write about three pages every count time, three counts each day, and now I have over a thousand pages in here that I need to edit down and get published. I figured, as long as I am here, I might as well be productive." I opened the file and showed him the handwritten pages to see for himself while he smiled and nodded.

"Good for you, Walker, good for you. There is, however, one slight problem we have. You aren't authorized to take that with you to county. You need to mail it out of here, and I can only assume your books were closed over the weekend."

"That's right, sir, they were."

"I tell you what…" He paused and thought about his next comment for a full minute while I waited quietly. "This definitely doesn't fall under my job description, but here is what I am personally going to do for you. Divide the whole thing into thirds and put it in the three manila mail folders you still have and address them to your attorney. I will personally take them to the post office tomorrow and have them mailed to him. I am not supposed to be doing things like this for inmates, but I admire your dedication and have witnessed your determination daily, so I am willing to help you out."

I couldn't believe what he was going to do for me. If I tried to take it with me, the manuscript might have been seized or maybe even read. Who knew what kind of trouble that might have gotten me into.

"Thank you, sir. I appreciate it. I wanted to continue with it when I got to county, but I can just get more paper and a pen when I get there."

"Well, even if I let you take it with you, who knows if it would show up where it is supposed to? Those bags get lost all the time or left at the wrong county jail, never to be seen again. After all the time you put in on this, I would hate for you to lose it."

"Thank you, sir. If I were to be honest and confess to something that happened a few months ago, could I still get in trouble for it now, sir?"

"Depends on how serious the offence was. You murdered someone, I don't have a choice. What is it you want to get off your chest, Mr. Walker?"

"Remember the roll that you found in the snow on Thanksgiving, sir?"

"That was your work, Mr. Walker?"

"Yes, sir. I just thought you might like to know."

"I saw you fidgeting when I confronted the unit. I also picked it up right before I saw you getting ready to stand up, am I right?"

"Yes, sir."

"I didn't want to ruin anybody's holiday, but I did make my point. It's probably tough enough to be stuck in here on a holiday, and a purple card on top of that. Can't say I even blame you too much. I don't agree with the two-meal system, and being purple during Thanksgiving week must have been difficult to deal with. Nine meals in four days, I think. Meanwhile, the rest of the country has tables stacked with all their favorites."

"I admit, it wasn't very easy smelling and watching all the consumption on the one holiday specifically designated for feasting and being excluded."

"Well, don't worry about the roll, Mr. Walker. You more than compensated for it with the fire safety issue you addressed. It told me a lot about you when you came up with that idea. It was long overdue and might even save a life someday. It was some good work done for the greater good of the community. Good luck with your book, and make sure you don't come back to see us."

"I won't be back, sir, and thank you."

He shook my hand, and I walked out of the bubble feeling like we were more friends than CO and inmate. Something inside told me that somehow, somewhere, I would see this man again under different circumstances.

CHAPTER

57

THE NEXT MORNING, THE CHEETOS were called out to segregation in the middle of the morning meeting. We were given the pretransport strip search, shackled, handcuffed, and loaded on the bus heading south. I stared at the compound as we pulled out, wondering if I would be coming back in a month or two like Mr. Wells. I felt for the new guys who arrived yesterday, knowing what was in store for them, but I was also proud of all I had accomplished while I was in Cottonwood. Did this place changed my life? Possibly. Only time would be able to answer that question, but I knew I would never forget my time here and the people I had met and bonded with. Part of me would somehow miss this place even though I was more than happy to finally be leaving.

The snow was much deeper on the way home, and the rugged landscape was buried in deep drifts. It was much softer than the picture my mind had painted on the way up. We listened to the Blue Collar Comedy tape on the way back, and that had everybody laughing and in a good mood. Most of the way back, everybody told stories about the strange things that occurred on their own personal rider and talked about the differences between the COs and the units. Even the CO driving the bus seemed to be just a little nicer to us than they had been on the way up.

When we pulled into Canyon County, McGladrey and around ten others parted ways with us. I knew somehow that I would see him again. As we finally got to Ada County, I was surprised, thinking back to when I left and just how fast the time had gone by during my journey. We were booked in, and I couldn't wait to get back to the dorms. As Wiley had predicted, some of the bags didn't make it, and they wouldn't let us take anything into the jail except our portfolio. The rest of our belongings were put in our property bags for us to retrieve once we were released.

The first round of bad news came from the booking lady when I asked about the dorms. She told me that riders waiting to go to court were housed in MCU after a couple of days in the intake dorm. That meant until classification and then off to MCU and thirty-hour lock-down. I hoped I would be in court Thursday, and that would only mean one day in the MCU before leaving.

I was dressed in red and marched down the corridor to unit 5. As I passed dorm 6, I looked in to see if there were any familiar faces. I saw something that put the fear of God in me. Pacing back and forth, five weeks after leaving Cottonwood, was my old buddy Mr. Albert. He waved when he saw me, but since communication was forbidden between units, I had no chance to talk to him before being herded into dorm 5. Seeing him still here after the perfect rider he pulled off meant only one thing: anyone could be staying here for a long time no matter how well they performed up north if Albert was still here. If the riders waiting to go to court were housed in MCU, the only deduction I could make was that he had already been sentenced and ended up getting more county time on top of his rider. That was the only possibility I could think of as panic rushed through me. If he had flopped, he would be at the pen or back at RDU, heading back to Cottonwood. If he got probation, he should have been released already, unless it took five or six weeks until you went to court. This was not a good sign, and seeing him in there made me nervous about what awaited me.

I immediately resumed my walking routine in the dorm and tried to find something worth reading after being spoiled by the library at Cottonwood. Since everybody in here was new, nobody had any pen or paper to store out to me, and that was the only good thing about MCU. The guys in there had been there for extended periods and had all the amenities for their new cellmates. That was two days away, and I would have to make do until then.

I talked to Beth the next day, and she was the bearer of bad news that she had managed to get off the internet. Once I was booked in

Ada County, my court date had been set, and she found it on the court docket twenty-two days from now. That meant three weeks of being stressed out and worried about what my future held.

Two days later, I was moved to the MCU and settled in for three weeks, waiting for my court date. I hated MCU and the restrictions that came with it. The freedom of Cottonwood and the dorms was a luxury I had gotten used to, and being locked down for hours and hours on end was something I would never get used to. These guys did have some good books, and even the paper and pens that I had to have, but the trade-off wasn't worth it to me. It was impossible to pace in MCU, and with us having only four hours out of the cell each day, the county jail drug and legal discussions got old all too quickly. What happened to Albert had me extremely worried and fearful of what the judge might have in store for me.

Two of my cellmates were Mexican nationals who were here illegally. They had done their time for the offense they committed and were now waiting to be deported to Mexico. One of them was sentenced to sixty days and was now going on a year in here, just waiting to be sent back. They said the county was keeping them for so long because they could profit from the daily rate they charged the federal government for housing them until they were deported. The county was in no hurry to get rid of money-generating prisoners who couldn't fight the system anyway. The concept didn't seem right, and with it coming from these two, I wasn't too sure on the accuracy of their comments anyway. If it was true, then the county was basically kidnapping these two guys and holding them as long as possible for the ransom money. Maybe the feds were really that slow and this was just part of the normal process.

During tier time, while pacing, I received yet another dose of bad news. While walking past one of the cell doors, I noticed one of the guys from Cottonwood. He had been in unit 4 with me and had left the same week as Albert did. I talked to him briefly, and he had told me he was sentenced to thirty days after his rider and was now taking care of that before he would be out. Between him and Albert,

I could only assume that doing more time after you went in front of the judge would not be an uncommon occurrence. Just as you get excited to go home, the judge pulls the rug out from under you and makes you stay another month. Sounded like a total mind game to me. Just like letting a man out of jail only to arrest him as he walked out the door and put him back in like they did with Rodger before I left for Cottonwood.

Friday, at about 3:00 or 4:00 p.m., I couldn't help but smile for a while knowing that right now Mr. Chang was getting his commissary bag. McGladrey and I had filled out a new commissary sheet for him that week because of what he did to Mr. Edgar. Instead of coffee and candy this week, Mr. Chang would be receiving a variety of hygiene products, including tampons, panties, and ladies' socks, but absolutely no food. Some of the best humor takes place when you are not there to witness it, but I did tell Mr. Edgar what to watch for. True, it takes out some of the pleasure not to be there when it happens, but just knowing what was going to happen even after we were gone made it worth it.

The next three weeks were a boring, never-ending string of spades games, drug stories, and lots of reading. After the freedom of Cottonwood, MCU seemed like solitary confinement. Finally, my court date arrived, and with it the anxiety of facing the unknown. With nothing to do for three weeks but stress out over what might happen, I had worked myself into frenzy. I grabbed my book and my portfolio when they called me down to go, and I took the long corridor to the chain-up area, hopefully for the final time.

Sitting in the courtroom was a nerve-wracking experience I wouldn't wish on anyone. Of course, with my consistently bad luck, I had to endure two and a half hours until my name came up, but the girl before me provided a valuable lesson for me. She had violated her probation and was getting sentenced for her long list of violations, and the judge was not pleased with her noncompliance.

"Ms. Johnson," he began, "it says here that you have violated no less than five of the nine conditions of your probation, and you now stand before me again. You have frequented a place that is known for drug activity and are currently living with your ex-husband, whom you were told to stay away from. You have not kept the probation people updated on your address, you are not attending your drug and alcohol classes as ordered by this court, and apparently, you failed a UA when you were finally arrested. Do you have anything to say on your behalf before I sentence you?"

"No, sir." Her head was down, and her voice crackled.

"Well, since you have absolutely no regard for the conditions of your probation, it is the decision of this court to sentence you to two years at the Idaho Women's Penitentiary, starting immediately." He threw the book at her, and she burst into tears instantly. I hoped it wasn't a preview of the judge's mood and his anger wouldn't, in any way, be reflective of what I should expect.

Finally, after four months of waiting, it was my turn. The judge looked over my file and looked up at me. All I could think of were Wells and Albert while my heart was pumping a mile a minute. The last time I was in this situation, I almost had a heart attack after the sentencing.

"Mr. Walker, I don't profess to know what goes on up at NICI, and for the life of me, I can't figure out why you weren't given the drug and alcohol classes I asked that you receive." My heart was pounding. I thought, *Here comes the part when I join Mr. Wells and end up back on compound for my second rider because they didn't do what he wanted them to.* "Nevertheless, your records state here that you exemplified the ideals of the program and successfully completed your rider as instructed, so it is the decision of this court to grant you probation, provided you can abide by all the rules set forth. You just witnessed what happens if you fail to adhere to these rules. Understand?"

"Yes, sir, I do," I replied.

I was free. Finally, the long wait and my worst nightmares were finally going to end. I was going to walk out of Ada County Jail later today. I couldn't believe it was finally over.

When I got back to MCU, I gave my entire commissary to my cellmates even though it was considered bad luck to do so. Inmates say if you leave your stuff here, you are destined to return here. It was a good thing I wasn't superstitious, or these guys would have watched me walk out without giving them a thing. They were all jealous, and to be honest, I felt bad for them having to stay, especially knowing the messed-up situation they were stuck in. They had been good to me when I joined them three weeks ago, so it was payback time.

A couple of hours after lunch, my name was called, and I heard the best thing a man can hear in jail. "Walker, roll it up. You're going home."

At two in the afternoon, the booking area was deserted, and I remembered how much I enjoyed the antics all around me during in-processing 187 long days ago. After forty-five minutes of out-processing, I walked out of the Ada County Jail. I went straight to the railroad tracks where, six months ago, I had stashed my last $20 cash and headed straight for Sonic to get myself a good burger. I stopped at the store along the way and got a half-gallon of milk and chugged half of it before I even got to the cash register. Beth had arranged for me to be at the Extended Stay America for the next few days until I was cleared by the probation office to leave the state. I was required to have a travel pass to leave the state without violating my probation, and I had no intention of doing that. I was a free man, finally. No more time schedules, uniforms, jumpsuits, 6:00 a.m. wake-up calls, or COs with power-tripping issues to deal with. I had been locked up for 187 days, read eighty-three books, and had written over a thousand pages of what I hoped would eventually become a book, or maybe even a movie. I was proud of what I had accomplished while so many others had floundered.

My next stop was the probation office a couple of miles away, and the walk in the fresh air after MCU was extremely refreshing. As luck would have it, that night was the once-a-week orientation class for new people who had just been released, and attendance was mandatory. That coincidence saved me from staying in Boise for six extra days, and I would be released tomorrow. I sat through the two-hour class and then caught a ride to my hotel from a guy from MCU. On the way to the hotel, he told me of his friend who came back from the library one day with black circles on his ears. Imagine that!

I was once again the master of the house. I could lie in a nice big bed with the remote in my hand and eat whatever the hell I wanted. I most likely wouldn't be allowed to go to Washington until Monday or Tuesday, but Beth, knowing this was the case, was going to spend a couple of days here with me over the weekend.

When she showed up the next day, she looked even more beautiful than I had remembered. It had been so long since I last saw her that we just held each other in the parking lot for a few long minutes before going inside. After six months apart, it was almost awkward for a little while, until we got back in our groove and then we erupted into conversation about what we had each been going through with 398 miles between us. There was a lot of catching up to do, and there was no way it could all be covered in one weekend, but we did make some headway. It was nice to lie there, holding her in my arms, with the stress and worry of prison life behind me.

What was supposed to be a few weeks away from home had become a six-month roller coaster of emotional bullshit I wouldn't wish on my worst enemy. Acceptance of my situation and that I was the one responsible for it, along with a positive, productive attitude, enabled time to fly by and for me to benefit from the experience. The choices and freedoms we have grown accustomed to on a daily lifelong basis are much sweeter appreciated after their absence.

My own bathroom, shower, TV, and home were among the things I had always assumed were my God-given rights as a hardworking American. It had taken the last six months for me to realize that drug use, no matter how often or severe, will eventually ruin your life. I had gone from a hardworking businessman, father, boyfriend, and citizen into a strung-out, lying, unreliable addict in less than one seriously dysfunctional year. My thought process had become so delusional from drugs that even after all the security issues at the airport after 9/11, I tried to go from Seattle to Boise and back without giving up my drugs and paraphernalia. I had to be pretty messed up to be busted by the TSA screening station at the Boise airport with ten grams of crack on me. The copper screens I smoked it through in my pipe set off the metal-detection wand they were searching me with and changed my life forever.

I vowed to learn from my mistake and not return to conditions of probation. I would never not appreciate the freedoms I had taken for granted for so long. I was glad to be here with that and would do everything I could to never get incarcerated again. All kinds of snacks and goodies whenever I felt like it. There was also a refrigerator in my room that was well stocked with all the ice-cold, fresh, chuggable milk I could drink. It wasn't a tiny, eight-ounce jailhouse carton but more like three gallons. Thank God I was finally out. Thank God Beth had stood by me, and thank God for milk!

ABOUT THE AUTHOR

FIRST-TIME AUTHOR JOHN BEATON WAS walking over twenty miles a day. Now, as a free man, he is walking over twelve miles a day all over Snohomish County, Washington, and the entire West Coast. *Incarcerated Walker* is his story of incarceration and recovery, told through the eyes of fictional character Garrett Walker.